To —
Aunt Ditty & G C —
With my compliments.
Walter

AF678342

Mark-to-market Accounting

This thought-provoking and immensely readable collection of articles, speeches and letters by Walter Schuetze, one of the world's most distinguished accounting practitioners, is a work for our time.

In the wake of the largest surprise corporate failures and retrospective financial restatements in corporate history, Walter Schuetze and Peter Wolnizer (as editor) turn their attention to what they call the syndrome of "Enronitis."

They contend that the unheralded collapse of companies such as Enron and WorldCom in the USA, and HIH Insurance in Australia, shows the failure of conventional accounting and auditing practices to provide high-quality financial information for investors as intended by law. It is little wonder, therefore, that public confidence in financial reporting, auditing and corporate regulation is at an all-time low.

This book argues that it is time to base financial reports on up-to-date prices – current selling prices for assets and current settlement prices for liabilities – and to disclose the details of those who provide the market price data.

In this strongly practical case for mark-to-market accounting, the authors demonstrate how such a regime would put a stop to earnings management and establish a firm financial foundation for corporate governance and independent auditing. Providing nothing less than "true north" in financial reporting.

This book will be essential reading for advanced students and academics in the field of accounting.

Walter P. Schuetze is a certified public accountant. He was chief accountant to the Securities and Exchange Commission (1992–5) and chief accountant of the commission's Enforcement Division (1997–2000).

Peter W. Wolnizer is dean of the Faculty of Economics and Business and a professor of accounting in the University of Sydney. He is author of *Auditing as Independent Authentication* and has written extensively on financial accounting and auditing.

Routledge New Works in Accounting History
Series editors: Richard Brief, Leonard N. Stern School of Business, New York University; Garry Carnegie, Deakin University, Australia; John Richard Edwards, Cardiff Business School, UK; Richard Macve, London School of Economics, UK

The Institute of Accounts
Stephen E. Loeb and Paul J. Miranti

Professionalism and Accounting Rules
Brian P. West

Accounting Theory
Essays by Carl Thomas Devine
Edited by Harvey Hendrickson and Paul Williams

Mark-to-market Accounting
"True north" in financial reporting
Walter P. Schuetze, edited by Peter W. Wolnizer

Mark-to-market Accounting

"True north" in financial reporting

Walter P. Schuetze,
edited by Peter W. Wolnizer

Routledge
Taylor & Francis Group
LONDON AND NEW YORK

First published 2004
by Routledge
11 New Fetter Lane, London EC4P 4EE

Simultaneously published in the USA and Canada
by Routledge
29 West 35th Street, New York, NY 10001

Routledge is an imprint of the Taylor & Francis Group

© 2004 Walter P. Schuetze and Peter W. Wolnizer

Typeset in Baskerville by Taylor & Francis Books Ltd
Printed and bound in Great Britain by Biddles Ltd, Guildford and King's Lynn

All rights reserved. No part of this book may be reprinted or reproduced or utilized in any form or by any electronic, mechanical, or other means, now known or hereafter invented, including photocopying and recording, or in any information storage or retrieval system, without permission in writing from the publishers.

British Library Cataloguing in Publication Data
A catalogue record for this book is available from the British Library

Library of Congress Cataloging-in-Publication Data
A catalog record for this title has been requested

ISBN 0–415–29955–1

To our wives Jean and Gaye

Contents

Notes on author and editor

Walter P. Schuetze was chief accountant to the Securities and Exchange Commission (SEC) of the United States of America from January 1992 through March 1995, when he retired. He was appointed chief accountant of the SEC's Enforcement Division in November 1997 and served through mid-February 2000, when he retired again. He was a consultant to the Enforcement Division from March 2000 through March 2002 on matters involving accounting and auditing.

Mr Schuetze is currently a consultant in various litigations as an expert in accounting and auditing. He is also an executive in residence in the College of Business at the University of Texas in San Antonio and a member of the boards of directors and chairman of the audit committees of Computer Associates International Inc. and TransMontaigne Inc.

He was a charter member of the Financial Accounting Standards Board, serving as a member from April 1973 through mid-1976. He was a member then chairman of the Accounting Standards Executive Committee of the American Institute of Certified Public Accountants. He was a member of the Steering Committee of the International Accounting Standards Committee dealing with intangible assets, business combinations, and impairment of assets. He has delivered occasional lectures on accounting at the business schools of St Mary's University in San Antonio, the University of Texas in San Antonio and the University of Southern California in Los Angeles.

Walter Schuetze began his career in accounting in 1957 with the public accounting firm of Eaton & Huddle in San Antonio, which merged with Peat, Marwick, Mitchell & Co. (now KPMG LLP) in 1958. He was a partner in KPMG from 1965 to 1973, when he was appointed to the Financial Accounting Standards Board, and from 1976 to 1992, when he was appointed to the position of chief accountant to the Securities and Exchange Commission.

He served in the US Air Force from 1951 to 1955. He received a Bachelor of Business Administration degree, with honors, from the University of Texas at Austin in 1957. He is a certified public accountant, a member of the American Accounting Association and the American Institute of Certified Public Accountants, and a member of the Beta Alpha Psi and Beta Gamma Sigma honorary societies. He was born on 2 August 1932.

February 2003

Peter Wolnizer is dean of the Faculty of Economics and Business and a professor of accounting in the University of Sydney, Australia. Previously, he held the foundation chair of accounting and finance in Deakin University (1989–99), where he served as foundation dean of the Faculty of Business and Law (1991–99). Prior to those appointments, he held lecturing positions in the University of New South Wales (1973–5) and the University of Sydney (1976–87), and a readership in the University of Tasmania (1987–8). Before entering academic life, he worked for six years in industry, commerce and the accounting profession.

Professor Wolnizer has also been appointed to visiting professorial or research fellowship positions by the Universities of Canterbury, Glasgow, Kansas, Pittsburgh and Utah – most recently as the James Cusator Wards Visiting Professor in the University of Glasgow (1993 and 1998), Visiting Professor at the Czech Management Center in Prague (1995), and Visiting Erskine Fellow in the University of Canterbury (1998).

He is chairman of the Board Education Committee and Professional Education Board of CPA Australia, the Asia-Pacific member of the Education Policy Committee of the International Association of Financial Executives Institutes, and a member of the Research and Publications Committee of the Committee for Economic Development of Australia (CEDA). He served as a member of the Council of the Scots College (Sydney) from 1999 to 2002, a member of the Council of Scotch College (Melbourne) from 1998 to 2001, and a member of Australia's Corporations and Securities Panel from 1995 to 1998.

Peter Wolnizer has a Bachelor of Economics degree from the University of Tasmania, and the degrees of Master of Economics and Doctor of Philosophy from the University of Sydney. He is a Fellow of both CPA Australia and the Institute of Chartered Accountants in Australia. His fields of expertise are financial accounting, auditing, and corporate governance. He is the author of *Auditing as Independent Authentication* (Sydney University Press, 1987) and editor of five books. His articles have been widely published in scholarly and professional journals; several having been reproduced in anthologies, journals and textbooks published in the USA, UK and Australia.

February 2003

Foreword

Were an anthropologist from Mars to descend upon our financial world, observing companies presenting their financial positions, what an Orwellian experience it would be. The language of statutory obligation demands that they give a true and fair view. Yet there is no explicit obligation for that truth and fairness to be grounded upon the actuality of current market selling prices for assets and their reciprocals for liabilities. Our Martian would, if of historical bent, identify precisely when the rot set in: 1844, when the Joint Stock Companies Act was passed in the United Kingdom. For that research, we are indebted to the late Professor Ray Chambers and his former pupil, now professor and dean, Peter Wolnizer, at the University of Sydney's Faculty of Economics and Business. He is the thoughtful and discerning editor of this collection, adding important linking essays of his own.

It is rare to find an intellectual lineage that starts in the 1950s with an Australian progenitor, Ray Chambers, who pioneered with Walter Schuetze many of these seminal ideas. They proceeded on largely parallel tracks, like Leibniz and Newton devising calculus. It must be rarer still to find a disciple, again Australian, who collaborates with Professor Chambers, then engages in an intense and deeply reflective exchange with Walter Schuetze in the United States. Those connections are the intellectual underpinning of Professor Wolnizer's discerning editorial work, in which he brings to the Australian context a theme of international importance. That theme is one of outstanding simplicity, intuitively convincing, yet nowhere adopted as mandatory policy for corporate reporting. I refer to "mark-to-market accounting," so far the preserve only of those parts of a business that invest in marketable securities.

That Walter Schuetze early in his career studied Russian has, for me, a literary resonance. Tolstoy wrote a memorable short story about an archetypal character of Russian literature, the holy simpleton. The story was entitled, as I recall it, "The Shoemaker." This was a character of profound simplicity. He is not to be confused with Chauncey Gardner, the Peter Sellers character in the film *Being There*, a character of profound inanity. Tolstoy's shoemaker gently disarms untruth. He does so by unselfconscious intuition about what is right, expressed in simple terms; in the supposedly "real" world, an ingénue. Walter Schuetze is in some respects of that character, with his Texan directness, colloquial and jargon-free. For his paradigm is "accounting my sister would understand." He is also a person whose personal character was severely tested when a partner at KPMG. When asked to give auditing dispensation to the thrifts and saving associations, with their shonky pseudo-partnerships masquerading as loans, he, with the backing of his firm and at real cost, simply refused. If only the same had been done with Enron's audit.

But what impact has Walter Schuetze made in Australia? Some months after a memorable dinner in the Great Hall at the University of Sydney on 27 November 2001, at which Walter Schuetze gave the R.J. Chambers Memorial Research Lecture, I was approached by a critic: "this was a very unfortunate affair, did you not see how uncomfortable some of our invited guests were, especially some of the accountants, at Schuetze's radical views?" (I add that most of the accountants there were full of praise.) For those that would listen, he was telling us that in the world of corporate emperors many were overdressed; but beneath the Zegna suits they had no clothes at all.

The critic's observation, made after Enron had emerged, allowed me the perfect riposte. It was that Schuetze had shown extraordinary prescience in his appreciation of what was to come. Those accountants who were skeptical would have done well to heed his words rather than stone the prophet.

This book is a tribute both to its editor and to those who inspired it, but most especially to Walter Schuetze. It deserves a wide and discerning audience who take its message seriously. For what is at stake is nothing less than a fundamental underpinning of our capitalist system. It is a call, yet to be heeded, for accounts we can understand, who tell it like it is.

The Honorable Justice G.F.K. Santow, Chancellor, University of Sydney,
31 January 2003

Letter from Fred Talton

The following note, in handwritten form, was received by Walter P. Schuetze in June 2002 from Fred W. Talton, who was a partner in PMM&Co. in the Raleigh, North Carolina, office in the 1980s at a time when Mr Schuetze was a partner in PMM&Co.'s Department of Professional Practice.

2728 Branch Road
Raleigh, North Carolina 27610
28 June 2002

Dear Walter,

As a CPA who retired from PMM&Co. in 1987, I have reflected many times on various accounting and audit situations that I encountered during my career. In seeking help in these matters from the Department of Professional Practice, you were quite often the person that I called on for help. The responses that I received from you were always well thought out and reasonable, though not always what our clients wanted to hear. During that period, I felt that, in working with you, I was always working with the ultimate professional.

Over the years, and especially in the most recent years, I have often thought that all of our audit partners owe you a real debt of gratitude for being such a professional in dealing with client matters. I believe some of the thoughtful, reasonable positions you took have saved the firm and its partners many millions of dollars and great embarrassment.

Please allow me to express my own appreciation and respect for your service.

Sincerely,
Fred W. Talton

Acknowledgments

For his scholarly advice, encouragement and support for this work, we express our sincerest appreciation to Professor Richard P. Brief of the Leonard N. Stern School of Business in New York University, an eminent scholar of the history and development of accounting thought. And we are honored by, and deeply grateful to the Honorable Justice Kim Santow, a Judge in the Court of Appeal, Supreme Court of New South Wales, and Chancellor of the University of Sydney, for writing the foreword.

We acknowledge, with gratitude, the permissions given by publishers to reproduce in this volume the eight previously published articles and lectures by Walter P. Schuetze; and the permissions given by Sir Bryan Carsberg and Mr Fred Talton to reproduce their letters to Walter Schuetze.

Ron Ringer provided invaluable technical and editorial assistance in transforming dozens of differently formatted documents into the uniform style prescribed by Routledge, for reading and checking the entire manuscript, and for coordinating the project. Sincere thanks are also extended to Carl Harrison Ford, Walter P. Schuetze and Dr Robert R. Sterling for reading and providing constructive comments on the editorial essays.

We are indebted to the editorial staff of Routledge (London) for their very helpful advice and ready cooperation in respect of all publishing-related matters.

For the provision of a research grant to support this work, we express our sincere appreciation to the Accounting Foundation within the University of Sydney.

Permissions

The authors gratefully acknowledge permission to reproduce the following articles in full:

"Keep it simple," reproduced by kind permission of *Accounting Horizons*, American Accounting Association, Vol. 5, No. 2, June 1991, pp. 113–17.

"What is an asset?" reproduced by kind permission of *Accounting Horizons*, American Accounting Association, Vol. 7, No. 3, September 1993, pp. 66–70.

"Disclosure and the impairment question," © 1987 from *The Journal of Accountancy* by the American Institute of Certified Public Accountants. Opinions of the authors are their own and do not necessarily reflect policies of the AICPA. Reprinted with permission.

"The liability crisis in the US and its impact on accounting," reproduced by kind permission of *Accounting Horizons*, American Accounting Association, Vol. 7, No. 2, June 1993, pp. 88–91.

"A memo to national and international accounting and auditing standard setters and securities regulators (a Christmas pony)," 2001 R.J. Chambers Memorial Research Lecture in the Great Hall, the University of Sydney, Australia, 27 November 2001, reproduced by kind permission of the Accounting Foundation within the University of Sydney.

"Reporting by independent auditors on internal controls," reproduced by kind permission of *The CPA Journal*, October 1993.

"A mountain or a molehill?" reproduced by kind permission of *Accounting Horizons*, American Accounting Association, Vol. 8, No. 1, March 1994, pp. 69–75.

"What are assets and liabilities? Where is true north? (Accounting that my sister would understand)," *Abacus: A Journal of Accounting, Finance and Business Studies*, Vol. 37, No. 1, February 2001, pp. 1–25, Blackwell.

Speeches by Walter Schuetze in his capacity as a member of staff of the SEC are in the public domain. Letters written by Walter Schuetze are copyright to the author.

1 Walter P. Schuetze

Accounting reformer

Peter W. Wolnizer

This is a unique and timely work. While pertinent to the era of the modern corporation, it is especially a work for such a time as this. For corporate financial reporting and auditing are again sharply under the spotlight of governments and regulators around the world – this time, in the wake of the most significant unexpected corporate failures and surprise retrospective financial restatements in corporate history, a syndrome we call "Enronitis."

The recent and unheralded failures of Enron and WorldCom in the USA, and of HIH Insurance, One.Tel, and Ansett in Australia – and the unexpected retrospective restatements by a large number of public companies in the USA[1] – have occurred when, by law, investors, creditors, and others are to be informed truly and fairly of the up-to-date financial position and performance of the reporting enterprises. But, again, as we have seen repeatedly in the past, the financial instrumentation system by which investors and creditors are to be so informed (financial accounting and reporting), and the quality control system by which the reliability of that financial instrumentation system is to be assured (auditing), have failed to provide the reliable and high-quality financial signals and informative safeguards for the investing public intended by the Corporations and Securities Laws. The syndrome of Enronitis is not new. In the USA, for example, there were the unexpected collapses of Equity Funding and Penn Central in the 1970s, and the savings and loan fiascos of the 1980s and 1990s. In the UK, there was Pergamon in the 1970s, and Maxwell Corporation and BCCI in the 1990s. In Australia, there were Reid Murray, Latec Investments, Stanhill, and H.G. Palmer in the 1950s and 1960s; Minsec, Cambridge Credit, Mainline and Associated Securities Ltd in the 1970s; and Bond Corporation, Rothwells, Adsteam, Westmex, and Qintex in the 1990s.[2] And those are just a few of the notable corporate catastrophes.

This book addresses the prevalent and recurrent accounting and auditing problems highlighted again in the most recent corporate financial debacles. It contains an autobiographical essay and a collection of seven articles, eighteen speeches and addresses, and sixteen letters written by an eminent accounting practitioner, standard setter and corporate regulator – Walter P. Schuetze. Though addressed to diverse, but expert, audiences about specialist and often technically complex matters, their distinctive, plain English style makes them intelligible to all who are interested in financial accounting and reporting, and their function in informing financial decision making and capital markets.

Without drawing on the ideas and work of others, Schuetze sets forth, in a compelling and highly readable fashion, his ideas about financial accounting and reporting, auditing, accounting standard setting and corporate regulation. The work is novel in many respects, most of all perhaps because those ideas evolved throughout a career in accounting practice spanning more than forty years – many of them spent at the zenith of the accounting profession (as a partner in KPMG), accounting standard setting (as a charter member of the Financial Accounting Standards Board, a member of the Financial Accounting Standards Advisory Council and chairman of the Accounting Standards Executive Committee of the American Institute of Certified Public Accountants), and securities regulation (as chief accountant to the Securities and Exchange Commission in the USA and chief accountant of the Enforcement Division of the Securities and Exchange Commission). Schuetze's ideas fundamentally challenge the conventional accounting and auditing wisdom and advocate deep change and major reform. They offer a solution to the widely recognized problem of earnings management, and a cure for Enronitis.

The observations, ideas and arguments contained in this collection are born of personal experience, an encyclopedic knowledge of accounting and auditing standards and practices, an analytically incisive mind and a razor-sharp intellect. They are informed by direct personal observation of what styles of accounting do and do not work and by a professional passion to improve the quality of financial accounting and reporting in the interests of better informing capital markets and the financial decisions of investors and creditors. They are founded on an unshakable commitment to the highest ideals and standards of professional ethics and personal integrity. Walter Schuetze is an independently minded and thoughtful man who is given to measured and informed judgment – a consummate professional, a true reformer.

Schuetze's ideas and proposals for accounting and auditing reform are no recitation of the wisdom of others. His writings contain remarkably few citations or references. They contain no appeals to authority or support in the academic and professional literature. Although he is well and widely read, his ideas are shaped by intuition, common sense, observation and experience. Walter Schuetze's distinguished career, professional standing, expertise and strength of character speak loudly.

His autobiographical essay is highly informative and a delight to read. It reveals how a boy reared on a farm in south-central Texas was shaped by the education he received at two small schools, and of the tremendous impact and legacy left to him by a few highly dedicated teachers. It tells of his early ambition to teach, of his passion for the English and Russian languages developed during his undergraduate education at the University of Texas at Austin, of his service in the US Air Force during the Korean War, of his subsequent keen interest in accounting, and of what was to be an outstanding career – one that, uniquely, spanned accounting practice, standard setting and regulation at the highest levels. It provides helpful and fascinating insights into the challenging life and work of a senior practitioner, standard setter and securities regulator. Importantly, it illuminates the question "how did you arrive at mark-to-market (market selling price) accounting?" especially when the idea of market selling price accounting has received little support from the academic community notwithstanding its rigorous theoretical foundations and, except for accounting for marketable securities, negligible support from the practicing profession.

It is my great respect for the ideas and my enjoyment of the style and turn of phrase in Walter Schuetze's articles published in *Accounting Horizons* in the early 1990s, together with my curiosity about how and why such an experienced practitioner arrived at mark-to-market accounting, that stimulated my quest to make available in a single volume not only his eight published pieces (seven articles and the R.J. Chambers Research Lecture) but also his thirty-four hitherto unpublished speeches, addresses and letters. His writings date from 1986 to 2002, the majority coinciding with his appointments as chief accountant to the Securities and Exchange Commission (1992–5) and chief accountant of the Enforcement Division of the Securities and Exchange Commission (1997–2000).

Following this introduction and an autobiographical essay by Schuetze, the collection is arranged thematically in three sections as follows:

1 Schuetze on accounting for assets and liabilities;
2 the implications of accounting practices for auditing; and
3 accounting standard setting and regulation.

Apart from the autobiographical piece, each section is prefaced by an editorial overview of each article, speech, address and letter, essentially in chronological order. The editorial essays seek to provide a helpful guide to the topical matters under notice in each document, and to identify major drifts of argument. Drawing on his vast professional experience, and often writing as chief accountant to the Securities and Exchange Commission, Schuetze provides fascinating insights into the most fundamental and current issues confronting accounting standard setters and securities regulators as they determine and oversee the quality of financial accounting and reporting and corporate auditing.

The major themes throughout Walter Schuetze's writings are as follows:

- The function of accounting is to inform financial decision making by investors and creditors. Consequently, accounting standard setters and corporate regulators should adopt a "capital markets perspective" in determining the kind of financial information that should be provided in general-purpose financial statements.
- Investors and creditors would be better served by a simple, relevant and transparent style of accounting in which assets are defined in terms of exchangeability and valued at current market selling prices; and in which liabilities are defined in terms of legally enforceable claims against an entity

and valued at current settlement prices. Consequently, conventional cost-based accounting should be replaced by mark-to-market accounting.

- The Securities and Exchange Commission should require public companies to mark all assets and liabilities to market, and to disclose the names of the persons or entities that provide the market price data in the financial statements.
- Auditing should entail the gathering of competent evidence of the value of assets and liabilities from the marketplace, independently of the management of the reporting enterprise. Consequently, the ethical rules and ideals pertaining to auditor independence and due care would be transformed – from a singular, but blurred, focus on the auditor–client relationship to the independence of audit evidence and testing, and the independence of audit judgment. Auditing would thus become the rigorous process of independent authentication and control over the quality of financial reporting that the Corporations and Securities Laws intend it to be.
- Auditors should carefully guard their social interactions with clients to avoid any real or apparent threat to their ability to maintain an appropriate level of professional skepticism.

A call for accounting and auditing reform

The most recent financial imbroglios have caused particular consternation, perhaps, because of the sheer magnitude of the financial consequences of the corporate failures already mentioned, and of the retrospective financial restatements of the likes of Waste Management, Sunbeam, Cendant, Livent, MicroStrategy, and Global Crossing. Governments and corporate regulators around the world are properly concerned about the potentially detrimental economic consequences of a diminution of investor confidence in financial markets occasioned by the failure of financial reporting and auditing to provide informative, reliable and transparent financial information as a basis for financial decision making by investors.

No one would attribute corporate failure to accounting *per se*. Nor are we suggesting that accounting can prevent corporate failures. Some business enterprises fail in competitive markets. Rather, the point at issue is that the financial reporting by these corporations and the auditing of their financial statements failed to provide factual and up-to-date information about their actual financial position and solvency at the time of their collapse – and of their financial performance in the period prior to their collapse. However, it could be that defective accounting contributed to the magnitude of the financial losses associated with their collapse and led to involuntary redistributions of wealth.

Schuetze argues that the solution to the financial reporting problem does not lie in improved corporate governance measures alone. He argues that the current fixation on strengthening corporate governance arrangements, including enhancing the independence of auditors – as desirable as those arrangements might be – will not fix the problem. Focusing on the independence of auditors from the management of their clients, while ignoring the substantial dependence of auditors upon management for the reported accounting numbers, is to look in the wrong direction for a solution to the corporate financial accounting and reporting dilemma. The fundamental problem, argues Schuetze, is a technical accounting problem. I agree with him.

In his recent testimony before the US Senate Committee on Banking, Housing and Urban Affairs, Schuetze (2002: 2–3) demonstrates that:

> Under our current financial reporting rules promulgated by the Financial Accounting Standards Board, management of the reporting corporation controls and determines the amounts reported in the financial statements for most assets. ... The external auditor cannot require that the reported amount of an asset be written down to its estimated selling price; the external auditor cannot even require the corporation to determine the estimated selling price of the asset and disclose that price in its financial statements. So, when it comes time to sell assets to pay debts, there often are surprise losses that investors see for the first time. ... And under the FASB's definition of an asset, corporations report as assets things that have no market price whatsoever; examples are goodwill, direct response advertising costs, deferred income taxes, future tax benefits of operating loss carried forward, costs of raising debt capital, and interest costs for debt said to relate to acquisitions of fixed assets. I call these non-real assets. Today's corporate balance sheets are laden with these non-real assets; this is the kind of stuff that allows stock prices to soar when in fact the corporate balance sheet is bloated with hot air. Of course, when it comes time to pay bills or make contributions to employees' pension funds, this stuff is worthless. The same goes for liabilities. Corporate management determines the reported amount of liabilities for such things as warranties, guarantees, commitments, environmental remediation, and restructurings. Again, this is as per the FASB's accounting rules. The upshot is that earnings management abounds.

With his characteristic ability to get to the nub of a problem, Schuetze goes on in that testimony to describe the financial reporting dilemma in the following terms:

> I liken our current accounting system to bridges built from timber, which bridges keep collapsing under the weight of eighteen-wheelers. The public demands that expert consulting engineers be called in to oversee the building of replacement bridges. But the replacement timber bridges keep collapsing under the weight of eighteen-wheelers. More expert consulting engineers will not make the timber bridges any stronger. What needs to be done to fix the problem is to build bridges with concrete and steel. The same goes with accounting. In the 1970s, after the surprise collapse of Penn Central, the auditing profession instituted peer reviews – where one auditing

firm reviews the work and quality controls of another auditing firm. In the 1970s, auditing firms also instituted concurring partner reviews, where a second audit partner within the public accounting firm looks over the shoulder of the engagement audit partner responsible for the audit. These procedures have been ineffectual as shown by the dozens of Enrons, Waste Managements, Sunbeams, MicroStrategies, Cendants, and Livents that have occurred since then. Coincidentally, the Financial Accounting Standards Board also came on the scene in the 1970s; it was going to write accounting standards that would bring forth financial statements based on concepts. What happened was that the FASB wrote a mountain of rules that produce financial statements that nobody understands and that can be and are gamed by corporate management. What all of that amounted to was continuing to build timber bridges that keep collapsing under the weight of eighteen-wheelers. We need to stop building timber bridges. We need to build concrete and steel bridges. We need to mark to market all assets and liabilities.

"True north" in financial accounting and reporting

Schuetze is the world's leading practitioner exponent of mark-to-market accounting. He stands with the world's leading intellectual exponents of mark-to-market accounting – Raymond J. Chambers and Robert R. Sterling – and with this writer in explaining the significant benefits of mark-to-market accounting for auditing and auditors, and for corporate governance.

Chambers' theory of Continuously Contemporary Accounting (CoCoA) is comprehensively set forth in Chambers (1966, 1991) and in several other works (see Chambers and Dean 1986, 2000). As a theory, CoCoA associates financial information with financial decision making and market action. Sterling's major theoretical treatise on exit price accounting was published in 1970, and the scientific foundations on which this is based in 1979. By applying the theory of measurement to accounting and to the determination of enterprise income, Sterling demonstrates how marking to market all assets and liabilities yields financial information that is relevant to all financial choices (see many of his other published works in Lee and Wolnizer 1997). That mark-to-market accounting would transform auditing into a rigorous process of quality assurance and elevate the notion of independence in auditing to include the independence of audit evidence, testing and judgment is demonstrated in Wolnizer (1987).[3]

Unlike Chambers and Sterling, Schuetze is not concerned with establishing rigorous theoretical foundations for the measurement of wealth and income. Nor is he concerned with the theoretical foundations of auditing as a process of independent verification. Rather, he is fundamentally concerned with the definition and financial quantification of assets and liabilities – with an accounting that works in the sense of informing the financial decisions of investors and creditors. However, his formulation of mark-to-market accounting, which he calls "true north," is entirely consistent with the drift of the theoretical arguments of

Chambers (1966), Sterling (1970) and Wolnizer (1987). The most comprehensive descriptions of "true north" are found in Schuetze (2001a; 2001b).

After examining the FASB's definition of an asset as a probable future economic benefit – "a high-order abstraction" – he said:

> I think we should account for real things such as trucks, not abstract future economic benefits. I suggest that we adopt a different definition of an asset. A simple one. ... I suggest that we adopt the following definition: cash, contractual claims to cash, things that can be exchanged for cash, and derivative contracts having a positive value to the holder thereof.
>
> Schuetze 2001a: 15.

Like Chambers and Sterling, Schuetze defines an asset in terms of exchangeability for cash. He argues that assets should be valued at fair value, which he defines as follows:

> The estimated amount of cash the asset would fetch in an immediate sale whether or not under duress, without recourse or guarantees, less the estimated amount of cash that would have to be paid out to accomplish the sale. This suggested definition is clear and permits no judgments about the state of the market or the willingness of the seller to sell at prices being offered or bid by potential buyers.
>
> *ibid.*: 20.

He argues that his definition of an asset

> would vastly simplify the practice of accounting. Vastly simplify financial accounting and reporting. I believe that it would appeal to investors, creditors, and other users of financial statements. I think the results of applying my definition would appeal to ordinary men and women who walk up and down Main Street in the USA, and those who walk up and down Main Street in other countries as well. They would understand the result. My sister would understand the result. I think that ordinary people who are not accountants think that when they see an asset on a balance sheet that the asset is something real, and that the dollar amount associated with the asset represents value, that is, that the asset can be exchanged for cash for approximately the dollar amount at which the asset is represented in the balance sheet.
>
> *ibid.*: 16.

Turning to liabilities, he said:

> The FASB's definition of a liability [as probable future sacrifices of economic benefits] is as infirm as its definition of an asset. ... I suggest we define liabilities by reference to future cash outflows required by negotiable instruments,

> by contracts, by law or regulation, by court-entered judgments or agreements with claimants, and derivative contracts having a negative value.
>
> *ibid.*: 18.

He argues that liabilities should also be valued at fair value, which he defines as follows: "The least amount of cash that the counterparty would accept in an immediate and complete liquidation of his/her/its claim against the reporting enterprise" (*ibid.*: 20).

Schuetze (*ibid.*: 20–4) elucidates twelve benefits of adopting the "true north" formulation of mark-to-market accounting, the most important being:

1 that financial statements in which all assets and liabilities are marked to market would be intelligible and transparent to all users of financial statements;
2 that the information contained in financial statements would be reliably verifiable by recourse to commercial evidence that can be independently corroborated;
3 that opportunities for earnings management and fraud in audited financial statements would be significantly reduced; and
4 that the currently complex institutional and political accounting standard-setting apparatus and arrangements would be replaced with a single agency charged with responsibility for providing guidance on, and refining the measurement techniques for, estimating market prices.

Schuetze acknowledges that the greatest challenge to implementing mark-to-market accounting is "estimating cash selling prices for assets for which there is no ready market" (*ibid.*: 24). He believes that the provision of guidance on that matter should be the principal role of the FASB. While acknowledging that "developing that guidance no doubt would give rise to debates about how to estimate those prices … that debate would, however, be about something that would be important and relevant for making investment and credit decisions" (*ibid.*: 25). Much of the opposition to the market selling price accounting proposals of Chambers and Sterling focused on the feasibility of obtaining market price data (McDonald 1968: 38). These unfounded criticisms prompted inquiries about the availability of market price data for several classes of commodities in different countries.[4] All of those studies demonstrated that up-to-date price data were readily available at little cost. While no generalizations can be made from those studies, they do suggest that the practical problems associated with the implementation of mark-to-market accounting may not be as significant as is sometimes surmised. Furthermore, the recent professional moves to adopt "fair value" accounting in limited settings such as accounting for financial instruments is another confirmation of the availability of market price data.

In determining what information is understandable by "ordinary folk" and what information is most relevant for making investment and credit decisions, Walter Schuetze said:

> I use my sister as a guidepost when I think about accounting issues. She has no university education. She runs a successful small business located near my home town of Comfort, Texas. She prepares financial statements for her business to run her business and so that the other owners of the business may see how well the business has done under her leadership. In the financial statements of her business, assets are cash, contractual claims to cash, and things that the business owns and that can be sold for cash – all at fair value, that is, the amount of cash any of the non-cash assets would fetch in an immediate sale for cash less cost to sell the asset. When she consults me about the preparation of the financial statements for her business and I try to explain to her the standards that we accountants use to prepare financial statements, her eyes glaze and she blames my "accountababble" on my having sat for too long in the hot Texas sun.
>
> Schuetze 2001a: 5.

Hence the subtitle of his article in *Abacus* (*ibid.*): "Accounting that my sister would understand." It is a style of accounting that hundreds of respondents to comprehensive surveys administered in Australia, Canada and Singapore also understand.[5] It is a style of accounting that investors, creditors, regulators, corporate managers and corporate directors – as well as accountants – will understand. A style of accounting that will provide factual, up-to-date, decision-relevant and reliably verified financial information to, and be transparent in, capital markets. According to Schuetze, mark-to-market accounting is "intuitively" obvious. It is not rocket science. It is readily understandable by all who have experience of normal commercial activity, of buying and selling, of lending and borrowing – of financial and market action.

In his testimony before the US Senate Committee on Banking, Housing and Urban Affairs (2002), Schuetze presented a pithy summary of "true north." In addressing the questions "how do we stop earnings management," which entails taking "control of the reported [accounting] numbers out of the hands of corporate management," he said:

> We do it by requiring that the reported numbers for assets and liabilities … be based on estimated current market prices – current cash selling prices for assets and current cash settlement prices for liabilities. And by requiring that those prices come from, or be corroborated by, competent, qualified, expert persons or entities that are not affiliated with, and do not have economic ties to, the reporting corporate entity. And by requiring that the names of the persons or entities furnishing those prices, and the consents to use their names, be included in the annual reports and quarterly reports of the reporting corporate entity so that investors can see who furnished the prices.
>
> Schuetze 2002: 3.

To my knowledge this is the most profoundly reformist proposal in respect of financial accounting and reporting, and corporate auditing, to come from the pen of an accounting practitioner. It is informed by a highly expert understanding of an accounting that has been shown repeatedly in corporate failures and litigated cases to be technically defective and to yield financial information that lacks intelligibility, transparency and relevance for financial decision making – conventional historical cost accounting.[6] It is also informed by extensive, high-level experience that suggests that market selling price accounting can be implemented in practice.

Schuetze's "true north" proposals are consistent with and are based on rigorous established – and to my knowledge largely unrefuted – theoretical foundations: the association between financial information and market action (Chambers 1966, 1991); the application of measurement theory to accounting (Sterling 1970, 1979); and auditing as a process of independent authentication and quality control (Wolnizer 1987).

Mark-to-market accounting: historical and contemporary perspectives

It may be thought that the idea of market selling price accounting is of relatively recent origin – perhaps since the mid-twentieth century. It is not. While the ground-breaking and major theoretical treatises on market selling price accounting by Chambers and Sterling date from the 1950s and 1960s, respectively, the notion that assets are legally owned objects and rights that are exchangeable for cash – and that should be valued at current market selling prices – predates the UK Joint Stock Companies Act of 1844. This is the Act from which the occurrence of such phrases as "true and correct" and "true and fair" as statutory specifications of the quality of financial statements is generally dated.

The meaning of "true and correct" or "true and fair" as the statutory quality standard for financial reporting has never been clarified by statute, case law or statements promulgated by professional accounting bodies or regulatory agencies. Consequently, it has been a matter of debate over the last thirty-five years or so. However, largely absent from that debate has been a consideration of the subjects of which a "true and fair view" is to be provided: namely, the dated financial position and financial performance of firms. Lacking specification of those subjects, the debate has been largely fruitless – notwithstanding the overriding rule (of truth and fairness in financial reporting) and the apparently critical importance of the meaning of the phrase (see Chambers and Wolnizer 1990).

Being curious about the origins of the description "true and correct" or "true and fair," Chambers and Wolnizer (1991) searched statutory references, contractual references and bookkeeping manuals dated prior to 1844 for any indications of the meaning and intention of the statutory quality standard for financial reporting. The material presented in that study was considered by the authors to have established a *prima facie* case for two propositions:

> (a) that "true and correct" and "true and fair" and like terms are simply expressions in the vernacular of the intent that financial accounts and summaries shall be false to the dated financial facts of companies in no material respect; (b) that in respect of property and other assets, the use of market selling prices ... and not cost prices would give the required view of a dated state of affairs and dated profits or results.
>
> Chambers and Wolnizer 1991: 211.

Twenty-four partnership agreements (1714–1829) and seventy deeds of settlement (1827–43) were examined in that inquiry. The lengths to which a deed of settlement might go are indicated in the 1827 deed of the Huddersfield Banking Company. That deed stipulated that the directors:

> shall cause to be provided and kept ... all necessary and proper books of account, wherein shall be entered in a fair, regular and plain method, an account of all receipts, payments, transactions and dealings ... and of all profits, gains and losses ... [and shall twice yearly] take and make up a fair, accurate, and just statement and account of the stock and capital ... so that the real state of the affairs of the company may in such statement plainly appear.
>
> *ibid.*: 203.

The deed goes on to stipulate how the property (or assets) of the bank were to be valued:

> in each such stock-taking, reference shall be had to the then value of the funded and all other property of the company which shall be estimated, not at the cost, but at the then selling price thereof; so that the real state of the affairs of the company may in such statement plainly appear.
>
> *ibid.*: 208.

Of the fifty-five bank deeds examined that gave a general valuation rule, twenty-six were of the style "not at the cost but at the then selling price ... so that the real state of affairs may plainly appear" twenty-nine were of the style "at the then fair estimated value ... for fully manifesting the state of affairs" (*ibid.*: 208).

Characteristic of the wording of the partnership agreements and deeds of settlement was the use of two or more words to describe the financial reporting required: for example, "true state or representation," "well and truly," "fairly and regularly," "fairly and impartially," "true and fair," "just true plain perfect and particular." These phrases forcefully express the idea that the financial affairs of an entity were to be conducted and reported with the utmost circumspection.

In his R.J. Chambers Research Lecture (2001b: 3), Walter Schuetze provides the following interesting insight into the introduction of mark-to-market accounting in the USA:

> Few people know that to the extent that we have mark-to-market accounting today, the credit for that belongs to the Securities and Exchange Commission, and primarily to Chairman Breeden. Incidentally, none of those commissioners in 1990 was an accountant. ... When the SEC endorsed mark to market on bonds in 1990, the banking, thrift, and insurance companies community had to be dragged, kicking and screaming, into the world of relevant, mark-to-market accounting. In a sense, the FASB was also dragged along by the SEC because none of the FASB's constituencies was in favour of mark to market, and the FASB itself was not out in front leading the charge for mark to market. But, come around it did, and now the FASB is moving forward on mark to market for all financial assets and liabilities.

Most recently, the Australian government – under the auspices of the Commonwealth Treasury – has called for fundamental accounting reform and the introduction of mark-to-market accounting. I believe this to be a world first. In 1997, the Australian government introduced the Corporate Law Economic Reform Program (CLERP). Its first reform proposal is contained in a paper titled "Accounting Standards: Building International Opportunities for Australian Business" (hereafter CLERP 1, 1997). While CLERP 1 advocates the international harmonization of accounting standards (and CLERP 9, 2002, requires Australian companies to report in accordance with IASB standards from 2005), the burgeoning literature on CLERP is overwhelmingly concerned with the harmonization issue while inadvertently neglecting, or choosing to remain silent about, the more far-reaching and significant reform agenda of mark-to-market accounting.

CLERP 1 (1997: 1) states that "It should be made clear in legislation that accounting standards should be interpreted from a commercial perspective to promote compliance by preparers of accounts, not only with the black letter of the standard, but also its overall purpose." CLERP 1 articulates the meaning of "commercial perspective" in the following words: "By a commercial perspective, it is intended that more weight should be given to the objectives of the standards and what is generally considered in the relevant market to be good commercial practice" (*ibid.*: 15). And that purpose? "The basic purpose of accounting standards is to facilitate the provision of financial information about entities to enable investors, analysts, creditors and the entities themselves to make informed decisions about the allocation of resources. Accounting standards are essentially about disclosure and, in many respects, are at the heart of market efficiency" (*ibid.*: 13).

The consistency between CLERP 1 and what Schuetze describes as a "capital markets approach" to accounting standard setting is clear:

> Accounting standards that result in the provision of accurate and comparable information about the true financial performance and position of business entities promote investor confidence and market integrity, thereby

> ultimately reducing the costs of capital throughout the economy. Public confidence in the integrity of the financial reporting framework is central to maintaining and expanding a sophisticated domestic capital market.
>
> *ibid.*: 13–14.

Having regard to that objective of promulgating accounting standards, CLERP 1 states:

> it should be specifically stated, either in the charter of the standard setter or in the legislation under which it is established, that in designing accounting standards, the standard setter should seek to ensure that compliance with accounting standards leads to the production of relevant, reliable, neutral and comparable financial information for users of financial statements.
>
> *ibid.*: 14.

While advocating that Australian companies adopt IASB standards in the "immediate future," CLERP 1 does not contemplate that conventionally prepared financial statements possess the attributes of relevance, reliability, neutrality and comparability:

> In a world of often rapidly changing asset and liability values ... fluctuating interest rates and other market developments, measurement based on historical cost can be largely meaningless for the purpose of assessing the financial standing or solvency of an entity.
>
> In view of the need for informed capital markets, there is a need to move away from the current historical cost accounting framework and to introduce a disclosure regime based on market value and risk accounting.
>
> *ibid.*: 59.

Furthermore, "Australia should be promoting moves internationally to introduce market value accounting and working cooperatively to address fundamental issues such as measurement" (*ibid.*: 59).

By market value accounting – or mark-to-market accounting – CLERP 1 means the following:

- in the case of an asset – the amount which could be expected to be received from the disposal of the asset in an orderly market; and
- in the case of a liability – the amount which could be expected to be paid to extinguish the liability in an orderly market.

ibid.: 60.

While Schuetze's "true north" proposal makes no presumptions about the state of markets and hence removes any ambiguity about whether a market is orderly or otherwise, the directive force of mark-to-market accounting in CLERP 1 is fundamentally consistent with "true north." (Like Schuetze, Sterling insists on cash selling – or exit – prices at the date of the balance sheet. Like CLERP 1,

Chambers contemplates market selling prices at the date of the balance sheet "in the ordinary course of business.")

CLERP 1 acknowledges that "While market value principles have been included in a number of Australian accounting standards (for example, in accounting for the general insurance industry), the method is not favoured by the business community" (*ibid.*: 60). Notwithstanding this opposition, CLERP 1 advocates mark-to-market accounting because it "would enable the markets to operate more efficiently through a reliance on enhanced transparency from institutions and corporations in relation to their operations. In particular, market value accounting would provide a more informative means of financial reporting for investors, market participants and regulators" (*ibid.*: 60). According to CLERP 1, the advantages of mark-to-market accounting are that it provides greater transparency, better reflects risk management practices and obviates the need for ledger accounting (*ibid.*: 60).

So we have solidly established and unrefuted theoretical foundations for mark-to-market accounting, evidence that the basic ideas of mark-to-market accounting have a rich history, evidence of the ready availability of market price data for a variety of commodity classes and evidence that at least one distinguished accounting practitioner and the Australian government (at least in CLERP 1) believe that mark-to-market accounting can and should be implemented.

The cost of implementing mark-to-market accounting

With earnings management rampant, and with a widely acknowledged crisis of confidence in the integrity and reliability of financial reporting and auditing, it is reasonable to ask "what would it cost to implement mark-to-market accounting?" There is no definitive answer to that question. However, it is a question that was raised and addressed by Schuetze in his testimony before the US Senate Committee on Banking, Housing and Urban Affairs.

Returning to his analogy of wooden versus concrete and steel bridges, he asked:

> Can we afford to build concrete and steel bridges? My response is that we cannot afford not to build concrete and steel bridges. How much of the cost of the S&L bail-out was attributable to faulty accounting; the amount is unknowable but no doubt was huge. How much does an Enron or Cendant or Waste Management or MicroStrategy or Sunbeam cost? The answer for investors is billions, and that does not count the human anguish when working employees lose their jobs, their 401k assets, and their medical insurance, and retired employees lose their cash retirement benefits and medical insurance. By some estimates, Enron alone cost $60–70 billion in terms of market capitalization that disappeared in just a few months. Waste Management, Sunbeam, Cendant, Livent, MicroStrategy, and the others also cost billions in terms of market capitalization that disappeared when their earnings management games were exposed. And, these costs do not

> include the immeasurable cost of lost confidence by investors in financial reports and the consequent negative effect on the cost of capital and market efficiency.
>
> By my estimate, annual external audit fees in the United States for our 16,000 public companies, 7,000 mutual funds, and 7,000 broker/dealers total about $12 billion. Let's say that $4 billion is attributable to mutual funds and broker/dealers. (Incidentally, mutual funds and broker/dealers already mark to market their assets every day at the close of business, and we have very few problems with fraudulent financial statements being issued by those entities. Mark to market works and is effective.) That leaves $8 billion attributable to the 16,000 public companies. Assume that the $8 billion would be doubled or even tripled if the 16,000 public companies had to get competent, outside valuation experts … to determine the estimated cash market prices of their assets and liabilities. We are then looking at an additional annual cost of $16–24 billion. If we prevented just one Enron per year by requiring mark-to-market accounting, we would easily pay for that additional cost. And, when considered in relation to the total market capitalization of the US corporate stock and bond markets of more than $20 trillion, $16–24 billion is indeed a small price to pay.
>
> Schuetze 2002: 5.

A small price indeed for factually informative and reliably audited financial reports, and a solid foundation for corporate governance.

Who should mandate mark-to-market accounting?

Both Chambers and Schuetze have addressed that question. In his R.J. Chambers Research Lecture (2001b: 11), Schuetze said:

> I have been in this business since August 1, 1957. I think that I have seen every side and dimension of this [earnings management] problem. … The SEC must make deep and fundamental changes to the [accounting] system. Unless and until the SEC requires that assets be reported at estimated selling prices, which of course means that only things that have a market price could be represented as assets, nothing will change. Unless and until the SEC requires that liabilities be reported at estimated settlement prices, nothing will change. Unless and until the SEC requires that … external auditors get evidence about those selling and settlement prices from persons or entities outside the reporting enterprise, nothing will change.

Again, in his testimony before the US Senate Committee on Banking, Housing and Urban Affairs (2002: 5), Schuetze stated:

> I recommend that there be a sense of the Congress resolution that corporate balance sheets must present the reporting corporation's true economic

> financial condition through mark-to-market accounting for the corporation's assets and liabilities. I recommend that Congress leave implementation to the SEC, much the way it is done today by the SEC for broker/dealers and mutual funds.

Like Schuetze, Chambers anticipated that the introduction of mark-to-market accounting will require legislation. As chairman of the Accounting Standards Review Committee appointed by the New South Wales Government (1978), he suggested that the following two sentences in the Corporations Act would be sufficient:

> No balance sheet shall be deemed or declared to give a true and fair view of the state of affairs of a company unless the amounts shown for the several assets, other than cash and amounts receivable, are the best available approximations to the net selling prices in the ordinary course of business of those assets in their state and condition as at the date of the balance sheet.
>
> No profit and loss account shall be deemed or declared to give a true and fair view of the profit or loss of a company unless that profit or loss is so calculated as to include the effects during the year of changes in the net selling prices of assets and of changes in the general purchasing power of the unit of account.[7]

In Australia, the CLERP would be a convenient vehicle for introducing such a requirement into the Corporations Law.

A concluding comment

I am delighted and honored to be a friend and colleague of Walter Schuetze. We first met in Washington in 1998 while he was chief accountant to the Enforcement Division of the SEC. Since then, we have enjoyed countless conversations about accounting and auditing in Washington, Houston, San Antonio and Sydney. We maintain a regular dialogue as the unwelcome financial and professional consequences of the spread of Enronitis continue unabated and, from our observation of the pronouncements of accounting standard-setting bodies, without a cure in prospect. My admiration of his reformist accounting ideas and professional ideals has grown increasingly as I have read and reread his articles, speeches and letters in the course of preparing this volume.

In compiling this anthology I acknowledge my debt to Walter. Over the last five years, I have learned more about the intricacies of accounting and auditing practices and standards than I could ever have imagined. And I have been fascinated to learn about the world of accounting practice, accounting standard setting and corporate regulation. Importantly, he has greatly stimulated my thinking about the practical benefits and possibility of implementing mark-to-market accounting.

Having had the personal pleasure and intellectual privilege of completing my PhD under Ray Chambers' rigorous supervision, and of undertaking my post-doctoral studies under Bob Sterling's stimulating mentoring, it has been my very good fortune to learn about the practicalities of implementing mark-to-market accounting from Walter Schuetze. While the theoretical case for mark-to-market accounting, established by Chambers and Sterling, is compelling and substantially unchallenged, Walter Schuetze is the first practitioner to argue the case on practical grounds. In the light of the most recent experiences of Enronitis, the cases put by Chambers, Schuetze and Sterling for mark-to-market accounting seem unassailable. They merit the most serious and urgent consideration by national and international accounting and auditing standard setters and corporate regulators.

I hope that all who read this book will benefit as much as I have from the extensive experience, penetrating insights and informed understanding of one of the most eminent accountants in the world in relation to financial accounting and reporting and corporate auditing: Walter P. Schuetze, accounting reformer.

Notes

1 The US General Accounting Office found 919 retrospective restatements of financial statements for accounting irregularities by 845 public companies between January 1997 and June 2002 (see GAO-03-138, "Financial statement restatements – trends, market impacts, regulatory responses, and remaining challenges," 4 October 2002).

2 For a comprehensive analysis of several of those corporate failures, covering their accounting, ethical and regulatory dimensions, see Clarke *et al.* 2003.

3 See also Chambers 1973; Lee 1993, Sterling 1968, 1970; Wolnizer 1978, 1995.

4 McDonald 1968; Foster 1969; McKeown 1971; Gray 1975; Wolnizer 1977, 1983; see also Dean and Wells 1984.

5 Chambers and Falk 1985; Chambers and Clarke 1986; Chambers *et al.* 1987.

6 See, for example, Chambers 1973; Clarke *et al.* 2003; Stamp *et al.* 1980; Sykes 1994.

7 See Chambers, 1973: 219; Chambers *et al.* 1978: 97; Chambers and Wolnizer 1990: 366.

Bibliography

Chambers, R.J. (1966) *Accounting, Evaluation and Economic Behavior*, Englewood Cliffs, NJ: Prentice Hall.

Chambers, R.J. (1973) *Securities and Obscurities. A Case for Reform of the Law of Company Accounts*, Melbourne: Gower Press.

Chambers, R.J. (1991) *Foundations of Accounting*, Geelong: Deakin University Press.

Chambers, R.J. and Clarke, F.L. (1986) *Varieties and Uses of Financial Information*, Sydney: University of Sydney Accounting Research Centre Monograph No. 6.

Chambers, R.J. and Dean, G.W. (eds) (1986) *Chambers on Accounting*, Vols 1–5, New York: Garland.

Chambers, R.J. and Dean, G.W. (eds) (2000) *Chambers on Accounting*, Vol. 6, New York: Garland.

Chambers, R.J. and Falk, H. (1985) *The Serviceability of Financial Information: A Survey*, Vancouver: Canadian Certified General Accountants Research Foundation.

Chambers, R.J., Ma, R., Hopkins, R. and Kasiraja, N. (1987) *Financial Information and Decision Making: A Singapore Survey*, Singapore: Singapore Institute of Management and University of Sydney Accounting Research Centre.

Chambers, R.J., Ramanathan, T.S. and Rappaport, H.H. (1978) *Company Accounting Standards*, report of Accounting Standards Review Committee to NSW Attorney General, Sydney: NSW Government Printer.

Chambers, R.J. and Wolnizer, P.W. (1990) "A true and fair view of financial position," *Company and Securities Law Journal* 8, 354–68; reprinted in *Economia Aziendale*, X: 183–203 and also in R.H. Parker, P.W. Wolnizer and C.W. Nobes (eds) (1995) *Readings in True and Fair*, New York: Garland, 153–68.

Chambers, R.J. and Wolnizer, P.W. (1991) "A true and fair view of position and results: the historical background," *Accounting, Business and Financial History* 1, 197–213; reprinted in G.G. Kaufman (ed.), *Research in Financial Services: Private and Public Policy*, 5, 1–17 and also in R.H. Parker, P.W. Wolnizer and C.W. Nobes (eds) (1995) *Readings in True and Fair*, New York: Garland, 5–21.

Clarke, F.L., Dean, G.W. and Oliver, K.G. (2003) *Corporate Collapse: Regulatory, Accounting and Ethical Failure*, 2nd (revised) edn, Melbourne: Cambridge University Press.

Commonwealth of Australia (1997) "Accounting Standards: Building International Opportunities for Australian Business," *Corporate Law Economic Reform Program: Proposals for Reform*: Paper No. 1, Canberra: Treasury.

Commonwealth of Australia, (2002) "Corporate disclosure – strengthening the financial reporting framework," *Corporate Law Economic Reform Program: Proposals for Reform*: Paper No. 9, Canberra: Treasury.

Dean, G.W. and Wells, M.C. (eds) (1984) *The Case for Continuously Contemporary Accounting*, New York: Garland.

Foster, G.J. (1969) "Mining inventories in a current price accounting system," *Abacus* 5, 99–118; reprinted in G.W. Dean and M.C. Wells (eds) (1984) *The Case for Continuously Contemporary Accounting*, New York: Garland, 367–86.

Gray, S.J. (1975) "Price changes and company profits in the securities market," *Abacus* 11, 71–85; reprinted in G.W. Dean and M.C. Wells (eds) (1984) *The Case for Continuously Contemporary Accounting*, New York: Garland, 405–19.

Lee, T.A. (1993) *Corporate Audit Theory*, London: Chapman & Hall.

Lee, T.A. and Wolnizer, P.W. (eds) (1997) *The Quest for a Science of Accounting: An Anthology of the Research of Robert R. Sterling*, New York: Garland.

McDonald, D.L. (1968) "A test application of the feasibility of market based measures in accounting," *Journal of Accounting Research* 6, 38–49; reprinted in G.W. Dean and M.C. Wells (eds) (1984) *The Case for Continuously Contemporary Accounting*, New York: Garland, 355–66.

McKeown, J.C. (1971) "An empirical test of a model proposed by Chambers," *Accounting Review* XLVI, 12–29; reprinted in G.W. Dean and M.C. Wells (eds) (1984) *The Case for Continuously Contemporary Accounting*, New York: Garland, 387–404.

Schuetze, W.P. (2001a) "What are assets and liabilities? Where is true north? (Accounting that my sister would understand)," *Abacus* 37, 1–25.

Schuetze, W.P. (2001b) "A memo to national and international accounting and auditing standard setters and securities regulators", R.J. Chambers Memorial Research Lecture, Sydney: Accounting Foundation within the University of Sydney.

Schuetze, W.P. (2002) prepared statement by Mr Walter P. Schuetze, chief accountant, Securities and Exchange Commission 1992–5, hearing on "Accounting and Investor Protection Issues Raised by Enron and Other Public Companies: Oversight of the

Accounting Profession, Audit Quality and Independence, and Formulation of Accounting Principles," US Senate Committee on Banking, Housing, and Urban Affairs, http://banking.senate.gov/02_02hrg/022602/schuetze.htm.

Stamp, E., Dean, G.W. and Wolnizer, P.W. (eds) (1980) *Notable Financial Causes Célèbres*, New York: Arno Press.

Sterling, R.R. (1968) "A glimpse of the forest," *The Accountant's Journal*, November: 589–94; reprinted in T.A. Lee and P.W. Wolnizer (eds) (1997) *The Quest for a Science of Accounting: An Anthology of the Research of Robert R. Sterling*, New York: Garland, 375–80.

Sterling, R.R. (1970) *Theory of the Measurement of Enterprise Income*, Lawrence: University Press of Kansas.

Sterling, R.R. (1979) *Toward a Science of Accounting*, Houston: Scholars Book Co.

Sykes, T. (1994) *The Bold Riders: Behind Australia's Corporate Collapses*, Sydney: Allen & Unwin.

Wolnizer, P.W. (1977) "Primary production inventories under current value accounting," *Accounting and Business Research* 28, 303–10; reprinted in G.W. Dean and M.C. Wells (eds) (1984) *The Case for Continuously Contemporary Accounting*, New York: Garland, 421–8.

Wolnizer, P.W. (1978) "Independence in auditing: an incomplete notion," *Abacus* 14, 31–52.

Wolnizer, P.W. (1983) "Market prices v. cost indexation in accounting for steel inventories," *Abacus* 19, 171–88.

Wolnizer, P.W. (1987) *Auditing as Independent Authentication*, Sydney: Sydney University Press.

Wolnizer, P.W. (1995) "Are audit committees red herrings?" *Abacus* 31, 45–66.

2 Autobiography

Walter P. Schuetze

I was born on 2 August 1932 in Comfort, Texas, USA. I was raised on a farm located in south-central Texas in Kerr County between Comfort and Center Point, Texas, about fifty miles northwest of San Antonio and about one hundred miles west and slightly south of Austin, the capital of Texas.

Grades one through seven from September 1938 through May 1945 were in a one-room schoolhouse in Kerr County on the banks of the Guadalupe River. (A second room was added in about 1943, where we ate our cold lunches brought from home.) It was called the Union Valley School. There were three children in my class for all seven years, Lorraine Boerner, Leroy Pressler, and me. I don't recall exactly, but at most there were about twenty-five children in the Union Valley School. From 1938 to 1942, our teacher was Bodo Burrow. In 1942, he entered the US Navy on account of World War II. He was succeeded by an eighteen-year-old woman, Helen Spenrath, who had just graduated from high school. She taught all twenty-five of us reading, writing, arithmetic, geography, and history – in one room. We all learned together. She was wonderful.

I then went to Center Point High School for grades nine through twelve. (No grade eight.) On graduation in 1949, I was the class valedictorian. It was there that two teachers – Grace Wallis and Frank Gilliland – took me under their wings, mentoring me for three years. They took me with them wherever they went – to bull fights in Mexico, to the opera in San Antonio, and to open-air symphony concerts in Boulder, Colorado. They took me with them to college at Stephen F. Austin State College in Nacogdoches in east Texas in the summer of 1949, where they took postgraduate courses and I started my college learning. I cannot express how much I enjoyed their company and how much I am indebted to them for opening my eyes to the world around me.

I moved from Stephen F. Austin to the University of Texas at Austin in the fall of 1950. My major was in English language, and my minor was in foreign languages. I was going to be an English teacher. I enrolled in a course in Russian language in 1950, because a course in Spanish language, which I wanted to take, was not available. That course in Russian language changed the course of my life.

In January 1951, the Korean conflict was in full throttle, and I enlisted in the US Air Force. When the military learned that I knew some Russian, I was shipped off to the Army Language School in Monterey, California, and I spent six months learning more Russian. I became a Russian language specialist in the Security Service of the Air Force. From the summer of 1952 through May 1955, I was stationed in England and Scotland, where I, and others in the Air Force, monitored the voice and telegraphic traffic of the Soviet army and air force in East Germany and Europe. It was in Scotland that I met and married my wife Jean.

While in Scotland, I read an article in a magazine, maybe *Time*, about accountants and accounting. Somehow, I was attracted to the idea of being an accountant. So, after I finished my tour of duty in the Air Force in 1955, I went back to the University of Texas at Austin and began to study accounting. I liked it. I still do.

My accounting teachers at the university included George Newlove (cost accounting), Glenn Welsch (advanced accounting), and John White (introductory accounting). In the 1950s, they were leaders in accounting in academia and had all written textbooks.

I graduated from the university with honors in the summer of 1957. My degree is a Bachelor of Business Administration. I was and am a member of Beta Alpha Psi and Beta Gamma Sigma honorary societies.

I need to mention here that but for the GI Bill of Rights, I would not have been able to finish college as I did not have the money to do so. Pursuant to the GI Bill, every veteran of World War II and the Korean War was entitled to receive a stipend to attend college. That stipend, about $89 a month as I recall, allowed me to attend college and get my degree. I am grateful to the American public for that stipend. It was a godsend.

On 1 August 1957, I started work as a junior staff accountant with a small public accounting firm in San Antonio, Eaton & Huddle. Although I had received offers of employment from all of the companies and firms that I had interviews with – two Fortune 500 companies, three of the then big eight accounting firms, and Eaton & Huddle – I decided to join the last of these. I had been interviewed on campus by Thomas L. Holton of Eaton & Huddle. After my visit to the firm's offices and meeting the people there, Tom Holton made me an offer; I decided to join Eaton & Huddle because I liked the cut of Tom Holton's jib and because I thought that I would get more varied experience in a small firm and at the same time be closer to the partners than in a large firm. Eaton & Huddle had three senior partners, led by Marquis Eaton, who at the time was president of the American Institute of Certified Public Accountants. The firm had four junior partners, including Tom Holton, and about thirty staff. Marquis Eaton died in the spring of 1958. On 1 July 1958, Eaton & Huddle merged with Peat, Marwick, Mitchell & Co., now KPMG LLP. Tom Holton would later be elected chairman of Peat Marwick.

I received my public accounting certificate from the state of Texas in 1959.

My first six years in public accounting were in San Antonio. Audit and tax clients were primarily small oil and gas exploration and production companies, oil and gas drilling companies, banks, savings and loan associations, and insurance companies. For the most part these clients were not public companies, although a few were. Financial institutions were just beginning to have audits of their financial statements performed by independent public accountants (in addition to examinations by regulators such as the banking authorities). Peat Marwick was to the fore in auditing the financial statements of financial institutions. I participated in many of those audits, first as a staff accountant and then at progressively higher levels. Peat Marwick performed the first external audit of the financial statements of Chase Manhattan Bank in either 1959 or 1960, and I went from San Antonio to New York to participate in that audit. I spent about four weeks working on that audit. What a wonderful experience.

In the 1950s and 1960s, many small and medium-sized companies were becoming public companies so as to raise money, grow, and compete. The public accounting profession was growing by leaps and bounds. So was Peat Marwick. To deal with this growing number of public company clients, among them many financial institutions, Peat Marwick created its Department of Professional Practice in New York, known as DPP. The department started with two partners, John Peoples and George Shepherd, one career manager and three newly minted managers, one from Philadelphia, one from Los Angeles, and me from San Antonio. (At the time of writing in 2002, DPP had a hundred partners and senior managers.) John Peoples was the firm's representative on the AICPA's Accounting Principles Board and had been the firm's representative on the AICPA's Committee on Accounting Procedure. The managers were to spend two years in DPP in New York and then go back to an operating office. I stayed for seven years.

What DPP did, in those early years, was help partners and managers in practice offices to deal with accounting and auditing problems (mostly accounting problems), review clients' financial statements after their issuance to detect areas for improvement in future years, review the financial statements of non-clients to determine best practices, prepare firm bulletins and manuals and disseminate those to practice offices, and serve as staff to the firm's committees of senior partners who dealt with accounting and regulatory matters arising primarily with respect to public company clients that filed financial statements with the US Securities and Exchange Commission.

I worked in DPP from the summer of 1963 to the summer of 1970. I was admitted to the partnership in 1965. I worked with John Peoples and then with Joseph P. Cummings, who succeeded John Peoples on the Accounting Principles Board. From 1965 to the summer of 1970, I was Joe Cummings' technical adviser and attended meetings of the Accounting Principles Board as an observer. (Joe Cummings was the second chairman of the International Accounting Standards Committee in the 1970s after the APB was dissolved.) The APB met for about three days every other month. I watched as the APB deliberated and wrote Opinions 9 through 17. In fact, I did more than watch. Observers, and there were seven or eight of us, would, overnight, draft portions of Opinions that the APB had deliberated that day for the APB to review, re-deliberate, and re-vote the next day. Many times, the APB changed its mind the next day, and we observers went back to the drafting table to craft new language based on new instructions from the APB. Fascinating work. "Work" is not the right word; it was, to me, a labor of love. I am to this day fascinated with writing the words of accounting standards, observing how financial statements are prepared using those standards, and observing how those financial statements are then used by investors in making investment decisions.

While in DPP, I prepared, with the help of a number of partners and managers located in operating offices, the firm's Accounting and Audit Manual for Savings and Loan Associations, worked on other technical manuals and bulletins, reviewed filings by clients with the Securities and Exchange Commission, and assisted partners in operating offices of the firm in responding to accounting and auditing matters that arose in practice.

My stay in DPP started in 1963, and in 1970 Joe Cummings insisted that I go out to an operating office and deal with clients on a day-to-day basis. So, in the summer of 1970, I transferred to the firm's Los Angeles office and worked as an audit engagement partner and SEC reviewing partner. (It was the firm's policy that all client registration statements filed with the Securities and Exchange Commission be reviewed by a designated SEC reviewing partner who was not the audit engagement partner.) While in Los Angeles, I served as the audit engagement partner to Bourns Inc., City Investing Company, Max Factor, Motel 6, Southern California Savings and Loan Association, and Western Airlines.

Late in 1972, I was invited to serve as a member of the newly formed Financial Accounting Standards Board. In March 1973, the FASB began operations, and I moved from Los Angeles to Stamford, Connecticut, where the FASB was originally located. (It is now located in Norwalk, Connecticut.) I served on the FASB until 30 June 1976. My term on the FASB ran for five years, from 1973 through 1978, but I decided to go back to public practice in 1976.

The early years at the FASB were fascinating. Board members did nitty-gritty, pick-and-shovel work, drafting discussion memoranda, exposure drafts, and final statements of financial accounting standards. Board meetings often ran late into the night. Board members and staff understood why the AICPA's Committee on Accounting Procedure and the Accounting Principles Board had not achieved their desired measure of success, and we very much wanted to prove to the world, and to ourselves, that we could succeed in setting standards where our predecessors had not. There was a great sense of camaraderie and a can-do spirit. I signed FASB Statements of Financial Accounting Standards 1–12 and Interpretations 1–9. Statements 3, 4, 6, 7, 10, and 11 dealt with very narrow issues and continue in force today. Statements 1, 8, 9, and 12 have been superseded by subsequent statements. Statement 2, R&D costs, and Statement 5, loss contingencies, were and are broad in scope and application and continue in force today.

In those early days of the FASB, we did not have a written conceptual framework as the FASB has now. We relied on our experiences, judgment, and intuition in writing the early standards that were issued by the FASB. In retrospect, I think that we were not very successful. FASB Statement 2 – expense

R&D costs as incurred – has survived but is under attack by many who would like to see some or all R&D costs capitalized or who would like to see the value of a company's R&D represented on its balance sheet. (I like the results of Statement 2 because I think that only things that can be exchanged for cash may be represented as assets in balance sheets and, incidentally, that costs can never be assets. The reason given in Statement 2 for charging to expense all R&D costs as incurred is that the future benefit is uncertain, not that things that are represented in balance sheets as assets must be exchangeable and that costs may not be represented as assets.) FASB Statement 8 on foreign currency translation was faithful to the historical cost notion as to non-monetary assets, but it lasted only a few years and was replaced by Statement 52. Corporations would not accept the income-statement results produced by Statement 8, primarily because cost of inventory was translated at the historical rate instead of the current rate, which put the effect of exchange rate changes into the period of the sale of the inventory instead of when the exchange rate changed. Statement 52 makes a pig's breakfast of balance sheets, what with (1) domestic non-monetary assets at historical cost and foreign non-monetary assets at historical cost but translated at the current exchange rate instead of the exchange rate in existence at the time of the acquisition of the asset and with (2) deferral of transaction gains and losses on management-designated economic hedges of net investments in a foreign entity and translation adjustments.

FASB Statement 5 on loss contingencies (warranties, bad debts, claims against the corporation by outsiders, and the like) looks and sounds good but does not work in practice. The two standards in Statement 5 – probable that a loss has been incurred and the amount of loss is reasonably estimable – allow for so much judgment and leeway that in practice they amount to no standard at all. Witness the manner in which commercial banks measure their bad debt allowances – almost any amount that they want. I have told the FASB on numerous occasions that Statement 5 does not work.

The FASB has now had a written conceptual framework for about fifteen years, but I think that the FASB's standards, said to be based on that framework, are producing financial statements that are not very useful in the hands of investors trying to make investment decisions. I have made several speeches and written several articles expressing my views about financial statements that are being produced nowadays as a result of the FASB's standards; the most recent and most comprehensive article is entitled "What are assets and liabilities? Where is true north? (Accounting that my sister would understand)," which appeared in *Abacus* in February 2001. Rather than repeat or summarize that article here, I refer the reader of this piece to that article.

In July 1976, I returned to KPMG's DPP in New York as a partner in the firm. (When I left the firm in 1973, I severed all ties with it and had no agreement or understanding that I would or could return. It just so happened that when I decided in 1976 to leave the FASB and go back to public practice, the partner in KPMG's DPP who was in charge of the Accounting Group function had become ill, and there was an opening for a person with my background, skills, and experience.) I served in DPP until January 1992, when I was appointed chief accountant to the US Securities and Exchange Commission.

In DPP, I was the partner in charge of the Accounting Group and had responsibility for the preparation and maintenance of the firm's Accounting Manual and related bulletins and letters. I was vice-chair of the firm's Committee on Accounting Practice. I also served as an SEC reviewing partner. As the partner in charge of the Accounting Group and as an SEC reviewing partner, I was extensively involved in consultation with engagement partners in the firm's operating offices on financial accounting and reporting issues and with the staff of the Securities and Exchange Commission and various banking and savings and loan association regulators.

While in DPP, I was the firm's representative for about eight years on the AICPA's Accounting Standards Executive Committee, which I chaired for three years. The Accounting Standards Executive Committee is the AICPA's senior technical committee authorized to speak for the AICPA on all accounting matters. That committee prepares statements of position and clears all AICPA Accounting and Audit Guides and other documents that speak to accounting matters. As chair of the Accounting Standards Executive Committee, I was an observer at meetings of the FASB's Emerging Issues Task Force with the privilege of the floor but no vote. As chair of the Accounting Standards Executive Committee, I was a member of the Financial Accounting Standards Advisory Council for three years.

While in DPP, I worked on dozens of important accounting issues for both the firm and the profession. But one issue stands out in my mind as the most important, from the standpoint of both KPMG and the profession. This particular issue had a life span of ten to twelve years, so I will describe it only briefly.

After the second Arab oil embargo in 1976, asset prices began to spiral upward in the USA, and interest rates began to climb. KPMG was at that time the dominant thrift auditor in the profession, serving as auditor to thrifts having about 45 percent of total thrift deposits. The thrift industry invested primarily in thirty-year mortgage loans and funded its asset base with short-term deposits. In or about the late 1970s, insurance for deposit accounts was raised by Congress from $40,000 to $100,000. At about the same time, brokers such as Merrill Lynch were allowed to broker deposits, which theretofore had been gathered only at the local level. Short-term interest rates rose to very high levels, in excess of the rates that many in the thrift industry were earning on their investments in mortgage loans. At or about this same time, thrifts were allowed to invest in loans secured by land and land acquisition, development, and construction projects – at 100 percent of the value of the underlying collateral. Anxious to eliminate or reduce their negative spreads (paying more in interest on deposits than they were earning in interest on their loan portfolios), many thrifts began to make so-called loans on ADC projects. These thrifts funded 100 percent of the developers' cost of land and improvements to the land. Because the project owners had no investment in the ADC projects other than their sweat, the project owners were willing to "pay" large up-front points to the thrift lender, sometimes as much as 5, 6, 7, or 8 percent of the amount of the loan; the "payment" was not made in cash but was added to the loan balance or deducted from the loan proceeds. Then, as construction proceeded, interest during construction was added to the loan balance as well as construction "draws." At the end of the construction phase, the balance of the construction loan – cash advanced to the ADC project owner plus points plus accrued and uncollected interest – was rolled over into a semi-permanent loan. The interest rate being charged by the thrift lender was very high – greater than the thrift was paying on its deposit accounts. In addition, in many cases, the thrift lender would, on the ultimate sale of the project, participate with the ADC project owner in the profits on the sale of the project. The thrifts were crediting to earned revenue the uncollected up-front points and the accrued but uncollected interest.

We at KPMG saw all this revenue piling up in the balance sheets of the thrift lenders as uncollected points and interest and concluded that the thrift lenders were in fact jointly venturing with the ADC project owners in the ADC projects. So, early in 1983, we stepped hard on the revenue-recognition brakes and notified our thrift clients that no more revenue could be recognized until the ADC projects were sold and cash was collected. Well, everyone went through the windshield. Our clients screamed bloody murder.

We notified all the other major accounting firms, the thrift regulators, and the staff of the SEC of our position. Many thrift regulators were taken aback. The other accounting firms thought we were daft. Too far out in front, one of them told me. Of course they were happy to take our clients. Fortunately, not too many clients left our firm, although many were extremely unhappy. But we did not get some prospective new clients when our position became known to them. (Tom Holton was chairman of the firm at this time.)

It took the rest of the profession and the thrift regulators and the SEC several years to come to the same position that KPMG had in early 1983. But, by then, huge amounts of reported revenue had piled up in thrift balance sheets as uncollected receivables for points and accrued interest. In the savings and loan bail-out by the US federal government in the late 1980s, the US taxpayer paid for that faulty asset/revenue recognition. Ultimately, in the early 1990s, the large accounting firms that were auditors to the thrift industry paid the US government huge amounts of money as a result of having certified thrift financial statements that included those faulty receivables and revenue. But not KPMG, because of the stand we had taken in 1983.

I was appointed chief accountant to the Securities and Exchange Commission in January 1992 and served in that capacity until March 1995, when I retired for the first time.

Richard Breeden was the chairman of the SEC in 1992. The commission, in testimony that Richard Breeden had given to Congress in September 1990, had taken the position that commercial banks should mark to market their bond holdings, which up till then banks had reported at amortized cost. I had for many years promoted the idea that banks and other entities should mark to market their assets, so my views and Richard Breeden's views were in sync. I spent a lot of time from January 1992 through March 1995 convincing banks, banking and thrift regulators, and the FASB that banks, thrifts, and insurance companies should mark to market their bond holdings.

The chief accountant is the SEC's principal adviser and spokesperson on matters involving accounting and auditing. The Office of the Chief Accountant monitors the activity of the Financial Accounting Standards Board and the AICPA's Accounting Standards Executive Committee, Auditing Standards Board, and SEC Practice Section, which includes the Public Oversight Board, to determine whether those bodies are acting in the public interest. As chief accountant, I attended meetings of the FASB's Emerging Issues Task Force and the Financial Accounting Standards Advisory Council with the privilege of the floor.

The chief accountant interacts with the staff of the US Congress, the staff of the General Accounting Office and the Comptroller General, and the staffs of other federal regulatory agencies such as the Federal Reserve Board, the Comptroller of the Currency, the Federal Insurance Corporation, and the Office of Thrift Supervision.

The chief accountant, in the day-to-day administration of the securities laws, has the final say on accounting and related disclosure by corporate registrants, and a significant amount of my time was spent on corporate registrants' accounting and disclosure problems. My decisions could, of course, be appealed by registrants to the chairman of the commission and ultimately to the full commission. In the three plus years that I was chief accountant, only one of my decisions was appealed to the chairman, and he reversed my decision. I will describe that situation briefly.

A very small company was in the business of originating "reverse mortgage loans," which is an instrument whereunder senior citizen homeowners can monetize the equity in their homes primarily in order to meet day-to-day cash needs. The lender makes periodic, generally monthly, cash advances to the homeowner. When the homeowner dies, the home is sold, and the proceeds are used to repay the lender's cash advances plus interest, with any remaining balance going to the heirs of the homeowner. If the proceeds on sale are insufficient to repay to the lender the amount of cash advances plus interest, the lender bears the loss.

This company wanted to "go public" through the offering of common stock. This company's major asset was its portfolio of reverse mortgage loans. Accounting for the portfolio of reverse mortgage loans was critical.

The company had accounted for the cash advances as loans and had added the amount of contractual, uncollected interest to the balance of the loan. The company credited earned interest revenue with the amount of the contractual, uncollected interest. I took exception to the company's accounting. I told the company that it should account for the reverse mortgage loan as an investment in real estate; thus, contractual interest would not be credited to income. Instead, on the owner's death and sale of the home, gain or loss would be recognized at that time. I took this position because of two factors. One, the company was exposed to what is called the risk of adverse selection. What this means is that the company's homeowner borrowers were likely those who were in very good health and thus would outlive the actuarial tables, thereby saddling the company with the risk that cash advances plus accrued interest over a very long period would be greater than the proceeds on sale of the home at the owner's death. Second, the company was exposed to garden-variety real estate risk; that is, the value of the home might decline, thereby exposing the company to the risk that proceeds on sale of the home upon the owner's death would be less than cash advances plus uncollected interest.

One of these risks, namely real estate risk, was the same as the savings and loans had faced with ADC loans as discussed above. Moreover, and more importantly, the entire cash proceeds to this company would come from the sale of real estate, not from the borrower's cash flow as in the case of other, normal lending.

Although this company was very small, the company's founders were well connected with the senior citizen, banking, and housing lobbies in Washington. Moreover, the business of reverse mortgage lending was just getting started and, politically, a lot of very prominent people in Washington and elsewhere very much wanted this little company's initial public offering to be a success. My accounting meant that this company's income statement looked very sickly, and the initial public offering, which was keenly anticipated, would not come off. The company and its followers appealed to the chairman, who instructed me to accept the company's original accounting. I think that the chairman knew that my accounting was correct, but he was unwilling, at that time, to take on another political challenge in addition to the opposition he was facing in the banking industry in getting the banks to mark to market their bond portfolios. I decided to accept the chairman's instructions and not resign my position as chief accountant, primarily because the company was very small and there were no other companies with a similar asset base where there would be a similar problem. In addition, I very much wanted to succeed in getting banks to mark to market their bond portfolios, and I could not do that if I resigned.

Interestingly, as I write this piece in 2002, the federal government now has an insurance program available to reverse mortgage lenders whereunder the lender may buy insurance from the government at a very low, government-subsidized price to cover any shortfall in the proceeds upon the death of the homeowner, which would protect the reverse mortgage lender against the risks I have described above. The apparent reason for the insurance program is that Congress must have concluded that reverse mortgage lending is desirable and that the risks need to be taken on by the federal government in order to encourage this type of lending. This program came into being after my encounter in the early 1990s with the small company described above.

Between March 1995 and November 1997, while in retirement, I delivered a few lectures on accounting subjects to students of St Mary's University in San Antonio, Texas, and the University of Southern California in Los Angeles. Also, while in retirement, at the invitation of the AICPA, I served on the International Accounting Standards Committee's steering committee dealing with intangible assets, business combinations, and impairment of assets. I resigned from that steering committee when I rejoined the staff of the SEC.

In November 1997, I came out of retirement when I was appointed chief accountant of the Enforcement Division of the SEC, which position I held until mid-February 2000, when I retired again.

The chief accountant of the Enforcement Division of the SEC oversees those aspects of SEC investigations and administrative proceedings dealing with audit and accounting matters, including auditor independence. The SEC's enforcement cases involve civil law. The chief accountant also becomes involved sometimes, on a consultative basis, in investigations and prosecutions by the US Justice Department and various state law enforcement authorities into securities law violations involving criminal law, particularly in cases involving parallel investigations and prosecutions of securities law violations by both the SEC and criminal authorities. The involvement with criminal authorities is fairly slight, but it is significant.

At the time of this writing in 2002, I am retired. From March 2000 through March 2002, I was a consultant to the Enforcement Division of the SEC. Currently, I serve on the boards of directors of Computer Associates International Inc. and TransMontaigne Inc. and chair their audit committees. I am also an expert witness on accounting and auditing matters in several litigations. In August 2002, I was appointed an executive in residence at the School of Business at the University of Texas at San Antonio.

My mother is now 87 and still lives in the town where I was born. My father died in 1976. My sister and two brothers also live in Texas.

My wife Jean and I live in a small town called Fair Oaks Ranch, Texas (mailing address is 8940 Fair Oaks Parkway, Boerne, Texas 78015), twenty-five miles from San Antonio airport and twenty-five miles from Comfort. We have three boys, aged 44, 43, and 39, and two grandchildren, aged 16 and 8.

Addendum

One day, in our many conversations about accounting and auditing, Peter Wolnizer asked me how I had got onto mark-to-market accounting (MTMA). He said to me, "You surely did not learn mark-to-market accounting in college. How did you come upon it?" So I decided to write this addendum to try to explain how I got onto it.

Well, no, I did not learn about MTMA in college, but, for reasons that I don't remember, I had thought about it a lot in college. I remember my first days and years at Eaton & Huddle in San Antonio, when the young staff would gather at lunch and talk about accounting. I remember talking about and promoting MTMA as to assets in those sessions in the 1950s. Tom Holton will attest that I have been talking about and promoting MTMA as to assets since the 1950s. I remember doing audits of the financial statements of oil and gas companies in the 1950s and 1960s and how we accountants argued interminably about the correctness of successful efforts accounting versus full cost accounting and how we pushed numbers around on yellow working papers when the whole exercise was pointless in that what investors really wanted to know was the quantities of oil and gas reserves held by the reporting enterprises and the values of those reserves. I remember doing audits of the financial statements of insurance companies where bonds were accounted for at cost and where management could manage earnings at will by deciding when to sell bonds and thus time the recognition of gain or loss. I remember interminable arguments about deferring gains and losses on the sale of bonds and adding or subtracting the loss or gain to the cost of the replacement bonds and then amortizing the deferred gains and losses as adjustments of interest income, and I thought we should just mark the bond holdings to market so that investors could see the results of changes in market prices right on the faces of the financial statements.

I remember endless arguments in the 1960s as the Accounting Principles Board debated the relative merits of pooling-of-interest and purchase accounting and wondered why we did not just mark to market all of the assets and liabilities of both the acquiring and acquired corporation and stop the arguments.

I was a member of the Financial Accounting Standards Board from April 1973 through June 1976. When the board addressed accounting for marketable securities in 1974 and 1975, the result of which was FASB Statement 12, "Accounting for Certain Marketable Securities" (which has now been superseded), I wanted to require that all marketable securities be marked to market. So did two other members of the board, Arthur Litke and Robert Sprouse. But the other four members did not; they wanted lower of cost or market for each portfolio of securities. Because the board at that time needed five votes to issue a standard and because the board's constituents said that a standard, some standard, was needed because of the diversity in practice, I decided to bite my tongue, not dissent, and agree to the issuance of Statement 12, which required lower of cost or market for each portfolio of securities. Statement 12 was an awful standard; lower of cost or market is simply not a relevant number. I got so frustrated with the board over Statement 12 that I decided to leave, which I did on June 30, 1976. The market prices of marketable securities are always relevant. And those prices are very easy to obtain, generally just by looking in the *Wall Street Journal*. I concluded that if the board would not agree to MTMA when getting the number was as easy as looking in the newspaper then there was little hope of my persuading the board of the relevance of MTMA in situations other than those involving marketable securities. So I left the board.

I stumbled around, mentally, for a number of years over how to deal with liabilities such as bond liabilities and pension liabilities. Should the bond liability be reported at the amount of original proceeds adjusted for amortization of discount or premium, or should the bond liability be adjusted to the market price at each balance sheet reporting date? Should the pension liability, that is the vested pension liability, be reported at its discounted amount using the risk-free rate or the rate implicit in the liability assuming settlement with the pensioner at the balance sheet reporting date? I had argued to the Financial Accounting Standards Board in 1995 and to the International Accounting

Standards Board in 1997 that the discount rate should be the risk-free rate. In a most persuasive letter of response to me in 1997 (which unfortunately I have since lost), Sir Bryan Carsberg of the International Accounting Standards Board argued that the rate should be the rate that takes into account the obligor's credit standing. As a result of Carsberg's letter, I changed my mind. Restated by me, the pension liability is the amount of cash that the pensioner would accept, given the obligor's credit standing, in settlement of his/her vested pension benefits. Thus, conceptually, both the pension liability and the bond liability are reported at their estimated cash settlement prices at the balance sheet reporting date. I have since referred to this amount as the current cash settlement price of liabilities.

Despite the fact that the Financial Accounting Standards Board and the International Accounting Standards Board have not endorsed MTMA, I have not given up on MTMA. I continue to believe that current market prices of assets and current settlement prices of liabilities are the most relevant information that accountants can provide to investors, as set out in various pieces in this anthology. See, for example, "True north" appearing in *Abacus* in February 2001, my Chambers Lecture in November 2001, and my US Senate Banking Committee testimony in February 2002.

Let me just close by saying that the historical cost of assets and the historical proceeds of liabilities, which is the way reporting is mostly done today, are seldom relevant and are often misleading to investors. Current selling prices of assets and current settlement prices of liabilities are never misleading and are always relevant to investors. That is the kind of accounting that my sister would understand.

Part I

Accounting for assets and liabilities

3 Schuetze on accounting for assets and liabilities

Peter W. Wolnizer

This section contains Walter Schuetze's major intellectual and practice-informed contributions to accounting. It is here that he makes a cogently argued case for the adoption of mark-to-market accounting. With care and insight informed by an extensive experience of accounting practice, standard setting and corporate regulation at the highest levels, he establishes the practical foundations for valuing assets at their current selling prices and liabilities at their current settlement prices.

Schuetze deals with fundamental accounting matters – the definition and quantification of assets and liabilities. He tackles the most vital, but still problematical and controversial, questions at the heart of corporate financial reporting – the representation of a company's dated financial position or state of affairs and a company's periodic financial performance or profit/loss. However, he reaches beyond these big questions to deal with accounting regulation generally and with several specific accounting matters, such as accounting for restructurings, good will, stock options, asset impairment, contingencies and financial instruments. In many ways, it is in his incisive analytical dissection of particular, but complex, accounting matters that Schuetze's already compelling case for mark-to-market accounting really shines.

Comprising three articles, six speeches and fifteen letters, this is the largest section in the book.

The articles

These articles are substantial contributions to the literature not for their content alone but because they are from the pen of a practitioner whose views are informed not so much by theoretical argumentation as by observation and experience of what style of accounting works – and informs investors' choices – in practice. Hence we find a plea to those responsible for promulgating accounting rules and standards to "Keep it simple" – the title of his first article in *Accounting Horizons* (1991) but a recurrent theme throughout his writings in this section. A recurrent theme, yes, but one richly and poignantly illustrated by reference to a plethora of APB Opinions and FASB Statements, including FASB Statement 133 (derivatives and hedging instruments), Statement 96 (income taxes), Statement 87 (pensions) and Statement 13 (leases).

While he observes, in various places, that the accounting standards issued by the FASB are "far too complicated," "vastly too voluminous," "too detailed," "too abstruse" and of "mind-numbing complexity," he looks for elegant solutions that work – "simple bright-line rules" he calls them. He argues that the idea of simplicity should be transported to the conceptual framework – and he does, starting with perhaps the most basic question, the definition of an asset.

The FASB definition of an asset, as "probable future economic benefits obtained or controlled by a particular entity as a result of past transactions or events," he describes as "an abstraction" and "mind-boggling stuff":

> Most accountants do not understand it. Ordinary folk are mystified by it. We have not been able to solve accounting problems by using that definition. Almost any expenditure fits into that definition because it does not discriminate. We need a simple definition. How about defining assets as CASH, contractual claims to CASH and things that can be sold for CASH? That definition would do away with goodwill, pre-opening costs, employee training costs, and other junk now called assets.

He elaborates: "Abstractions – probable future economic benefits – cannot be sold for CASH. Only real things can be sold for CASH. Only real things can be assets." It is clear that exchangeability (for cash) is the crucial attribute of an asset. In this article, he argues that assets should be measured at "current value, i.e. the price of the assets in a current sale for CASH, at least for financial instruments." Later, he elaborates on current value or fair value: "I would define fair value of assets as follows: the estimated amount of cash the asset would fetch in an immediate sale whether or not under duress, without recourse or guarantees, less the estimated amount of cash that would have to be paid out to accomplish the sale."

Schuetze developed this line of argument further in a speech delivered at the 20th Annual National Conference on Current SEC Developments in Washington in January 1993, when he was chief accountant to the SEC. That speech, published as "What is an asset?" in *Accounting Horizons* (1993), was delivered against the background of the SEC promoting mark-to-market accounting for marketable debt and equity securities to the FASB and the financial community. Having attended a conference for accounting standard setters from around the world at the FASB following the World Congress of Accountants in Washington in October 1992, he states that he was "taken by the lack of agreement on basic concepts about financial accounting and reporting. One of those conceptual issues is the definition of an asset. It is clear that one of the major roadblocks to resolving accounting issues here in the United States is lack of agreement on the definition of an asset."

The FASB's definition of an asset, he argues, is "so all-inclusive and so vague that we cannot use it to solve problems. It does not require exchangeability, and therefore it allows all expenditures to be considered for inclusion as assets. That definition does not discriminate and help us to decide whether something or anything is an asset. That definition describes an empty box. A large empty box.

... Almost everything or anything can be fit into it. Some even want to fit losses into the definition." It comes as no surprise when, as chief accountant to the SEC, he revealed that:

> We see situations at the Commission, particularly in enforcement cases, where there are long-winded briefs by registrants, their lawyers, their independent auditors, and their expert witnesses quoting extensively from the FASB's Concepts Statement 6 to support a debit balance in the balance sheet as a fit and proper asset, fully meeting the FASB's definition of an asset. One sees even longer, long-winded briefs in private, civil litigation. In that litigation, both sides, and all of their expert witnesses are citing the same passages from the FASB's Concepts Statement 6 in support of their positions regarding the worthiness or unworthiness of a debit balance in a balance sheet as an asset. What we have, then, in the lawyers' words are teams of swearing accountants – one swearing "thus and so" and another swearing "such and that" – and they cannot resolve what should be a simple question: whether something is an asset.

And nearly another decade has passed, and nothing has changed.

In "What is an asset?" he expands his definition of an asset to include "contractual claims to services," an addition he subsequently deleted in "What are assets and liabilities? Where is true north? (Accounting that my sister would understand)" (*Abacus*, February 2001).

Defining assets in terms of exchangeability and measuring them at their current market selling prices "would vastly simplify the practice of accounting ... would appeal to investors and other users of financial statements ... would appeal to ordinary men and women who walk up and down Main Street ... would dispense with all of the long-winded briefs about the fitness of debit balances as assets and the teams of swearing accountants ... would tend to make balance sheets less prone to challenge and thereby reduce litigation against registrants and auditors. It would make balance sheets rock solid."

In this latest and most comprehensive article, he elucidates his views about the definition and quantification of assets and liabilities in a formulation he calls "true north."

Building the case for simplicity in accounting, he outlines the voluminous body of literature that constitutes "generally accepted accounting principles" – the FASB's Statements on Financial Accounting Standards, Accounting Research Bulletins issued by the AICPA and the APB Opinions, in addition to the FASB's "special reports" and the "consensuses" issued by the FASB's Emerging Issues Task Force. He claims that the "volume and complexity of those pronouncements have become overwhelming – on a par with the Internal Revenue Code and the related regulations in the USA" and "too much for (a) those insiders who are responsible for and prepare financial statements and reports, (b) those outsiders who audit those financial statements and reports, (c) those outsiders such as investors, creditors, underwriters, boards of directors and audit committees, and analysts who use those financial statements and reports, and (d) those outsiders who regulate the preparation, audit, and dissemination of financial statements and reports." The result, he declares, is "a cacophony … nothing but noise. It is as if each musician in the orchestra is playing from his or her self-selected sheet of music, one of the Three Tenors is singing in Italian, the second in German and the third in French, all without a conductor."

So he looks for accounting rules that "ordinary folk" can understand and apply: an "accounting that my sister would understand." Such an accounting must be intelligible to "ordinary people, chief executive officers, line operating managers, members of boards of directors, investors and creditors and regulators, who are not accountants." Why? Because "it is the non-accountants who use financial statements and reports to make investment, credit, and regulatory oversight decisions, not to mention corporate governance decisions."

Having dealt with the definition and measurement of assets, he turns to liabilities. He argues that the FASB's definition of liabilities as "probable future sacrifices of economic benefits arising from present obligations of a particular entity to transfer assets or provide services to other entities in the future as a result of past transactions or events" (FASB Concepts Statement 6, para. 35) "is as infirm as its definition of an asset. … We cannot solve the question, at the margin, of what is and what is not a liability because the definition is so open-ended." Schuetze proposes an alternative definition: "I suggest that we define liabilities by reference to future cash outflows required by negotiable instruments, by contracts, by law or regulation, by court-entered judgments or agreements with claimants, and derivative contracts having a negative value." He would value liabilities at "fair value," which he defines as "the least amount of cash that the counter party would accept in an immediate and complete liquidation of his/her claim against the reporting enterprise."

Such an accounting, says Schuetze, would be simple. "It would have a simple, singular focus – cash. All assets and liabilities would be stated at fair value. We all would know where north lies on that accounting compass."

The speeches and addresses

The six speeches and addresses in this section, dating from 1992 to 2002, were delivered to diverse audiences including accounting and legal practitioners, academics, accounting standards setters, and regulators, students and politicians.

The first, delivered on 7 January 1992 to the 19th Annual AICPA National Conference on Current SEC Developments in Washington, was his maiden speech as chief accountant of the SEC. He called it "New chief accountant's wish list." In crisp focus were the two related themes of simplicity and relevance in financial accounting and reporting. In a fresh approach to these desirable objectives in accounting, he said:

> I suggest that we all stand back and try to put ourselves into the shoes of the investor and creditor and ask whether this welter of complexity that we have

> created [generally accepted accounting practices], and continue to create, really helps those people to make lending and investing decisions. My judgment is that we have gone too far.

He suggests that we have arrived at voluminous and complex accounting rules because broad, general standards do not work:

> At best, that approach results in extensive non-comparability amongst and between reporting entities. At worst, that approach results in abuse and perhaps even fraud. People will, in good faith, interpret broad, general rules in just that way: some people will be conservative, some liberal, and some in between; and that provides wide non-comparability in financial reporting. Given that kind of broad, general standard, independent auditors have no benchmark or guideline to judge whether their clients have complied with the standard or rule. … Investors and creditors need to be able to make comparisons among and between alternative investments, and we should help them do that, not make it difficult or opaque.

This leads him to suggest that standards have some bright lines "that will result in uniform application of the standards and comparability among and between reporting enterprises, not only in this country but others as well."

From a call for simplicity in accounting rules, Schuetze proceeds to call for relevance in financial reporting and mark-to-market accounting – in full support of the commission's advocacy of mark-to-market accounting for financial institutions as set forth by SEC Chairman Breeden in testimony before the US Senate Committee on Banking, Housing and Urban Affairs of the United States on 10 September 1990. "My views about mark-to-market accounting versus historical cost are on all fours with the views of the commission as articulated in the 1990 testimony. Indeed, I will go one step further and suggest that this issue has been studied enough in the laboratories of academic journals and needs to be tested in the crucible of practice." He concludes that "Market value information about assets and liabilities, intuitively, has to pass everyone's test of relevance." Simplicity in accounting rules, relevance for financial decision making and mark-to-market accounting "go hand in glove."

In the second speech, delivered at the annual meeting of the American Accounting Association on 12 August 1992, he sets forth six reasons why historical cost accounting should be "jettisoned" and mark-to-market accounting adopted for marketable securities: (1) to enhance usefulness for investment or lending decisions; (2) to stop income or earnings management; (3) to recognize the effectiveness of managing interest rate risk; (4) to recognize credit losses as the credit standing of bond issuers declines; (5) to enhance market efficiency; and (6) to report accurately on capital adequacy.

He illustrates the misleading outcomes of using historical cost accounting by reference to the savings and loan debacle. "The use of historical cost did not cause the S&L problem, but the use of historical cost is to blame for the loss of some of that money down the S&L hole. … If the S&Ls had been forced to disclose, never mind account for, the fair value of their ADC [acquisition, development and construction] portfolios and their bond and mortgage loan portfolios, does anyone honestly believe that the S&L hole would have gotten as deep as it got? I think the fair answer to that question is 'No'."

The speech concludes with a challenge to the profession to "pull on its own bootstraps," to deal with the underlying causes of litigation against itself:

> The profession will not go to its clients and tell those clients that their balance sheets have to have realism in order to elicit unqualified opinions. … The profession, again with an exception or two, will not go to the FASB and support realism in financial accounting and reporting. The profession will not reach tough and unpopular decisions. Why is that? Is it because the profession has become so beholden to its clients that it will not speak to them about realism and relevance and credibility in financial accounting and reporting?

This argument will be picked up again in the next section. Suffice it to say at this point that Schuetze illustrates his point with five – of many possible – situations where the profession has "become a cheerleader for its clients": troubled debt restructurings, pension plan values, deferred tax assets, investment versus trading and SEC filings.

His plea to the profession is "to give some thought to the public that it serves, to the investors and creditors and employees who put up their money and their labor to make investments in the profession's clients." His plea to the FASB and the profession is "to address the issues of relevance and credibility in financial accounting and reporting so as to maintain their own relevance and credibility." A timely clarion call to the accounting profession and standards setters indeed.

Schuetze's address to the Theta Chapter of Beta Alpha Psi at the University of Texas at Austin on 12 November 1993, on the occasion of their naming him Accountant of the Year, expounds the vital role that accounting plays in capital markets: "Accounting is the lubrication that allows this country's capital markets engine to turn at very high RPMs without overheating." He explains how public and private companies, state and local governments, churches and temples, colleges and universities, and charitable organizations all need and use accounting and accountants. And he leaves those bright, aspiring accountants with an observation and sage advice: "the one thing that I have found to be the most important as I have traveled through this world of business and accounting for thirty-six years. That is, high ethical standards. … It has been my observation that those who are the most fulfilled are those who not only do good work but who do it on the up and up, on the straight and narrow, with no corners rounded. It is they who are sought out most often by their colleagues, by their superiors, by their clients, by new clients, by the public."

The fourth and sixth speeches deal with accounting for restructurings. They were delivered to the Financial Executives Institute in New York on 8 November 1994 and the 19th Annual Ray Garrett Jr Corporate and Securities Law Institute at Northwestern University on 22 April 1999. The 1994 speech is set against the background of the SEC's request to the FASB's Emerging Issues Task Force to address accounting for restructurings. Schuetze had observed the substantial growth in the number of restructurings and the concomitant increase in restructuring charges. He had also observed that while a large proportion of those charges related to employee-related costs, the ingredients of restructuring charges were diverse, including a variety of write-downs and write-offs of costs incurred in past periods, and expenditures expected to be made in the future for the benefit of future operations.

Noting that as a charter member of the FASB he had signed FASB Statement 5 dealing with accounting for contingencies, he explains how he would account for restructuring charges, exit costs and related balance sheet liabilities or reserves. He argues that accounting for restructurings has become an abuse and states that the FASB's definition of a liability in FASB Statement 6 would not accommodate liabilities recognized pursuant to management's declaration in a restructuring and that such liabilities amounted to contingency reserves that are precluded by FASB Statement 5. Consequently, he argues that the Emerging Issues Task Force should not approve such accounting for restructurings. Notwithstanding that advice, nine days later, on 17 November 1994, the Emerging Issues Task Force approved the establishment of restructuring reserves.

In the speech delivered at Northwestern University, he again addressed accounting for restructuring charges and restructuring reserves – one of the accounting "hot spots." He suggests that a better title for the speech may have been "Accounting for general reserves, contingency reserves, rainy day reserves, or cookie jar reserves." Lacking a robust definition of what constitutes a restructuring, he notes that "Accounting for so-called restructurings has become an art form" because restructuring charges are frequently reported below the line. Hence earnings are reported before charges. In other words, accounting for restructurings has become just another way of manipulating earnings.

He points out that two consensuses of the FASB's Emerging Issues Task Force that deal with the recognition of liabilities on the occasion of a restructuring or merger (EIFT 94-3 and 95-3) "allow for the recognition of liabilities based on a representation by management that the company will make certain expenditures but before a cash outflow is required pursuant to a law or a contract. In all other cases except in accounting for pensions and OPEBs, liabilities are not recognized until some event has occurred and a cash outflow therefore is required, either by law or regulation or under an enforceable contract." Furthermore, companies may establish reserves for some restructurings and not for others. And the numbers ascribed to those reserves, being management's assertions, cannot be verified by the auditors.

In his 1999 speech on restructurings, he states:

> Well, my instinct in 1994 has been confirmed by practice. What has happened since 1994 is that general reserves, contingency reserves, rainy day reserves, and cookie jar reserves, now are in vogue for those who want to use them. Based on what I see in the Enforcement Division [of the SEC], there apparently is no limit to what ingredient may be included in the reserves or the amount ascribed to it.

The fifth speech, delivered at the 1998 annual meeting of the American Accounting Association, deals primarily with the question of whether purchased goodwill is an asset. Before tackling that question, however, he opens with the theme of cooking the books by using examples such as premature revenue recognition, deferral of operating costs, and recognition of treasury stock and barter trade credits as assets.

In that context, he returns to the use of reserves to manipulate earnings:

> I have found that reserves are like crab grass. They are everywhere. ... Need a penny a share to meet Wall Street's expectations? Need two pennies? A nickel? A dime? Two bits? Dip into the chocolate chip cookie jar reserve. The mere existence of reserves is a chocolate chip cookie jar that management cannot resist when the earnings need a sugar high. We need to fix reserve accounting. It's time to make another pass at reserves; we need a Year 2000 version of FASB Statement 5.

Schuetze notes that the FASB had tentatively concluded that the cost of purchased goodwill meets the board's definition of an asset. With careful and skilful analysis, he demonstrates how purchased goodwill fails to meet all the criteria set forth by the board in Concepts Statement 6 for the recognition of an asset. Calling the cost of purchased goodwill "the lump," he demonstrates that the lump is not a future economic benefit; the lump is just a cost, nothing more; the lump cannot be controlled; the lump cannot be measured reliably. The lump cannot be used to produce anything of value. The lump cannot be used to settle a liability. Using the board's own words, he demonstrates that the future economic benefit criterion of an asset is not met in the case of goodwill.

The letters

There are fifteen letters in this section. They are addressed to the FASB, IASC, *Barrons Magazine*, *Journal of Accountancy* (submitted when Schuetze was in private practice and withdrawn in January 1992 when he was appointed as chief accountant to the SEC); and to Sir Bryan Carsberg and Senator Charles Schumer. These letters are packed with illustrations, examples and analogies that bring life to the analytical argumentation. They are compelling reading.

Dating from 1986 to 2002, the letters cover a wide range of topics, including accounting for goodwill, asset impairment, liabilities, contingent liabilities, transfers of receivables and stock options, the discount rate to be used in determining pension liabilities, and the disclosure of market values of financial instruments.

The letters to the IASC (18 September 1997) and FASB (15 June 2000 and 16 March 2001) are responses to exposure drafts dealing with internally generated and purchased goodwill. His letter to *Barrons Magazine* is on the same topic. In those letters, he analyzes why internally generated and purchased goodwill should not be capitalized. He argues that costs are not assets, even under the conventional accounting definition of an asset, and that goodwill is neither separable from the enterprise nor exchangeable for cash.

In his letters to the FASB, he calls the cost of purchased goodwill "a glob" and argues that the recognition of the glob as an asset is precluded by the FASB's own words in Concepts Statement 6. He also argues that goodwill represents expected, "hoped for future profits," which are "contingent gains" that should not be recognized as assets until they are earned and in the hand as cash or something that can be sold for cash. He urges the FASB to go back to first principles and to re-examine its definition of an asset. In particular, he argues that exchangeability should be the crucial test for recognizing something as an asset. Goodwill, he demonstrates, is not exchangeable in and of itself for cash. In his letter to *Barrons Magazine*, he argues that the vast majority of CPAs do not understand the FASB's definition of an asset: "Only FASB accountants know what it means, but they can't explain it in plain English that my sister, who runs a successful business, can understand."

He argues that the IASC and FASB exposure drafts on internally generated intangible assets and purchased goodwill "will not work": "There will be no comparability whatsoever in the accounting from one enterprise to another for internally generated intangible assets. Investors will not be well served. ... What will work is a requirement to charge to expense when incurred all costs related to internally generated intangible items and purchased goodwill." He argues that:

> Two rationales support this approach, both of which fit within the IASC's framework. One rationale is that costs *per se* are not assets and should not be recognized as if they were assets ... The other rationale is that the ... future economic benefits from expenditure (or fair value of securities issued) for intangible items that are not separable and saleable and for which a fair value cannot therefore be established are so indeterminate and so speculative that expenditure (or fair value of securities issued) for such items should not be represented as an asset.

In his letters of 23 July 1997 to the IASC and 7 November 2000 to the FASB, Schuetze comments on exposure drafts dealing with the impairment of assets. These are also very interesting pieces, for he addresses the fundamental differences between "value in use" and "fair value." By fair value, he intends "the estimated amount of cash the asset would yield in a sale to an unrelated party, that is, a market participant." He argues that the IASC's proposal to require that management make its estimate of "value in use" to determine whether the carrying amount of an asset is impaired will produce unreliable and irrelevant information for users of financial statements. He makes the same argument in relation to the FASB's proposal that impairment be determined by a comparison of management's estimate of the undiscounted cash flows of the asset with the carrying amount of the asset even though the selling price of the asset is less than the carrying amount. He argues that the carrying amount of an asset should be its fair value, or market selling price: "Fair value is an amount that generally can be verified by reference to information outside the enterprise and thus is reliable. Value in use, being an internal, private estimate cannot be verified and thus is not reliable."

He makes a telling point: "The holders of assets may do their own, internal, private accounting any way they want to … But, the chief concern of the IASC is financial accounting and reporting for investors and creditors. The information that is produced for investors and creditors must be relevant to them, and the information must be reliable (verifiable). Value in use fails on both counts."

The 7 November 2000 letter also addresses the timing of the recognition of liabilities associated with the disposal of assets. He points out that the FASB's proposal in its Exposure Draft *Accounting for the Impairment of Long-Lived Assets and for Obligations Associated with Disposal Activities* is inconsistent with its own definition of a liability in FASB Statement 6 because it would allow for the recognition of a liability before there is a "present obligation" to pay cash to an obligee. He writes: "We have seen enough downright awful earnings management under Consensuses 94-3 and 95-3 issued by the FASB's Emerging Issues Task Force where liabilities may be recognized when managements of reporting enterprises want to and then reversed when those managements want to. The FASB itself should not issue a standard that will allow this shoddy, reprehensible practice to continue."

The letters to the FASB (13 February 1986), to the *Journal of Accountancy* (December 1991) and to Senator Schumer (25 March 2002) also concern accounting for assets and expenses. In his letter to the FASB, Schuetze urged the board to require companies to disclose the fair value of all on- and off-balance sheet financial instruments. It appears that this letter may have been very influential on the board's deliberations, for in a personal note to Schuetze by Halsey Bullen (16 October 1992), a senior FASB staff person, he writes: "I'm not sure how much credit we gave you at the time, but it was [your letter] that led to our [FASB] Statement 105 [*Disclosure of Information about Financial Instruments with Off-Balance Sheet Risk and Financial Instruments with Concentrations of Credit Risk*] and [FASB] Statement 107 [*Disclosure About Fair Value of Financial Instruments*]."

In his article submitted to the *Journal of Accountancy* in December 1991 but withdrawn in January 1992 upon his appointment as chief accountant to the SEC, Schuetze tackled a then pressing problem – accounting for transfers of receivables. Against the background of the corporate collapses of the late 1980s and the subsequent liquidity crunch, many US corporations were seeking to increase their liquidity and equity and decrease their borrowings. Hence there was a push to get loans, including receivables, off their balance sheets.

Consequently, accounting for receivables generally, and transfers of receivables in particular, was "hugely important."

In that letter, Schuetze describes how, under FASB Statement 77, transferors of receivables who retain various risks, such as credit risk or interest rate risk, in connection with the transfer are reporting false gains on sales of the receivables, because Statement 77 does not require the recognition or measurement of those retained risks by the transferor. Schuetze argues that the retained risk should be recognized as a put liability and priced at fair (market) value at every reporting date. He claims that the IASC's Exposure Draft (E40) on accounting for receivables and transfers of receivables, if adopted, would "put the accounting for receivables and especially transfers of receivables, back into the Dark Ages." He analyzes how the IASC's proposal to deal with retained risk by accounting for the transfer of the receivable as a borrowing produces phantom assets, liabilities, revenues and expenses in the transferor's financial statements and those of subsequent transferors as well: hence the reference to Tom, Dick and Harry.

In his recent letter to Senator Schumer (25 March 2002), Schuetze returns to the problematic conventional definition of assets as future economic benefits. At issue in this letter is accounting for stock options. Under the conventional definition of an asset, issuance of a stock option to an employee produces an expense. Schuetze argues that under his definition of an asset, where assets are real things and not future economic benefits, the stock of a reporting enterprise would never be regarded as an asset, and expenses would be the using up of an asset or the decline in the market value of an asset. Under that scenario, the issuance of stock options to employees would not give rise to an expense.

Letters to the IASC (9 September 1997) and FASB (1 May 2001) deal with liabilities. Responding to the IASC's Exposure Draft E59 on "Provisions, Contingent Liabilities and Contingent Assets," wherein it is proposed that a liability be recognized when an enterprise has no realistic alternative but to transfer economic benefits to another party, Schuetze argues that "liabilities should [only] be recognized … when transfers of economic resources are required by law, by contract, or because an enforceable claim exists against the enterprise and the amounts can be measured reliably." He claims that the IASC's proposal is ill-founded and illogical: "That idea could be applied in logic to tomorrow's salaries and electricity resulting in the recognition of a liability today for such items."

Against the IASC's notion that provisions and contingencies may not need to be disclosed if such disclosure would be prejudicial to the reporting enterprise in negotiations with another party, he argues that the financial statements of public companies must be transparent so that investors are fully informed, and non-disclosure should not be permitted at any price.

His letter of 1 May 2001 to the FASB concerns the board's Exposure Draft 213-B *Accounting for Financial Instruments with Characteristics of Liabilities, Equity or Both* and its Exposure Draft 213-C, a proposal to revise the definition of liabilities. He argues that the FASB's proposal to require that certain obligations that must or may be settled by issuance of the enterprise's share be classified as liabilities is incorrect because it "implies that a corporation's shares, which will be used to settle the obligation, are assets of the corporation. That is an incorrect implication."

Referring to the FASB's proposal (in 213-B) to require that proceeds received on the issuance of a compound instrument be allocated to the various parts as, for example, allocation to the equity and debt features of a bond, he states: "That's as-if accounting – as if a corporation had issued two instruments, a debt instrument and an option to buy shares of the corporation, when in fact only one instrument was issued. Financial statements should report what happened and what is, not what might have happened and what might be." He likens this style of accounting to "accounting for hypothetical, as-if deferred income taxes" – just another "time-consuming, money-consuming, hypothetical, as-if allocation that has no real world meaning."

In his letters to the FASB (25 September 1995) and Sir Bryan Carsberg (17 April 1997), Schuetze argues that the discount rate used for determining pension liabilities and liabilities for nuclear decommissioning and environmental remediation should be the risk-free rate. In conversation, Schuetze recalls that "Sir Bryan took me to task for faulty thinking, saying that the determination of the rate should take into account the credit standing of the borrower or obligor. Largely based on Sir Bryan's arguments, I changed my mind." Schuetze now argues that liabilities should be reported at fair value (or settlement price), which would implicitly take into account the obligor's credit standing. That definition is clear in "True north."

In many ways, his latest two letters to the FASB, dated 14 July 2002 (concerning accounting for guarantees) and 6 September 2002 (concerning "special-purpose entities"), demonstrate how a straightforward, rigorous application of mark-to-market accounting would do away with the ambiguous and open-ended accounting that currently prevails.

In the letter on accounting for guarantees, he points out that while the FASB requires guarantee liabilities to be measured initially at fair value, it is silent about how those liabilities should be measured subsequently. He states: "Guarantee liabilities should always be measured and reported at fair value, and the Board should say so. If the Board leaves the matter open, as in the proposed interpretation, practice likely will be mixed, which obviously is not in the best interest of financial reporting. That's no way to run a railroad."

The FASB's proposed interpretation of the consolidation of certain special-purpose entities (SPEs) exemplifies the kind of knee-jerk accounting that Schuetze decries. In his letter of 6 September 2002, he states:

> In its determination and rush to get off-balance-sheet liabilities of SPEs onto someone's balance sheet after Enron's implosion last year and the subsequent publicity about Enron's off-balance-sheet activities and the publicity about the Board's inaction for a decade or more about accounting for SPEs, the Board now proposes to contaminate the liability side of corporate balance sheets by putting onto corporations' balance sheets "debt" that

> the reporting corporations do not owe. In the process, the Board now also proposes to contaminate the asset side of corporate balance sheets by putting onto corporations' balance sheets "assets" that the reporting corporations do not own, cannot sell, cannot pledge as collateral, cannot give to charity, and cannot distribute to shareholders – assets that belong to SPEs.

This section of twenty-six pieces is a rich repository of analytical arguments, examples and illustrations that demonstrate how valuing assets at current market selling prices and liabilities at current settlement prices would yield a more contemporary, factual, informative and intelligible accounting not only for investors and creditors but for all interested users of financial statements. Schuetze exposes serious technical flaws in the conventional definitions and quantification of assets and liabilities and demonstrates how they yield accounting fictions, inconsistent and unintelligible accounting practices, and misleading signals for investors and other users of corporate financial reports.

4 Keep it simple

Accounting Horizons, Vol. 5, No. 2, June 1991

The Financial Accounting Standards Board is getting a lot of advice these days. The advice comes from the American Institute of Certified Public Accountants, the Business Roundtable, the Financial Executives Institute, the chairmen of the large accounting firms, the Financial Analysts Policy Committee, the Securities and Exchange Commission and its staff, and banking and thrift regulators. I will add my voice to the chorus. My theme (plea) in this piece is for the FASB to keep it simple.

Some of the FASB's recent and not so recent statements are far too complicated. FASB Statement 96 (income taxes), Statement 87 (pensions), and Statement 13 (leases) are examples of mind-numbing complexity. Those statements are so complicated that ordinary people cannot understand and apply them. The best analogy that I can think of is one of automobiles. When I look at FASB Statement 96 on income taxes, I see a Formula 1 racing machine. One has to be a Fittipaldi or Luyendyk to drive a racing machine at Indianapolis at an average speed of 167 or 186mph. Most of us can handle and afford only a production-line automobile, and the speed limit for us is 55mph (65mph in certain states), not something in excess of 160mph.

How did we get here? How did accounting standards get so complex? Some of the responsibility for the complexity lies with the Securities and Exchange Commission and its staff. Regulation S-X, Regulation S-K, the various registration forms, and the periodic reporting forms with which public companies must comply are complicated. Over the years, the SEC has layered complexity on top of complexity. The SEC's staff for years has written detailed letters of comments to registrants; it is said that the staff is picking the bugs from the bed linen. Some of the complexity arises because transactions are complex. However, by far most of the recent complexity arises because preparers of financial statements and their CPA firms have asked for it. An example is pension accounting (FASB Statement 87). Pension accounting is complicated because most preparers, and their CPA firms, are unwilling to see changes in market values of plan assets and settlement values of plan liabilities entered into earnings as those values change. Spread those changes, they say. A large part of FASB Statement 87 is devoted to smoothing the hills and valleys of change. FASB Statement 106 on accounting for post retirement benefits other than pensions is complex for the same reason. Income tax accounting (FASB Statement 96) is complicated because the auditing profession was unhappy with a simpler rule that left unanswered a lot of details and because old APB Opinion 11 does not fit into the FASB's conceptual framework and had to be changed for that reason.

We have the Emerging Issues Task Force because our current accounting rules are not detailed enough to answer all the accounting questions that arise in a complex business world, and the independent auditing profession wants detailed answers to respond to pressures from clients to do things in a less than conservative way.

The board needs to keep it simple in future statements. But the board cannot just set forth a simple standard, state the objective of the standard and leave it to the judgment of preparers and their CPAs to implement the standard, as it now is in vogue to suggest.[1] That approach will not work. The world needs simple bright-line rules.

We have tried the simple approach that requires judgment. For example, in APB Opinion 5, the Accounting Principles Board said that lessees should recognize on their balance sheet those leases that are in substance installment purchases of property – those that result in creation of a material equity in the property. That was a general standard, requiring judgment to implement. It did not work. Very few leased assets and corresponding lease obligations were recognized by lessees. As a result, the Financial Accounting Standards Board issued very detailed, complex rules on accounting for leases in FASB Statement 13. But now, Statement 13, even with all its amendments and interpretations, does not work. And, to make things worse, the Securities and Exchange Commission's staff and the Emerging Issues Task Force keep adding layers of complexity to it. The Accounting Principles Board, in APB Opinion 9 on earnings per share, said that an outstanding security is a residual security (now called a common stock equivalent) if it derives a major portion of its value from its conversion rights or its common stock characteristic. That was a general standard requiring judgment to implement. It didn't work, The CPA firms could not agree on the meaning of "major portion." Some thought 90 percent, others 51 percent. APB Opinion 9 had to be replaced by APB Opinion 15, which is far too complex and needs to be simplified. The predecessor rule (Accounting Research Bulletin 48) to the pooling-of-interest rules in APB Opinion 16 was simple but judgmental. It did not work. And now APB Opinion 16 is not working because its detailed, complex rules do not cover new situations not thought of when it was issued in 1970.

FASB Statements 77 (transfers of receivables) and 80 (futures contracts) are fairly simple but leave a lot of room for judgment. Neither one works in practice. What is a sale and what is a financing under Statement 77 is judgmental. A fairly large segment of Wall Street earns a living figuring out how to best the CPA firms and Statement 77. Statement 80 allows for so much judgment about correlation and anticipated transactions that preparers, auditors, and banking and thrift regulators cannot agree on what to do in practice. (One thrift,

Franklin Savings, and its regulator, the Office of Thrift Supervision, are in court in a disagreement over how to interpret FASB Statement 80.)

Let's look at some simple, non-judgmental standards that have been successful. FASB Statement 14 on segments says that if 10 percent or more of total revenue is from a segment, then data for the segment shall be reported separately. No ifs, ands, or buts; 10 percent is 10 percent and FASB Statement 14 has been successful. (Except that many users of financial statements would like segment reporting on a quarterly basis, one seldom hears about problems with Statement 14. Could it be that the success of a standard is measurable by the lack of complaint about it?) FASB Statement 85 says that a convertible bond that has a cash yield of less than two-thirds of the long-term corporate bond rate at the time of its issuance is a common stock equivalent for the purpose of earnings per share computations. No ifs, ands, or buts; two-thirds of that bond rate is easy to compute and that standard has been successful. APB Opinion 15 says, in a footnote, that if the dilutive feature of a convertible bond or preferred stock or option or warrant does not reduce earnings per share by at least 3 percent, then fully diluted earnings per share need not be reported. The 3 percent rule has been effective. It's simple, and it works.

How might such a simple yet effective bright-line be applied to two live recognition and measurement problems?

Lease accounting by lessees will never be right or correct insofar as all the interested parties (lessees, CPAs, the SEC's staff, and users of financial statements) are concerned. FASB Statement 13, with all its amendments and interpretations, is not the answer because only a few of us know how to apply Statement 13. (And sometimes we don't know what's "right" until we ring up the SEC's staff and check with them.) We cannot explain the result. We need simple bright-line rules to fix that problem, at least as to lessees. Either capitalize (recognize) all lease obligations or none of them. If all leases are to be capitalized, specify the rate to be used to discount the lessee's contractual cash outflows: for example, use the 10-year US government bond rate to discount the cash payments. That rate will not correspond exactly with the lessee's incremental borrowing rate, but there is no harm done by using that rate as a surrogate for the lessee's incremental borrowing rate – it's only an estimate, not perfection. We need not measure things to the sixth degree. The light is not worth the cost of the candle. Users of financial statements will understand that approach; it is easy to explain and understand.

Deferred tax accounting under FASB Statement 96 is incredibly complex, what with scheduling and hypothetical tax-planning strategies for every temporary difference in every taxing jurisdiction. If we must have deferred tax accounting, and I question whether we should,[2] why not just assume that all of the assets are sold for cash at their book amounts and all of the liabilities are settled for cash at their book amounts and the corporation files a final tax return on the day following the balance sheet; the amount of tax payable or recoverable on that hypothetical final tax return would be the deferred tax to be reported in the corporation's balance sheet. Simple. No scheduling. No hypothetical tax planning strategies. Under this approach, there would be no debate about whether to discount the tax asset or liability; no discounting would be necessary. Moreover, that simple answer could be explained to and even understood by ordinary people. The results of APB Opinion 11 and FASB Statement 96 cannot be explained and understood.

We could transport the idea of simplicity to the conceptual framework. Look at the FASB's definition of an asset and its characteristics:

> 25 Assets are probable[18] future economic benefits obtained or controlled by a particular entity as a result of past transactions or events.
>
> 26 An asset has three essential characteristics: (a) it embodies a probable future benefit that involves a capacity, singly or in combination with other assets, to contribute directly to future net cash inflows, (b) a particular entity can obtain the benefit and control others' access to it, and (c) the transaction or other event giving rise to the entity's right to or control of the benefit has already occurred. Assets commonly have other features that help identify them – for example assets may be acquired at a cost,[19] and they may be tangible, exchangeable, or legally enforceable. However, those features are not essential characteristics of assets. Their absence, by itself, is not sufficient to preclude an item's qualifying as an asset. That is, assets may be acquired without cost, they may be intangible, and although not exchangeable they may be usable by the entity in producing or distributing other goods or services. Similarly, although the ability of an entity to obtain benefit from an asset and to control others' access to it generally rests on a foundation of legal rights, legal enforceability of a claim to the benefit is not a prerequisite for a benefit to qualify as an asset if the entity has the ability to obtain and control the benefit in other ways.
>
> ---
>
> 18 "Probable" is used with its usual general meaning, rather than in a specific accounting or technical sense (such as that in FASB Statement No. 5, *Accounting for Contingencies*, para. 3), and refers to that which can reasonably be expected or believed on the basis of available evidence or logic but is neither certain nor proved (*Webster's New World Dictionary of the American Language*, 2nd college edn, New York: Simon & Schuster, 1982, p. 1132). Its inclusion in the definition is intended to acknowledge that business and other economic activities occur in an environment characterized by uncertainty in which few outcomes are certain (paras 44–8).
>
> 19 Cost is the sacrifice incurred in economic activities – that which is given up or forgone to consume, to save, to exchange, to produce, and so forth. For example, the value of cash or other resources given up (or the present value of an obligation incurred) in exchange for a resource measures the cost of the resource acquired. Similarly, the expiration of future benefits caused by using a resource in production is the cost of using it.

Egad! That is mind-boggling stuff. Most accountants do not understand it. Ordinary people are mystified by it. We have not been able to solve accounting problems by using that definition. Almost any expenditure fits into that definition, because it does not discriminate. We need a simple definition. How about defining assets as CASH, contractual claims to CASH, and things that can be sold for CASH?[3] That definition would do away with goodwill, pre-opening costs, employee training costs, and other junk now called assets.[4] The current definition is an abstraction. Under that definition, the asset that I call a truck is not the FASB's asset. The FASB's asset is the present value of the net cash flows that truck will produce by hauling coal or lumber or steel, *viz.* the "probable future economic benefit." I call it a truck. Trucks can be sold for CASH. Abstractions – probable future economic benefits – cannot be sold for CASH. Only real things can be sold for CASH. Only real things can be assets. Mario Gabelli, John Neff, and Martin Zweig will understand and appreciate that approach.[5]

Small and medium-sized companies will understand and appreciate that approach. Many FASB standards are so complex that most small and medium-sized companies do not have the staff to implement the standards. And they do not want to pay their CPA firms to help to accumulate the information that is used only to prepare financial statements but is not understood by or useful to the owners of the company and their bankers. The Alliance of Practicing CPAs has called for a "moratorium on new [FASB] standards" and/or a "separate, simplified set of accounting standards for non public companies."[6] Small and medium-sized companies and their CPA firms cannot afford to follow the FASB's lead on complex standards.

International standard setters also will not follow the FASB's lead in issuing complex, detailed standards. If the International Accounting Standards Committee were to issue a standard as detailed as FASB Statement 96 on income taxes, the IASC would lose its following, which is beginning to grow. That approach would be not only foolhardy but also suicidal for the IASC.

Can you imagine a men's shoe manufacturer in Lyon, France, who needs money wanting to come to the United States to issue debt or equity securities or American depository receipts? This French company has been preparing its financial statements using French francs and the French language and French generally accepted accounting principles and has a French auditor who practices only in France. When the management of the French shoe manufacturer goes to issue securities in the USA, it will learn that it must reconcile its net income and shareholders' equity to that which would result under US generally accepted accounting principles. The management of the shoe manufacturer will learn that in order to do that reconciliation both it and its auditor will have to learn the FASB's accounting pronouncements and those of its predecessors, the Emerging Issues Task Force, and perhaps even the utterances of the Accounting Standards Executive Committee of the American Institute of Certified Public Accountants. The management of the French company will be dismayed and discouraged. The management will say "We make shoes; we just want to raise a few dollars; we don't want to be fodder to be crushed by your accounting machines; we will go to Hong Kong or Singapore or Geneva to raise money." Repeat that for shoe makers in Frankfurt, Osaka, Vancouver, and Edinburgh and you begin to see how stifling the competition is here in the USA.

Accounting standards have to be implemented by ordinary people. Financial reports are used by ordinary people. The standards and the results of applying the standards have to be understandable to ordinary people. Beyond understandability of new standards, the cost of change to a new standard and the cost of continued compliance should not exceed the benefit. This cost–benefit test is a judgment call, and my judgment is that we have to change the way we write standards. It's perhaps acceptable to have as an objective the construction of a Formula 1 racing machine, and to state the objective of a standard in that fashion. But let's remember some practical constraints: automobiles for ordinary people are built on production lines, not in high-tech hotrod garages. We drive our cars to work, school, and Friday night softball games. The speed limit for us is 55/65mph on the highway, 30mph in town, not 167 or 188 mph. Keep it simple.

If we keep it simple then the users of the information will have the information that they can use. (What can users do with an intangible asset arising from smoothing out pension expense except to ignore the asset?) The smaller CPA firms and their clients will be able to keep up with the rest of the world. Preparers of financial statements can stop fussing over things that cost a lot of money and have little usefulness, like the "corridor" in pension accounting and scheduling temporary differences for deferred income tax computations, and do things to improve the quality of US products in the world marketplace. And the FASB will stand a better chance of promoting its ideas in Australia, Canada, France, Germany, Great Britain, Italy, Japan, Russia, Pacific Rim countries, and at the IASC.

Notes

1 I have heard it said at meetings of the Financial Standards Advisory Council, "Write simple rules and leave it to the preparer and auditor of the financial statements to use their judgement." What happens under that approach is that the first time that a preparer does not like its CPA's answer, then a way will be found to take the question to the Emerging Issues Task Force in an attempt to overturn the CPA's answer.

2 I do not like hypothetical, as-if accounting. Deferred tax accounting is hypothetical, as-if accounting.

3 This definition says nothing about how we might measure assets – cost or current value. I think it ought to be current value, i.e., the price of the assets in a current sale for CASH, at least for financial instruments.

4 We would have to fix FASB Statement 87 on pensions to do away with intangible assets that arise under that statement. Deferred tax assets would disappear.

5 Mario Gabelli (Gabelli Asset Management Company), John Neff (Vanguard's Windsor Fund), and Martin Zweig (Zweig Fund) are investment portfolio managers.

6 Quote from the 30 November 1990 issue of *Public Accounting Report*.

5 What is an asset?

Accounting Horizons, Vol. 7, No. 3, September 1993

I am pleased to make my second appearance on the program of this annual national conference on current SEC developments.

The year gone by has been one where the staff has concentrated on promoting the commission's drive for mark-to-market accounting for marketable debt and equity securities. That policy was set out in congressional testimony in September 1990 by Chairman Breeden and in December 1990 by James Doty, the commission's former general counsel.

We have continued to encourage the Financial Accounting Standards Board, and the financial community in general, to embrace the idea of mark to market for marketable securities. Contrary to the perception by some, we have not been promoting mark to market for other assets, such as plant and equipment, patents and copyrights, or commercial loans held by banks. However, what the staff has done is to suggest the idea that, when one is looking to identify impairment of the carrying amount of assets such as stocks, bonds, loans, plant, and patents, it is appropriate to look at the fair value of the asset and compare that fair value with the carrying amount of the asset. And then, when one goes to measure impairment, fair value of the asset would be the appropriate attribute to look at in order to obtain the best and most relevant measure of the impairment. This approach is consistent with the measurement of foreclosed assets and in substance foreclosed assets as announced in Financial Reporting Release 28, issued in 1986. In that release, the commission said that market value should be used to measure foreclosed assets and in substance foreclosed assets, even in a situation where those market values come from an auction market where assets are being bought for speculative purposes.

Also, during the past year, the staff has had discussions with numerous registrants, mostly holding companies of financial institutions, regarding their accounting for marketable debt securities. A good number of those registrants have reclassified all or a portion of their bond holdings from the category of so-called "long-term investments" accounted for at amortized cost to a category of "held for sale" or "available for sale" accounted for at the lower of cost or market or, in the case of certain insurance companies, at market. These reclassifications were in acknowledgment by registrants that their own actions indicated bonds they owned were in fact not being held to maturity or for the long term.

Those registrants also revised their stated accounting policies to bring them into line with the registrants' actual practices of buying and selling bonds, instead of buying and holding bonds to maturity. I want to make the point here that the staff was enforcing, administratively, the current literature based on cost and not market value; the staff was not moving toward mark-to-market accounting by way of the back or side door as has been suggested in some quarters.

[Schuetze referenced the FASB's then pending projects on impairment and of marketable securities, to be discussed at the conference by James Leisenring of the FASB.]

What I would like to spend the balance of my remarks on is a more fundamental issue, namely, the definition of an asset.

Last October, after the meeting of the World Congress of Accountants in Washington, the FASB invited standard setters from around the world, and a few other individuals, to meet at the FASB's offices in Norwalk, Connecticut, for a day and a half to share ideas about standard setting in various countries and at the "international" level. During that conference, to which I was invited by the FASB, I was taken by the lack of agreement on basic concepts about financial accounting and reporting. One of those conceptual issues is the definition of an asset. It is clear that one of the major roadblocks to resolving accounting issues here in the United States is lack of agreement on the definition of an asset. As work on international standards proceeds, that may be a problem as well.

So today I wish to offer, for the consideration of standard setters and others who seek to improve the state of financial accounting and reporting, an alternative definition of an asset. I suggest this alternative definition to be provocative and to stimulate thought and discussion. I do not mean to imply that this is a definition that the commission or its staff is proposing or will incorporate into its rules and regulations or even impose in the day-to-day administration of the securities laws.

Most articulated definitions of an asset refer to "economic benefit" or "future economic benefit" or "probable future economic benefit." For example, the FASB's definition is "probable future economic benefit." The full definition of assets from the FASB's Concepts Statement 3, which originally was issued in 1980 and which is now included in Concepts Statement 6, is as follows:

> Assets are probable future economic benefits obtained or controlled by a particular entity as a result of past transactions or events.

The FASB lists three essential characteristics of an asset, as follows:

> (a) it [an asset] embodies a probable future benefit that involves a capacity, singly or in combination with other assets, to contribute directly or indirectly to future net cash inflows, (b) a particular entity can obtain the benefit and control others' access to it, and (c) the transaction or other event giving rise to the entity's right to or control of the benefit has already occurred.

The FASB goes on, in the same paragraph of Concepts Statement 6, to say:

> Assets commonly have other features that help identify them – for example, assets may be acquired at a cost and they may be tangible, exchangeable, or legally enforceable. However, these features are not essential characteristics of assets. Their absence, by itself, is not sufficient to preclude an item's qualifying as an asset. That is, assets may be acquired without cost, they may be intangible, and although not exchangeable they may be usable by the entity in producing or distributing other goods or services.

The FASB's definition is so complex, so abstract, so open-ended, so all-inclusive, and so vague that we cannot use it to solve problems. It does not require exchangeability, and therefore it allows all expenditures to be considered for inclusion as assets. The definition does not discriminate and help us to decide whether something or anything is an asset. That definition describes an empty box. A large empty box. A large empty box with sideboards. Almost everything or anything can be fitted into it. Some even want to fit losses into the definition. When I said in March 1992, as the SEC observer at the Emerging Issues Task Force, that losses on "hedging" instruments related to anticipated transactions do not qualify as assets under that definition, a lot of people objected to my conclusion, including some members of the Emerging Issues Task Force. At the commission, we often see proposals for the recognition as assets of operating losses of retail operations in the start-up mode and operating losses of plants in their shakedown phase. The definition seems large enough to some people to accommodate these losses.

We see situations at the commission, particularly in enforcement cases, where there are long-winded briefs by registrants, their lawyers, their independent auditors, and their expert witnesses quoting extensively from the FASB's Concepts Statement 6 to support a debit balance in the balance sheet as a fit and proper asset, fully meeting the FASB's definition of an asset. One sees even longer, long-winded briefs in private, civil litigation. In that litigation, both sides, both the defendant and the plaintiff, and all of their expert witnesses are citing the same passages from the FASB's Concepts Statement 6 in support of their positions regarding the worthiness or unworthiness of a debit balance in a balance sheet as an asset. What we have, then, in the lawyers' words, are teams of swearing accountants – one swearing "thus and so" and another swearing "such and that" – and they cannot resolve what should be a simple question: whether something is an asset.

What generally happens in practice, under the FASB's definition of an asset, is that assets are not recognized unless the reporting enterprise acquires them by paying cash or agreeing to pay cash in the future or someone contributes something to the reporting enterprise in return for an ownership interest in the enterprise. Then an asset is said to have a cost. In fact, we accountants sometimes think of the asset and talk about it in terms of its cost, not in terms of the asset itself or the future benefit that may flow from it. That is, the asset is the cost, or the cost is the asset. For example, if an enterprise discovers something of value, say, oil or gold, we do not recognize it as an asset because the enterprise has no cost. When the FASB proposed several years ago that business enterprises recognize as assets things received from others in a so-called non-reciprocal exchange, for example land received from a government, some people objected. One of the reasons for the objection was that the enterprise receiving the asset had no cost in the asset. I refer to this phenomenon as the cost *per se* is the asset syndrome.

I will cite some examples:

- The AICPA's Accounting Standards Executive Committee has outstanding an exposure draft of a statement of position entitled "Reporting on advertising costs" that says so-called direct-response advertising costs may be reported as assets if the advertising activity resulted in probable future economic benefits. Thus, the cost is the asset. In oil and gas accounting, either successful efforts as described by the FASB in FASB Statement 19 or full cost as described by the SEC in Regulation S-X, the asset represented in the balance sheet is the cost of finding the oil and gas reserves, not the reserves themselves.
- In FASB Statement 60, the cost of acquiring insurance contracts is an asset.
- In AICPA Statement of Position 90-8, the cost of originating or acquiring continuing care retirement community contracts is an asset.
- In FASB Statement 86, the asset is the cost of the computer software, not the future benefit that will flow from the software.
- In the AICPA Accounting and Auditing Guide "Audits of casinos," pre-opening costs are assets.
- In the AICPA Accounting and Audit Guide "Audits of airlines" and the related Statement of Position 88-1, costs of training flight crews and maintenance crews, pre-revenue flight expenses, insurance, and the depreciation expense of new aircraft are assets.
- In the AICPA Accounting and Audit Guide "Audits of government contractors," learning, start-up, or mobilization costs incurred for anticipated but unidentified contracts are assets.
- In Accounting Principles Board Opinion 21, costs of raising debt finance are assets.
- In FASB Statement 80, losses on future contracts related to anticipated but not firmly committed transactions are assets.
- And, finally, in APB Opinion 16, the cost that is left over in a business combination after the purchase price is allocated to all other assets and liabilities is an asset; it is called cost of acquisition in excess of net assets acquired, or goodwill. Along this same line, the International Accounting Standards Committee has proposed that development costs, the "D" in R&D, may be recognized as an asset under certain conditions.

In all of these cases, it is the cost itself that is identified as the asset, not a probable future economic benefit. It is this same line of reasoning, that a cost can be an asset, that leads some people to suggest that the FASB should reconsider FASB Statement 2 and allow for recognition of research and development costs as an asset. Note that in none of the cases is the asset represented on the balance sheet exchangeable.

The cost of many assets does not represent anything close to the "probable future economic benefit" to be derived from the asset. For example, the probable future economic benefit of a successful, direct-response advertising campaign may be many multiples of the cost. The future benefit of a discovery of mineral deposits generally bears no relationship whatsoever to the costs of finding the deposits. The future benefits of successful research and development also bear little or no relationship to the costs incurred. The Concepts Statement 6 definition of an asset and the historical cost model that we know and use today do not mesh.

Defining an asset as a probable future economic benefit is to use a high-order abstraction. Under such an approach, if an enterprise owns a truck, the truck *per se* is not the asset. The asset is the present value of the cash flows that will come from using the truck to haul lumber, or coal, or bread. Yet, in today's practice, the asset represented on the balance sheet is a truck, and users of the financial statements see it as a truck. The users do not see it as the economic benefit that will come from using the truck to haul lumber. I think most people are more comfortable thinking of the asset as a truck instead of as an abstraction, instead of the present value of future cash flows or the economic benefit to be derived from it.

I suggest that we try an alternative definition. A simple one. One that is not a large empty box. One that is not a high-level abstraction. I suggest that we try the following definition: "Cash, contractual claims to cash or services, and items that can be sold separately for cash."

The suggested definition would comprehend only real things, not abstractions. Real things such as trucks can be sold. Real things can be pledged as collateral. Real things can be given to charity. Abstract probable future economic benefits cannot be sold, pledged, or given away. The definition would not accommodate a cost as being an asset. Losses would not fit into that definition. Exchangeability is a critical element in that definition.

Let me list a few of the things this alternative definition would include. Obviously, cash. Obviously, claims to cash such as trade receivables, loans receivable, demand deposits at banks, certificates of deposit, cash surrender value of life insurance policies, bills, notes, and bonds issued by governments, corporations, partnerships, individuals, and trusts. Cash paid in advance for the future use of land and buildings would be included. That definition would include raw materials, finished goods, common stocks, land, buildings, equipment, mineral deposits, air rights, water rights, landing slots at airports, broadcast rights, patents, and copyrights. Work-in-progress inventory and fixed assets in the process of construction would also be included, on the theory that they can be sold for cash when completed.

Let me list what would be excluded: any cost as such, such as pre-opening costs. Proportions of assets that arise in proportional consolidation, such as 33 percent of cash or accounts receivable or plant held by a joint venture in which venture the reporting enterprise has a one-third interest would be excluded. (However, the one-third interest in the joint venture itself would be an asset.) Receivables sold with recourse and thus owned by another enterprise would be excluded. Assets leased by lessees would be excluded for the same reason. So would deferred taxes. Goodwill would be excluded because it cannot be sold apart from the business.

I submit that use of that alternative definition would vastly simplify the practice of accounting. Intuitively, I think it would appeal to investors and other users of financial statements. I note, in that regard, that the Association of Investment Management and Research has recently recommended that the cost of goodwill no longer be recognized as an asset. Intuitively, I think the alternative definition would appeal to ordinary men and women who walk up and down Main Street, USA, and those who walk up and down Main Street in other countries. They would understand it. I think that ordinary people who are not accountants think that when they see an asset in a balance sheet the asset is something real, and that it represents value; that is, if it is not cash or a claim to cash, that it can be sold separately for cash. Accounting should not be done for the benefit of accountants. Accounting should result in financial statements that ordinary people will understand and therefore be able to use to make investment and credit decisions.

Accountants would also understand that alternative definition. They could use it to identify things to be reported as assets on balance sheets. They could use it to identify, through exclusion, things not to be reported as assets on balance sheets. We would dispense with all of the long-winded briefs about the fitness of debit balances as assets and the teams of swearing accountants. Assets would be real things, exchangeable things. Defining assets as real things would also tend to make balance sheets less prone to challenge and thereby reduce litigation against registrants and auditors. It would tend to make balance sheets rock solid. As this audience knows well, auditing the recoverability of a cost, or the impairment of a cost, is hard enough when the cost is associated with a real thing where one can look to the market value of the real thing to test for impairment. Auditing the recoverability or impairment of something that is just a cost, a cost not associated with a real thing, is more than hard.

Another benefit to be gained would be improved comparability in financial accounting and reporting. In practice, many of the costs recognized as assets are not recognized as assets by all enterprises. Some enterprises, motivated by income tax considerations or conservatism, or for other reasons, charge to income such costs when incurred, whereas other enterprises recognize the cost as an asset. Thus, in practice, there is a significant degree of non-comparability in financial accounting and reporting with respect to such costs or such assets. Where non-comparability is most evident, because of the size of the amounts, is in the accounting for the cost of goodwill. The cost of goodwill must be reported as an asset by enterprises domiciled in the USA and reporting under US generally accepted accounting principles but may be charged to shareholders' equity or "reserves" by enterprises domiciled in other countries and not reporting under US generally accepted accounting principles.

Using that alternative definition of an asset of course would not govern or suggest which attribute of the asset ought to be or could be selected for recognition and measurement and reporting on the face of the balance sheet. The acquisition price, or historical cost, could be used for non-monetary operating assets. Or historical cost updated for changes in the general price level. Or the current cost of similar productive capacity. Or the present value of future cash flows. Or the estimated selling price of the non-monetary asset. As to financial instruments such as marketable stocks and bonds, the acquisition price or current market value could be used, and I would, of course, suggest market value. Or one could be eclectic and select from the menu of attributes of assets to be recognized and measure that attribute which is judged to provide the most relevant information possible for decision making by investors and creditors, limited of course by cost–benefit constraints.

The definition of an asset that is in use today is too inclusive, overly complex, and vague. I suggest that standard setters take another look at the definition.

6 What are assets and liabilities?

Where is true north? (Accounting that my sister would understand)

Abacus, February 2001

This is an article about what I think financial accounting and reporting ought to look like – about my vision that the singular focus of financial accounting and reporting should be on cash, that is, cash itself, contractual claims to cash, things (assets) that can be converted into cash, and obligations to pay cash, and that assets and liabilities should be stated at fair value in corporate balance sheets. I call this formulation "true north."

I have previously written about how we should keep financial accounting and reporting simple ("Walter Schuetze on keep it simple," *Accounting Horizons*, June 1991, pp. 113–17). I have also written about how assets should be defined for accounting purposes ("What is an asset?" *Accounting Horizons*, September 1993, pp. 66–70). This article builds on those two earlier ones. It deals with definitions of assets and liabilities that should be recognized (that is, displayed, shown, or reported) in corporate balance sheets and how the recognized assets and liabilities should be measured when reported in those balance sheets.

Key words: accounting; fair value; measurement; simplicity.

The rules for financial accounting and reporting in the USA have become vastly too voluminous, too detailed, too complex, and too abstruse. At this writing in July 2000, the Financial Accounting Standards Board has issued 139 statements on financial accounting standards (SFASs). Public companies in the USA, and foreign companies whose securities are listed in the USA, must follow these standards in the preparation of their financial statements or in the reconciliation of their home-country financial statements to US standards. Because some of those 139 superseded a prior standard, the count of currently effective standards is about 100. In addition to standards, there is previously issued literature inherited by the FASB at its formation in 1973 from the American Institute of Certified Public Accountants, namely Accounting Research Bulletins and Accounting Principles Board Opinions. This legacy literature has the standing and authority of a standard. The FASB itself has also issued numerous interpretations of standards and has issued technical bulletins prepared by the FASB's staff.

The FASB's staff has also issued numerous special reports dealing with various accounting matters dealt with in standards, for example *A Guide to Implementation of Statement 125 on Accounting for Transfers and Servicing of Financial*

Assets and Extinguishments of Liabilities, and guidance for implementation of SFAS 133, *Accounting for Derivative Instruments and Hedging Activities*. The FASB's Emerging Issues Task Force has issued several hundred "consensuses," each dealing in extreme detail with quite specific accounting problems. (The issues summaries for the July 2000 meeting of the task force run to more than 300 typewritten pages, many of which are single spaced.)

The American Institute of Certified Public Accountants has issued numerous audit and accounting guides, statements of position, and practice bulletins, most of which have been vetted by the FASB and its staff prior to the issuance of those documents by the AICPA. The AICPA has also issued technical practice aids, which are not vetted by the FASB or its staff prior to issuance.

As well, the Securities and Exchange Commission and its staff have issued numerous rules, regulations, releases, and bulletins dealing with financial accounting and reporting.

All of this literature constitutes generally accepted accounting principles, which is required accounting by public companies in the USA. As well, the large public accounting firms have issued their own guidance or interpretation or "how to" guides that instruct the firms' partners and staff on various FASB, AICPA, and SEC pronouncements. These firm-prepared documents often run to hundreds of pages. For example, shortly after the FASB issued Statement 133, *Accounting for Derivative Instruments and Hedging Activities*, in June 1998, itself more than 200 pages in length, several accounting firms issued their own guidance on how to apply Statement 133 – which guidance constituted more than 400 pages in the case of one firm and 500 pages in the case of another. I have all of these documents in my office, but many are on the floor because my bookcase is full. And all of this is before mentioning standards issued by the International Accounting Standards Committee since its inception in 1973.

The volume and complexity of those pronouncements have become overwhelming – on a par with the Internal Revenue Code and the related regulations in the USA. The volume and complexity have become too, too much for (1) those insiders who are responsible for and prepare financial statements and reports, (2) those outsiders who audit those financial statements and reports, (3) those outsiders such as investors, creditors, underwriters, boards of directors and audit committees, and analysts who use those financial statements and reports, and (4) those outsiders who regulate the preparation, audit, and dissemination of financial statements and reports.

The hapless user of the financial statements and reports has almost no grip on the rules governing financial reporting and thus, in many cases, does not understand the financial statements and reports. Indeed, in a survey of 140 star sell-side analysts, Epstein and Palepu (1999) found that "Footnotes [where asset and liability recognition and measurement are described] seem to frustrate analysts the most. When asked which components of the annual report they often have a hard time understanding and which they would like explained more, star analysts rated the footnotes first. Thirty-five percent of the analysts have difficulty understanding the footnotes, and 55 percent would like further explanation of the footnotes." Imagine that. Star, sell-side analysts do not understand the accounting. Buy-side analysts (institutions) cannot be any better equipped to understand the accounting. Is it any wonder that the London School of Business advertises a financial seminar for senior managers that enables senior managers to "decode published financial statements" (*The Economist*, 14 November 1998, p. 101)?

Financial analysts are not alone. I was chief accountant to the SEC (January 1992 to March 1995) and chief accountant of the SEC's Division of Enforcement (mid-November 1997 to mid-February 2000). While on the staff of the commission, I tried to explain relatively simple accounting issues and accounting rules to the commission's legal staff and its litigators, FBI agents, US postal inspectors, and assistant US attorneys in the Department of Justice so that they could bring and prosecute civil and criminal cases before administrative law judges, Federal judges, and juries. I had minimal success even on simple issues. The litigators and prosecutors are very reluctant to bring accounting fraud cases unless smoking guns are evident, such as, for example, fake invoices, boxes filled with bricks instead of laptop computers, or incriminating memos.

Financial accounting and reporting should be based on intuition, not inculcation. There really should be nothing complicated about it. It is not like medicine. It is not like the law. It is not rocket science. Ordinary people, chief executive officers, line operating managers, members of boards of directors, investors and creditors and regulators, who are not accountants, should be able to look at financial statements and reports and understand the information portrayed and conveyed. After all, it is the non-accountants who use financial statements and reports to make investment, credit, and regulatory oversight decisions, not to mention corporate governance decisions. But ask members of boards of directors, members of audit committees of boards of directors, members of the investing and credit-granting public, financial analysts, and members of regulatory oversight bodies to explain, in plain English, the meaning of the representations in the financial statements and reports they use to make decisions and there is no response. I repeat – there is no response. They must turn to the accountant to furnish the explanation. The accountant's explanation turns out to be not in plain English at all but in arcane jargon understandable only by other accountants, and not necessarily all other accountants but only the initiated ones. The much proclaimed transparency in corporate financial accounting and reporting in the USA is in fact a considerable illusion insofar as the numbers (dollar amounts) in the financial statements and reports are concerned. The numbers are not very transparent at all. Only accountants know how the numbers are derived, and sometimes only a very few accountants.

I say again, preparation of financial statements and reports, their use, and their regulation should be based on intuition, not inculcation. The way it is now, however, to be fully conversant with all of the financial accounting and reporting requirements means that one has to live in a medieval, unheated, stone building in the Pyrenees, wear a brown robe with a rope belt, a skull cap, and clogs, and memorize accounting literature (dogma). I recently received a mailing from the

AICPA advertising a two-day course on accounting for business combinations at a price of $1,295 or at $1,035 for AICPA members. Can you believe that? Two days and over a thousand dollars to learn about one accounting problem.

There are more than 330,000 CPAs in the USA. No more than a few hundred of them know the workings of the standards on (1) leases, (2) foreign currency translation, (3) pensions, (4) post-retirement benefits other than pensions, (5) interest (whether and when to capitalize interest cost), (6) deferred income taxes, (7) investments in debt securities, (8) impairments of carrying amounts of loans receivable or long-lived operating assets, (9) transfers and servicing of financial assets and extinguishments of liabilities, and (10) derivative instruments and hedging activities. Moreover, each one of these areas has such detailed, complex, and abstruse rules that the few hundred CPAs who are expert in accounting for derivatives often are not the same few hundred CPAs who are expert in accounting for pensions. Each monk knows just one book of the Bible.

I liken the use of financial statements and reports to driving an automobile. Automobiles are powered by internal combustion engines, but drivers of autos do not need to know anything about what makes the auto go except that gasoline (or petrol) is necessary and that the engine oil needs to be replaced occasionally. That is virtually all that I know about my auto. Comparing accounting to the auto, one needs to be the equivalent of a mechanical engineer to use and drive the auto called financial accounting and reporting. We accountants are doing accounting for accountants' sake, not for use by investors, creditors, underwriters, analysts, boards of directors, and regulators, who are the people that we accountants should aim to please.

How overwhelming today's accounting is can be demonstrated by the response to a proposal for improving the effectiveness of audit committees. The Blue Ribbon Committee on Improving the Effectiveness of Corporate Audit Committees, co-chaired by John Whitehead and Ira Millstein, in one of its ten recommendations about improving the effectiveness of audit committees, recommended that the audit committee, in the annual report to shareholders, attest that audit committee members believe, based on discussions with management and the external auditor, that the financial statement conforms to generally accepted accounting principles (see Recommendation 9 of the *Report and Recommendations of the Blue Ribbon Committee on Improving the Effectiveness of Corporate Audit Committees*, issued in 1999). That recommendation was soundly rejected by commentators in financial and legal circles. In response to a reporter, the general counsel of the Securities and Exchange Commission said that "The reference to generally accepted accounting principles has created some fear and confusion because audit committee members have been concerned that they don't know the intricacies of the accounting rules. Audit committees understand accurate, full and fair disclosure, and that things may not be materially misleading, but they don't necessarily understand the nuances of generally accepted accounting principles" (*Wall Street Journal*, 14 July 1999, p. C14). The SEC, in its new rule on audit committees, did not require that the audit committee give the opinion suggested by the Blue Ribbon Committee. Instead, the SEC amended its rule to require only that the audit committee publicly state that it had reviewed and discussed the audited financial statements with the auditor and that the audit committee recommends the inclusion of the audited financial statements in the form 10-K or 10-KSB. (SEC Release 34.42266, 22 December 1999.) The new rule does not require the audit committee to give an opinion about compliance with generally accepted accounting principles. In my opinion, most members of audit committees, if not virtually all members of audit committees, could not give the opinion suggested by the Blue Ribbon Committee, because the accounting is beyond their ken. Incidentally, I think it is a fair question to ask: how can boards of directors and audit committees satisfy their governance responsibilities if they do not understand the accounting numbers?

I use my sister as a guidepost when I think about accounting issues. She has no university education. She runs a successful small business located near my home town of Comfort, Texas. She prepares financial statements for her business to run her business and so that the other owners of the business may see how well the business has done under her leadership. In the financial statements of her business, assets are cash, contractual claims to cash, and things that the business owns and that can be sold for cash – all at fair value, that is, the amount of cash any of the non-cash assets would fetch in an immediate sale for cash less cost to sell the asset. When she consults me about the preparation of the financial statements for her business and I try to explain to her the standards that we accountants use to prepare financial statements, her eyes glaze and she blames my *accountababble* on my having sat for too long in the hot Texas sun. She recently bought out one of her competitors and paid about $100,000 in excess of the fair value of the identifiable net assets acquired. The competitor agreed not to compete against my sister's business for five years. I told her that the $100,000 represented the cost of the non-compete agreement and purchased goodwill, which, under generally accepted accounting principles, should be reported as assets. She laughed at me. Try to pay salaries, rent, the electric, or dividends with those assets, she said. That kind of accounting may be okay for Wall Street but not for Main Street in Comfort, Texas. Moreover, she said, those so-called assets will not earn a penny. The $100,000 is gone – irretrievably gone. It is spent money. Whether her business earns any additional net after-tax cash flows as a result of buying out her competitor and getting him to agree not to compete with her business for five years will be decided by the former competitor's customers – whether they decide to patronize her business and buy her business's services. She does not control what those potential customers may do. Not an asset today, she says. Maybe tomorrow, if and when those customers buy her business's services and generate additional after-tax cash for her business. Not a fit and proper asset to be recognized in advance of sales to customers, however. In short, in accounting parlance, the $100,000 is a quintessential "gain contingency" that should not be recognized as an asset until it materializes in the form of cash.

Moreover, there is no overarching theme to this huge body of literature governing financial statements and reports to which the uninitiated, or even the initiated, may refer. The FASB says that the information in financial statements and reports has to have "decision usefulness." But the numbers in balance sheets for reported assets and liabilities are the result of mechanically applying all of the rules and literature described above without regard to whether the result is understood by and makes sense to the people who actually use it. Remember my reference earlier to the findings of Epstein and Palepu about star, sell-side analysts who do not understand the notes to the financial statements. As a guide or standard, "decision usefulness" is so non-specific and allows so much judgment and leeway that it is not helpful. What we need instead is a definition of true north in accounting. Everyone knows where north lies on a compass, and we can navigate towards it in our daily journeys in accounting. Decision usefulness, on the other hand, can lie anywhere on the compass.

Under the current rules, in addition to cash, we have the following as to assets representing contractual claims to cash:

1 Receivables, generally at the amount of cash expected to be collected and generally not reduced for the time value of money or otherwise reduced to fair value. This category includes such items as trade receivables, amounts due to the reporting enterprise by a counterparty under a currency or interest rate swap agreement, insurance premiums due from the owner of an insurance policy, income tax refunds, and amounts due from vendors/suppliers under cooperative advertising agreements. Amounts of receivables not yet billed are included in this category. For example, companies that perform construction work for the US government often show "unbilled receivables" as assets on their balance sheets.
2 Loans receivable having fixed or determinable amounts. Examples are commercial or residential mortgage loans and loans made by banks and insurance companies to individuals as a result of the individuals' using credit cards to buy goods and services, to small businesses, and to large commercial customers, at the present value of the amount of cash expected to be collected based on the effective interest rate in the loan. If the carrying amount of a loan is deemed not to be collectible in full, then the carrying amount of the loan is reduced to (a) the fair value of any collateral, (b) the market price of a similar loan if such a price exists, or (c) the revised expected cash flows reduced for the time value of money using the interest rate implicit in the loan at its inception. (The cost of originating loans is added to the "cost" [cash advanced to the borrower] of the loans.)
3 Securities representing an interest in indeterminate cash flows from "securitized" loans receivable, at the fair value of the security, with changes in that fair value being recognized (a) in income by traders such as broker/dealers and some banks and (b) in shareholders' equity (net assets) by other holders such as banks if the security is classified as "available for sale." Classification of such a security as "held to maturity" by the owner would have the security being reported at historical cost. These kinds of securities arise in

transactions where the originator of loans, such as mortgage loans and automobile loans, sells tranches of the loan portfolio to investors such as insurance companies, mutual funds, and trusts administered by banks.

4 Securities representing contractual, fixed or determinable cash flows, such as bonds, based on fair value or historical cost of the security.

5 Refundable cash deposits, such as the portion of an insurance premium that would be recaptured if the policy were to be cancelled.

As to assets such as inventory, land, plant, equipment, and patents (sometimes called non-monetary items) that are not cash and claims to cash, we have the following:

6 The amount of cash paid, at some time in the past, for an item other than cash or a claim to cash plus related expenditure, which is called "historical cost." For example, the amount of cash paid for land plus brokers' fees, legal fees, appraisal fees, documentary fees, and other fees applicable to the acquisition of the land. These fees could be material in relation to the cash price paid for the land. Other examples include amounts of cash paid for such things as plant, equipment, copyrights, patents, and TV or radio broadcasting rights. The amount of cash paid – the cost – is reduced by periodic charges made to income so as to allocate the cost to periodic income on what is said to be a rational and systematic basis.

7 The portion of a lump-sum purchase price paid for two or more assets acquired together, as, for example, in a business combination, that is allocated to one of the assets acquired, which amount would generally be the fair value of the asset. For example, the amount of cost allocated to land acquired in a business combination would be the fair value of the land but would not include the various fees described in 6 above.

8 The fair value of an asset at the time it was received by the reporting enterprise in return for the issuance of a debt or equity instrument, also said to be "historical cost" of the asset: for example, the fair value of land contributed to the reporting enterprise in exchange for stock. However, if the land is contributed to the reporting enterprise by a promoter or controlling shareholder, then the cost to the reporting enterprise is not the fair value of the land but instead is the historical cost of the land to the contributor (an SEC rule). (Note that the "historical cost" of land under 6, 7, or 8 could be three different, possibly materially different, amounts for the same parcel of land.)

9 Net realizable value, the amount of proceeds expected on sale of an asset such as work in progress or finished goods less cost to complete and cost to sell.

10 Current market prices in the case of certain equity securities but not others, such as when the owner of the equity security is said to have significant influence but not control of the investee, in which case the so-called equity method of accounting is required (see 11).

11 Historical cost of certain equity securities plus the arithmetic share of the investee's earnings and other changes in the investee's net assets said to be attributable to the investor (accounting by formula).
12 Fair value of assets at the date of the write-down of the carrying amount of those assets whose carrying amount was deemed to be impaired, which carrying amount after the write-down is then said to be "new historical cost."
13 Fair value of exchange-traded and over-the-counter derivative contracts having a positive value.
14 Deferred income taxes, which are solely the result of computations done only by accountants, reduced, in some cases, by an allowance, the need for and amount of which is determined solely by management based on its judgment.
15 Valuation allowances for certain assets; some allowances involving discounting, such as allowances for losses on individual loans where the discount rate is the rate of interest inherent in the loan when it was originated; and some allowances involving no discounting, such as allowances for deferred tax assets and allowances for loan losses that are said to relate to portfolios of loans instead of individual loans. The amounts of these allowances are determined solely by management based on its judgment.
16 The amount of cash paid for certain services to be received in the future such as advertising (prepaid advertising), placement of a manufacturer's product on shelves in grocery stores (slotting fees), and cash advances to writers for books or movies to be written or scripted, at the amount of cash paid reduced by periodic charges made to income to allocate to income the amount paid on what is said to be a rational and systematic basis.
17 The right, perhaps through a so-called barter exchange or by use of barter credits issued by a barter exchange, to buy goods or services at a price less than the posted price or rack price. Examples are advertising space, radio or TV time, or hotel "nights." Such rights also arise when vendors agree that customers may, based on the volume of their prior purchases, buy goods or services in the future at a discount from the posted price. (Do you have credits for airline miles that you have earned that you can use for upgrades to first class or for free tickets?) Some people believe that such a right or credit is a future economic benefit that should be recognized as an asset. Let me illustrate with an example. Suppose I buy groceries from the nearby supermarket. The bill is $42.00. When the cashier checks me out and gives me my receipt, the cashier also gives me a coupon that allows me to buy a bottle of 100 aspirin tablets at $5.75 instead of the shelf price of $6.75. The price reduction of a purchase in the future of a bottle of aspirin tablets at $5.75 instead of $6.75 is, in the minds of some, a future economic benefit that should be recognized as an asset under today's generally accepted accounting principles – recognized as an asset by allocating a portion of the $42 to the "value" of the coupon, I suppose. I am not making this up. But that is the kind of goofy answer that one can get under today's accounting for "future economic benefits" (more on "future economic benefits" later). My sister would shake her head in disbelief.

18 The amount of cash paid for certain things that only accountants call assets: for example, the cost incurred by banks to originate loans receivable, the cost incurred by insurers to originate certain types of insurance policy, the cost of so-called direct-response advertising, interest cost, and finally, the cost of purchased goodwill. (At this writing, some commentators are urging the FASB to rescind FASB Statement 2 [and Interpretation 4 thereof], which requires that the cost of R&D be charged to expense when incurred; those commentators would have corporations recognize as an asset some or all of its R&D expenditure.)
19 Some items that are solely the result of computations done only by accountants, such as amounts produced by applying the standards related to pensions and deferred income taxes.

As to liabilities, under the current rules, some amounts are:

1 What is to be paid in cash to vendors (accounts payable), to employees (wages payable), to counterparties under derivative contracts, to owners (dividends declared and payable), to taxing authorities, sometimes based on tax returns as filed and sometimes based on what management of the enterprise says will be the final tax payable after negotiation or litigation with taxing authorities.
2 Proceeds of borrowings.
3 Refundable cash collected from customers in advance of delivery of goods or services to those customers.
4 Deferred or unearned revenue, which is an amount representing cash collected from a counterparty in return for services to be rendered, reduced by credits to earned revenue that are determined based on services rendered or on what is said to be a systematic and rational basis.
5 Mandatory redeemable stocks generally measured at the redemption amount (an SEC rule, not a standards rule).
6 A calculated amount for promises to repair or replace faulty products.
7 Fair value of exchange-traded and over-the-counter derivative contracts having a negative value.
8 Deferred income taxes, which are based solely on computations done only by accountants.
9 Whatever management of the reporting enterprise says will be a cash outflow in the future in respect of non-contractual bonuses to employees, "restructurings," plant closures, or similar events.
10 A calculated amount for pensions and post-retirement benefits other than pensions.

The preceding discussion about various assets and liabilities assumes that the US dollar is the unit of measurement in the financial statement. If the unit of measurement is not the US dollar but a foreign currency, then another complexity is added in that the foreign currency amounts, determined using US generally accepted accounting principles, would be "translated" into US dollars using the current exchange rate. This procedure produces different "historical cost" amounts for identical assets if there has been a change in exchange rates between the time the assets were acquired and the date of the balance sheet; for example, three identical IBM computers, bought at the same time for the same price and located in different countries, say Canada, Mexico and the USA, would be shown at three different historical cost amounts in the balance sheet.

Then, because all of these amounts are expressed in Arabic numbers, we add them up as if they were cut from the same bolt of cloth and call them "total assets" and "total liabilities." And reporting services such as Moody's, Standard & Poor, and Value Line and analysts and investors compute and use things like return on assets and return on equity based on this potpourri of numbers.

What a cacophony! What the user of the financial statement hears is nothing but noise. It is as if each musician in the orchestra is playing from his or her self-selected sheet of music, one of the Three Tenors is singing in Italian, the second in German and the third in French, all without a conductor.

How did all of this happen? Well, its origin lies mainly in the fact that the staff of the SEC, in its early days (and lately as well), would not accept write-ups of assets to fair value and did not require write-downs to fair value except in extreme cases, because it thought the fair value numbers were too soft. Because we accountants were told by the SEC that we could not put current fair values in balance sheets but instead had to use historical cost, we accountants set about trying to make income the right number. Since the 1930s, when our federal securities laws were enacted, we have been trying to recognize, measure, and present income as opposed to assets and liabilities or net assets. In trying to get the right income number, we often put debits and credits on the balance sheet so as not to "distort" income. So as to time the recognition of these debits and credits in income when it is thought to be "right" or based on management's intent. It is as if the balance sheet is a holding pen for expenditure to be released to expense sometime in the future when the time is right. (Visualize a pen full of sheep awaiting their turn to be sheared.) We defer costs on the balance sheet and try to attach them or match them with revenue or allocate them to income on a causal basis or what is said to be a systematic and rational basis. We use different inventory costing methods: average cost; first in, first out; and last in, first out. A reporting enterprise may use almost any inventory costing method except what is called "base stock." On occasion, we see companies changing from one acceptable inventory cost method to another. Methods of calculating depreciation, depletion, and amortization expense run from accelerated methods to straight line to units of production. We often see changes in method. Estimated useful lives and salvage values or end values of the same kinds of fixed asset can vary significantly from company to company. Whether the carrying amounts of fixed assets are impaired is a judgment by management, for it is management that estimates the future cash flows from the asset in making the assessment about impairment. None of these deferrals, allocations, estimates of future cash flows, or formula-driven amounts can be verified or authenticated by reference to an actual phenomenon in the marketplace.

Most of this accounting is, in the end, highly judgmental. This accounting is what I call "feel-good" accounting. The AICPA's Committee on Accounting Procedure (1939–59) promulgated accounting rules designed to get income to be the correct number through feel-good accounting. That is, we like the financial statement results even though we may not be able to articulate why the results are what they are except by referring to the manner in which the amounts were determined. The accounting results, in many cases, cannot be audited or verified or authenticated by reference to any evidential matter coming from an outside source, but somehow we feel good about the numbers. An extreme example of feel-good accounting is from the Committee on Accounting Procedure in chapter 10 of Accounting Research Bulletin No. 43, *Taxes: Section A, Real and Personal Property Taxes*, paragraphs 10–13, which reads as follows:

> 10 In practice, real and personal property taxes have been charged against the income of various periods, as indicated below:
>
> a Year in which paid (cash basis),
>
> b Year ending on assessment (or lien) date,
>
> c Year beginning on assessment (or lien) date,
>
> d Calendar or fiscal year of taxpayer prior to assessment (or lien) date,
>
> e Calendar or fiscal year of taxpayer including assessment (or lien) date,
>
> f Calendar or fiscal year of taxpayer prior to payment date,
>
> g Fiscal year of governing body levying the tax,
>
> h Year appearing on tax bill.
>
> 11 Some of these periods may coincide, as when the fiscal year of the taxing body and that of the taxpayer are the same. The charge to income is sometimes made in full at one time, sometimes rateably on a monthly basis, sometimes on the basis of prior estimates, adjusted during or after the period.
> 12 The various periods mentioned represent varying degrees of conservatism in accrual accounting. Some justification may be found for each usage, but all the circumstances relating to a particular tax must be considered before a satisfactory conclusion is reached.
> 13 Consistency of application from year to year is the important consideration and selection of any of the periods mentioned is a matter for individual judgment.

The best way to sum up all of those alternatives of how to account for property taxes is to say that the accounting is whatever makes us feel good.

The AICPA's Accounting Principles Board (1959–73) also issued feel-good accounting rules; witness pooling-of-interest accounting and amortization of the cost of purchased goodwill over forty years. To a large extent, the FASB is doing the same; witness gains and losses on derivative contracts not being entered into earnings until the time is right; witness deferred gains and losses under pension accounting; witness the manner in which the carrying amount of fixed assets is to be assessed for impairment by reference to management's estimate of future cash flows from the asset instead of the fair value of the asset; witness the judgmental nature by which valuation allowances for loans receivable and deferred income tax assets are determined. Feel-good accounting rules can be set only by and through a political process; that is, who has the most votes or who can shout the loudest. Feel-good accounting produces numbers for non-cash assets and liabilities that are the result of keeping income smooth or steady, or better yet, steadily increasing, but smoothly. To take what otherwise would be variable, lumpy earnings and smooth those earnings. (Visualize a huge yellow Caterpillar bulldozer pushing the hills of economic change into the valleys of economic change.)

The FASB has been in business since 1973. It said, in its Concepts Statement 3, issued in 1980, that it "expects most assets and liabilities in present practice to continue to qualify under the definition [in Concepts Statement 3]." These words were carried forward by the FASB in Concepts Statement 6 issued in 1985 (paras 170, 177). The board in Concepts Statements 3 and 6 thus blessed – and poured into concrete – what was practice in the early to mid-1980s, which practice continues in large measure today in 2000 in the USA. Unless the FASB changes its conceptual framework, or unless the FASB itself is changed, there will not be much movement away from feel-good accounting. The question arises: is it time to start thinking about changing the FASB?

Today, most articulated definitions of an asset refer to "economic benefit" or "future economic benefit" or "probable future economic benefit." For example, the FASB's definition is "probable future economic benefit." The full definition of assets from the FASB's Concepts Statement 3, which was originally issued in 1980 and which is now included in paragraph 25 of Concepts Statement 6, is as follows: "Assets are probable future economic benefits obtained or controlled by a particular entity as a result of past transactions or events." In paragraph 26 of Concepts Statement 6, the FASB lists three essential characteristics of an asset, as follows: "(a) it [an asset] embodies a probable future benefit that involves a capacity, singly or in combination with other assets, to contribute directly or indirectly to future net cash inflows, (b) a particular entity can obtain the benefit and control others' access to it, and (c) the transaction or other event giving rise to the entity's right to or control of the benefit has already occurred." The FASB goes on, in the same paragraph, to say: "Assets commonly have other features that help identify them, for example, assets may be acquired at a cost and they may be tangible, exchangeable, or legally enforceable. However, these features are not essential characteristics of assets. Their absence, by itself, is not sufficient to preclude an item's qualifying as an asset. That is, assets may be acquired without cost, they may be intangible, and although not exchangeable they may be usable by the entity in producing or distributing other goods or services." That is mind-boggling stuff! I can tell you from experience that most accountants that I know do not understand the FASB's definition of assets. Ordinary folk – investors, creditors, analysts, underwriters, CEOs, line managers, members of boards of directors and audit committees, journalists, judges, and juries – are mystified by that babble. (That is one reason why I no longer tell people at dinner parties that I am an accountant. When I did, they appeared to feel sorry for me, averted their eyes, and silently hoped that the hostess had seated all the accountants together at one table away from the other folk.)

The FASB's definition of an asset is so complex, so abstract, so open-ended, so all-inclusive, and so vague that we cannot use it to solve problems. It does not require exchangeability of that which is called an asset; therefore it allows all expenditures to be considered for inclusion as assets. The definition does not discriminate and help us to decide whether something or anything on the margin is an asset. That definition describes an empty box. A large empty box. A large empty box with sideboards. Almost everything or anything can be fitted into it. The FASB, in its 7 September 1999 exposure draft of *Accounting for Business Combinations and Intangible Assets*, is even proposing to put the cost of purchased goodwill into that box. The five FASB members who assented to the publication of that exposure draft believe that the cost of goodwill is an asset. The two dissenters, who dissent for reasons unrelated to the initial accounting for the cost of purchased goodwill at the date of the business combination, in *obiter dicta*, say that they too think that the cost of purchased goodwill is an asset. A very large box indeed!

I have seen numerous situations at the SEC, particularly in litigated enforcement cases, where there are long-winded briefs by issuer-registrants, their independent auditors, and their expert witnesses, quoting extensively from the FASB's Concepts Statement 6 to support a debit balance in the balance sheet as a fit and proper asset, fully meeting the FASB's definition of an asset. One sees similar long-winded briefs in private, civil litigation. In that litigation, both sides, both the defendant and the plaintiff, and all of their expert witnesses, are citing the very same passages from the FASB's Concepts Statement 6 in support of their positions regarding the worthiness or unworthiness of a debit balance in a balance sheet as an asset. What we have, then, in the lawyers' words, are teams of swearing accountants – one swearing "thus and so" and another swearing "such and that," both invoking the same words in the same literature – and they cannot resolve what should be a simple question: whether something is an asset.

What generally happens in practice under the FASB's definition of an asset is that assets are not recognized in the balance sheet unless the reporting enterprise acquires them by paying cash or agreeing to pay cash in the future, or someone contributes something to the reporting enterprise in return for a debt or equity security issued by the enterprise. An asset is then said to have a cost. In fact, accountants sometimes think of the asset and talk about it in terms of its cost, not in terms of the asset itself or the future benefit that may flow from it. That is, the asset is the cost, and the cost is the asset. For example, if an enterprise discovers something of value, say, oil or gold, we do not recognize it as an asset, because the enterprise has no cost in that something. When the FASB proposed some time ago that business enterprises recognize as assets things received from others in a so-called non-reciprocal exchange, for example, land received from a government, some accountants objected. One of the reasons for the objection was that the enterprise receiving the asset had no cost in the asset. I refer to this phenomenon as the cost *per se* is the asset syndrome.

I will cite some examples of costs equal assets. (I am aware that the FASB has said in paragraph 179 of Concepts Statement 6 that costs are not themselves assets. In my experience, however, most preparers and auditors of financial statements continue to equate costs with assets in their conversations and in the way they prepare and audit financial statements. After all, the FASB said in Concepts Statements 3 and 6 that then "present practice" would continue, and in that practice costs equal assets.) The AICPA's Accounting Standards Executive Committee, without objection from the FASB, issued a statement of position entitled *Reporting on Advertising Costs*, which says that so-called direct-response advertising costs are to be reported as assets if the advertising activity results in probable future economic benefits. Thus, the cost is the asset. In oil and gas accounting, either successful efforts as described by the FASB in Statement 19 or full cost as described by the SEC in Regulation S-X, the asset represented in the balance sheet is the cost of finding the oil and gas reserves, not the value of the reserves themselves at the time of discovery or any time thereafter. In FASB Statement 34, interest cost is an asset. In FASB Statement 60, the cost of issuing insurance contracts is an asset. In FASB Statement 86, the asset is the cost of developing computer software, not the future benefit that will flow from the software. In Accounting Principles Board Opinion 21, the cost of raising debt finance is an asset, a "deferred charge." And, finally, in APB Opinion 16 and in the FASB's September 1999 exposure draft dealing with *Accounting for Business Combinations and Intangible Assets*, the cost that is left over in a business combination after the purchase price is allocated to the identifiable assets and liabilities is an asset; it is called cost of acquisition in excess of the fair value of net assets acquired, or cost of purchased goodwill. (In a letter dated 15 June 2000 to the FASB commenting on the FASB's September 1999 exposure draft of *Accounting for Business Combinations and Intangible Assets*, I called it a glob.) Along this same line, the International Accounting Standards Committee says that development costs, the D in R&D, may be recognized as an asset under certain conditions. In all of these cases, it is the cost itself that is identified as the asset, not the probable future economic benefit. It is this same line of reasoning, that a cost can be an asset, that leads some people to suggest that the FASB should reconsider FASB Statement 2 and allow for recognition of research and development costs as an asset.

Generally, when assets are acquired for cash, the fair value of the assets acquired, or the future economic benefit, is approximately equal to the cash paid (laying aside the difference between bid and ask prices and costs of actually buying assets, such as brokers' fees). So, at least at the date of acquisition of the asset, cost equals fair value and future economic benefit. (We all know that, soon after the acquisition of an asset, say, land, cost and fair value begin to diverge and often become quite far apart.) The cost of many assets recognized under the FASB's definition does not, at the time of acquisition, represent anything close to the "probable future economic benefit" to be derived from the asset. For example, the probable future economic benefit of a successful direct-response advertising campaign may be many multiples of the cost. The cost of prepaid advertising or direct-response advertising only by chance will be equal to the present value of increased net cash flows that may result because of the advertising. The future economic benefit of a discovery of mineral deposits generally bears no relationship whatsoever to the cost of finding the deposits. The future economic benefits of a successful research and development project also bear little or no relationship to the cost incurred.

Defining an asset as a probable future economic benefit is to use a high-order abstraction. Under such an approach, if an enterprise owns a truck, the truck *per se* is not the asset. The asset is the future economic benefit, that is, the present value of the cash flows that will come from using the truck to haul lumber, or coal, or bread. Yet, in today's practice, the asset represented on the balance sheet is a truck. Readers of the financial statements see the asset as a truck. The readers do not see it as the economic benefit that will come from using the truck to haul lumber. I think most people, even most accountants, think of the asset as a truck instead of an abstraction, instead of the present value of future cash flows, or the future economic benefit, to be derived from using the truck to haul lumber.

I think that we should account for real things such as trucks, not abstract future economic benefits. I suggest that we adopt a different definition of an asset. A simple one. One that is not a large empty box. One that is not a high-order abstraction. I suggest that we adopt the following definition: "cash, contractual claims to cash, things that can be exchanged for cash, and derivative contracts having a positive value to the holder thereof."

My definition would comprehend only real things, not abstractions. Real things such as trucks can be sold for cash. Real things can be pledged as collateral for a borrowing of cash. Real things can be given to charity. Exchange-traded derivative contracts having a positive value can be closed out for cash. The positive value of an over-the-counter derivative contract can be turned into cash by entering into an equal and offsetting contract. Abstract probable future economic benefits cannot be sold, pledged, or given to charity. My definition would not accept a cost as being an asset. A critical feature in my definition is exchangeability of the asset, which is explicitly not a feature of the FASB's definition of an asset (see FASB Concepts Statement 6, para. 26).

Let me list a few of the things that my definition would include. Obviously, cash. Obviously, claims to cash such as trade receivables, loans receivable, demand deposits at banks, certificates of deposit, cash surrender value of life insurance policies, bills, notes, and bonds issued by governments, corporations, partnerships, individuals, and trusts. Cash paid in advance for the future use of land and buildings would be included as an asset if the cash could be recaptured from the lessor by the lessee at its option. That definition would include raw materials, finished goods, common stocks issued by other enterprises, land, buildings, equipment, mineral deposits, air rights, water rights, broadcast rights, patents, and copyrights.

Work-in-progress inventory and fixed assets in the process of construction might be included if they can be sold for cash in their present condition or state. Growing crops would be excluded, because a crop generally cannot be sold separately from the land, but the value of the growing crop would increase the fair value of the land, which can be sold. Also included would be futures, forward, option, swap, and swaption contracts having a positive value; exchange-traded derivative contracts can be closed out with the receipt of cash, and over-the-counter derivative contracts can be offset with equal and opposite contracts, thereby producing cash.

Let me list some of the things that would be excluded: any cost as such, such as pre-opening costs, debt issue costs, interest cost, and advertising cost. Costs of opening new stores or branches. Employee training costs. Costs of restructuring a business. Assets that arise in proportional consolidation, such as 33 percent of cash or accounts receivable or plant held by a joint venture in which venture the reporting enterprise has a one-third interest would be excluded. (However, the one-third interest in the joint venture itself would be an asset.) Receivables sold with or without recourse and thus owned and controlled by another enterprise would be excluded, because the receivables were sold and are not owned by the seller and cannot be sold again by the seller. Assets owned by others and leased by the reporting enterprise would be excluded for the same reason unless the lease itself was transferable either directly or through a sublease and had a positive value. "Prepaid advertising" would be excluded unless the advertiser could get back its money at its option or could sell the advertising space, say, a billboard or an appearance on someone else's website. Costs of R&D or only D would not be an asset. Nor would so-called deferred tax assets be assets. Cost of purchased goodwill, or any other goodwill, would be excluded. It is significant to note, in this regard, that the Association for Investment Management and Research, which represents stock analysts in the USA, has recommended that the cost of purchased goodwill not be recognized as an asset (see *Financial Reporting in the 1990s and Beyond*, Association for Investment Management and Research, 1993, pp. 48, 49; and AIMR's letter to the FASB dated 7 December 1999, which is AIMR's response to the FASB's exposure draft of *Accounting for Business Combinations and Intangible Assets*).

The use of my definition of an asset would vastly simplify the practice of accounting. Vastly simplify financial accounting and reporting. I believe that it would appeal to investors, creditors, and other users of financial statements. I think the results of applying my definition would appeal to ordinary men and women who walk up and down Main Street in the USA, and those who walk up and down Main Street in other countries as well. They would understand the result. My sister would understand the result. I think that ordinary people who are not accountants think that when they see an asset on a balance sheet that the asset is something real, and that the dollar amount associated with the asset represents value, that is, that the asset can be exchanged for cash for approximately the dollar amount at which the asset is represented in the balance sheet. That the asset can be pledged as collateral for a borrowing. That the asset may be given to the Red Cross. Accounting should not be done for the benefit of accountants. Accounting should result in financial statements and reports that ordinary people can understand and therefore be able to use to make investment and credit decisions and regulatory oversight decisions.

Accountants could use my definition as a working tool. They could use it to identify things to be reported as assets on balance sheets. They could use it to identify, through exclusion, things not to be reported as assets on balance sheets, which is not possible today. We would dispense with all of the long-winded legal briefs about the fitness of debit balances as assets and the teams of swearing accountants. Assets would be real things. Exchangeable things. Defining assets as real things, and reporting those real things at their fair value, would make balance sheets rock solid and less prone to challenge and thereby reduce litigation against companies and their auditors. Would make balance sheets relevant, living documents instead of what they are now – dimly lit basement parking garages for collections of antique costs. Assessing and auditing the recoverability or impairment of something that is just a cost, a cost not associated with a real thing, is more than hard. It's impossible. One cannot look to the marketplace and find the value of a cost. All that the auditor can do is look at numbers that management puts on a sheet of paper or a computer monitor about how management believes that cost will be recovered. That's not gathering competent, evidential matter. That's not auditing. If an auditor is allowed to accept management's assertion about the value of that which is reported as an asset instead of having to find competent, evidential matter from sources outside the reporting enterprise to support that value, then audits have no purpose or worth. Scrap audits and save the cost of audits.

I repeat, the definition of an asset that is in use today is too inclusive, overly complex, and vague. It does not work. I suggest that standard setters take another look at the definition and include the feature of exchangeability.

The FASB's definition of a liability suffers from a similar infirmity to its definition of an asset. The FASB says in Concepts Statement 6, paragraph 35, that "Liabilities are probable future sacrifices of economic benefits arising from present obligations of a particular entity to transfer assets or provide services to other entities in the future as a result of past transactions or events." Footnote 22 expands on those words in the definition as follows:

> *Obligations* in the definition is broader than legal obligations. It is used with its usual general meaning to refer to duties imposed legally or socially; to that which one is bound to do by contract, promise, moral responsibility, and so forth (*Webster's New World Dictionary*, p. 981). It includes equitable and constructive obligations as well as legal obligations.
>
> paras 37–40.

Most people know what a legal obligation is. But most people do not know what an equitable or constructive obligation is, or what an obligation arising from moral responsibility is. Even the FASB does not know, for it has not articulated what those obligations are and what their characteristics are so that we can recognize them when we see them. Therefore, every time the FASB wants to require some accounting because of what it sees as an equitable or constructive obligation, or what an obligation arising from a moral responsibility is, the FASB has to write a detailed rule for accountants to use in drawing up financial statements. Look, for example, at our accounting in the USA for workers' pension benefits. Long before any benefit is vested in the employee, the FASB instructs us to recognize a pension liability. The idea is that the workers are earning the pension benefit over time, and a liability for an equitable or constructive obligation should be recognized prior to vesting of the benefits. But only the FASB knows what that equitable or constructive obligation is, how it is defined, when it should be recognized, and how it should be measured. The ensuing liability number, computed as per the FASB's formula, cannot be audited or verified except by checking the calculation, which is no audit at all. A perfect example of feel-good accounting.

Yet another example of feel-good accounting is a recent phenomenon in the USA, dating from the late 1980s and early 1990s. That is the accounting for so-called restructurings. The FASB's Emerging Issues Task Force, in Consensuses 94-3 and 95-3, said that it is okay to recognize a liability to pay termination bonuses or stay bonuses to workers that will be discharged before the workers' rights to that bonus are vested. EITF 94-3 and 95-3 are the ultimate in feel-good accounting. Management of the enterprise recognizes a liability if it says that it will make future expenditures, although there is no requirement for those expenditures to be made; in fact those expenditures may be avoided at will. The rationale is that management creates, by its proclamation to make the expenditures, a constructive or equitable obligation. If management does not make a proclamation about future expenditures for termination bonuses or stay bonuses but simply lays off workers and pays the workers termination bonuses in the ordinary course of business, then there apparently is no constructive or equitable obligation in advance of the cash disbursement to the terminated employee. I wonder how loud management's proclamation must be in order to create an accounting liability.

The FASB's definition of a liability is as infirm as its definition of an asset. We cannot solve the question, at the margin, of what is and what is not a liability, because the definition is so open-ended.

I suggest that we define liabilities by reference to future cash outflows required by negotiable instruments, by contracts, by law or regulation, by court-entered judgments or agreements with claimants, and derivative contracts having a negative value.

I think that a liability recognizable for accounting purposes should be one of the following:

1 A future cash outflow required by a negotiable instrument, such as a recourse promissory note, issued by the reporting enterprise, and accrued interest thereon. (The unpaid amount of a non-recourse note secured only by a specific asset would be netted against the fair value of the asset, for it is only the net amount of cash that the owner could get on sale of the asset. If the amount of unpaid debt exceeds the fair value of the asset, there is no liability to report, because the future cash outflows related to the debt may be avoided at will by walking away from an asset having a net value of zero.)

2 A future cash outflow required by the terms of a contract under which the counterparty has completed his/her/its obligations. Examples are (a) accounts payable to suppliers of goods, which goods have been delivered to and accepted by the reporting enterprise, (b) accounts payable to suppliers of services where the counterparty has performed according to the terms of the contract, (c) salaries and wages for work done by employees, (d) deposit accounts of banks and thrifts, (e) death benefits payable to beneficiaries under life insurance policies as a result of the insured's death (not an actuarially determined amount but the actual amount payable to the owner's estate or other beneficiaries), (f) vested pension benefits as to working and retired employees in excess of the fair value of any pension plan assets held by trustees, which assets may be used to pay only pension benefits, (g) amounts payable to counterparties under derivative contracts, (h) outstanding stock of the reporting enterprise, which stock must, by its terms, be redeemed for cash by the reporting enterprise (mandatorily redeemable stock), and (i) future "dividends" on issued and outstanding stock that unconditionally must be paid in cash by the reporting enterprise, including cumulative dividends on so-called perpetual preferred stock.

3 A future cash outflow required by a contract at the option of the counterparty. Examples are (a) sales returns by customers, (b) warranties related to defective product (in which case the cash outflow may be for parts and labor to fix the product), (c) cash surrender value of life insurance contracts issued (not an actuarially determined amount but the actual amount refundable to owners of the policies at the owners' requests), (d) refundable portion of magazine subscriptions, (e) refundable portion of fire, flood, and other casualty insurance premiums, (f) refundable portion of cash collected in advance from a counterparty prior to the reporting enterprise's having delivered goods or services to the counterparty, as to which amount the counterparty would have an enforceable claim if the reporting enterprise fails to deliver the goods or services, and (g) claims payable to insureds under various kinds of insurance policies.

4 A future cash outflow required by a federal, state, or local law or regulation. Examples are (a) amounts withheld from employees' salaries to be remitted to a governmental body by the reporting enterprise, (b) sales tax, value-added tax, or similar tax collected by the reporting enterprise from its customers to be remitted to a governmental body by the reporting enterprise, (c) tax based on taxable income or taxable capital of the reporting enterprise (the amount is to be determined by reference to the tax return filed or to be filed, not some greater or lesser amount to take into account contestable or negotiable matters), (d) decommissioning of nuclear plants, and (e) remediation of contaminated water or ground.

5 A future cash outflow that would be required on default or rescission of an executory contract that is unperformed as to both counterparties. Examples of executory contracts are those for the use of property (leases) and those to acquire property (inventory purchases).

6 Derivative contracts (futures, forwards, options, swaps, and swaptions) having a negative value over and above the amount of cash currently payable, which is included in 2 (g) above.

7 A future cash outflow required by a court-entered judgment or an agreement with a claimant. An example is a future cash outflow to an employee or an outsider as a result of a claim relating to a bodily injury.

Under the above definition of a recognizable liability, a proclamation by management that it intends to make certain future cash disbursements, no matter how loud that proclamation, would not qualify as a recognizable liability. For example, a proclaimed intention to pay year-end cash bonuses to employees would not be a recognizable liability if management may change its mind and not pay the bonuses and if no law or regulation requires that the bonuses be paid. An announced intention to pay termination bonuses, or stay bonuses, to employees who eventually may be terminated pursuant to a "restructuring" also would not be a recognizable liability if no contract or law or regulation requires the enterprise to terminate the employees and pay the termination bonuses. An announced intention to spend more money than is required by law to remediate contaminated ground would not be a recognizable liability, for the expenditure may be avoided at will without penalty.

No "reserve" or "valuation allowance" or "provision" of any kind would be a recognizable liability or an offset to any asset amount. Journalists, judges, and other ordinary folk think that "reserves" or "provisions" are vessels containing green money. This is evident from reading the *Wall Street Journal*, *The New York Times*, legal briefs, and court opinions. We need to get rid of the terms "reserves" and "provisions."

Computed amounts would not be recognizable liabilities under the definition, for example, deferred tax liabilities, actuarially determined amounts of pension benefits to be paid to working and retired employees, and actuarially determined amounts payable to owners of life insurance policies or the beneficiaries of those policies.

As I define assets to be recognized in balance sheets, they are the reporting enterprise's cash, claims to cash, and other things that are owned by the reporting enterprise and are exchangeable for cash. As I define liabilities to be recognized in balance sheets, they are the reporting enterprise's future cash outflows. All recognized assets and liabilities would be reported at fair value. True north.

"Fair value," of course, needs to be defined. The FASB's definition of the fair value of an asset is as follows, from paragraph 7 of FASB Statement 121: "The fair value of an asset is the amount at which the asset could be bought or sold in a current transaction between willing parties, that is, other than a forced or liquidation sale." (The definition of fair value for a financial instrument in FASB Statement 107 is, except for a minor difference of wording, the same.) That definition does not work very well. Owners of assets often contend that they would not be willing sellers at the prices offered by potential buyers. Owners also often contend that, because of lack of liquidity, "abnormal" market conditions, whatever abnormal is, or for other reasons, prices being offered by potential buyers are for "forced" or "liquidation" sales. Those matters are so judgmental that the FASB's definition does not work at the margin. I have seen it not work in enforcement cases at the SEC, where respondents will not write down the carrying amount of assets because they say the prices being bid are for forced or liquidation sales and that the respondents would not be willing sellers at those prices. So the standard does not work.

I would define fair value of assets as follows: the estimated amount of cash the asset would fetch in an immediate sale whether or not under duress, without recourse or guarantees, less the estimated amount of cash that would have to be paid out to accomplish the sale. This suggested definition is clear and permits no judgments about the state of the market or the willingness of the seller to sell at prices being offered or bid by potential buyers.

I would define the fair value of liabilities as follows: the least amount of cash that the counterparty would accept in an immediate and complete liquidation of his/her/its claim against the reporting enterprise.

Let me list a few of the beneficial effects that adoption of my proposal would have.

1 Users of financial statements and reports would understand the line-item descriptions and numbers in the balance sheet, namely, what the reporting enterprise owns and what it owes, with all measurements based on immediate cash prices. True north. There would be no balance sheet deferrals followed by (arbitrary) allocations of those deferred amounts to future periods. There would be no need for pages and pages of footnotes that describe the recondite procedures used to calculate amounts in financial statements, as is now the case. However, there would need to be disclosures about the assumptions made in estimating the fair value of assets and liabilities so that users of the financial statements would be fully informed.

2 Financial accounting and reporting under my approach (a) would be vastly simpler than what we have today and (b) would be understood by investors, creditors, underwriters, CEOs, line operating managers, analysts, journalists, editors, lawyers, judges, US senators and representatives, and ordinary folk. Members of boards of directors and audit committees would understand the line-item descriptions and numbers in the balance sheet. Corporate governance would take a quantum stride forward.

3 Fraud in audited financial statements would virtually cease to exist, because opportunities for cooking the books would no longer be available. Auditors would be responsible, as they are today, for auditing cash and other transactions involving assets (as defined herein). Auditors would confirm with banks the amount of cash on deposit. Auditors would confirm with counterparties the amounts owed to the enterprise. Auditors would confirm payables with counterparties. Auditors would observe inventory counts. Auditors would go to outsiders to get opinions regarding what the outsiders believe are the fair values of the enterprise's individual, exchangeable assets. Auditors would go to outsiders to get opinions about the fair value of the enterprise's liabilities. Auditors could not accept management's opinion about the fair value of assets or liabilities unless that opinion was corroborated by outsiders. In other words, auditors would get competent evidence supporting management's assertions in the balance sheet. That's what auditing should be about. For an exhaustive discussion of what auditing should be about, I commend to all Peter Wolnizer's book *Auditing as Independent Authentication* (1987).

We in the USA have seen many frauds that were perpetrated by so-called improper revenue recognition. We have labored to try to write rules for when and in what amount revenue may be recognized. We have lots of rules telling us when revenue may be recognized and how to measure it. The latest iteration is the SEC's Staff Accounting Bulletin 101, issued 3 December 1999. But, looking at revenue recognition as being the problem is to look down the wrong end of the pipe. Every line item and every amount in the income statement (or in a statement of changes in net assets as I would have in my scheme of things) is fathered in the balance sheet. There is no sales transaction to report until the enterprise receives cash or a promise by the counterparty to pay cash. Auditors should look at the balance sheet. That's where the DNA is. Auditors should ask a commercial bank or a factor what amount of cash it would pay, without recourse or guarantees, for the receivable arising from the sale. If the bank or factor says 100 or 95 or 84 or 39 or zero, then report the receivable, and therefore the sale, at that amount. Then disclose the name of the bank or factor that gave the opinion so that users of the financial statement will know who gave the opinion. Under my scheme of things, fraudulent financial reporting because of improper revenue recognition would disappear.

4 The FASB could stop writing complex accounting rules, which no one except accountants understand, and not very many accountants at that. The FASB, or some other body, would have to develop standardized valuation

> techniques for use by reporting enterprises and outside valuation experts when estimating the cash sale price of an asset if there is no liquid market for that kind of asset. Guidance would be necessary to estimate the cash sale price of many fixed assets, for example a railroad between Massachusetts and Florida, a petrochemical plant in Texas, a shoe factory in Brazil, a semiconductor manufacturing facility in Taiwan, or a salmon farm in Scotland.

Nowadays, we have amounts in balance sheets for fixed assets that are just numbers; the numbers have no information content whatsoever. Depreciation methods and salvage values are (almost) whatever management wants them to be. Whether the carrying amount for those fixed assets is impaired is determined by reference to all of the future, undiscounted cash flows attributable to the assets – cash flows projected by management as far as the eye can see. What an irrelevant methodology.

Let's assume that a company owns a fleet of commercial aircraft having a cost of 100. The value of aircraft declines to 80 because the price of fuel goes up, but the owner of the aircraft cannot put through increases in the price of tickets sold to passengers. Under the current standard in the USA, so long as all future net cash flows related to the aircraft, projected as far as the eye can see, without reduction for risk and the time value of money, equal or exceed 100 no write-down is made to reduce the carrying amount of the aircraft to 80. I used as an example a fleet of aircraft because we can learn the going price of aircraft fairly easily and at little cost. The concept is the same for any asset as to which there are not readily available price quotations, such as a railroad or a petrochemical plant or a shoe factory or a computer chip manufacturing plant or a salmon farm. (I would point out that there are many kinds of asset as to which the fair values can be obtained from outside parties at a relatively small cost considering the information value of those fair value amounts. Examples are land-, air-, and ocean-going transportation equipment, pipelines, office buildings, apartment buildings, shopping malls, warehouses, mineral reserves, and maybe even satellites.)

FASB Statement 15, *Accounting by Debtors and Creditors for Troubled Debt Restructurings*, was issued in 1977. Before being amended by FASB Statement 114, Statement 15 said that the total of all future cash inflows related to a receivable were to be compared with the carrying amount of the receivable to measure any loss on the receivable. So long as the undiscounted future cash inflows, no matter how distant, equalled or exceeded the carrying amount of the receivable, no loss was to be recognized. Never mind that the fair value of the receivable or the underlying collateral might be far less than its carrying amount. Statement 15, issued in 1977, retarded the thinking of an entire generation of accountants and significantly increased the US government's losses in the S&L mess in the 1980s because losses kept growing, and piling up on balance sheets, but were not recognized as such in income statements under Statement 15 until the federal government took over the assets. US taxpayers then took the hit in the S&L bail-out. Although the FASB somewhat, but not completely, fixed the loan-loss measurement problem in FASB Statement 114, *Accounting by Creditors for*

Impairment of a Loan, issued in 1993, the board then repeated the same mistake in 1995 when it issued Statement 121, *Accounting for Impairment of Long-Lived Assets to be Disposed Of.* Statement 121 says to look to the total of future cash inflows from long-lived assets, no matter how distant, compare that undiscounted amount with the carrying amount, and recognize no loss unless the total cash inflows are less than the carrying amount, even though the fair value of the asset might be significantly less than the carrying amount. The thinking of yet another generation of accountants is being retarded now under Statement 121.

5 The debate over purchase versus pooling accounting would disappear. With all assets (as defined herein) and liabilities (as defined herein) being reported as such in the balance sheet, and all at fair value, every business combination would be reported by combining the assets and liabilities of each party to the business combination – all at fair value. No debate about who acquired whom. No debate about whether the cost of purchased goodwill is an asset.
6 The debate over accounting for stock options issued to employees would not exist. No cash or other asset goes out of the enterprise, and no obligation to pay cash arises when a stock option is granted or exercised, so there is no decrease in assets or net assets and therefore nothing to account for except for the cash received when the option is exercised. When the attention is on cash inflows and cash outflows and changes in the fair values of real assets and liabilities, as it is in my proposal, it is clear that the issuance of stock options to employees, and exercise of those options, is a rearrangement of the ownership interest between the various owners and potential owners, not a decrease in corporate assets. The value of what one owner relinquishes to a potential new owner or a new owner is not imputed to the reporting enterprise. The reporting enterprise accounts for its assets and changes in them, not its owners' assets.
7 Earnings management would disappear as an issue. In the USA, I have seen earnings being managed almost at will by chief executive officers and chief financial officers. Loading accrued liabilities or "reserves" in good times and drawing them down in lean times. Or drawing down reserves or estimated liabilities, such as for warranties, whenever it is necessary to "make the numbers." Changing assumptions so as to time the recognition of write-downs of the cost of long-lived assets instead of when the value actually declined. Projecting net cash inflows, or increasing net cash inflows, as far as the eye can see to justify not writing down the cost of long-lived assets. Earnings management is a scourge in the USA. Earnings management is the ultimate in accounting gimmickry. By participating in this gimmickry, accountants not only have cheapened their image but also have raised serious questions about the substance of what they do.
8 We could stop arguing with banks about the size of their allowances for loan losses. Whether such allowances may be recognized only for loans that are already bad or for loans that may go bad as well. The loans would be

reported at their fair value, which comprehends all credit risk. I know that we will need guidance from the FASB, or some similar body, on how to estimate those fair values, but at least then we would be trying to get a relevant number that can be audited by reference to an outside source instead of an allowance that is determined judgmentally by management, as it is today.

9 We would no longer be arguing with banks and insurance companies about whether their bond holdings are for trading, held for sale (not trading), or held to maturity, with each of the three approaches producing a different income number. Going through these convoluted discussions gives accounting and accountants a bad name. Ordinary folk think that we accountants are practicing a dark art.

10 Huge gains and losses, mostly losses, on sale or discontinuance of assets would disappear. Users of financial statements today have a hard time interpreting how these gains and losses should be factored into previously reported income from an analytical standpoint. Changes in fair value of assets would be recognized as changes take place, not on sale or discontinuance.

11 It is now in vogue in the USA for the directors to discuss with the outside auditor what the auditor thinks about the "quality" of the company's accounting (see Recommendation 9 of the *Report and Recommendations of the Blue Ribbon Committee on Improving the Effectiveness of Corporate Audit Committees*, issued in 1999, and the AICPA's Practice Alert 2000–2, dated February 2000, entitled *Quality of Accounting Principles – Guidance for Discussions with Audit Committees*). That dialogue would not be necessary under my proposal. The basis of every company's financial statements would be the same as every other company's: what the company owns and what it owes, with the fair values of those things being determined by reference to facts or opinions received from outsiders instead of being based on a management-determined number. True north.

12 Students who aspire to be accountants could learn financial accounting and reporting in a very short time. As it is now in the USA, students must have five years of university study to become certified public accountants. Although I taught a few staff training courses when I was in public practice, I have no training on how to teach. However, I venture that I could teach students in one year, maybe less, how to do financial accounting and reporting my way. Thus, graduating students would not be so deeply in debt on student loans as they are today when they graduate.

Estimating cash selling prices for assets for which there is no ready market would be the largest challenge in implementing my proposal. We cannot look up prices for most assets in business publications. We would need guidance from the FASB, or some similar body, on how to estimate those prices. The FASB will soon face that issue if and when it requires that all financial instruments be reported at fair value. Developing that guidance no doubt would give rise to debates about how to estimate those prices. What kinds of model to use in estimating those prices.

what the inputs to the models should be. However, that debate would be about something that would be important and relevant for making investment and credit decisions. Currently, the debates that the FASB has with its constituencies about when to report and how to measure various assets and liabilities are not debates but are (shouting) arguments about whether a particular expenditure is an asset or an expense and recondite procedures to be used to compute financial statement amounts, for example pension liabilities and deferred taxes. The only reason that the FASB wins these arguments is a political one, to wit, the SEC requires that public companies in the USA follow the FASB's rules. Resolution of such debates should turn on relevance of information, logic, merit and substance, not political clout.

My accounting would be simple. It would have a simple, singular focus – cash. All assets and liabilities would be stated at fair value. We all would know where north lies on that accounting compass. The results of the accounting could be audited or verified or authenticated by auditors by reference to facts and opinions about the fair values of assets and liabilities – facts and opinions obtained from people outside the reporting enterprise. Real auditing. Investors, creditors, underwriters, analysts, CEOs, line managers, members of boards of directors and audit committees, lawyers, judges, regulators, journalists, editors, US senators and representatives, and ordinary people would understand that accounting. My sister would understand it.

References

AICPA Practice Alert (2000) *Quality of Accounting Principles – Guidance for Discussions With Audit Committees*, AICPA, 2 February 2000.

Association for Investment Management and Research (1993) *Financial Reporting in the 1990s and Beyond*, AIMR.

Blue Ribbon Committee on Improving the Effectiveness of Corporate Audit Committees (1999) *Report and Recommendation of the Blue Ribbon Committee on Improving the Effectiveness of Corporate Audit Committees*, available on www.nvse.com.

Committee on Accounting Procedure (1953) *Taxes: Section A, Real and Personal Property Taxes*, Accounting Research Bulletin No. 43.

Epstein, M.J. and Palepu, K.G. (1999) *Strategic Finance*, Institute of Management Accountants.

Schuetze, W.P. (1991) "Walter Schuetze on keep it simple," *Accounting Horizons*.

Schuetze, W.P. (1993) "What is an asset?" *Accounting Horizons*.

Wolnizer, P. (1987) *Auditing as Independent Authentication*, Sydney University Press.

7 New chief accountant's wish list

Address to the Nineteenth Annual AICPA National Conference on Current SEC Developments, Washington, 7 January 1992

I wish to thank Mr Huff and the AICPA's SEC Regulations Committee for the invitation to address the conference this morning.

My position here today is unique. I will not take up my post as chief accountant to the commission until two weeks hence. And my separation from my firm will not occur until shortly before I take my post at the commission, which will allow me to take a few days of accumulated vacation. So, I need to issue the standard SEC disclaimer that the views I express here are mine and do not necessarily reflect those of the commission or members of the staff of the commission. By like token, the views I express here today do not reflect the views of KPMG or its partners and staff.

What I want to discuss today are some broad, general themes that I intend to pursue and develop at the commission. First, I want to state that I intend to observe the policy of the commission as set forth in Accounting Series Release 150, which was issued in 1973, regarding the establishment of financial accounting and reporting standards. In ASR 150, the commission said that, while it reserved its authority and responsibility under the Securities Acts, it would look to the Financial Accounting Standards Board in the private sector to set standards. So I do not intend to take pen in hand and rewrite old standards or write new ones unless I believe that is necessary for the protection of investors.

I want to discuss two themes, namely, simplicity and relevance in standard setting and financial accounting and reporting. Uniting those two themes and objectives, and keeping them always in sight, I think will be in the best interests of users of financial information, both in the short term and long term. And I think that those two themes and objectives are so fundamental and common that all of us in this room and standard setters and regulators, wherever situated around the world, can embrace them.

I wrote an article entitled "Keep it simple," which was published as commentary in *Accounting Horizons* in June of last year. In that article, I suggested that the FASB write simpler accounting standards than it has in the past.

I do not mean to criticize the board's prior standards by that call for simpler standards in the future. Indeed, I think that many of us have participated for the last ten to twenty years in complex standards. I know that I have. I did some of that while I was technical adviser to Joe Cummings on the Accounting

Principles Board in the 1960s, while I was at the FASB in the 1970s, while I was on the AICPA's Accounting Standards Executive Committee in the 1980s and 1990s, and when I participated at meetings of the Emerging Issues Task Force in the 1980s and 1990s. The SEC's staff has, over the years, also been a party to making the rules for financial accounting and reporting complex. We can all say that we helped out. I suggest that we all stand back and try to put ourselves into the shoes of the investor and creditor and ask whether this welter of complexity that we have created, and continue to create, really helps those people to make lending and investing decisions. My judgment is that we have gone too far.

Having said that, however, let me also say that I do not agree with the call for broad, general standards that are left to the judgment of the preparer of the financial statements to implement and its independent auditor to audit the results of that implementation. We have tried that approach in the past in this country and it did not work. For example, there was a broad, general standard on pooling-of-interests accounting in Accounting Research Bulletin 48, but it did not work. We had a broad, general standard on lease accounting, in Accounting Principles Board Opinion 5, but it did not work in that very few lessees recognized any leased assets and related liabilities on their balance sheets. We have a broad, general standard on when to recognize credit losses in FASB Statement 5 on contingencies, which I signed, and it does not work very well in that the results under it are too widely dispersed. Holders of large loans, which are primarily financial institutions, and independent auditors of those institutions, under that broad, general standard, do not have a good grip on when to recognize credit losses or how to measure them. I think because those and other broad, general standards did not work, we went into the detailed and complex standard-writing business.

As a concept, I am attracted to the idea of regulators and standard setters issuing broad, general standards. However, I have been at this business long enough to know that that will not work very well. At best, that approach results in extensive non-comparability among and between reporting enterprises. At worst, that approach results in abuse and perhaps even fraud. People will, in good faith, interpret broad, general rules in just that way; some people will be conservative, some liberal, and some in between; and that produces wide non-comparability in financial reporting. Given that kind of broad, general standard, independent auditors have no benchmark or guideline to judge whether their clients have complied with the standard or rule.

That approach of broad, general standards or rules, allowing for latitude in interpretation, does not help investors and creditors, who need to be able to make comparisons among and between alternative investments, and we should help them do that, not make it difficult or opaque.

Well, where does that lead me? Where it leads me is to suggest that standards have some bright lines – perhaps arbitrary – that will result in uniform application of the standards and comparability among and between reporting enterprises, not only in this country but also in others.

Some people say that business arrangements are more complex than they used to be, so the accounting has to be equally complex. And some say that they object to bright lines because it eliminates judgment. I understand those arguments, but I do not agree with the answers that are produced as a result.

Let me move to my second major theme, that is, relevance in financial reporting and mark-to-market accounting, which, in my opinion, go hand in hand with my ideas about simplicity in accounting standards.

The commission's views on mark-to-market accounting were set forth by Chairman Breeden in testimony before the Committee on Banking, Housing, and Urban Affairs of the United States Senate on 10 September 1990. In that testimony, Mr Breeden said that there should be a move to mark to market by financial institutions:

> The [Senate Banking] Committee's last question focuses on a matter that is also a major area of current Commission concern: the valuation of financial instruments held by financial institutions. Under current practice, GAAP [generally accepted accounting practices] for banks and thrifts are based principally on a historical cost framework. These institutions are permitted to carry assets on their books at amortized cost, even in instances where the current value of the assets has eroded substantially, and where a market-based standard would provide a far more accurate measure of the institution's financial health.
>
> As we enter the decade of the 1990s, we should consider a fundamental shift in the goal we set for the accounting standards for financial institutions. Such institutions are in the business of buying and selling financial instruments, all of which have a value measured in terms of current market conditions. Determining the current value of an institution's assets ... should increasingly be the goal toward which we must work.

In that same testimony, speaking in a broader context than only financial institutions, Chairman Breeden also said:

> Steps currently being taken to clarify the accounting treatment for investment portfolios should be part of a broader move in the direction of mark-to-market accounting. The benefits of market-based accounting warrant consideration of a broader shift in this direction. The presumption that market-based information is the most relevant financial data attribute should be recognized. It may be appropriate to utilize historical cost only where specifically justified by the circumstances ....
>
> The Commission recognizes that the move to a full-scale application of market-based accounting requires careful and deliberate planning. The Commission is aware that strong views are held and valid concerns exist concerning a shift to market value accounting. In particular, great care must be taken to ensure that the costs of implementation and ongoing compliance do not exceed the expected benefits. With respect to reliability of

> market value information, additional work will be necessary to develop reasonable and cost effective valuation techniques for those assets and liabilities that do not have a liquid market. We need to explore ways to reduce subjectivity of estimates to an acceptable level. The Commission does not underestimate the significance or importance of these and other issues. However, we believe that their resolution must be aggressively pursued.

My views about mark to market versus historical cost are on all fours with the views of the commission as articulated in the 1990 testimony. Indeed, I will go one step further and suggest that this issue has been studied enough in the laboratories of academic journals and needs to be tested in the crucible of practice.

Last year at this conference, Chairman Breeden said that he was looking for a chief accountant who was a combination of Genghis Khan, Confucius, and Superman. What he got is a south Texas country fellow that likes mark-to-market accounting.

Intuitively, market value information about assets and liabilities has to pass everyone's test of relevance. If you, as a user of financial information, were to be offered a smorgasbord of financial information about an enterprise, including the historical cost/proceeds of its assets and liabilities and market value of its assets and liabilities, but were told that you could select only one item, which would you select? No doubt exists in my mind, or any user of financial information that I have ever talked to, that the one datum that you would select is market value of the enterprise's assets and liabilities.

The trick, of course, will be to find the point of trade-off or equilibrium between the obvious benefits and the cost of getting market value information that is sufficiently reliable to be published for use by investors and creditors.

We now have the FASB's Statement 107, which requires disclosure about the fair value of the financial assets and liabilities, both on and off the balance sheet. I applaud the FASB for getting that document on the street. Up to now, disclosure of fair value of financial instruments has been limited to assets such as marketable equity securities and certain bond-type securities. The disclosures under Statement 107 will be much more extensive and robust, and I suspect that some enterprises will go so far as to make the disclosures all in one place so that users of the financial statements, in one glance, can see the fair value of all of the financial instruments of the enterprise.

I look forward to seeing the results of Statement 107. I also look forward, eagerly look forward I might say, to other uses of fair value/market value information now being addressed by the FASB, namely, formal recognition in the financial statements of fair value of both stocks and bonds and the measurement of impaired loans by the application of market discount rates to revised estimated cash flows under the loan contract. I understand that Mr Leisenring will discuss both these projects later today.

The final matter that I want to mention is harmonization or internationalization of accounting standards. This issue does not involve a general theme, except that I think one can usefully think about simplification and the relevance of mark-to-market accounting as being related to the way we and others around the world perhaps should approach and work on achieving greater harmony in accounting standards. While I have not yet formulated thoughts as to how to approach this issue, I know that it has been the position of Chairman Breeden that the commission does not want to see a relaxation of our general approach of being neutral in formulating accounting standards or in the results that are reported under current standards. The commission has resisted pressure to remove the requirement that foreign registrants reconcile their earnings and equity using US generally accepted accounting principles and disclosing the differences from their home-country presentation.

In closing, I wish to indicate that George Diacont, who has been acting chief accountant for about a year, has been very helpful in briefing me on current items at the commission. I look forward to working with him and all of the other members of the staff and members of the commission. That said, I also should say that there are important staff positions to be filled, such as that of the deputy chief accountant and several GS-14 slots. We will be posting those slots, or some of them, in due course, and I would appreciate your bringing to my attention the resumés of good people either in this audience or among your colleagues back home.

I will be here today and tomorrow to listen to the discussions. I look forward to informal conversations with many of you during the course of the conference.

8 Relevance and credibility in financial accounting and reporting

Address to American Accounting Association, 12 August 1992

I am quoted as follows in the June 1992 issue of *The Journal of Accountancy*.

> I do not think the users of financial statements have been well served over the last 10 to 15 years ... I think financial accounting and reporting have lost some of their credibility, and we need to improve their relevance.

I want to continue that theme today.

Almost all of Washington and almost all of the banking, insurance, and thrift industries are pleading with the Financial Accounting Standards Board not to adopt mark-to-market accounting for debt securities held as assets. Congressmen, banking regulators, and the Secretary of the Treasury are saying that it would be wrong to change from historical cost to mark-to-market accounting for debt securities such as US treasuries, agencies, state and local governments, and mortgage-backed securities held by banks, thrifts, credit unions, and insurance companies.

Why do I think we should jettison historical cost accounting and adopt mark to market for marketable securities? The reasons are simple and straightforward.

The first reason is usefulness. One does not use historical cost numbers to make investment or lending decisions. No banker has ever made a collateralized loan to a customer based on the customer's historical cost of the collateral; the banker insists on knowing the market value of the collateral. No investor in any asset ever made an investment based on the seller's cost of the asset. No investor in a bank's stock, or a depositor with funds in excess of $100,000, or an annuitant or other insurance company policyholder, should be asked to rely on the historical cost of a bank's or insurance company's investment in bonds. Congress established in ERISA that pensioners need to know the market value of pension plan assets; no pensioner would be satisfied with the historical cost numbers for pension plan assets. Congress, in the Investment Company Act of 1940, required that all mutual funds mark to market their assets; broker/dealers do the same under the 1934 Act; mark to market is necessary so that customers and investors have up-to-date useful information to make investment and credit decisions. People who invest in or lend money to banks, thrifts, insurance companies, and credit unions deserve the same treatment.

The second reason is managed income. Historical cost accounting for debt securities allows the management of an enterprise to manage income; that is, management can select when it sells securities and thereby trigger a realized gain or loss. Preparers of financial statements often object to volatility of income in general. In this case, volatility is recognized in the period that management wants it to be recognized, not when the volatility actually occurs in the market value of the securities. The same amount or degree of volatility is present; it is just recognized in a different accounting period.

Moreover, if management wants to paper over a bad quarter or year because of, for example, bad debts being charged to income or because a hurricane requires an insurer to pay a lot of claims, management "cherry picks" some winners from the bond or stock portfolio and sells them so as to offset the bad debt loss or the hurricane claim losses. We have observed that phenomenon repeatedly.

More importantly, this discretion promotes wide non-comparability in reported income and capital (shareholders' equity). We all know that 1991 was a good year for bonds. Some holders of bonds sold the bonds, reaped the gains, and thereby increased income and capital. Other holders of bonds did not sell; those holders have unrealized gains residing in their balance sheets. Even with disclosure of realized and unrealized gains and losses, that condition makes it very hard for the investing public to compare, for example, Bank A or Insurance Company A with Bank B or Insurance Company B. Financial accounting and reporting should make comparable things look comparable, and should make comparison easier not harder.

The third reason is interest rate risk. Historical cost is used for debt securities provided management has the intent and ability to hold those assets on a long-term basis or to maturity, so-called accounting by psychoanalysis. Many financial institutions currently use their bond investments to "manage" interest rate risk, to manage foreign exchange risk, to manage taxable income, to manage liquidity, and to respond to loan demand. As we have seen in the last several decades, interest rates fluctuate widely. So do foreign exchange rates. So does loan demand. Managers of financial institutions respond by buying or selling securities. Management is responding to outside, uncontrollable forces. These responses are inconsistent with representations about intent to hold for the long term or to maturity. It is not credible to assert that one intends to hold bonds in the bond portfolio for the long term or to maturity while saying in the same breath that the investment securities portfolio is used to manage interest rate risk or is sold in response to loan demand.

A stated intent to hold to maturity or for the long term is an empty promise, an incorrect assertion, if it is broken or contradicted when interest rates change, loan demand rises, or some other uncontrollable event comes along and management decides to sell so-called investment securities.

A fourth reason for the use of market value involves credit losses. Holders of corporate bonds should, at least in theory, recognize credit losses as the credit standings of bond issuers decline. But that's theory. In practice, holders of corporate bonds do not recognize credit losses until the bond issuer is bankrupt or nearly so. Independent auditors condone this practice because the accounting rule is so judgmental and abysmally lax that loss recognition is delayed far beyond reason. The Federal Deposit Insurance Corporation, the Office of Thrift Supervision, and state insurance regulators learned that, too late.

On that score, we now have an exposure draft of a new accounting standard from the FASB on the recognition and measurement of credit losses, which the board calls loan impairment. Under the proposal, loan impairment would be recognized "when, based on current information and events, it is probable that a creditor will be unable to collect all amounts due according to the contractual terms of the loan agreement." When a loan is judged to be impaired under the standard of probability, the creditor would measure impairment by reference to the present value of the expected future cash flows of the impaired loan using the effective interest rate of the loan. For loans with no discount or premium or net deferred costs or fees, the effective rate is the coupon rate. The FASB considered using a market rate instead of the effective rate but decided on the effective rate. The board apparently never considered any other measure of impairment than the probability standard applied to expected cash flows.

I am very disappointed in the board's conclusions on both of those matters. First, the probability standard does not work; that has been demonstrated by the wide variability in current practice. The General Accounting Office has been extremely critical of that approach; the GAO's criticism is based on its review of failed banks, where the allowances for credit losses were badly understated. Saying that it must be probable that the principal and interest will not be collected is looking down the wrong end of the pipe; a lender assumes that principal and interest will be collected as per the loan agreement and then allows for risk through the rate.

Second, despite some cautionary words, the draft allows the measure of impairment to be made independently of market prices and what market participants think about a debt issuer's credit. Assume that a bond is traded on the New York Bond Exchange and that interest rates have not moved a tick since the bond was issued. The bond can be quoted at an amount less than 100, say, 95, 90, or 85, yet the holder of that bond judgmentally may conclude that it is not probable that the loan will not be collected as per schedule and therefore no impairment need be recognized. Under FASB Statement 107, the fair value of that bond will have to be disclosed somewhere in the financial statements of the holder of that bond. I think that the public will not understand how it can be that two values are being reported and disclosed for the same bond, 100 and an amount less than 100. I think the public will be confused. I think the public will conclude that impairment as measured by the market is the relevant measure of impairment and not the amount as measured under the FASB's standard. I think that the FASB's proposal will diminish its standing in the eyes of the public.

However, what I am most concerned about is the measurement of capital. This is more than one accountant's debate with another accountant about the best way to allocate a cost among various accounting periods. I am talking about more than accounting elegance. How we measure loan impairment concerns whether financial institutions should be required by the cognizant regulator to raise more capital or reduce their asset holdings and liability levels, or, indeed, whether they may keep open their doors.

A fifth reason for mark-to-market accounting is market efficiency. Free markets are wonderful things. Ours are marvelous. Markets price assets daily, hourly, and by the minute, at no cost. Use of historical cost for assets and such notions as intent to hold to maturity and "other than temporary declines" in price interfere with market efficiency. To the extent that marketplace participants believe that the reported numbers have been skewed by artificial restraints, the market exacts a penalty in pricing the securities issued by reporting companies.

A sixth and final reason concerns capital adequacy. Financial institutions have explicit or implicit capital-adequacy requirements. Banks, for example, must have $8 of capital for every $100 of "risky" assets, such as loans. Under the accounting rules, declines in market values of debt securities are not recognized if the holder has both the intent and ability to hold the securities to maturity or on a long-term basis. Whenever the price of a debt security goes below the historical cost of the security, reaching a conclusion that the enterprise has the ability to hold the security to maturity implicitly requires an interest rate forecast. First, management of the reporting enterprise must conclude that, even though interest rates have risen, that condition will not persist for so long that the enterprise will be forced to sell the security at its reduced price to get cash to meet obligations. Alternatively, the management must conclude that interest rates will fall in the near term, the price of the security will increase, and the enterprise will not have to sell the asset at a loss. Then the enterprise must get its independent auditor to agree to that forecast, at least implicitly.

Second, the reporting enterprise must conclude that its regulator will allow it to continue to operate and not force it to sell the security at its reduced price even though the real capital of the enterprise is impaired. The enterprise must get its independent auditor to agree with that conclusion as well, at least implicitly.

I think that it is not within the competence of independent auditors to make interest rate forecasts, and independent auditors should not be responsible for judgments about forbearance from laws and regulations. I think that it is the responsibility of banking, thrift, insurance, and credit union regulators, and ultimately Congress and the public, to decide when forbearance from laws and regulations is appropriate, not independent auditors. Besides, once an independent auditor has agreed that a decline in market value below cost need not be recognized and thereby not reduce the reported amount of capital, he or she then becomes wedded to that decision and will not reverse it, because to do so is to admit error, or at least fallibility, not to mention the exposure to litigation. The auditor then has a vested interest in the client's interest rate forecast and psychologically may no longer be independent in the deepest meaning of that word.

However, the critical point here is regulatory forbearance. Under a recent FASB standard – FASB Statement 107 – all entities will have to disclose the market value of their marketable securities portfolios, both debt and equities. Many assert that with those disclosures the cognizant regulator has all the information necessary to make regulatory decisions. True. Marking to market right on the face of the financial statement will not change the facts; what marking to market will do is require regulatory authorities to make explicit decisions about whether regulated enterprises have met their capital requirements, whether those enterprises need to raise more capital, reduce their assets and liabilities, or indeed whether they may keep their doors open to the public. Those explicit decisions then cannot be postponed or sloughed off as they can if the mark to market is only in the footnotes and not formally accounted for on the face of the financial statement. I am talking about something more than bean counting by people wearing green eyeshades. I am talking about more than accounting elegance. I am talking about whether financial institutions that are entrusted with the public's money are allowed to keep open their doors and take in more of the public's money.

Look what the use of historical cost got us in the savings and loan debacle. The final tally will not be in for years, but the cost to the American taxpayers, and society in general, will be enormous.

The use of historical cost did not cause the S&L problem, but the use of historical cost is to blame for the loss of some of that money down the S&L hole. Because the S&Ls could say that the acquisition, development, and construction arrangements were loans and not real estate, and were fully collectible, but did not have to disclose their fair value, never mind write the ADC loans down to fair value, ADC loans kept growing and growing on S&L balance sheets. Accounting income from such loans also kept growing, even though no cash income was being collected. For the marketable securities and regular residential mortgage loans that S&Ls held, and which were significantly under water in the high interest rate environment of the early to mid-1980s, no write-down was required by the applicable accounting standard, or at least practice under that standard, so long as the S&L had the stated intent and ability to hold the securities and loans to maturity. Historical cost was OK.

So, even though it was known by the S&L regulator that the real equity of the S&Ls was a huge negative number, the S&Ls were allowed to stay open and to keep making risky investments with taxpayers' money. They kept rolling the dice. When the FSLIC and FDIC took over the failed S&Ls and savings banks, however, they found that the size of the hole was huge. But under generally accepted accounting principles, no hole, or only a small hole, had been reported. None of the S&Ls, or their auditors, had critically examined whether the S&Ls had the ability to hold those assets. That ability was wholly dependent on the S&Ls not being shut down by the regulator and was therefore of very questionable fact. The analysis was circuitous. The regulator implicitly said that the S&Ls would not be shut so long as reported equity was positive, and the S&Ls kept accounting for their marketable securities and mortgages at cost so long as the regulator did not shut the doors; the circle was closed; thus the parties involved were able to say that the ability-to-hold criterion was met.

If the S&Ls had been forced to disclose, never mind account for, the fair value of their ADC portfolios and their bond and mortgage loan portfolios, does anyone honestly believe that the S&L hole would have gotten as deep as it did? I think the fair answer to that question is "No."

Let me turn to a closely related matter, namely litigation against public accounting firms, which also involves relevance and credibility in accounting. Litigation is said to threaten to obliterate a significant portion of the profession, at least that portion of the profession that audits the financial statements of public companies. The profession is going to various state capitals and to Capitol Hill in Washington asking for relief from various laws. The profession claims that it is the subject of abusive and frivolous lawsuits by shareholder/investors. Members of the profession also cite cases where their "deep pockets" have been opened to pay for the sins of more culpable, but now insolvent, audit clients. The profession is lobbying hard for litigation reforms, including a major push to restrict joint and several liability.

I am very concerned about abusive litigation against accountants. So is the commission. The commission has suggested that Congress look at proportional versus joint and several liability. The commission has stated its support for RICO reform. The commission has stated its support for the proposition whereby the loser of non-meritorious litigation pays the winner's costs. However, getting reform through federal Congress and the various states will take a long time, if it ever comes.

Meanwhile, the profession, with a few exceptions, is not doing anything about the underlying causes of litigation against itself. It will not pull on its own bootstraps. The profession will not go to its clients and tell those clients that their balance sheets have to have realism in order to elicit unqualified opinions. Why not? Well, that could involve being tough with a client. Maybe make the client angry. Maybe the client will go across the street to another auditing firm and that firm will agree to report on a balance sheet that has outdated or irrelevant representations in it.

The profession, again with an exception or two, will not go to the FASB and support realism in financial accounting and reporting. The profession will not reach tough, unpopular decisions. Why is that? Is it because the profession has become so beholden to its clients that it will not speak to them about realism and relevance and credibility in financial accounting and reporting? Let me list only a few situations where the profession has become a cheerleader for its clients.

1 *Troubled debt restructurings*. The profession, in response to its bank clients, asked the FASB to issue Statement 15 more or less as the FASB did back in 1977. That document allows for restructured loans to be reported at 100 cents on the dollar even though that dollar will earn no interest and will not be collected until many years in the future. FASB Statement 15 has plunged an entire generation of accountants into darkness. Fortunately, the FASB is now proposing to change that standard so as to remove that part of it which is so grossly bad, but the new FASB proposal itself is flawed because of

measurement of the loss on in substance foreclosed assets by using the effective rate rather than a market rate.

2 *Pension plan values.* When pension accounting was being reconsidered, the profession, at the behest of its commercial and industrial clients, went to the FASB and suggested that the volatility in pension plan assets and liabilities not be recognized immediately and in full in income and equity. They argued that the FASB should create an artifice to keep the income statement and shareholders' equity from being affected too much by changes in the values of plan assets and liabilities. The FASB obliged in Statement 87, and now we have delayed recognition of changes in values of plan assets and liabilities.

3 *Deferred tax assets.* APB Opinion 11 produced deferred tax asset and liability numbers that no one could explain. When the FASB fixed that problem in Statement 96 a few years ago and permitted the recognition of deferred tax assets only when the amounts could be recovered through the operation of a carryback, the profession, at the behest of its clients, let out a howl. Even though it clearly was not in their best interests to do so, all the large accounting firms went to the FASB and pleaded with the board to allow recognition, on a judgmental basis, of deferred tax assets that will be recovered, if at all, years and years into the future and only if there is future taxable income.

The FASB obliged in Statement 109. The claim was, under old Opinion 11, that the deferred tax liability was a "UGO," an "unidentified growing object," because the amount kept getting larger and larger. The deferred tax asset under FASB Statement 109 has the potential to be a "UGO" in reverse. What are the users of financial statements going to do when they see those deferred tax assets? If they are sophisticated, they are going to exclude those assets from income and equity or discount them heavily. If they aren't sophisticated, I don't know what they will do. What is going to happen when those deferred tax assets are not realized? I know what will happen. The accounting firms will be sued.

4 *Investment versus trading.* In 1990 and 1991, we have seen financial institutions sell 25 percent, 50 percent, 75 percent, even 95 percent of their entire self-designated investment securities portfolios during the year despite their assertions in the footnotes that they intend to hold the securities to maturity or for the long term. One insurance company turned its long-term US Treasury bond portfolio eight times in 1991. Yet, remarkably, every one of those institutions' financial statements received the unqualified opinion of its outside auditor.

5 *SEC filings.* In SEC filings, we sometimes see what I call incredible accounting. When our staff challenges the incredible accounting, it becomes clear that the auditor did not concur with his or her client's accounting but nonetheless signed an unqualified opinion hoping that our staff would challenge and object to the accounting and thereby become the bad guy. Our staff is being used as the auditor's leverage, but only after the auditor agrees to the incredible accounting.

I could list other examples, but I have made my point.

What is the purpose of my bringing this issue to the fore? Well, I think that instead of thinking simply of its clients and itself, the profession needs to give some thought to the public that it serves, to the investors and creditors and employees who put up their money and their labor to make investments in the profession's clients.

I suggest that the profession go to the FASB and ask it to issue accounting standards that produce more relevant, more understandable, more useful, and more credible financial statements than what we now have. That the profession ask the FASB to issue accounting rules that produce bulletproof balance sheets instead of what we now have. Bulletproof in the sense that assets are not stated in excess of market values. That the profession ask the FASB to issue accounting rules that respond to and correspond with real-world, outside-of-accounting phenomena, like market values of assets instead of such arcana as undiscounted cash flows and delayed recognition of changes in value of pension plan assets and liabilities. That the profession ask the FASB to issue accounting rules that result in financial statements that investors can understand and use instead of accounting rules that are arcane and idiosyncratic and produce financial information that only other accountants can understand.

The accounting profession keeps saying that instead of reporting real assets, hard assets, at current value, its clients should continue to be able to use historical costs and deferrals and allocations of costs and losses and that the profession should then be able to apply its judgment to the recoverability of the amounts of deferrals reported by its clients. But the profession then says, when it is sued, that it should not be held responsible when those deferrals and those judgments turn to clabber instead of cream. I submit that if reporting companies published relevant, credible balance sheets that are bulletproof the profession would not get sued. Or, if it got sued, the plaintiffs would not prevail on the merits.

What if those who are crying wolf are right? What are the implications of a major firm being bankrupted by damage awards because of overstatement of asset values? I truly hope that does not happen. That would be tragic for any firm and the individuals involved. Investors would suffer. But what if it did happen? What would that imply for the Securities and Exchange Commission? Would that suggest that the commission step into the accounting standard-setting process and require that assets not be reported in balance sheets at amounts in excess of market values? Would that suggest that the commission mandate rotation of auditing firms so as to make it more likely that auditors who know they will be replaced will not allow clients to report assets in excess of market values? I do not know the answer to those questions, and I do not want to find out.

I urge the Financial Accounting Standards Board and the accounting profession to address the issues of relevance and credibility in financial accounting and reporting so as to maintain their own relevance and credibility.

9 Why are we all here anyway?

Speech delivered at the University of Texas at Austin Theta Chapter of Beta Alpha Psi on the occasion of the Accountant of the Year award, 12 November 1993

Good evening. It is indeed a pleasure and honor to be recognized by the Theta Chapter of Beta Alpha Psi as your Accountant of the Year.

I especially want to thank you for inviting my wife, Jean, and several members of our family to be here this evening to join us: my mother and stepfather, Mr and Mrs Milton Taylor, my aunt and her husband, Durinda and G.C. Slough, and our son and grandson, Brian and Bryce Schuetze.

I remember an evening such as this one thirty-seven years ago, when I was inducted into this chapter of Beta Alpha Psi. I would like to say that I remember it well, but that would be a bit of a stretch. The speaker was an officer from Humble Oil & Refining Company in Houston, now Exxon USA. I have tried to locate him. I thought that perhaps he might remember the theme of his talk because I do not. However, I have not been able to track him down.

The accounting professors who may have been here that evening included Jim Ashburne, Bob Grinaker, George Newlove, C. Aubrey Smith, Glenn Welsch, John White, and Charles Zlatkovitch. And going through my file, I was surprised to find a newspaper clipping about Dean Dennis Ford's addressing the BBA Wives Club, where Mrs Edwin Pickett was elected president and my wife was elected secretary. The Picketts live in Dallas and, after all these years, we still keep in touch with them through the exchange of Christmas greetings. I also found a program for the Eighth Annual Honors Day, held on Saturday, 7 April 1956 in Hogg Auditorium, where Dr Logan Wilson, then president of the university, recognized the faculty and honor students, and where the Honors Day address was by Dr Benjamin Wright, the president of Smith College. Fond memories indeed.

Since World War II and since I graduated here in 1957, our economy has been in a long-term upward trend. In 1957, on 1 July, the Dow Jones Industrial Average stood around 500. About two weeks ago, the Dow Jones Industrial Average, on an intraday basis, briefly breached the 3,700 mark and closed just an eyelash under 3,700. When I started in the practice of public accountancy in 1957, a ten million share day on the New York Stock Exchange was such a blizzard of paper that the brokerage houses could not keep track of all the ownership of shares, and dividends to shareholders sometimes floated in the system for months. Now, daily volume on the New York Stock Exchange routinely exceeds 250 million shares and was over 600 million in October 1987 when the market crashed. A new house, a so-called starter house, cost about $12,000 – at least that's what our first one in San Antonio was. The USSR had not launched it first Sputnik, and of course no one had walked on the Moon. Now, trips into space last for weeks, even months, and no one seems to notice very much. Only CNN now televises our space launches live, and I wonder how long that will last.

The price of oil was about $3 a barrel, and a gallon of gas was about 15 cents. The price of natural gas was about 10 cents an MCF. Wheat was about $1.90 a bushel. Corn $1.12. My starting salary in August 1957 was $425 a month.

I do not remember how many accountants there were in 1957, or in 1959 when I passed the CPA exam and joined the American Institute of Certified Public Accountants. Today, there are about 300,000 members in the AICPA, about half of them in the practice of public accountancy. In the state of Texas, there are about 55,000 CPAs licensed by the Texas State Board of Public Accountancy. The so-called Big Six accounting firms are now international service organizations. Those six firms, in the United States alone, generate about $11.6 billion in revenue and have about 8,350 partners and 72,000 professional staff.

Savings and investment have also been spectacular during that timespan. There are now more than 51 million individual investors in this country. People like us in this room. Open-ended mutual funds alone have about $1.8 trillion of assets under management. Look in your daily newspaper, say *USA Today*, and you will see listed about 4,000 open-ended mutual funds. They range from giants like Fidelity's Magellan and Vanguard's Windsor to very small funds. In addition, there are vast institutional holdings of stocks, bonds, loans, real estate, and the like, mostly through pension funds. TIAA/CREF, the college school system retirement vehicle, has assets of $110 billion; it is the largest in the world. The Texas State Teachers Retirement System manages upwards of $31 billion of assets. The California Public Employee Retirement System has about $69 billion in assets. The various pension and retirement plans of General Motors have assets of about $40 billion; GE's exceeds $36 billion. Not to mention the assets held by about 12,000 commercial banks, 2,000-plus savings and loans and savings banks, thousands of insurance companies, credit unions, and broker/dealers such as Merrill Lynch and Charles Schwab.

You may ask, what has all of that got to do with why we are all here tonight? What has that got to do with accounting anyway? Well, I'm here to tell you that it has got everything in the world to do with accounting.

Accounting is the lubrication that allows this country's capital markets engine to turn at very high RPMs without overheating. There are about 13,400 public companies in this country. Like General Motors, General Electric, General Dynamics, General Mills, and General Reinsurance. 4,000 mutual funds. 8,000 broker/dealers, 20,000 banks, thrifts, credit unions, and insurance companies. Every one of them keeps books and records. Everyone of them prepares financial statements at least annually and most of them quarterly. All of them, except for the very smallest, are required by some law or regulation to have their financial statements audited by independent certified public accountants. Over and above those public companies and financial institutions, there are thousands, millions, of small, closely held, private companies. The local hardware store. The dry cleaner. The construction company. The bakery. And all of them need financial statements, mostly for their bankers and their owners and the owners' families.

Wait, I am not finished. There are fifty state governments. Thousands, dozens of thousands, of cities, counties, water and sewer districts, bridge and tunnel authorities, and toll roads. They all prepare financial statements. Most of these financial statements need to be audited.

There is more. Churches and temples. Colleges and universities. Charities like Boy Scouts and Girl Scouts and United Way. Thousands of them. They prepare financial statements, and most of them need audits.

There is still more. The US Treasury and various states need money to run, and we all prepare tax returns so as to compute the amount of money to send to Washington and state capitals and in some cases to cities that have income tax systems.

And, finally, in order to prepare all these financial statements and all these tax returns, we need accounting systems. Indeed, to run all of these businesses, governments, schools, churches, charities, and what have you, we need accounting systems to gather and produce information. Who does all of that? Accountants do all of that. That is why we are here this evening.

Let me spend just a few minutes with you on the one thing that I have found to be the most important as I have traveled through this world of business and accounting for thirty-six years. That is, high ethical standards. Whatever your chosen field, management accounting, financial accounting, tax accounting, or accounting systems, you will of course want to be proficient in that field. You will prosper financially if you do good work, for good work is its own best referral.

It has been my observation that those who are the most fulfilled are those who not only do good work but who do it on the up and up, on the straight and narrow, with no corners rounded. It is they who are sought out most often by their colleagues, by their superiors, by their clients, by new clients, and by the public.

In my opinion, the next thirty-six years hold great promise for you young people in this audience. To be sure, right now our economy and the economies of the major industrial countries are in somewhat of a slowdown. It could be that the slowdown will get worse before it gets better. But, for you in this audience, that will be but a momentary blip on the radar screen of life. Let me tell you why I say that.

Three years ago, the Berlin Wall came down. Communism is no longer a way of life for people behind the Iron Curtain. From Budapest to Vladivostok, there are more than 300 million people who are making the conversion to democracy and capitalism. We in the West, in the USA and other Western countries, will be able to sell those people tractors, fertilizer, TVs, autos, plants to build tractors and autos, Coca-Cola, Pepsi, and plain old soap. About six years ago, during Gorbachev's regime, the coal miners in Siberia went on strike. They went on strike because after working ten hours in the mines they came out to wash up but there was no soap. There was no soap. Proctor & Gamble will be glad to sell them soap. There are 1.1 billion people in China. They need tractors and cars and computers and Coke and Pepsi and TVs and maybe even soap. The same goes for 800 million in India. Millions more in Pakistan.

Right here, south of the border, are 90 million Mexicans to whom we can sell cars and computers. The same goes for Brazil. And I haven't even mentioned the African continent.

I see a huge demand for all kinds of good and services to be sold to these millions of people. That means that economies around the world are going to grow and expand. And you accountants will be needed to help it to grow and expand. To gather the information and report on it. To do the accounting.

It has indeed been a pleasure to be here this evening.

10 Accounting for restructurings

Address to Financial Executives Institute, Current Financial Reporting Issues Conference, New York Hilton Hotel and Towers, 8 November 1994

Thank you for inviting me to speak again at your annual conference. This is now the third time I have appeared here. My remarks are mine and mine alone. I do not speak for the commission or any of the other staff.

Last year, at this conference, Robert Bayless, in his remarks, discussed accounting for restructurings. In the question and answer session that followed, in which both Robert Bayless and I participated, it became clear that there was not a meeting of minds between FEI people in the audience and the SEC's staff on accounting for restructurings.

Restructurings are not new. There is an SEC Staff Accounting Bulletin – SAB 67, issued in 1986 – that deals with restructurings. SAB 67 deals with the geography of restructuring charges in the income statement and what disclosures there should be about restructurings in management's discussion and analysis. SAB 67 does not address when restructurings should be recognized, what the ingredients thereof ought to be, or how restructuring charges should be measured.

After that FEI conference, we went back to our office and began to look into what companies were doing in the area of restructurings. We found that restructurings had, in the past several years, grown substantially in number, and the amounts of the restructuring charges had increased dramatically. We also found that the ingredients of restructuring charges were diverse. We found that a large fraction of many restructuring charges were employee-related costs, such as termination and other related benefits. Benefits for employees that were to be terminated not just in the following year but planned to be terminated two, three, five years hence. Also included in restructuring charges were write-downs or write-offs of costs incurred in prior periods, such as plant cost, where decisions had been taken to dispose of assets and estimated proceeds to be received on sale and the assets were expected to be less than cost, or simply to abandon the assets in some cases. We also found an odd assortment of other things, which mostly were to get rid of sundry old costs that had accumulated on balance sheets over the years. Lastly, we found that restructuring charges included expenditures to be made in the future for the benefit of future operations; included in this category were future expenditures for equipment such as computers, software for those computers or computers already on hand, relocating and retraining employees, advertising and legal services, consulting services, expected adverse factory overhead variances on future production runs, expected increases in returns and allowances on future sales, increased warranty liabilities on future sales, and the like, all related to future operations.

The upshot of our investigation was that in January we asked the Financial Accounting Standards Board's Emerging Issues Task Force to address accounting for restructurings. The task force discussed accounting for restructurings at its March, May, June, and September meetings and will discuss it again next week.

In May, with respect to termination benefits, the task force concluded as follows:

6 At the May 19, 1994 meeting, the Task Force discussed when an employer should recognize a liability for the cost of termination benefits that management decides to provide to involuntarily terminated employees. That discussion addressed the accounting for involuntary termination benefits that are not associated with a disposal of a segment or a portion of a line of business and are not paid pursuant to the terms of an individual deferred compensation contract. The discussion covered situations in which employees would be terminated as a result of management's decision and would receive termination benefits that they would not have otherwise been entitled to under any pre-existing arrangements. Further, the benefits would not be ongoing for employees not terminated in connection with the current plan of termination.

7 In those situations, the Task Force reached a consensus that a liability for employee termination benefits should be recognized in the period management approves the plan of termination if all of the following conditions exist:

a Prior to the date of the financial statements, management having the appropriate level of authority to involuntarily terminate employees approves and commits the enterprise to, the plan of termination and establishes the benefits that current employees will receive upon termination.

b Prior to the date of issuance of the financial statements, the benefit arrangement is communicated to employees. The communication of the benefit arrangement should include sufficient detail to enable employees to determine the benefits they will receive if they are terminated.

c The plan of termination specifically identifies the number of employees to be terminated, their job classifications or functions, and their locations.

d The planned terminations will occur within one year from the date that management approves the plan of termination unless circumstances outside the control of the enterprise (in other words, legal or contractual restrictions on the enterprise's ability to terminate employees) are likely to delay the termination date (for example, existing union contracts or enacted legal restrictions concerning the length of notice required to terminate employees).

After discussions in July and September, the task force tentatively concluded that liabilities for future expenditures for computers, computer software, relocating and retraining employees and other items that will benefit future operations should not be recognized early and included in restructuring charges. However, the task force also tentatively concluded, after discussion in July and September, that future expenditures related to a plan to exit an activity may be recognized as a liability prior to the time the activity is exited and prior to the time a liability would be eligible for recognition without such an exit plan. The minutes of the September meeting of the task force read as follows on this latter point:

13 At the September 21–22, 1994 meeting, the Task Force discussed when an enterprise should recognize a liability for costs, other than employee termination benefits, that are directly associated with a plan to exit an activity (exit plan) including certain costs incurred in a restructuring. That discussion focused on identifying costs that should be recognized as liabilities at the time that management commits the enterprise to an exit plan (commitment date). The Task Force observed that the tentative conclusions in paragraphs 14–21 of this Issue do not apply to the disposal of a segment of a business accounted for under Opinion 30 or to asset impairments arising from an exit plan. The Task Force also observed that the accounting for impairment of long-lived assets will be addressed when the Exposure Draft of the proposed FASB Statement, Accounting for the Impairment of Long-Lived Assets, issued 29 November 1993, is a final statement.

14 The task force reached a tentative conclusion that a decision by an enterprise's management to execute an exit plan that will result in the incurring of costs that have no future economic benefit represents an obligating event for those costs meeting the criteria in paragraphs 15–17 of this issue.

15 The Task Force reached a tentative conclusion that a commitment date for an exit plan occurs when all of the following conditions are met:

a Management having the appropriate level of authority approves and commits the enterprise to an exit plan.

b The exit plan specifically identifies all actions to be taken to complete the exit plan, activities that will not be continued, including the method of disposition and location of those activities, and the expected date of completion.

c Actions required by the exit plan will begin as soon as possible after the commitment date and the period of time to complete the exit plan indicates that significant changes to the exit plan are not likely.

16 The Task Force reached a tentative conclusion that only costs resulting from an exit plan that are not associated with or that do not benefit activities that will be continued would be eligible for recognition as liabilities at the

commitment date. Costs meeting that requirement should be recognized at the commitment date if they meet either criterion (a) or (b) and also meet criterion (c) below:

a The cost is incremental to other costs incurred by the enterprise in the conduct of its activities prior to the commitment date and will be incurred as a direct result of the exit plan. The notion of incremental does not contemplate a diminished future economic benefit to be derived from the cost but rather the absence of the cost in the enterprise's activities immediately prior to the commitment date.

b The cost represents amounts to be incurred by the enterprise under a contractual obligation that existed prior to the commitment date and will either continue after the exit plan is completed with no economic benefit to the enterprise or be a penalty incurred by the enterprise to cancel the contractual obligation.

c The cost is not associated with or is not incurred to generate revenues after the exit plan's commitment date.

17 The Task Force agreed to define costs that meet the criteria of paragraphs 15 and 16 of this Issue as exit costs. The Task Force observed that the overall exit plan may be composed of many different components. The Task Force agreed that it is not necessary for an enterprise to be able to reasonably estimate the individual costs of every component of the exit plan at the commitment date. A liability should be recognized at the commitment date for those exit costs that can be reasonably estimated. The remaining exit costs should be recognized when they can be reasonably estimated.

18 The Task Force reached a tentative conclusion that the results of operations after the commitment date of an activity that will not be continued are not exit costs. The Task Force also reached a tentative conclusion that for assets to be disposed of as part of the exit plan, costs to sell those assets are not exit costs. Expected gains from the sale of those assets should be recognized when realized (in accordance with Statement 5) and should not be used to offset the liability for exit costs recognized at the commitment date.

19 The Task Force discussed whether the cash flows for certain costs not otherwise qualifying as exit costs would be included in determining an asset's fair value based on the proposed FASB Statement on Impairment of Long Lived Assets. The Task Force was not asked to reach a consensus on this issue and agreed to continue discussion of that issue at a future meeting.

20 The Task Force agreed that costs that do not qualify as exit costs should not be recognized as liabilities at the commitment date. Costs not qualifying as exit costs should be recognized as liabilities when an obligation exists to pay cash or otherwise sacrifice enterprise assets.

As some of you may know, I was one of the charter members of the FASB. I signed FASB Statement 5, which was issued in 1975. As you may recall, Statement 5 deals with catastrophe reserves and contingency reserves. Today, I would like to give you my analysis of how I think restructuring charges and exit costs and related balance sheet liabilities or reserves fit into the accounting literature.

The FASB's definition of a liability in its Concepts Statement 6 is as follows:

> Liabilities are probable future sacrifices of economic benefits arising from present obligations of a particular entity to transfer assets or provide services to other entities in the future as a result of past transactions or events. [Footnotes omitted]

I am struggling with how the liability to be recognized by a corporation for the termination benefits pursuant to the May consensus of the task force fits the FASB's definition of a liability. Based on the facts discussed by the task force, it looks to me as if the "past event" that will make the corporation liable for the termination benefits is that the employee continues to work up to the time he or she is terminated involuntarily. If the employee voluntarily leaves prior to the termination date, he or she receives no benefits. I question how a decision by the corporation's management to pay benefits constitutes such a "past event," because that decision itself does not obligate the corporation; the corporation becomes obligated only if the employee works up to the scheduled termination date. Moreover, I question how a communication of the decision of the management of the corporation to the employees after the balance sheet date but prior to the issuance of the financial statement constitutes such a "past event" inasmuch as that communication also does not obligate the corporation; again, the corporation becomes obligated only if the employee works up to the scheduled termination date. The benefit does not vest in the employee until the involuntary termination date. (I recognize that pension benefits and post-retirement healthcare benefits are recognized as liabilities prior to when those benefits are "vested," but that is where there is a contractual benefit plan, which is not the case in the matter discussed by the task force in May.)

As indicated above, the task force has also tentatively concluded that costs to exit an activity including certain costs incurred in a restructuring would be recognizable as liabilities when the management of a corporation has determined that such costs will be incurred. I am struggling with how the liability to be recognized for such costs, which liability would be recognized based on a decision by management to incur a cost, meets the FASB's definition of a liability. I do not see a "past event" triggering a liability.

As I understand the FASB's definition of a liability, a liability arises under a contract or pursuant to laws or regulations. When employees work, they are entitled to receive money for their work, and the corporation is obligated to pay the money. There is a contract between the employer and the employee. When a vendor supplies goods or services to a corporation, the corporation owes the vendor money pursuant to the contract between the vendor and the corporation. When corporations borrow money, they must repay the money pursuant to the borrowing contract. Corporations must pay money to governments pursuant to various laws and regulations, such as income tax laws, excise tax laws, and property tax laws. Corporations must spend money to remediate polluted sites because of laws and regulations. In all of these cases, liabilities are recognized because of the existence of contracts or laws or regulations. In none of these cases is a liability recognized based on a management decision to make an expenditure or public announcement of that decision.

It might be argued I suppose, in the case of a "restructuring," that a liability may be recognized because once management has decided to pay cash (or otherwise use corporate assets) that cash outflow is "probable" of occurrence – indeed it may be highly probable. But, under the FASB's definition of a liability, the probability of a cash outflow, in and of itself, does not create a liability. If probability of a cash outflow were sufficient alone to justify (or require) the recognition of a liability, then corporations would or could recognize as liabilities future cash outflows for salaries and wages, raw materials, advertising, rent, and the like, which is not done in accounting today.

Then there is the question of verifiability. The FASB concluded, in its Concepts Statement 2, that verifiability is one of the necessary qualities of representations in financial statements. Verifiability means that two or more measurers of something would reach approximately the same conclusion – that the accuracy of something can be determined. I question how the ingredients of restructuring charges, and the measure of them, can be verified by outsiders. Those things are known only to the management of the enterprise.

Moreover, I know of no auditing procedure that the external auditor can execute to determine whether management of an enterprise is contemplating to exit an activity or otherwise engage in a restructuring. Let me ask, rhetorically, if management does not announce to the auditor that an exit or restructuring is contemplated, what does the auditor do? Does the auditor, and the user of the financial statement, assume that none is contemplated? The task force has been unable to define what a restructuring is, so I would not know how to formulate an accounting standard or rule for when a restructuring is required to be recognized; likewise, there is no way to formulate an auditing procedure that requires a search for something that is not defined.

Let me ask, rhetorically, about enterprises that do not announce restructurings or exit plans and consequently do not recognize liabilities related thereto early but simply account for expenditures the "regular way" when liabilities arise under contracts. Their financial statements presumably will be OK under generally accepted accounting principles. Thus, allowing liabilities to be recognized based on a management decision to recognize the liabilities would appear to result in non-comparability among and between enterprises.

Finally, I think that we will continue to have definitional problems. What will constitute a "restructuring?" What will constitute an "activity" that is planned to be exited? I do not see ready answers for those questions.

Based on this analysis, I suggest that the liabilities to be recognized for termination benefits, exit costs, and other costs said to be incurred in restructurings are not liabilities but are in the nature of contingency reserves, which were precluded by Accounting Research Bulletin 50, issued in 1958, and brought forward by the FASB in Statement 5 in 1975.

We have all struggled together for almost a year now working on accounting for restructurings. I hope my analysis – from the perspective of one who signed FASB Statement 5 – is useful and of interest to you.

11 Enforcement issues, and is the cost of purchased goodwill an asset?

Speech to the Financial Accounting and Reporting Section, American Accounting Association Annual Meeting, New Orleans, 17 August 1998

When Bob Swieringa called several months ago and asked me to speak here today, he suggested that I talk about some of the financial accounting and reporting issues that I see on the enforcement side of the Securities and Exchange Commission and about my views on accounting for intangible assets.

First to enforcement. There is nothing new under the sun on the accounting side at the Enforcement Division. Over the years, I have heard every chief accountant of the division speak at forums like this one, and they have all said the same things. I have been the chief accountant of the Enforcement Division since November 1997, and I have seen nothing new except that some of the frauds are now on the Internet. There are only so many ways to cook the books. I too am going to sound like a broken record.

Let me illustrate the kind of problems that we accountants in the Enforcement Division actually work on. In the nine months that I have had to look at the problems since I became chief accountant, I see that we do not deal much with esoteric accounting problems such as foreign currency translation or the ins and outs of pension accounting or post-pre-retirement benefits other than pensions. We deal with more pedestrian issues.

Premature revenue recognition appears to be the first choice for cooking the books. Recognizing revenue in advance of the customer's acceptance of the product. Recognizing revenue when right of return exists. Shipping product to company warehouses and employees' homes and recognizing sales revenue. Keeping the sales journal open after the end of the quarter or year but back-dating sales invoices.

Deferral in the balance sheet of costs that should have been reported in income as operating expenses. Assigning inflated, often outrageously inflated, dollar values to exchanges of non-monetary assets, particularly with related parties. Assigning inflated, often outrageously inflated, dollar values to non-monetary assets contributed to the corporation in exchange for stock of the corporation. Not disclosing the existence of related parties and transactions with related parties. Recognizing officers' salaries as receivables. Recognizing cash taken from the corporation by officers as cash in bank, or as an investment, or as a direct reduction of stockholders' equity instead of as a charge to expense. Bleeding into income, without disclosure, "reserves" established in business combinations or in so-called restructurings. In some recent cases, the bleeding has turned into hemorrhaging.

I thought that the "reserve" issue had been resolved in 1975 when the Financial Accounting Standards Board issued Statement 5 on "Accounting for Contingencies." But I have found that reserves are like crab grass. They are everywhere. Tax liability cushions. Deferred tax asset cushions. Inventory reserves. Bad debt reserves. Merger reserves. Restructuring reserves. They are everywhere. The Division of Corporation Finance, in its reviews of filings by issuers, sprays Roundup on issuers' balance sheets, but the crab grass reserves keep re-emerging. (For you apartment dwellers, Roundup is a herbicide that is supposed to kill weeds.) The reserves are being used to manipulate earnings. Need a penny a share to meet Wall Street's expectations? Need two pennies? A nickel? A dime? Two bits? Dip into the chocolate chip cookie jar reserve. The mere existence of reserves is a chocolate chip cookie jar that management cannot resist when the earnings need a sugar high. We need to fix reserve accounting. It's time to make another pass at reserves; we need a Year 2000 version of FASB Statement 5.

How about treasury stock carried as an asset in the balance sheet at market, with "unrealized" gains credited to unearned income and "realized" gains on sale of the treasury stock credited to income. I'm not making this up. How about increasing fixed assets and crediting cost of sales. Not booking all of the accounts payable; just put the invoices from suppliers into a desk drawer. Not writing down or writing off uncollectible receivables. Booking barter trade credits as if they represented US dollars. Such is the grist of our accounting mill. Not very esoteric stuff. If I draw an analogy with police work, what we see is stolen automobiles with fingerprints on the door handles, not murders where there are no clues except for dogs that did not bark.

On the audit side, I have now seen several non-audits since I came on board last year. Auditors accepting, with little or no evidential support, values ascribed to both monetary and non-monetary assets. Artwork by unknown artists booked as assets at huge amounts but without any support for the assigned value or no inquiry by the auditor about independent valuation of the artwork. Receivables acquired from collection agencies for pennies but booked at dollars without any documentation and no auditor inquiry as to the basis for the value. Auditors not doing substantive audit work but relying on so-called analytical procedures where the evidence, or lack thereof, cries out for substantive audit work. Auditors not doing cut-off work for sales and purchases. And, of course, we see cases where the auditors were lied to or were not given all of the documentation that they should have been given. But sometimes I wonder whether the auditors asked the right questions.

Now, on to intangibles, and specifically whether the cost of goodwill is recognizable as an asset. The FASB has on its agenda the broad question of accounting for business combinations and what to do about the cost of purchased goodwill. The board has tentatively concluded that the cost of purchased goodwill is an asset – that it meets the board's definition of an asset in its

Statement of Financial Accounting Concepts No. 6, *Elements of Financial Statements*, which I will refer to as Concepts Statement 6. Presumably, the board has also concluded that the cost of goodwill has all of the necessary characteristics to constitute an asset and that the measurement criterion is met although I am not sure that the board has had a thorough-going discussion about measurement.

In articles and speeches in 1991 ("Keep it simple," *Accounting Horizons*, June 1991, pp. 113–17) and 1993 ("What is an asset?" *Accounting Horizons*, September 1993, pp. 66–70), I proposed that accountants use as a definition of an asset the following: "Cash, contractual claims to cash, and things that can be sold separately for cash." I proposed that exchangeability be a required feature of anything recognized as an asset in a balance sheet. Under my proposal, the cost of goodwill would not qualify as an asset. The Financial Accounting Standards Board has not adopted those proposals, however. Thus, in addressing the question of whether the cost of goodwill should be recognized as an asset, I will use the FASB's definition in its Concepts Statement 6, namely, "Assets are probable future economic benefits obtained or controlled by a particular entity as a result of past transactions or events" and the board's enumerated characteristics of assets. Exchangeability is not a required feature of an asset in the board's conceptual framework.

The basis for the board's tentative decision is, as I understand it, as follows, in highly summarized form: (1) while the cost of goodwill itself lacks the capacity to generate future net cash inflows, it has the capacity in combination with other assets to contribute indirectly to those cash flows and therefore meets the "future economic benefit" test; (2) control over the cost of goodwill is provided by the acquirer's controlling financial interest in the acquired entity's equity or equity securities; and (3) the cost of goodwill obviously arises from a past transaction, which is the third condition in the definition. I do not agree with the board's analysis. I think that the analysis omits too much.

The board's articulation, in Concepts Statement 6, of the necessary characteristics of an asset says that (1) it, whatever it is, must have a probable future economic benefit, (2) a cost, by itself, is not an asset, and (3) in order for something to be an asset it must be controlled by the enterprise that calls the something its asset. I think that, ultimately, the board will not be able to demonstrate convincingly and persuasively that the cost of purchased goodwill satisfies each and every one of those three characteristics. I will explain why, using the board's own words.

In paragraph 172 of Concepts Statement 6, the board said, "Future economic benefit is the essence of an asset. An asset has the capacity to serve the entity by being exchanged for something of value to the entity, by being used to produce something of value to the entity, or by being used to settle its liabilities." The cost of purchased goodwill is simply the amount paid by one entity for the net assets of another entity, or for a controlling equity interest in another entity, in excess of the fair value of the individual, identifiable net assets (assets minus liabilities) of that other entity; the amount said to represent the cost of purchased goodwill is just the excess amount left over – in a word, the lump. But the lump cannot be exchanged for anything. The lump cannot be used to produce anything of value. The lump cannot be used to settle a liability. I conclude, therefore, using the board's own words, that the future economic benefit criterion has not been met.

In paragraph 179 of Concepts Statement 6, the board said, "Although an entity normally incurs costs to acquire or use assets, costs incurred are not themselves assets." The lump is just a cost, nothing more. It is not the cost of something that will, by itself or in combination with anything else, produce any identifiable positive future cash inflow or reduce any identifiable future cash outflow – which is what a future economic benefit is. As the board itself said, a cost is not an asset, so the lump fails to be an asset by the board's own words.

In paragraphs 183 and 184 of Concepts Statement 6, the board said, "To have an asset, an entity must control future economic benefit to the extent that it can benefit from the asset and generally can deny or regulate access to that benefit by others, for example, by permitting access only at a price ... The entity having an asset ... can exchange it, use it to produce goods or services, exact a price for others' use of it, use it to settle liabilities, hold it, or perhaps distribute it to owners." But the lump cannot be exchanged for anything; it cannot be used to produce goods or services; it cannot be leased or loaned to others for a price; it cannot be used to settle liabilities; it cannot be held the way one holds, for example, land or patents or marketable securities; and it cannot be distributed to owners. I conclude, therefore, using the board's own words, that the lump cannot be controlled.

Maybe my difference of opinion with the board represents a different view of what the financial statements of operating companies should show versus what the financial statements of investment companies should show.

There is no doubt, and I agree, that the owner of an investment in net assets, or an interest in net assets, controls that investment. If the financial statements are to show the investment, which investment implicitly includes the lump, and the results of holding that investment, then the balance sheet will show a one-line item representing the investment, perhaps at cost or perhaps at fair value, and the income statement will show dividends flowing from the investment and perhaps changes in the fair value of the investment. That is the way an investment, and the results of holding an investment, are shown in the financial statements of an investment company. In the financial statements of an operating company, however, the investment is not portrayed; instead the individual operating assets such as marketable securities, loans, inventory, land, plant, equipment, mines, and patents, and the results of using or holding those individual operating assets, are portrayed, for it is those individual operating assets that generate cash inflow, and only those operating assets. It is in the balance sheet of an operating company that the lump does not, in my opinion, satisfy the control criterion even though that criterion would be met in the balance sheet of an investment company as to the investment itself.

There is a final question to ask about whether the cost of goodwill should be recognized as an asset by an operating company, namely, whether there is reasonably reliable measurability. Assume, *arguendo*, that, somehow, one can argue convincingly that the cost of goodwill meets the definition of an asset. The problem does not end there. The next and conclusive step is that the future economic benefit from that asset be measurable, with reasonable reliability (see paragraphs 44–8 of Concepts Statement 6). Even at the date of acquisition, the cost of goodwill is not a reliable indicator of the value of any possible indirect future economic benefits. At the date of acquisition, the cost of things such as raw materials, land, equipment, computers, mines, and patents is approximately the amount that all market participants have judged to be the appropriate cash price (laying aside the difference between bid and ask prices). That cash price is the market participants' collective judgment about the future economic benefit (cash flows) embodied in the thing that was acquired, and one can look to that marketplace for a reliable measure of those benefits. Not so for the cost of goodwill, not even at the time of acquisition. No one would pay anything for it alone. And, no business person would sign his or her name to a purported appraisal value of goodwill standing alone. Thus the measurability criterion has not been met.

If the cost of purchased goodwill is not an asset in the financial statements of an operating company, whether because of definitional problems or measurement issues, then what is it? The cost of purchased goodwill is not the distribution of an asset (a dividend) to owners, which would be charged to equity. If the cost of purchased goodwill is not an asset, as I have argued, and as the cost of purchased goodwill is not a distribution of an asset to owners that would be charged to equity, the cost of purchased goodwill then must represent an expense at the time the cost is incurred. The cost of purchased goodwill is like other costs that are not assets under the board's definition of an asset: advertising new or existing products or services, recruiting employees, training new employees, training or retraining existing employees, scouting new locations, opening new stores, starting a new line of business, restructuring an existing business, writing software code to fix the Year 2000 problem, and researching possible new drugs, to name only a few; all such costs, not being assets under the board's definition of an asset, are charged to expense.

12 Cookie jar reserves

Speech delivered at the Nineteenth Annual Ray Garrett Jr Corporate and Securities Law Institute, Corporate Counsel Center of Northwestern University School of Law, 22 April 1999

One of the accounting "hot spots" that we are considering this morning is accounting for restructuring charges and restructuring reserves. A better title would be accounting for general reserves, contingency reserves, rainy day reserves, or cookie jar reserves.

Accounting for so-called restructurings has become an art form. Some companies like the idea so much that they establish restructuring reserves every year. Why not? Analysts seem to like the idea of recognizing as a liability today, a budget of expenditures planned for the next year or next several years in down-sizing, right-sizing, or improving operations, and portraying that amount as a special, below-the-line charge in the current period's income statement. This year's earnings are happily reported in press releases as "before charges." CNBC analysts and commentators talk about earnings "before charges." The financial press talks about earnings "before special charges." Funny, no one talks about earnings before credits – only charges. It's as if special charges aren't real. Out of sight, out of mind.

The occasion of a merger also spawns the wholesale establishment of restructuring or merger reserves. The ingredients of the merger reserves and merger charges look like the makings of sausages. In the Enforcement Division, I have seen all manner and kind of things that ordinarily would be charged to operating earnings instead being charged "below the line." Write-offs of the carrying amounts of bad receivables. Write-offs of cost of obsolete inventory. Write-downs of plant and equipment costs, which, miraculously at the date of the merger, become non-recoverable, whereas those same costs were considered recoverable the day before the merger. Write-offs of previously capitalized costs such as goodwill, which all of a sudden are not recoverable because of a merger. Adjustments to bring warranty liabilities up to snuff. Adjustments to bring claim liabilities into line with management's new view of settling or litigating cases. Adjustments to bring environmental liabilities up to snuff or into line with management's new view of the manner in which the company's obligations to comply with the EPA will be satisfied. Recognition of liabilities to pay for future services by investment bankers, accountants, and lawyers. Recognition of liabilities for officers' special bonuses. Recognition of liabilities for moving people. For training people. For training people not yet hired. For retraining people.

Recognition of liabilities for moving costs and refurbishing costs. Recognition of liabilities for new software that may be acquired or written, for ultimate sale to others. Or some liabilities that go by the title of "other."

It is no wonder that investors and analysts are complaining about the credibility of the numbers. A bank stock analyst was quoted in the *WSJ*'s "Heard on the street" on 1 April: "The reported profits number is now considered an accounting fiction." Warren Buffett's latest annual report to shareholders of Berkshire Hathaway has several pages of commentary about restructuring and merger reserves. He says that "many managements purposefully work at manipulating numbers and deceiving investors ... when it comes to restructurings and merger accounting." A major investment banking house has concluded that the P/E ratios of stocks and indexes of stocks are understated because of restructuring charges and merger charges being "below the line"; that, for example, the P/E of the S&P 500, instead of being, say, 31 should really be 34 or 35 because the special charges are not factored into the earnings part of the calculation.

The cover for these shenanigans is two "consensuses" of the FASB's Emerging Issues Task Force that deal with recognition of liabilities on the occasion of a restructuring or a merger, namely EITF 94-3 and 95-3. Generally, what EITF 94-3 permits is (1) the recognition as a liability today of future expenditures for involuntary termination benefits to be paid to employees and (2) the recognition of a liability today for future expenditures that are directly associated with a plan to exit an activity – provided those expenditures will have no future economic benefit and provided four conditions laid down by the EITF are met. EITF 95-3 expands on 94-3 to say that, in a business combination, expenditures to relocate employees may also be recognized as a liability at the time of the business combination, in addition to the employee termination benefits and exit costs covered by 94-3.

Those two utterances by the Emerging Issues Task Force allow for the recognition of liabilities based on a representation by management that the company will make certain expenditures but before a cash outflow is required pursuant to a law or a contract. In all other cases except in the accounting for pensions and OPEBs, liabilities are not recognized until some event has occurred and a cash outflow is therefore required, either by law or regulation or under an enforceable contract. For example, liabilities to suppliers of goods are not booked by the buyer until the supplier has delivered the goods to the buyer. Liabilities for salaries and wages are not booked until employees have worked and earned their pay. Liabilities for tomorrow's rent and electric are not booked until the premises have been used and the electricity has been used – both events of the tomorrow, not today. There is no liability to pay investment bankers, accountants, or lawyers until they have performed services. But, pursuant to the EITF pronouncements, it is OK to recognize a liability today for severance pay to employees that will be paid to them months or years in the future but only if they stay at their jobs until then. It's OK to recognize a liability today for other so-called "exit costs." It's OK to recognize a liability today for future costs that will have no future economic benefit. But, because the EITF could not define a restructuring, and therefore could not specify its ingredients, those two consensuses are, as a practical matter, largely optional. For example, looking at the *Forbes* article of 23 March 1998 on "Pick a number, any number," two of the companies interviewed, VF Corporation and Walgreen, said that they do not recognize restructuring charges, whereas many companies do. VF charged the $400 million cost of cutting 2,000 jobs and consolidating seventeen locations to five to current earnings instead of as a restructuring charge. Walgreen charged the cost of closing 400 stores over five years to current earnings instead of as restructuring charges. VF's CFO is quoted as saying, "Restructuring is an invention by Wall Street. It's a term for covering up debits. We don't play that game. It's short-sighted. It delays the inevitable." Jack Ciesielski, a CPA/analyst with R.G. Associates, in the 29 March 1999 issue of *The Analyst's Accounting Observer*, in footnote 8, says that following the consensuses is optional. Thus, Company A may establish a restructuring reserve and charge selected expenditures to that reserve if it wants to, but Company B need not establish such a reserve and may charge the expenditures to income in the regular way – even though both may be similarly situated and have the same auditors. Or both Company A and Company B may establish reserves for some restructurings but not others. To boot, the numbers ascribed to restructurings and thus included in the reserves cannot be verified by the outside auditor by reference to anything except management's assertion, which is no evidence or verification at all; the numbers are whatever management of the enterprise says they are. Moreover, I have seen the amounts of those initially established reserves arbitrarily increased for good measure. These excessive amounts of reserves are then leached, undisclosed, into subsequent operating income at a rate that is under someone's radar screen of materiality.

On the point about the inability to audit the numbers in these reserves, imagine a situation where a new management team comes in after year end and dramatically changes the amounts in various reserves established by the previous management. The new management issues restated financial statements for the prior periods. The same audit firm reports on both sets of financial statements without qualification. We also see, quite frequently, where restructuring reserve amounts are retroactively restated downward as a result of piercing, probing comment and inquiry by the Division of Corporation Finance, and the external auditors report without qualification on the financial statements with the reserve at its original amount and at its revised, decreased amount. So much for auditing reserves.

I was chief accountant in 1994 when EITF 94-3 was debated by the Emerging Issues Task Force. I pleaded with the EITF not to allow the recognition of liabilities today where there has been no past event, for example the performance of services by employees or the receipt of goods from suppliers or the receipt of cash in return for issuing a put option, which establishes that the reporting enterprise has an obligation to lay out cash tomorrow. I made a speech about that on 8 November 1994 to the Financial Executives Institute. As I recall, I sent a copy of that speech to EITF members. In that speech, I pointed out the conceptual flaw in the EITF's approach and the practical consequences of that approach. Nine days later, on 17 November, despite my pleas, the Emerging Issues Task Force said OK to the establishment of restructuring reserves.

What has happened since 1994? Well, my instinct in 1994 has been confirmed by practice. What has happened since 1994 is that general reserves, contingency reserves, rainy day reserves, and cookie jar reserves are now in vogue for those who want to use them. Based on what I see in the Enforcement Division, apparently there is almost no limit to what ingredient may be included in the reserves or the amount ascribed to it. I was recently in a conversation with a prominent Wall Street lawyer whose client established, improperly, a general contingency, rainy day reserve. This lawyer explained his client's rationale for the reserve that was established. I said to the lawyer that his description of his client's rationale was the description of a general contingency reserve, which was outlawed by the FASB in 1975. Whereupon, he called me a pencil pusher and said that all the Fortune 500 companies are doing the same thing his client did.

How does this problem get fixed? The FASB's definition of a liability in its Concepts Statement 6 says, in footnote 22, that "It [a liability] includes equitable and constructive obligations as well as legal obligations." The question is what constitutes a constructive obligation? Does an announcement by a company that it will lay off 100 or 1,000 employees create a liability for termination bonuses that are promised to be paid at termination but only if the employee remains as an employee until terminated by the company? Does a decision by a lessee that it will no longer use leased facilities give rise to a recognizable liability for the lease payments when there was no recognizable liability the day before the decision? The accounting for pensions and OPEBs is based on an idea of a constructive obligation, not on a vested-benefit notion, which is more akin to a legal obligation. Are management decisions, which obviously are always reversible, to terminate employees and no longer use facilities sufficient to either permit or require the recognition of liabilities before the obligation to pay cash becomes an obligation enforceable at law? The FASB has been working on such questions in three projects that it has on its agenda, namely, liabilities and equity, obligations associated with the retirement of long-lived assets, and impairment and asset disposal issues. It appears that the questions are very, very difficult. Getting agreement apparently is not easy. The SEC staff has been encouraging the FASB to complete work on these projects. Investors urgently need some guidance that can be applied uniformly by all issuers and their auditors so that investors receive better information and can make more informed decisions.

Meanwhile, however, the Division of Corporation Finance and the Office of the Chief Accountant are taking a close look at restructuring reserves and merger reserves. So is the Enforcement Division. I am going to take a pencil pusher's attitude to all such reserves and examine whether all of the ingredients of an issuer's reserve are explicitly permitted by the words in EITF 94-3 and 95-3 and the issuer has explicitly and in detail justified the reserve and the amount thereof and documented that justification.

If you have clients that have established restructuring reserves or merger reserves, I recommend that you and the audit committee get for yourselves copies of EITF 94-3 and 95-3, get your client's CFO and CEO into a conference room, and you and the audit committee do your own audit of the restructuring reserves and determine whether what your client has done fits into the authoritative literature.

13 Financial instruments

In 1992, I requested a copy of the attached letter of 13 February 1986 from me to the FASB regarding financial instruments (I had lost my copy of the letter). Halsey Bullen, one of the FASB's senior staff, sent the letter to me with a hand-written note as follows:

> Here is the letter you wanted. I'm not sure how much credit we gave you at the time, but it was this letter that led to our [FASB] Statement 105 [Disclosure of Information about Financial Instruments with Off-Balance-Sheet Risk and Financial Instruments with Concentrations of Credit Risk] and Statement 107 [Disclosure about Fair Value of Financial Instruments].
>
> Halsey Bullen 10-16-92.

Peat, Marwick, Mitchell & Co.
Certified Public Accountants
345 Park Avenue
New York, NY 10154
13 February 1986

Mr Halsey G. Bullen
Financial Accounting Standards Board
P.0. Box 3821
High Ridge Park
Stamford, CT 06905-0821

Dear Mr Bullen,
This letter is a follow-on to the meeting on February 5, 1986 at the FASB to discuss the scope of a possible Board project(s) on "Financial Instruments."

While I believe that a Board project is necessary, particularly in response to Mr Sampson's letter of June 1985 to Mr Kirk, I did not find the scope of the Board's project defined very clearly in the materials accompanying your letters of January 27 and 31, 1986. I am very much inclined to a different initial approach than where you appear to be headed, *viz.*, disclosure of market values of on- and off-balance-sheet financial instruments. (I agree with Mr Stewart that FAS 76 and 77 and FTB 85-2 need to be re-examined; they produce illogical, and sometimes inexplicable, results.)

Assets represented by financial instruments generally are reported at cost, not at market value. There are exceptions in FASB pronouncements: for example, FAS 12, market or lower of cost or market for marketable equity securities; FAS 52, market for foreign currency; FAS 60, market for common and non-redeemable preferred stocks; and FAS 65, lower of cost or market for inventory. Certain AICPA Industry Guides require certain assets to be reported at market; for example, the Broker/Dealer and Investment Company Guides for practically all assets and the Bank Guide for trading account securities. And the Bank and Savings and Loan Guides require disclosure of market value for investment account securities. But there is no single, across-the-board requirement to disclose market values of assets that readily can be, and in many cases are, bought and sold.

In the end, the Board will have to deal with *when* and *which* assets represented by financial instruments should be reported at market value in the basic financial statements. This is the "fundamental question" raised by Mr Sampson, or at least one of them. Before the Board can make an informed decision on the *when* and *which* questions, however, I think that the Board and its constituencies need information about (1) how difficult it is, if it is, to find market values for financial instruments that are not traded on exchanges or in a highly organized over-the-counter market and (2) how people would react to the introduction of market values of assets represented by financial instruments in the reporting of assets, equity, and income.

The first step essentially involves fact finding and should be a relatively simple task. The second step has to do with finding out about people's emotions and their perceptions of "economic reality." For the Board to find out about those things – those non-facts will require some period of introduction, acquaintance, and education. Both of these steps can best be done through mandated disclosure before introducing more market values into the basic financial statements, if that is the Board's decision.

As I said at the meeting, I would start with disclosure of market values for all on-balance-sheet assets representing financial instruments. Next, I would proceed to those financial instruments that currently are not shown on balance sheets and that are used to hedge, shift risks to others, take on risks of others, and, in some cases, to speculate.

As I also mentioned at the meeting, it was necessary for me to prepare a definition of *financial instruments* that I had in mind. That definition is attached as Appendix A.

Yours truly,
Walter Schuetze

cc: Members of 2647 Task Force
Laurel Bond – SEC

Appendix A

Financial instruments

1 A contract, whether firm or optional, whereunder the issuer thereof has agreed to deliver to the holder thereof, on a specified date(s):

a a specified amount of money (a *money* obligation on the part of the issuer of the contract),

b a specified measure of a specified commodity (a *commodity* obligation on the part of the issuer of the contract), or

c an uncertain amount of money with the final amount to be measured by reference to an independently determined interest rate, price of a commodity, including foreign money, or an index (an uncertain money/commodity/index obligation on the part of the issuer of the contract).

2 In order for a *commodity* to fall within the scope of this project, a fairly ready market must exist for it. Contracts involving the following are excluded:

a personal services,

b equipment,

c real estate (land and attachments to land, e.g. buildings),

d intangibles such as copyrights, patents, names, and franchises,

e minerals,

f air and water rights.

The aim would be to exclude specifically those that the Board would want to exclude; b–f might be included if they serve as collateral for other contracts.

3 Included in the scope of this project would be any item for which one can find price or yield quotations in financial or trade publications or as to which brokers and offer price or yield quotations. (The aim here would be to embrace in the project(s) *things* for which a fairly ready market exists.)

4 Contracts requiring payments of cash or the use of other assets by the issuer (writer) of the contract because of damages to life, health, or property or damages arising from torts, errors or omissions, and business interruption somehow should be excluded. Contracts relating to the performance of another party under a contract should be included, however.

5 Admittedly, this kind of definition (paragraphs 1–4) has some ambiguity, but the ambiguity would appear to be at a tolerable level.

14 Accounting for transfers of receivables (by Tom, Dick, and Harry)

When Walter Schuetze was appointed chief accountant to the Securities and Exchange Commission in January 1992, he withdrew this article, which he had submitted to the *Journal of Accountancy* in December 1991.

Peat Marwick
Certified Public Accountants
767 Fifth Avenue
New York, NY 10153
9 December 1991

Ms Barbara J. Shildneck
Executive Editor
Journal of Accountancy
1211 Avenue of the Americas
New York, New York 10036-8775

Dear Ms Shildneck,
I enclose an article on transfers of receivables (draft 12/9/91) that I would like you to consider for publication in the *Journal.*

Because the issue is so hot and topical right now (the IASC has requested comments on its exposure draft on financial instruments by the end of next May, and the FASB has just issued its discussion memorandum on financial instruments), I would like to get the article published very soon.

Please telephone me at 212-909-5644 to discuss.

Yours truly,
Walter Schuetze

Governments and regulators around the world are forcing banks to decrease their leverage or increase their equity (capital). Thrifts in the United States must do the same. Other enterprises such as insurers, retailers, and manufacturers want to reduce their leverage or increase their equity (capital) so that they will be perceived as better risks by those who lend money to them or invest in their stock, bonds, notes, and commercial paper, or buy insurance from them. The entire world is in a liquidity crunch, and all enterprises are competing in the worldwide marketplace to reduce leverage or raise equity. Just-in-time inventory controls are one response to that liquidity crunch. Another response is to sell receivables. All of these entities want and need to get receivables – consumer loans, automobile loans, retail receivables, mortgage loans, commercial loans, HLT loans, LDC loans, real estate loans, agricultural loans – off their balance sheets. Thus, accounting for receivables, and especially transfers of receivables, is hugely important.

Accounting for transfers of receivables in the United States is governed by Statement of Financial Accounting Standards No. 77, *Transfers of Receivables with Recourse*. It is one of the most controversial standards issued by the Financial Accounting Standards Board. Why? Because the financial statement results produced by following Statement 77 are counterintuitive. Because people do not understand, and therefore are bewildered by, the financial statement results produced by the statement. Because Statement 77 generally allows for sale accounting when receivables are transferred and certain risks related to the receivables are retained, but, at the same time, the statement does not require recognition and measurement of those retained risks in a meaningful way. In fact, under Statement 77, certain retained risks are not recognized at all by the transferor. Under Statement 77, originators of receivables are able to sell those receivables and report a gain – or no loss – retain certain risks inherent in the receivables, and not recognize and portray the value of those risks on their balance sheets. Gain may be recognized for accounting purposes when no economic gain exists. What accounting magic. Cut off the end of a blanket, sew it to the other end, and the blanket is longer than it was. Sadly, everyone who is a party to such a transaction – and the financial community as a whole – knows there is no gain.

The controversy about Statement 77 – and the financial stakes surrounding it – are so great that a legion of Wall Street investment bankers, lawyers, and accountants makes a handsome living figuring out how banks, thrifts, insurers, retailers, and manufacturers can get receivables off their balance sheets without recognizing losses in the process. Statement 77 is broken and needs to be fixed. It is being reconsidered by the FASB in its Financial Instruments Project, but resolution is a long way off. Many accountants, maybe most accountants, would fix Statement 77 by not permitting sale accounting on transfers of receivables if the transferor retains credit, interest rate, or foreign exchange risk. They would have the transferor account for the transfer as a borrowing instead of a sale. I disagree with that approach. It rejects what is right about the statement and ignores what needs correction, as will be illustrated, and it results in the recognition of phantom assets and liabilities. The FASB considered that approach in Statement 77 and rejected it. The FASB decided instead that control over a receivable should drive the accounting, not retention of risk. I agree with the FASB. However, Statement 77 needs to be modified so that risks retained by the transferor are adequately recognized in the transferor's financial statements.

The International Accounting Standards Committee recently (September 1991) issued an exposure draft of an International Accounting Standard[1] on accounting for receivables and transfers of receivables that would, if adopted by the IASC and then by the FASB in the spirit of international harmonization, put the accounting for receivables, and especially transfers of receivables, back into the Dark Ages.[2]

The IASC's proposal is based on accounting for risks and rewards inherent in receivables, not who controls the receivables. According to paragraphs 19 and 20 of E40, a receivable[3] has the following risks and rewards:

19 Financial instruments (receivables] result in an enterprise assuming or transferring to another party one or more of the financial risks described below.

Price risk

There are three types of price risk: currency risk, interest rate risk, and market risk. Currency risk is the risk that the value of a financial instrument will fluctuate due to changes in foreign exchange rates. Interest rate risk is the risk that the value of a financial instrument will fluctuate due to changes in market interest rates. Market risk is the risk that the value of a financial instrument will fluctuate as a result of changes in market prices, whether those changes are caused by factors specific to the individual security or its issuer or factors affecting all securities traded in the market. The term "price risk" embodies not only the potential for loss but also the potential for gain.

Credit risk

Credit risk is the risk that one party to a financial instrument will fail to discharge an obligation and cause the other party to incur a financial loss.

Liquidity risk

Liquidity risk is the risk that an enterprise will encounter difficulty in raising funds at short notice to meet commitments associated with financial instruments (also referred to as funding risk). Liquidity risk may result from an inability to sell a financial asset quickly at close to its fair value.

Changes in the market's perception of these risks give rise to fluctuations in the market price of a financial instrument. For example, the market price of a debt security is affected by changes in the market's perception of credit risk, as well as by changes in market interest rates and, in some cases, currency risk.

20 The rewards associated with a financial asset may include not only potential gains as a result of having assumed price risk but also rights to receive interest and payments of principal, to pledge the instrument as security for obligations, to dispose of the instrument for consideration and to use the instrument to settle an obligation. Financial liabilities usually arise from

transactions in which the enterprise has received some past benefit, such as a receipt of cash, and may also have the potential for future benefits as a result of exposure to price risk.

The IASC proposes, in E40:

1 An enterprise initially should recognize a receivable (a financial asset) when the risks and rewards associated with the receivable have been transferred to the [reporting] enterprise [paragraph 15]. [What curious words. I do not understand why the IASC used the phrase "transferred to." "Acquired by" would have been a more conventional and comfortable form of words.]
2 A receivable is not de-recognized – that is, a sale is not recognized – by the transferor if the receivable is transferred to others in a manner that involves the retention by the transferor of some of the original risks and rewards inherent in the receivable [paragraphs 29 and 30). In that case, the proceeds of sale are recognized as a liability by the transferor.

The IASC's proposal on initial and subsequent recognition/de-recognition of a receivable is based on whether the risks and rewards associated with the receivable have been transferred to [acquired by] or retained by the reporting enterprise. I think that initial and subsequent recognition/de-recognition of a receivable by an enterprise should be based on *control* – that is, who has title to the receivable, who will collect the cash proceeds from the debtor, who can sell/transfer the receivable or parts of it to someone else, who can pledge the receivable, who can use the receivable as collateral for a debt, who can forgive the receivable, and who can give the receivable to charity. The IASC's proposal would require the recognition of phantom assets and liabilities.

Under the IASC's proposal, if a bank originates a receivable, transfers it to another party, and guarantees that the debtor will pay on time and in full as per the receivable contract, then the bank would not de-recognize the receivable but would account for the transfer as a borrowing. Whereas if an enterprise other than the guaranteeing bank originates that same receivable and buys credit insurance from the bank in the form of a letter of credit, then the bank would not recognize and report the receivable as its asset. Yet, in both cases, the bank has exactly the same risk. Not consistent, logical conclusions. Tilt. To describe a receivable, or any other asset, in terms of its risks and rewards is oblique; describing it in terms of who has control of it is direct. Deriving accounting results based on the idea of control has a better chance of being consistent and logical.

What would be some of the consequences of the IASC's proposal on transfers of receivables if it were to be implemented?

1 If the originator/acquirer of a receivable – Tom – transfers (sells) the receivable to Dick and Tom retains one of the risks described above, say, credit risk, then Tom could not remove that receivable from his balance sheet. But to Tom that receivable is a phantom receivable after the transfer. Tom will not

collect the cash paid by the debtor, cannot sell the receivable again, cannot pledge the receivable, cannot forgive the receivable, and cannot give it away. And if the receivable that was sold is denominated in a foreign currency, then Tom would have to report phantom foreign currency gains or losses. Tom's hapless treasurer might even hedge that phantom receivable with a real foreign currency futures contract. What a thigh slapper that would be. How would Tom mark to market a receivable he does not own and cannot sell?

Tom would have to recognize a liability equal to the proceeds received from Dick. That presentation would imply that 100 percent of the receivables are bad or will go bad, and Tom will have to pay back to Dick all of the cash Dick paid to Tom. That implication is not in keeping with the facts; Dick would not buy receivables that are totally bad or are going to go totally bad. The liability that Tom would report will not require cash payments by Tom to Dick except to the extent that receivables go bad. Thus the liability that Tom would have to report is a phantom liability.

Tom would have to report phantom revenue, expenses, cash receipts, and cash payments related to the phantom receivable and liability. Tilt.

2 If Tom retained credit risk in the transfer and Dick acquired no credit risk, then Dick, under the IASC's proposal for recognition of a receivable (E40, paragraph 15), would not report the transferred receivable as an asset; Dick would report a receivable from Tom in the full amount of the price that Dick paid Tom for the receivable. If you are Dick's auditor, try to send a receivable confirmation to Tom and see what Tom says. Tom will say that he does not owe Dick any money. If Tom says that he does not owe Dick any money, how then can Dick report a receivable from Tom? Double tilt.
3 If Dick needs or wants cash before the receivable is fully collected, Dick may transfer the receivable, without recourse or guarantee, to Harry for cash. What asset would Harry report: the receivable itself, a receivable from Dick, or a receivable from Tom? I guess a receivable from Tom or Dick but not the receivable itself. But Harry owns the receivable itself and will collect the cash from the original debtor, not from Tom or Dick. Triple tilt.

Some may argue that the IASC's proposal for accounting for the transfer of receivables with recourse for credit loss is analogous to the accounting by a borrower for collateralized borrowings.[4] I disagree. A borrower who has pledged an asset that he/she/it owns as collateral for a debt can regain unrestricted, unconditional control of the pledged asset simply by extinguishing the debt. The transferor of a receivable cannot do that; the transferee owns the receivable; the transferor cannot regain control of the receivable unless the receivable goes bad. If the value of a pledged asset goes up, the borrower/owner can benefit from that event. If the value of a transferred receivable goes up, the transferee can benefit from that event, but the transferor cannot benefit. If the value of a pledged asset goes down, the borrower/owner suffers to the full extent. If the value of a transferred receivable goes down, the transferor suffers only to the extent he/she/it must pay the transferee for some or all of the decline under the contract surrounding the transfer. There are large, important differences between collateralized borrowings and transfers of receivables with retained risk for credit loss. The analogy is flawed.

As I said, Statement 77 is broken and needs to be fixed, but not along the lines of the IASC's proposals. The way Statement 77 needs to be fixed is to retain the notion of control currently in Statement 77 and to go on to require recognition, at *fair value*, of the risks and rewards retained by the transferor. This is, after all, how such transactions are priced by transferors and transferees. If the seller/transferor retains credit risk, then the seller should recognize, at fair value, the liability for the credit put written by the seller. If the seller retains interest rate risk, then the seller should recognize, at fair value, the liability for the interest rate put written by the seller. If the seller retains foreign exchange risk, then the seller should recognize, at fair value, the liability for the foreign exchange put written by the seller. Then, at each balance sheet date, the seller should reprice these written puts to their fair value and recognize that price change in income. The same goes for rewards; the seller should recognize at fair value the rewards – the calls – retained by the seller.

Let me be up-front about my proposal on how to fix Statement 77. What would be some of the consequences? Recognizing liabilities, at fair value, at the time of transfer for written puts for credit risk, interest rate risk, or foreign exchange risk, would significantly and dramatically reduce gains, or increase losses, on transfers of receivables compared with the results that we get today under Statement 77.[5] As it now stands, Statement 77 requires no recognition of any liability whatsoever for retained interest rate risk or retained foreign exchange risk. And it requires, with respect to retained credit risk, that the recourse obligation be measured by reference to FASB Statement 5. Statement 5, read in conjunction with Statement 77, is confusing and has been interpreted in different ways. Statement 5 requires that credit loss for receivables be recognized for those receivables that *have gone* bad, not those that *may go* bad. No one would buy bad receivables; sellers' written credit puts relate to receivables that may go bad in the future. If one looks at the recourse obligation as being related to receivables that will or may go bad – sort of like a warranty obligation for parts on machinery and equipment that will or may break – then one would measure the recourse obligation more appropriately and robustly. But that kind of measurement ignores a profit margin on the guarantee and the time value of money and does not get at the fair value of the written credit put. Reference to Statement 5 to measure the recourse obligation has proved to be unsatisfactory.

Determining fair values of put and call options that are retained by sellers of receivables will require difficult, and sometimes highly judgmental, estimations. But, such estimates now are made in the world of credit insurance and derivative instruments; in fact, real transactions for cash between real enterprises are based on such estimates. Such estimates are also made when businesses are acquired and lump-sum purchase prices must be allocated. Fair values can be estimated.

Estimating those values and accounting for those puts and calls will be better than subsuming losses in balance sheets, as is now done under Statement 77, and dribbling those losses into income over time. Better to estimate and account for something that is relevant – the puts and calls – than to report irrelevant and potentially misleading phantom assets and liabilities. More importantly, it is imperative that transferors of receivables who retain risks estimate, and constantly re-estimate, the fair value of the retained risks so as to make intelligent decisions about the business they are in, namely, risk guaranty.

Moreover, repricing written puts at every balance sheet date and including that price change in income may make for increased earnings volatility.[6] Reduced gains, or increased losses, and perhaps earnings volatility will make it difficult for some to accept this way of fixing Statement 77. But repricing is the best accounting measure of the results of the guaranty business.

However, the other way to fix Statement 77 is the way the IASC proposes. That fix will balloon transferors' balance sheets, create phantom assets, liabilities, revenue, expenses, and phantom cash receipts and payments in statements of cash flows. Reporting phantom assets and liabilities will cause ROAs around the world to decline. If bank regulators in the United States and other countries that signed the Basel Accord somehow believe that the phantom assets and liabilities are real, then they may require that $8 of equity be raised for every additional $100 of assets that will arise under the IASC's proposals.[7] If rating agencies somehow believe that the phantom assets and liabilities are real, those rating agencies will downgrade debt issued by highly leveraged enterprises. Investors and creditors will certainly be confused and may be misled. Only accountants will know how to interpret the financial statements under the IASC's proposals, but they do not use financial statements or make investment or credit decisions.

Notes

1 International Accounting Standard, proposed statement, "Financial instruments," Exposure Draft 40 (E40).

2 The Canadian Institute of Chartered Accountants also recently issued a proposal on accounting for financial instruments and transfers of receivables very similar to the IASC's. The United Kingdom's Accounting Standards Board also recently issued a proposal on "securitisations." The accounting proposed by the UK ASB for securitisations is roughly the same as that proposed by the IASC for transfers of receivables.

3 Under the IASC's proposal, "receivables" include trade accounts receivable, notes receivable, loans receivable, and bonds receivable, that is, a contractual right to receive cash in the future (E40, paragraph A3).

4 Two members of the FASB, Messrs March and Sprouse, so argued in their dissents to Statement 77. In Statement of Position 74-6, "Recognition of profit on sales of receivables with recourse," the Accounting Standards Executive Committee of the American Institute of Certified Public Accountants stated, in paragraph 41, that "Sales of receivables with recourse have significant characteristics of financing transactions in which monies are borrowed and assets are pledged as security thereon." In Statement of Position 74-6, the Accounting Standards Executive Committee considered and rejected the proposal that I advance in this article for retained credit risk; the committee believed that the value of the written credit put option could not be determined objectively. Statement of Position 74-6 was superseded by Statement 77.

5 Gains would be reduced, or losses increased, because the buyers of receivables from banks, thrifts, insurers, retailers, and manufacturers generally have a higher cost of capital than do the sellers; or the buyers are types of enterprise or individual that demand higher rates of return than do the owners of those enterprises that originate receivables. More importantly, pricing the written puts by reference to fair value – for example, what third parties would charge to write the puts – will significantly increase the liabilities of sellers of receivables who retain various risks over what is done under Statement 77.

6 But earnings "volatility" also results by charging income with losses arising from risk retention when cash payments are made; the "volatility" simply will come in later periods. The "volatility" does not go away.

7 If a transferor bank retains risk, US banking regulators' call report instructions are like the IASC's proposals in that the transferred receivable is not de-recognized, and those regulators require $8 of equity for each $100 of phantom assets. I would argue that regulators should base equity (capital) requirements on the fair value of the written put liability, which in some cases might be more than $8 on $100. If the regulators think that the amount of the put liability is too low or too high, they should adjust that liability for their purposes and not force banks to recognize and report phantom assets and liabilities.

15 Discount rate re cash outflows for nuclear decommissioning and environmental remediation

Director of Research and Technical Activities
Financial Accounting Standards Board
407 Merritt 7
P.O. Box 5116
Norwalk, CT 06856-5116
25 September 1995

Dear Sir,

Discount Rate re Cash Outflows for Nuclear Decommissioning and Environmental Remediation

According to its Status Report 151-A of 7 July 1995, The Financial Accounting Standards Board tentatively has concluded that cash outflows for nuclear decommissioning should be discounted at a rate consistent with that specified in FASB Statement 106 for cash outflows for retirees' healthcare benefits, namely, the rate of return on high-quality fixed-income investments or the settlement rate if settlement is possible (Statement 106, paragraph 31). Settlement for post-retirement healthcare benefits generally is not possible, so the settlement rate is not used.

The American Institute of Certified Public Accountants' Accounting Standards Executive Committee, on the other hand, in its 30 June 1995 exposure draft of a proposed statement of position on environmental remediation liabilities, would require that cash outflows be discounted at "a rate that will produce an amount at which the environmental liability theoretically could be settled in an arm's-length transaction with a third party and that should not exceed the interest rate on monetary assets that are essentially risk free and have maturities comparable to that of the liability" (paragraph B30).

I suggest that the ASEC selected the correct rate for cash outflows related to environmental liabilities and that the FASB should reconsider the rate for nuclear decommissioning liabilities. Otherwise, those liabilities, especially those with long payouts, will be significantly understated.

The objective should be to recognize and measure liabilities at their *fair value*. When money is borrowed, the *fair value* of the liability is the amount of money received from the lender, and the rate charged by the lender, either explicit or implicit, is known or may be calculated. In the absence of a borrowing and a schedule of contractually fixed cash outflows, estimating the fair value of a liability is a theoretical undertaking; it is made even more theoretical if there is no market in which liabilities such as the one being recognized and measured can be settled. If there were such a market, however, we could deduce how participants in that marketplace would price future cash outflows for things such as environmental remediation, nuclear decommissioning, post-retirement healthcare benefits, pensions, and warranties. In that marketplace, participants first would estimate future cash flows based on best estimates; then they would increase the amount of best estimate for the risk of having made an incorrect estimate (adverse deviation); and then they would make assumptions about investing the cash proceeds to be received on the transfer of a liability. Inasmuch as neither the FASB nor the ASEC allows for estimates of cash outflows for nuclear decommissioning or environmental remediation to include a factor for adverse deviation, the estimate of total cash outflows as allowed by the FASB and ASEC does not mimic what marketplace participants would do, and therefore understates the liability in the first instance. That understatement is compounded by using too high a rate for discounting the future cash outflows.

Assume that one could know exactly both the timing and amount of cash outflows for remediation or decommissioning. What amount of money would any transferee demand to take on those cash outflows: that amount which if invested in risk-free instruments (US Treasury securities in the United States) would exactly equal the cash outflows to be made for remediation or decommissioning. Why is that? It is because the transferee, if it is required, come hell or high water, to satisfy the cash outflow requirements, would not, indeed could not, take on credit risk or any other investment risk.

One can analyze the issue from a slightly different perspective. Assume again that both the timing and amount of cash outflows for decommissioning or remediation are known – exactly. Assume further that laws of the state allow for legal defeasance of the future cash outflows by the obligor's placing in trust today an amount of cash to satisfy the cash outflow when necessary. The state, and the state's citizens, *could* demand that cash sufficient to satisfy the cash outflow requirement – *with no investment whatsoever of that cash pending the cash outflow* – be deposited with the state. But that would not be equitable either as to the obligor or the citizens of the state, for the investment earnings would then benefit only the citizens. The citizens would, in equity, agree to receive today that amount of cash, which if invested in risk-free investments, would satisfy the cash outflow requirements. (The state, or any transferee, would also want a small, additional amount of cash for administration, or handling, but I have ignored that amount here.) The state would not take risk and thereby pass on to the citizenry through taxation any cash shortfall caused by a credit loss.

The ASEC selected the correct rate.

This analysis and conclusion have implications for the measurement of other liabilities for which there is no marketplace where one can look for pricing, for example retirees' pension and healthcare benefits and warranties. As well, the cash outflows for those items should be discounted using the risk-free rate.

Yours truly,
Walter P. Schuetze

cc: Mr G. Michael Crooch
Mr Michael H. Sutton
Mr E.W. Trott

16 Discount rate for pension liabilities

Sir Bryan Carsberg responded to my note of 17 April 1997 (attached). I have lost his note. As I recall, he took me to task for my faulty thinking, and he argued to me that a pension liability should be discounted taking into account the credit standing of the employer/obligor. Largely based on Carsberg's argument, I have changed my mind. I now think that a vested pension liability should be measured by reference to the amount of cash that the pensioner would accept in complete settlement of his/her claim against the employer/obligor. The pensioner no doubt would take into account the credit standing of the obligor.

Many pension benefits in the USA are guaranteed by the US federal government. In that case, the credit standing of the employer/obligor effectively is that of the US federal government; thus, the discount rate effectively would be the risk-free rate for those vested pension liabilities.

I do not recall whether Carsberg's argument in his note to me ran only to a *vested* pension liability. And I do not know whether Carsberg would agree with my revised thinking regarding the measurement of a vested pension liability.

17 April 1997
TO: Sir Bryan Carsberg, IASC
FROM: Walter P. Schuetze
RE: Discount rate for pension liabilities

I read with great interest the exchange between McGeachin/Whittington (Team 1) and Metcalf/Peirson/Upton (Team 2) in the March 1997 issue of *IASC Insight*. Team 1 argues for a "risk-adjusted rate" for discounting pension liabilities, while Team 2 argues for the "risk-free rate." In my opinion, Team 2 wins the argument hands down.

But Team 2 did not go far enough. Team 2 argues for using the rate derived from high-quality, fixed-rate corporate bonds. That is the same rate used by the Financial Accounting Standards Board in its Statements 87 and 106. That rate includes some factor, perhaps small, for credit risk, and using that rate will understate the amount of the pension liability in relation to its fair value. (That rate may also include some factor for coupon reinvestment risk.)

What is the fair value of a pension liability? It is the amount of cash the employer would have to pay to a third party to assume the pension obligation. If that third party must pay the pensioner, come hell or high water, the amount due the pensioner under the pension contract, the third party will be unwilling to take any credit risk (or reinvestment risk) whatsoever. So the rate that should be used is the rate available on zero coupon bonds, or bonds stripped of their coupons, issued by the sovereign state, which bonds will mature at the same time, and in the same amount, as money must be paid to pensioners. (Of course, that third party would want to be paid for its administrative costs plus some profit for its effort, but I have ignored those matters here, although those amounts might not be trivial.)

Attached is a copy of my letter of 25 September 1995 to the FASB, wherein I argued at more length about using the risk-free rate to discount certain liabilities.

17 Exposure Draft E55: *Impairment of Assets*

TO: The Secretary General, International Accounting Standards Committee
FROM: Walter P. Schuetze
RE: Exposure Draft E55: *Impairment of Assets*
DATE: 23 July 1997

The Exposure Draft on *Impairment of Assets* should not be issued as a final standard, for it is fatally flawed. The information produced by following E55, if issued in final form, would be unreliable and irrelevant and therefore misleading to investors.

The major flaw in E55 is that it requires that "value in use" be used to determine whether the carrying amount of an asset is impaired. To determine value in use of an asset, management of the reporting enterprise makes its own, private estimate of the future cash flows that the asset may produce – as contrasted with what unrelated third parties, i.e. market participants, would estimate as the future cash flows from that asset. Amounts in financial statements should – in order to be reliable – be based on information that is free from preparer bias. Thus fair value of the asset, not value in use, should be used to determine whether the carrying amount of the asset is impaired, with fair value being the estimated amount of cash the asset would yield in a sale to an unrelated party, that is, a market participant. Fair value is an amount that generally can be verified by reference to information outside the enterprise and thus is reliable. Value in use, being an internal, private estimate, cannot be verified and thus is not reliable.

Indeed, at the time an asset is acquired by paying cash for the asset, the value in use of that asset to the buyer may be an amount in excess of fair value, which is the amount of cash just paid for the asset. Were our accounting system one that allowed or required periodic revaluation of assets and were value in use a superior number to fair value in terms of its relevance to the reporting enterprise's investors, then we would see revaluations upward at the time assets are acquired whenever value in use is greater than fair value. I think that investors would not favor that idea.

Value in use of an asset to the holder of an asset is not a relevant amount to investors in the securities issued by the holder of the asset. The cost of an asset to the holder of the asset is relevant to the holder's investors at the time an asset is acquired, for at the time of acquisition the cost of the asset is the best estimate by market participants of the present value of the cash that may flow from the asset. But, just as value in use to the holder of an asset is not relevant to the holder's investors at the time the asset is acquired, neither is value in use relevant to those investors at some later date. Insofar as the holder's investors are concerned, the best estimate of the present value of cash that may flow from an asset is what marketplace participants think that amount is, not what the holder of the asset thinks it is.

The holders of assets may do their own internal, private accounting any way they want to; those holders of assets may decide what is relevant for their own, private purposes. But the chief concern of the IASC is financial accounting and reporting for investors and creditors. The information that is produced for investors and creditors must be relevant to them, and the information must be reliable (verifiable). Value in use fails on both counts.

In the invitation to comment on E55, on page 5, it is stated that "if no market exists for the asset, fair value would be estimated in a similar way to value in use as defined in the Exposure Draft." Wrong. That procedure requires the use of the same unreliable (and non-verifiable) information to estimate fair value as would be used to estimate value in use. An estimate of fair value requires the use of information external to the reporting enterprise.

For most assets, information regarding fair value of the asset or a similar asset is available from external sources at a relatively insignificant cost. This is true, for example, of land, land leaseholds, office buildings, apartment buildings, automotive equipment, commercial aircraft, earth-moving equipment, on- and offshore oil and gas drilling rigs, ocean-going vessels, mining equipment, mines, oil and gas reserves, unexplored oil and gas leases, taxicab licenses, fishing licenses, radio stations, TV stations, memberships of stock or commodity exchanges, copyrights, and patents. Even as to unique, one-of-a-kind assets, such as chemical processing plants and refineries, information from external sources about current input and output prices can be used by engineers and other knowledgeable people to estimate fair value of the asset. Only as a last resort, and then only when the cost of getting information from external sources is judged to be too high in relation to the benefit to investors, should a final standard allow for the use of internal, private information to estimate fair value; and, in that case, there should be a requirement for the reporting enterprise to disclose that the estimate of fair value was based on internal information as opposed to external information.

I recommend that the final standard on impairment of assets require that fair value of an asset be compared with the carrying amount of the asset to measure impairment, and that to the extent possible within cost/benefit constraints that fair value be estimated by reference to information external to the reporting enterprise, and that there be required disclosure if the estimate of fair value is made by reference to information internal to the enterprise.

18 Exposure Draft E59: *Provisions, Contingent Liabilities, and Contingent Assets*

The Secretary-General
International Accounting Standards Committee
167 Fleet Street
London EC4A 2ES
United Kingdom
9 September 1997

Dear sir,

This letter concerns the IASC's Exposure Draft E59, *Provisions, Contingent Liabilities, and Contingent Assets*.

The requirement in paragraph 14 to recognize a liability when an enterprise has no realistic alternative but to transfer economic benefits [to another party] is ill-founded and illogical. That idea could be applied in logic to tomorrow's salaries and electricity, resulting in the recognition of a liability today for such items. Maybe the IASC board would say in response that expenditure for tomorrow's salaries and electricity may be avoided by going out of business today and therefore expenditure for those items is not a liability today; if so, the expenditure for refunds to customers described in paragraph 17(a) and the expenditure to remove land contamination described in paragraph 17(b) are also not liabilities today, because those expenditures may be avoided by going out of business today.

Nor is the expenditure for tomorrow's "restructuring" a liability today, because that expenditure may also be avoided by going out of business today, just as tomorrow's expenditure for salaries and electricity may be avoided. Maybe the IASC board would say that expenditure for tomorrow's salaries and electricity is not a liability today because no "past event" will have occurred until employees work and electricity is used. If a past event, an "obligating event," is critical to the recognition of a liability, and I think it is, there will be no such event for the refunds to customers and for removing land contamination described in paragraphs 17(a) and (b) until the enterprise actually disburses cash; no obligating event for those disbursements occurs just because the enterprise says it has a liability because of its "policy," "published policies," or "past actions" as stated in paragraphs 17(a) and (b). (Likewise, there is no obligating event for the additional expenditure for environmental costs because of the company's "higher standard" described in Illustrative Example 3 in Appendix 1.) As well, no obligating event can arise for cash disbursements in "restructurings" until cash is actually disbursed. In short, enterprises should not be allowed to recognize liabilities just because they want to or because they have "policies" or "published policies" or because of their "past actions" or because they have "higher standards."

The "no realistic alternative" idea coupled with "constructive obligation" in paragraphs 16, 17, 18, and 19 will produce liability amounts that managements of some enterprises will recognize but others will not in circumstances that are similar. The liability amounts that may be recognized by those who choose to do so will not be verifiable by outside auditors or anyone else; the amounts simply will be what managements say the amounts are. We have ample evidence in the USA of "restructuring" liabilities that were understated or overstated or did not exist at all because circumstances changed and required either more or less expenditure than management had thought would be required or because management changed its mind and abandoned the "restructuring" altogether.

The ideas of "no realistic alternative" and "constructive obligation" look good outwardly, but they cannot be implemented consistently and comparably by all preparers of financial statements. The ideas should be scrapped. As I said in my letter of 12 February 1997 to you, wherein I commented on the Draft Statement of Principles on *Provisions and Contingencies*, "liabilities should be recognized as such in the balance sheet when transfers of economic benefits are required by law, by contract, or because an enforceable claim exists against the enterprise and the amounts can be measured reliably." Liability recognition based on "no realistic alternative" and "constructive obligation" will produce financial statement amounts that will be optional on the part of the issuer of the financial statement and that cannot be made reliable and should therefore be rejected.

Paragraphs 52, 53, and 85 would allow non-disclosure about provisions and contingencies if such disclosure would be prejudicial to the reporting enterprise in negotiations with another party. Non-public companies may disclose or not disclose anything they wish and deal with their security holders and potential security holders behind closed doors. However, public companies pay a price for being public and raising capital in the public marketplace and having their securities traded publicly; part of that price is that their financial reports must be transparent so that participants in the public marketplace have the necessary information with which to make informed decisions. Accounting standard setters should not superimpose their judgment on how much transparency is enough when parties have opposing interests. Accounting standard setters should require that disclosure which is necessary so that investors may make informed investment decisions. Non-disclosure should not be permitted in any circumstance.

Yours truly,
Walter P. Schuetze

P.S. I commented on the Draft Statement of Principles on *Provisions and Contingencies*; my comments were not accepted by the IASC board in the exposure draft. No doubt, some suggestions of other commentators were also not accepted. The exposure draft would have been a more complete and satisfying document had those comments and suggestions been summarized in the draft along with the board's reasons for not accepting them. I recommend that that be done in the final standard.

19 Exposure Drafts E60: *Intangible Assets*, and E61: *Business Combinations*

The Secretary-General
International Accounting Standards Committee
167 Fleet Street
London EC4A 2ES
United Kingdom
18 September 1997

Dear sir,
This letter concerns the IASC's Exposure Drafts E60, *Intangible Assets*, and E61, *Business Combinations*.

E60: *Intangible Assets*

Internally generated intangibles

This proposed standard, E60, as it relates to internally generated intangible assets, should not be issued in final form. When to recognize an internally generated intangible asset, when to capitalize the cost of the recognized asset, and how to determine that the capitalized cost of an internally generated asset not yet available for use is not in excess of recoverable amount, are so judgmental, so vague, so imprecise, and so open to interpretation that the standard, if issued in final form, will not be a standard except in name. Those enterprises that wish to capitalize costs, or at least some costs, or some costs in some reporting periods but not in other reporting periods, will be able to justify their actions. Those that wish to charge all or most costs to expense will be able to justify their actions. There will be no comparability whatsoever in the accounting from one enterprise to another for internally generated intangible assets. Investors will not be well served.

What then should the IASC board do? IAS 9 on R&D apparently is not working because its application to development costs has the same flaws as this proposed standard; enterprises may recognize development costs as an expense or as an asset, depending on very subjective and judgmental criteria. This proposed standard, E60, will not work. What will work is a requirement to charge to expense when incurred all costs related to internally generated intangible items and purchased goodwill. Two rationales support this approach, both of which fit within the IASC's framework. One rationale is that costs *per se* are not assets and should not be recognized as if they were assets; I have previously corresponded with the IASC in this regard and will not repeat that correspondence here. The other rationale is that the payback – future economic benefits – from expenditure (or fair value of securities issued) for intangible items that are not separable and saleable and for which a fair value therefore cannot be established is so indeterminate and so speculative that expenditure (or fair value of securities issued) for such items should not be represented as an asset. Couple a requirement to charge expenditure for intangible items (or fair value of securities issued) to expense when made with robust disclosure about expenditure (or fair value of securities issued) for intangible items, and investors will be well served and pleased.

Purchased goodwill

I have argued in previous correspondence with the IASC that the cost of purchased goodwill is not an asset. I will not repeat those arguments here. I will, however, respond to the counter-arguments presented by the IASC board in paragraphs 34, 35, and 51–3 of Appendix 3 of E60 in favor of recognizing the cost of goodwill as an asset and not having a separability criterion for the recognition of an asset.

The IAC board says in paragraph 34(a), in part, "the term 'resource' in the definition of an asset in IASC's framework should be interpreted broadly. Goodwill gives an enterprise rights and opportunities to future cash inflows such as the right to operate in a particular business name, the right to use particular premises, the opportunity to deal with existing customers of the business, the opportunity to employ the work-force with its know-how, etc."

I grant that the right to use a "particular name" may in and of itself be valuable, particularly if the name stands alone and its sale to another party may be accomplished without damaging the value of other assets of the enterprise, in which case the name should be recognized as a separate asset. In many cases, however, the name of the acquired enterprise is not used by the acquiring enterprise, and the old name disappears; there is obviously no value to the name in that case.

The value of the right to use "particular premises" is captured in the value of land or land leasehold and is included in the fair value assigned to the identifiable asset land or land leasehold, so there is no additional goodwill value in particular premises.

"Existing customers" of the business are not controlled by the business, as those customers may come and go as they please. The IASC board itself acknowledges in example B in paragraph 15 of the standard that banks' deposit customers are not controlled and therefore the so-called "core deposit" does not meet the definition of an intangible asset. (In example C of paragraph 15, the

IASC board also says that customer loyalty does not meet the definition of an intangible asset.) It is completely illogical to say that because deposit customers, no matter how loyal, are not controlled (control being a key part of the definition of an asset) the so-called core deposit intangible, if generated internally, may not be recognized as an asset but then to say in the next breath that the core deposit intangible must be recognized as an intangible asset called goodwill if the core deposit intangible is acquired through a purchase business combination.

The "existing workforce" as well is not controlled by the acquiree, and therefore the IASC board itself would not permit an asset to be recognized by the acquiree for developing that workforce (see example C in paragraph 15 of the standard). But if an existing workforce is acquired, then the IASC board says that the workforce is controlled and the asset must be recognized in the name of goodwill. Not logical.

In paragraph 34(b), the IASC board says "(b) the cost of goodwill is incurred willingly only because the access to future cash flows from the mix of the various rights and opportunities mentioned above [paragraph 34(a)] is effectively controlled by the acquirer. Control over goodwill, that is the power to obtain the future economic benefits from goodwill, can be exercised to ensure that the benefits from the mix of rights and opportunities acquired are received by the acquirer." I really do not know what to make of those words. It strikes me that the IASC board is saying something like "I breathe, therefore I control the air that I breathe."

In paragraph 35, the IASC board says "Some argue that whether or not goodwill meets the definition of an asset is not so important if the recognition of goodwill as an asset is a pragmatic and acceptable solution that settles a debate that went on at IASC for many years in the recent past." What this statement acknowledges is that indeed there has been and is contention within the IASC as to whether the cost of goodwill should be recognized as an asset, which calls into question why the IASC board says in paragraph 29 of Appendix 3 that it does not currently intend to reconsider the requirement for the recognition of goodwill as an asset. What this statement also says is that the IASC board (or some delegations to the board) will ignore its own definition of an asset in its own framework when the definition produces a result that is undesirable. How then are the IASC's constituents to view the definitions of an asset and a liability in the IASC's framework? Should constituents continue to look to the definitions for guidance? If the IASC will be guided by the definitions only when the result is deemed acceptable by the number of votes that it will attract a political solution, then should not IASC explicitly rescind its framework and go back to developing solutions to accounting problems on an *ad hoc* basis and so inform its constituents?

In paragraphs 34(c) and 51–3, the IASC board says that "separability" is not a criterion for asset recognition, because it is not a criterion set out in the framework (the framework is meaningful when the board wants it to be?) and no separability criterion exists or is even mentioned in IAS 16 on property, plant, and equipment. If separability is not a criterion for asset recognition, why is the board requiring in paragraphs 18 and 20 of the standard that future economic benefits must be *specifically attributable* to an asset in order for its recognition as an asset? I cannot think of an asset that will produce economic benefits specifically attributable to it and yet not be separable from the enterprise as a whole and transferable to another party for cash or other economic benefit. I would also point out that the framework is silent about separability; the criterion is not required to be met for asset recognition; nor does the framework say that things which are not separable may qualify for recognition as assets. The Board's reference to the framework is a *non sequitur*.

Saying that separability is not a criterion for recognition of property, plant, and equipment as an asset and therefore should not be a requirement for recognition of intangible assets, including goodwill, is a false argument. By their very nature, individual items of PP&E are separable. No one would even conceive of some item of PP&E not being separable, although some items would perhaps be separable only together as a unit. For example, a coal mine in the mountains needs a railroad to get the coal to market, so the coal mine and the railroad go together as an economic unit, but the economic unit – the thing that produces cash flows – is separable and transferable to another party for cash. That is impossible to do for goodwill unless one considers that the entire business to which the goodwill relates is considered separable. One could of course consider the entire business as the economic unit, but in that case the balance sheet would show the investment in the business as the asset not the individual assets and liabilities of the business. If the reporting enterprise is an investment company, then of course the asset of that enterprise is its investments in common stocks and its income is dividends plus or minus changes in value of its investment; but if the reporting enterprise is an operating company, then its assets are the individual operating assets that produce cash flows, and goodwill obviously is not one of those assets, for it produces no cash flow. And, obviously, the proposed standard is directed toward operating companies, not investment companies.

Finally, regarding separability, I do not understand the example of a license to operate a radio station set out in paragraph 53. The implication is that the license to operate the radio station and the transmitting equipment are not separable; I think that is not the case, at least in the USA. Radio licenses are transferable, with or without the transmitting equipment.

To sum up, the IASC board's arguments for recognizing the cost of goodwill as an asset are not strong.

E61: *Business Combinations*

Negative goodwill

In paragraph 51 of E61, the IASC board says, in part, "To the extent that negative goodwill relates to expectations of future losses and expenses that are identified in the acquirer's plan for the acquisition and can be measured reliably, but which do not represent identifiable liabilities at the date of acquisition …

that portion of negative goodwill should be recognized in income when the future losses and expenses occur."

The quoted words are an open invitation for issuers to manipulate their income after an acquisition. The words say that the amounts of future losses or expenses must be reliably measurable. But the amounts of future losses and expenses, because of their very nature, cannot be made reliable and will not be verifiable by outside auditors or anyone else. Issuers will say that such and such are the amounts of losses and expenses that are expected, and outside auditors will not be able to challenge those amounts. Then, in future quarters, half-years, and years, issuers will be able to release those amounts into income at will, and again outside auditors will not be able to challenge the amounts released. Investors will be misled.

The words quoted above from paragraph 51, and the words in paragraph 51(a), are an admission by the IASC board that negative goodwill does not meet the IASC's definition of a liability in its framework, yet the amount of negative goodwill will be displayed in the balance sheet as a liability. Why does the IASC board not follow its definition of a liability in its own framework? Should the IASC's constituents continue to look to the IASC's framework for guidance? The IASC's constituents will not know what is going on.

This proposed standard, E61, should not be issued in final form.

Yours truly,
Walter P. Schuetze

20 Business combinations and intangible assets

Director of Research and Technical Activities
File No. 201-A
Financial Accounting Standards Board
401 Merritt 7; P.O. Box 5116
Norwalk, CT 06856-5116
15 June 2000

Dear sir,

Business Combinations and Intangible Assets

This letter is a late response to the FASB's September 1999 exposure draft on accounting for business combinations and intangible assets.

At a meeting that I attended last month with Mr Jenkins and Mr Lucas, Chair and Director of Research, respectively, of the FASB, there was a discussion about the FASB's exposure draft and the accounting for the cost of purchased goodwill. In an exchange with Mr Jenkins, I said, in jest, that it would be OK for the cost of purchased goodwill to be recognized as an asset by an acquirer of another company or business "for a moment" before the cost is written off by the acquiring company. I retract that statement.

I think that the cost of purchased goodwill can never be an asset, not even for a moment. After subtracting from the purchase price of a company or a business the fair value of the acquired identifiable net assets (assets minus liabilities), the remaining amount of the purchase price is called cost of purchased goodwill. It is the amount left over. In a word, a glob. A glob of cost. It is a cost, only a cost, and nothing more. The glob should be charged to expense at the date of acquisition of the company or business.

The glob does not and cannot meet the FASB's own definition of an asset in Concepts Statement 6, paragraph 25: "Assets are probable future economic benefits obtained or controlled by a particular entity." A cost cannot be controlled. I paid $22,000 for my Buick automobile. I control my Buick. I can let it sit in my garage. I can sell it. I can use it to drive to work. I can lend it or lease it to someone else to use as a taxicab or drive to work. I can pledge it as collateral for a bank loan. I can give it to my grandson. Or the church. But there is no interpretation of the word "control" that says I control the $22,000. What I control is the Buick.

The FASB's definition of an asset requires that there be future economic benefit controlled by the reporting entity. As to the glob of cost of purchased goodwill, the board says, in paragraph 184 of the exposure draft, that it "concluded that control is provided by means of the acquiring enterprise's ability to direct the policies and management of the acquired enterprise." That is faulty thinking. The purchase price of a company or a business, to the extent it exceeds the fair value of the acquired identifiable net assets (which fair values can be verified by reference to the marketplace), represents the buyer's judgment about the present value of the future cash inflows of that company or business in excess of the fair value of the acquired identifiable net assets. Those future cash inflows can come from only one source: sales of goods and services to customers. Whether and in what amount or degree those customers will, in the future, buy goods and services from the reporting enterprise will be determined by those customers, not by the reporting enterprise. The reporting enterprise obviously does not control its customers' purchasing decisions. Thus the control element of the FASB's own definition is not met as to the glob.

It is instructive to look at what the FASB itself said about "control" in paragraph 184 of Concepts Statement 6:

> an asset of an entity is the future economic benefit that the entity can control and thus can, within limits set by the nature of the benefit or the entity's right to it, use as it pleases. The entity having an asset is the one that can exchange it, use it to produce goods or services, exact a price for others' use of it, use it to settle liabilities, hold it, or perhaps distribute it to owners.

The glob cannot be exchanged for anything; nobody would give a farthing for it; no creditor would accept the glob in settlement of a debt; no banker would accept the glob as collateral for a loan; the glob cannot be held the way things generally are held, for example, the way one holds inventory or land or bonds; the glob cannot be loaned or leased to anyone; the glob cannot be used to make anything that might be sold to others; the glob cannot be given to the Red Cross; and, finally, the glob cannot be distributed to shareholders. Thus the glob of cost of purchased goodwill does not meet a single one of the features of "control" of an asset that the FASB itself has described. Why won't the FASB eat its own cooking?

Following the FASB's approach to accounting for the glob, balance sheets of acquiring enterprises will look like dirigibles, filled with the hot air of the glob of cost of purchased goodwill. Investors will be misled into thinking that the glob has value as a real and separate asset when nothing could be further from the truth. The board would have recoverability of the amount of the glob be assessed pursuant to the procedures set out in FASB Statement 121, *Accounting for the Impairment of Long-Lived Assets and for Long-Lived Assets to Be Disposed of.* Auditors will be unable to determine whether the glob of cost of purchased goodwill is recoverable under Statement 121. Recoverability of the glob of cost of purchased goodwill cannot be verified by an auditor by reference to any competent, evidential matter whatsoever (an audit requirement). Management of the reporting enterprise can put numbers on a piece of paper or a computer monitor about its estimate of future earnings of the business or net assets acquired, but those numbers, which cannot be refuted or verified by the auditor, are not competent, evidential matter on which an auditor can base an opinion. (If the auditor is allowed to rely on management's assertion about the value of that which is called an asset instead of having to find competent, evidential matter from sources outside the reporting company regarding that value, then an audit has no worth. Scrap audits. Just accept the opinion of corporate management about the value of the reporting company's assets. Save the cost of audits.) Nor can recoverability of the glob of cost of purchased goodwill be assessed by an auditor by reference to a quoted market price or a price in a real market transaction. The glob does not exist in the marketplace and does not trade.

Incidentally, assessing whether the glob of cost of purchased goodwill is recoverable (or impaired) by reference to management's projection, no matter how distant (as far as the eye can see), of future undiscounted cash flows, as the board proposes and as set forth in FASB Statement 121, is a very bad idea. In practice today, under Statement 121, there are many examples where the glob was not written down or off until the soul had departed the body. That is so because management-determined undiscounted future cash flows almost always will be in excess of the amount of the glob, thus making the glob "recoverable" unless management itself decides otherwise. That practice will continue if the exposure draft becomes final.

When, ultimately, reporting enterprises have to write off the glob because of business downturns, because too much was paid in an acquisition, or for many other possible reasons, everyone will be damaged. The reporting enterprise will lose credibility in the marketplace. Auditors will be said to have been negligent or worse in the conduct of their audits; cries of "Where were the auditors?" will be heard. But it will be investors, investors who relied on the number in the balance sheet for the glob as a fit and proper asset, who will take the hit. The FASB should not let that happen. The FASB is supposed to be the investor's guardian.

I recommend that the FASB withdraw the exposure draft. Issuing the document in final form will be a huge mistake. If the FASB goes forward with the accounting for the glob as proposed in the exposure draft, the FASB will be inundated by a tsunami of rejection. Rejection by executive and line managers of corporations, boards of directors and audit committees of corporations, analysts, investors, creditors, underwriters, journalists, editors, and ultimately Congress.

There are, at bottom, two fundamental, confounding problems in today's accounting that are embedded in the exposure draft. Those two problems are that (1) the FASB's definition of an asset does not require that the thing called an asset, whatever it is, be exchangeable, that is, convertible into cash, and (2) in practice, with some exceptions for financial instruments and derivatives, writing up assets to fair value is not permitted. The first of these allows the presentation and representation of all kinds of junk as assets. Examples of such junk are the costs of direct-response advertising, the cost of bounties paid by Internet service providers to original equipment manufacturers for referrals of Internet subscribers (sometimes "paid" in stock not cash), and the costs of future advertising or other services purchased by one dot.com from another dot.com (often "paid" in stock not cash). In none of these cases is the junk something or anything that the reporting enterprise controls. The junk is spent money – money that is gone. Whether those expenditures of cash (or issuance of stock) will produce future net cash inflows is a matter that the company's customers will decide if and when they buy the reporting enterprise's goods and services; those customers' purchasing decisions obviously are not controlled by the reporting enterprise. The reporting enterprise cannot sell the junk, pay off a bank debt with it, pledge it to a bank, lend it or lease it to someone else, give it to the Red Cross, or pay a dividend with it. In short, it is junk that only an FASB accountant would call an asset. The FASB now proposes to anoint the glob of cost of purchased goodwill as another junk asset, perhaps the premier junk asset, but return of and return on investment with respect to all of that junk depends on the company's customers – customers whose purchasing decisions obviously are not controlled by the company that reports the junk as an asset. No control equals no asset. All of that junk would disappear from corporate balance sheets if the FASB required that things must be convertible into cash in order to be presented and represented as assets in corporate balance sheets. Something that ordinary folks such as CEOs, line operating managers, boards of directors and audit committees, analysts, investors, creditors, underwriters, journalists, editors, and US representatives and senators would understand.

The second problem is that in practice real assets, exchangeable things such as inventory, land, buildings, copyrights, and patents, are not written up to fair value except in the case of a business combination accounted for as a purchase. So what happens is that when one company acquires another, one company's real assets, for example, inventory, land, buildings, copyrights, and patents, are written up to fair value, but those of the other company are not. If Exxon buys Mobil, then Mobil's oil and gas reserves are written up to current fair value but not Exxon's. If Glaxo buys Wellcome, then Wellcome's patents are written up to fair value but not Glaxo's. The result is a balance sheet potpourri with some asset amounts being old, ancient, irrelevant amounts and others being current, relevant fair values all jumbled together, thereby obscuring the relevant new fair values. The prohibition in practice of writing up assets to fair value is, in large part, the responsibility of the Securities and Exchange Commission. In the early days of the commission, and more recent days as well, the staff of the commission has balked at writing up assets to fair value, saying that the numbers are too soft. Well, nowadays assets are being valued every day. Those valuations are being used in negotiating deals, in Internet auctions, and in accounting for bulk acquisitions of assets. The Commission's staff needs to step over the threshold of the new millennium and remove its objection to writing up assets to fair value.

Pooling-of-interest accounting was invented in part in response to the problem of not being able to write up assets to current fair value. Thus, for example, Exxon's and Mobil's and Glaxo's and Wellcome's old historical costs of assets could be added together using pooling accounting and the balance sheet asset amounts would have at least comparability if not relevance. If, instead, all assets were adjusted periodically to fair value, then when Exxon and Mobil or two dot.coms combine, two sets of real assets – both at fair value – would simply be added together. The FASB could call the accounting for such a business combination a "fair value pooling of interests," thus retaining the concept of pooling and simultaneously eliminating the glob of cost of purchased goodwill and attendant income statement amortization of the glob, and thereby make CEOs, line operating managers, boards of directors and audit committees, analysts, investors, creditors, underwriters, journalists, editors, and everyone else happy. The FASB could then celebrate victory in the war over accounting for business combinations and the glob.

I think that assets to be shown in corporate balance sheets should be defined as (1) cash, (2) claims to cash, for example an account or loan receivable, (3) that which can be sold for cash, for example, land, inventory, equipment, buildings, stocks, patents, copyrights, oil and gas reserves, salmon farms in Scotland, shoe factories in Brazil, semiconductor factories in Taiwan, seats on the New York Stock Exchange, and hack licenses issued by New York city, and (4) derivative contracts having a positive value to the holder, which value can be converted into cash by entering into an equal and offsetting contract. I think that all assets presented in corporate balance sheets should be stated at fair value, which is the amount of cash that the asset would fetch in an immediate sale for cash even if that sale were under duress. If the FASB defined assets as I suggest, and required them to be valued as I suggest, the controversy over pooling-of-interests accounting and accounting for the glob would disappear.

The question arises: should accounting abandon historical costs in favor of current fair values of assets? Answer: yes. Accounting must come into the new millennium. Current fair values of assets are obviously relevant to investors, creditors, and underwriters. Old, historical costs of assets are obviously not relevant to investors, creditors, and underwriters. Accountants should do things that help investors, creditors, and underwriters to make decisions. Getting fair values of assets will not be as easy as looking in the *Wall Street Journal* or *The Financial Times* and finding the price of many assets. It will take more work and money. But if that were done, the balance sheet would be relevant instead of what it is today – a dimly lit basement parking garage for a collection of antique costs. The balance sheet would become a living document – a relevant document.

A final question arises: how about just staying with the status quo as some have urged? Answer: no. The combination of using historical costs of assets and mergers and acquisitions of businesses causes so much friction that it is clear that the FASB must do something to fix the problem. I think that the FASB should define assets as I suggest and prescribe that all assets be presented at fair value in corporate balance sheets. There is no other solution to the problem of accounting for business combinations and the glob.

Under the status quo, the accounting for a business combination as a pooling of interests is subject to such a welter of ambiguous and uncertain rules that corporate issuers must, as a practical matter, pre-clear their accounting for business combinations as poolings with the staff of the Securities and Exchange Commission or potentially face restatements of financial statements. This situation subjects corporate issuers to the idiosyncratic judgment of the incumbent chief accountant to the commission or the incumbent chief accountant of the commission's Division of Corporation Finance. Accounting standards should be clear. Corporate issuers and accountants in New York, Hong Kong, London, Paris, Tokyo, and elsewhere should be able to account for business combinations without having to consult the commission's staff.

Moreover, many business combination transactions that would qualify for pooling-of-interest accounting can be engineered so as to achieve purchase accounting along with the resultant write-up of assets and recognition as an asset of the glob.

Thus, in many cases, pooling accounting is optional as a practical matter, which is not good public policy. We should not have either/or accounting. Still further, the pooling rules say that *bona fide* business transactions, such as treasury stock acquisitions, can preclude pooling accounting; accounting rules should not stand in the way of business transactions. And, under the status quo, the commission's staff often disagrees with the amounts allocated to in-process research and development and intangible assets other than the glob. The staff also often disagrees with the lives assigned by corporate issuers to the glob (and certain other intangible assets) for amortization of those asset amounts and often requires restatement of the financial statements. The upshot is that many corporate issuers and their auditors are not sure that their accounting for a business combination as a pooling and their accounting for the cost of intangible assets and the glob, and subsequent amortization, will pass muster at the Securities and Exchange Commission without an advance "no objection" from the staff. That's no way to run a railroad.

RECOMMENDATION: WITHDRAW THE EXPOSURE DRAFT AND START OVER.

Yours truly,
Walter P. Schuetze

P.S. According to the FASB's Action Alert 00-21, dated 7 June 2000, the board is considering whether to allow the glob to sit on balance sheets without income statement amortization thereof so long as its value is sustained by continuing investment in the acquired business; the glob would be considered impaired when the rate of profitability is permanently below that necessary to sustain the original acquisition value.

The assumptions and judgments made by management of a corporate issuer to make those determinations will be highly subjective. No auditor will be able to refute or verify the assumptions and judgments made by management and the resulting numbers. Great big globs – unauditable globs – will sit on balance sheets. Investors will be misled into thinking that those globs are fit and proper assets.

21 Accounting for the impairment or disposal of long-lived assets and for obligations associated with disposal activities

Director of Research and Technical Activities
File Reference 210-D
Financial Accounting Standards Board
P.O. Box 5116
Norwalk, CT 06586-5116
7 November 2000

Dear sir,
This letter concerns the board's proposed statement of financial accounting standards entitled *Accounting for the Impairment or Disposal of Long-Lived Assets and for Obligations Associated with Disposal Activities*.

Asset to be held and used

As to an asset to be held and used, the proposed statement would require that an impairment loss not be recognized so long as [estimated] undiscounted cash flows from the use and eventual disposal of the asset exceed the carrying amount of the asset even though the selling price of the asset is less than the carrying amount (paragraph 11). Those (estimated) undiscounted cash flows would be the entity's own estimates, not those of market participants (paragraph 120). The proposed statement provides that the asset be tested for impairment when events and changes in circumstances indicate that the carrying amount may not be recoverable and gives six examples that indicate that carrying amount may not be recoverable (paragraph 13) (this proposed standard is substantially the same as the standard currently embodied in FASB Statement 121). The upshot is that impairment losses will be recognized if and when, and only if and when, management decides to recognize those losses. Outside auditors will be unable to challenge a failure by management to recognize impairment losses on a timely basis just as under FASB Statement 121 because they will be unable to demonstrate that management's estimates are wrong and thus require recognition of impairment losses. When I was on staff at the Securities and Exchange Commission, I saw this happen many times under FASB Statement 121, and it no doubt will continue to happen using the standard in the proposed statement.

In fact, under FASB Statement 121, impairment losses often are not recognized until assets are disposed of, although the fact of loss is known long before disposal. The standard in the proposed statement is no standard at all. The board should not go forward with the proposed statement. Moreover, the board should rescind FASB Statement 121.

I think that the reported amount of every non-cash asset, to be relevant, ought to be the estimated selling price of the asset minus the estimated cost of selling it. In my scheme of things, the reported amounts of assets would be written up and down based on market prices. I can understand a standard that says reported amounts of assets ought never to be written up above original cost and always ought to be written down to market price, although I don't agree with that idea, because it results in financial statements containing irrelevant and potentially misleading information when market price is above cost no matter that the reported amount is described as being cost and no matter how fulsome that description is. But what I can't understand and what can't be explained to investors is a non-standard – one that says that reported asset amounts may be determined by management of the enterprise and not by economic events or conditions.

The board says that its answer is practical not conceptual (paragraph 115). But what the board does not acknowledge and cannot rationalize or defend is the practical result – the result that I saw when I was on staff at the Securities and Exchange Commission. That is, impairment losses are recognized when the management of the reporting entity wants to recognize the losses, including when assets are disposed of, which is also a management choice, not when the value of the asset actually declines below cost. Timing of impairment loss recognition based on management discretion instead of when the economic event of a decline in value occurs results in financial statements that are not credible.

If the board is unwilling at this time to require that all non-cash assets be marked to market, up or down, then the board ought at least to require that impairment losses be recognized whenever the carrying amount is greater than market price.

The board has proposed with respect to certain intangible assets that an impairment loss be recognized when the carrying amount of the intangible asset exceeds its observed market price (see paragraph 50 of the board's proposed Statement of Financial Accounting Standards entitled *Business Combinations and Intangible Assets*, dated 7 September 1999). It is incongruous, grotesquely incongruous, for the board to require the recognition of an impairment loss for an intangible asset when the carrying amount is in excess of its observed market price but at the same time to require that no impairment loss be recognized for a tangible asset when management-projected undiscounted cash flows exceed the carrying amount of the asset, even though an observable market price for the asset is less than its carrying amount. (Tangible assets have observable market prices just as intangible assets have observable market prices.) Consider the following example. Company X owns a medallion issued by New York city, which medallion allows Company X to operate a taxicab in New York city. Company

X's carrying amount (cost) of the medallion is $250,000. The market price of the medallion falls to $240,000 because of an increase in the price of fuel, which cannot be offset by an increase in taxi fares until New York city approves an increase, which may take a year or longer. Company X's carrying amount (cost) of the taxicab (a Ford automobile) is $20,000. The market price of the taxicab is $18,000. The projected undiscounted cash flows from operating the taxicab are in excess of $20,000, say $30,000. Company X would be precluded from recognizing an impairment loss of $2,000 with respect to the taxicab but would be required to recognize an impairment loss of $10,000 with respect to the medallion. That answer does not make sense.

Impairment losses for both tangible and intangible assets ought to be recognized when the carrying amount of the asset exceeds market price.

Obligations associated with disposal activities

The board's definition of a liability in Concepts Statement 6 requires that there be a "present obligation" in order for there to be a recognizable liability. But the three "conditions" set out in paragraph 49 of the proposed statement apparently allow for the recognition of a liability before there is a "present obligation" to pay cash (or transfer some other asset) to an obligee. This is evident (1) in paragraph 54, where the board would allow for the recognition of a liability by an employer to employees for termination benefits before their termination, although the employees must work until they are terminated in order to receive the termination benefits and (2) in paragraph 56, where the board would allow for the recognition of a liability by a lessee to a lessor for lease termination costs before the lease is terminated by the lessee. Until the employees are terminated or the lease is terminated, there is no "present obligation" for the reporting entity to pay cash (or transfer some other asset); until the employees are terminated or the lease is terminated, the obligation to pay cash (or transfer some other asset) is optional and at the discretion of the reporting entity. The board's own definition of a liability requires that there be a "present obligation" in order for there to be a recognizable liability. The board should respect its own definition.

Liabilities ought not be recognizable by reporting entities when their managements say so, which is what the three "conditions" in paragraph 49 apparently amount to. We have seen enough downright awful earnings management under Consensuses 94-3 and 95-3 issued by the FASB's Emerging Issues Task Force, in which liabilities may be recognized when managements of reporting entities want to and then reversed when those managements want to. The FASB itself should not issue a standard that will allow this shoddy, reprehensible practice to continue.

Yours truly,
Walter P. Schuetze

22 Business combinations and intangible assets

Accounting for goodwill

Director of Research and Technical Activities
File Reference No. 201-R
Financial Accounting Standards Board
401 Merritt 7; P.O. Box 5116
Norwalk, CT 06586-5116
16 March 2001

Dear sir,
This letter is in response to the FASB's 14 February 2001 limited revision of exposure draft issued 7 September 1999, entitled *Business Combinations and Intangible Assets – Accounting for Goodwill.*

Cost of goodwill is not an asset

The board continues to assert that the cost of goodwill is an asset. The board notes in paragraph 46, with apparent approval, that respondents to the 7 September 1999 exposure draft said "goodwill is an asset because it is paid for and future benefits are expected to arise from it in conjunction with the future benefits from other assets." Just because something was "paid for" does not make it an asset. I remind the board that in its own words in paragraph 179 in its own Concepts Statement 6 "costs incurred are not themselves assets."

As for the second statement by respondents in support of the cost of goodwill as an asset, namely that "future benefits are expected to arise from it in conjunction with the future benefits from other assets": that description is the description of a contingent gain. Contingent gains are not recognized as assets until realized. We don't count tomorrow's profits as assets today even if we paid for them. Those profits have yet to be earned. Indeed, we see many situations – the acquisition of a money manager is a prime example – where there are no "other assets" to speak of, where the only thing "paid for" is future profits. But that's precisely, exactly what the glob of cost called goodwill represents – expected, hoped-for future profits. Future profits aren't assets until they are earned and are in hand in the form of cash or something that can be converted into cash.

A critical feature of that which is reported as an asset is that it must be controlled by the enterprise that reports it as an asset. Future profits obviously are not controlled by the reporting enterprise. Whether future profits ever materialize depends on whether customers buy the reporting enterprise's goods and services and then, crucially, whether the selling price yields a profit. As I have argued in prior correspondence with the board (see my letter of 15 June 2000), the glob of cost called goodwill does not qualify as an asset.

If the FASB goes forward with this exposure draft, auditing the recoverability or "impairment" of the glob of cost called goodwill will be extremely difficult. Many of the "examples of events or circumstances that would require goodwill of a reporting unit to be tested for impairment" set out in paragraph 18 of the exposure draft are so subjective that the external auditor will often have no traction to require a client to test the glob of cost called goodwill for impairment. Add to that (1) the fact that the board will allow for organic goodwill (internally generated goodwill), previously unrecognized as an asset, to be recognized by silent and undisclosed stealth merger with purchased goodwill (see paragraphs 69 and 70), thereby effectively recognizing organic goodwill of some immeasurable amount as an addition to the cost of purchased goodwill; and (2) through a "reorganization" of reporting units (see paragraph 14), a strong reporting unit, having recognized or previously unrecognized goodwill, may be reorganized with a weak reporting unit having recognized but impaired cost of purchased goodwill, thereby propping up the impaired glob of cost of goodwill. What will happen is that unauditable individual globs of cost called goodwill will turn into an unauditable amorphous sludge of goodwill that will be written down because of "impairment" when and only when management of the reporting enterprise decides that the time is right for a write-down. That's no way to run a railroad. Investors will be misled.

Maybe my difference of opinion with the board about what the glob of cost called goodwill is represents a different view of what kind of financial statements should be presented to investors. There is no doubt, and I agree, that the owner of an investment in a business controls that investment. If the financial statements are to show the investment in a business, and the results of holding that investment, then the balance sheet will show a one-line item representing the investment, and the income statement or statement of changes will show dividends flowing from that investment and changes in the fair value of that investment. That is the way an investment, and the results of holding an investment, are shown in the financial statements of an investment company or holding company.

However, today's financial statement presentations are those of operating companies, not investment companies or holding companies. In the financial statements of an operating company, the investment itself is not portrayed. Instead, the individual operating assets of the business, such as marketable securities, loans, inventory, land, plant, equipment, mines, patents, and copyrights are portrayed. And the results of holding and using those individual operating assets are portrayed as operating revenue and operating expenses and operating cash flows, for it is those individual operating assets that generate cash flow; the glob does not and cannot generate cash flow. It is in the balance sheet of an operating company that the glob does not satisfy the control criterion even though that criterion is met in the balance sheet of an investment company or holding company as to the investment itself.

Words and what words represent are crucially important. It is a vast difference to call an investment in a business an asset as compared with profits that are yet to be earned. An investment in a business is controlled; it can be sold; it can be pledged as collateral; it can be given to charity; it can be distributed to shareholders. Not so with future profits. Profits that are yet to be earned cannot be assets today.

What the FASB could do is require a financial statement presentation as follows: a balance sheet showing the enterprise's investments in its various businesses and a statement of changes showing the cash dividends from those businesses and the changes in fair value of the enterprise's investments in those businesses, accompanied by balance sheets of the various businesses showing the operating assets (no glob called goodwill) and liabilities of those businesses and statements of changes for those businesses showing the operating revenues, operating expenses, and operating cash inflows and outflows of those businesses and changes in fair values of the operating assets and liabilities. That kind of presentation would have great transparency – a highly desirable objective – and would be very revealing and rich in informational content. Investors would be enthralled with such information; they would wallow in it. I would support such a presentation.

Acquired identifiable intangible assets

Paragraphs 5(a) and (b) set out criteria for the separate recognition of acquired identifiable intangible assets as follows:

a Control over the future economic benefits of the asset results from contractual or other legal rights (regardless of whether those rights are transferable or separable from other rights and obligations).

b The asset is capable of being separated or divided and sold, transferred, licensed, rented, or exchanged (regardless of whether there is an intent to do so or whether a market currently exists for that asset).

Paragraph 5 goes on as follows: "An intangible asset that cannot be sold, transferred, licensed, or exchanged individually meets criterion (b) if it can be sold, transferred, licensed, rented, or exchanged along with a group of related assets or liabilities. For example, although a financial institution depositor relationship cannot be transferred apart from the related deposits, it meets criterion (b) and should be recognized separately from goodwill."

Given the words in parentheses, I do not know what paragraph (a) means, and the basis for conclusions is no help. If an item is not transferable, how can it have a fair value? The term "fair value" means that something has a cash price. That which is not transferable cannot have a cash price. How can that which does not have a fair value (cash price) possibly qualify for separate recognition as an asset? The board needs to explain what that paragraph means. Better yet, delete it.

As to paragraph (b), how can the board possibly conclude that a "financial institution depositor relationship" meets the requirement of "control" in the board's own definition of an asset in Concepts Statement 6? Depositors' actions cannot be controlled by the financial institution where depositors keep their money. Demand depositors can withdraw their money at the drop of a hat without penalty. Time depositors can withdraw their money at the end of the term of the deposit without penalty. Even if time depositors withdraw their money before the term expires, the amount of any penalty is not earned until the depositor surrenders the amount of the penalty. What the value of a depositor relationship represents is the future profits to be earned by putting the depositor's money to work and earning a return over and above the return promised to the depositor and the costs of handling the depositor's money and the cost of insurance of deposits in the case of financial institutions in the USA. Again, future profits, just like goodwill.

What good does it do for the board to have a definition of an asset in its conceptual framework if it does not respect and follow that definition in the standards that the board itself issues? How can board members go around the country, indeed, the world, trumpeting the merits and usefulness of the board's conceptual framework when apparently the definition of an asset in that conceptual framework is not binding on the board itself. If the board does not like its definition of an asset, then it should put forth a new definition for review and comment by the public. I think that investors, the Securities and Exchange Commission, other federal and state regulators, Congress, and the public at large would welcome and benefit from a simple definition of an asset along the lines that I have suggested in published articles of which the board is well aware.

I think the FASB should scrap this project altogether. I think the FASB should go back to first principles. I recommend that the FASB undertake forthwith a re-examination of its definition of an asset with a view to including the feature of exchangeability in the definition, as I have recommended in published articles. In other words, require that for something to be reported as an asset that that something must be exchangeable for cash. Were the FASB to change the definition of an asset to include the feature of exchangeability, standard setting would get a lot easier. Auditing of financial statements by external auditors would improve immensely, because the FASB-approved junk in financial statements today can't be audited: for example, cost of direct response advertising, deferred tax assets, and now goodwill, to name just some of the FASB-approved junk that can't be audited. Financial reporting would take a quantum stride forward. Investors would be better off.

Yours truly,
Walter P. Schuetze

23 The FASB and accounting for goodwill

The FASB published the Statement of Financial Accounting Standards No. 142, *Goodwill and Other Intangible Assets*, in June 2001. That document was preceded by an exposure draft published by the FASB in October 1999 and a second exposure draft published by the FASB in February 2001.

The next document, dated 30 April 2001, was submitted by Walter P. Schuetze to the editor of *Barron's* magazine, but the editor did not publish it.

Brace yourself. This piece is about accounting. Be brave.

Since 1950, companies have accounted for stock-for-stock acquisitions of other companies as poolings. In 1970, the Accounting Principles Board, which was replaced by the FASB in 1973, issued very detailed, arbitrary rules that have to be followed in order for pooling accounting to be used in stock-for-stock deals. If those rules are not met in stock deals or if an acquisition is done with cash or debt, purchase accounting is required. In purchase accounting, the acquired company's tangible assets such as land and equipment and identifiable intangible assets such as patents and copyrights are revalued upward or downward to market, and any remaining purchase price is called goodwill, which is reported as an asset and written down over a period of up to forty years. Now, in 2001, the FASB proposes to do away with poolings. It also proposes that goodwill no longer be written down each reporting period but remain on the balance sheet and be assessed periodically for "impairment." If impaired, then goodwill would be written down or written off by way of a charge to operating earnings.

In my opinion, the FASB is repeating the mistake that the Accounting Principles Board made in 1970 when it concluded that goodwill is an asset.

Is goodwill an asset? Before answering, we need to ask what an asset is. The FASB defines assets in paragraph 25 of its Concepts Statement 6 as "probable future economic benefits obtained or controlled by a particular entity as a result of past transactions or events." Paragraph 25 is then followed by six paragraphs containing 612 words explaining what the words in paragraph 25 mean. There are 330,000 CPAs who are members of the American Institute of Certified Public Accountants; 329,000 of them don't understand the FASB's definition of an asset. Only FASB accountants know what it means, but they can't explain it in plain English that my sister, who runs a successful business, can understand. Using FASB jargon, a thing that my sister, other business people, and 329,000 CPAs call a truck is not an asset; the asset is the present value of the cash flows that can be earned by using the truck to haul lumber or bread, *viz.* the "probable future economic benefit." Thus abstractions instead of real things are assets.

I say that assets ought to be defined as real things, not abstractions. Call a truck a truck, not an abstract probable future economic benefit. I define assets by reference to CASH – something my sister understands. I define assets as (1) CASH, (2) claims to CASH, for example accounts and notes receivable, and (3) things that can be sold for CASH, for example trucks, land, oil and gas reserves, marketable securities, and patents. DO YOU UNDERSTAND MY DEFINITION?

What is goodwill? Take an example. DEF pays 100 cash for XYZ. XYZ has real assets worth 65; 35 then is goodwill. What is the 35? The 35 is the amount of cash that DEF paid for hoped-for profits that it may earn from future sales of goods and services. The FASB says the 35 is an asset because DEF "paid for it." Since when are hoped-for future profits assets today, even if we paid for them? Never. Dozens of cash outlays are made every day with the expectation and hope of future profit: advertising, R&D, operating new stores or branches at a loss, training new employees, retraining existing employees, and restructuring businesses are just a few of the things that are done and paid for today with the expectation and hope of profit tomorrow. But we don't call those cash outlays assets. The cash is gone; no one would call that spent cash an asset. But that's what the FASB says to do with the 35 – call it an asset. I say "nuts." Try to sell the 35. Try to borrow money using the 35 as collateral. Try to pay bills with the 35. Try to give the 35 to the Red Cross. Try to pay a dividend with the 35. It won't work.

The FASB also says the 35 is an asset because "future benefits are expected from it [goodwill] in conjunction with the future benefit expected from other assets." I would point out that the market value of the "other assets," the 65, already reflects the full earning power of those assets. Moreover, those quoted words sound like hoped-for future profits to me.

If the 35 isn't an asset, what is it? The owners of DEF did not receive the 100 paid to XYZ's shareholders, so we can't call the 35 a dividend and deduct it from DEF's shareholders' equity (retained earnings) the way we do with dividends to DEF's shareholders. If the 35 isn't an asset and isn't a dividend, the only explanation that is left, and one that my sister understands, is EXPENSE. Calling the 35 an expense doesn't mean that DEF's management was dumb and made a bad deal. The 35 is just like advertising. Just like R&D. Just like training employees. Just like restructuring a business. Maybe the 35 is a "probable future economic benefit" to the FASB, but my sister and I don't think it's an asset. We'll call it an asset when cash, or something that we can convert into cash, is in hand, which won't happen until DEF sells goods and services at a profit.

To be sure, charging the 35 to expense at the time of acquisition makes a hole in earnings. Maybe a deep hole. Maybe turns earnings into a loss. But that hole or loss can be explained just the way advertising, R&D, and dozens of other cash outlays are explained. Investors understand those explanations. What investors don't understand and what causes immense distrust and ill will, not to mention shareholder litigation and SEC investigations that take years to resolve and leave everyone scarred, is when cash outlays for things like R&D and advertising are capitalized and reported as assets and then later are written off to expense when hoped-for profits don't materialize. The same goes for goodwill.

Where are regulators and lenders in this debate? State insurance regulators do not allow goodwill to be counted as an "admitted asset"; policyholders and beneficiaries can't be paid with goodwill. State and federal banking regulators do not allow goodwill to be counted as an asset in call reports; depositors can't be paid with goodwill. The SEC does not allow a broker/dealer to count goodwill as an asset in determining net capital; customers and other creditors can't be paid with goodwill. Commercial bankers and other lenders routinely delete goodwill from borrowers' balance sheets. Those regulatory and lending practices have stood the test of time. Regulators and bankers know the difference between a truck and an abstract probable future economic benefit.

Maybe by now you agree with me that goodwill is not an asset and should be charged to expense in cash deals, but now you say let's keep poolings for true uniting of shareholder interests in stock-for-stock deals. That idea is a busted straight. First, the idea of "uniting of shareholder interests" is a fairy tale. (Kirk Kerkorian and Daimler Benz did not stay united.) Second, we accountants, and SEC staff, have tried to police pooling accounting since 1950, when the first accounting standard on poolings was issued, but business people and deal makers keep turning stock-for-stock deals into cash-for-stock deals in dozens of different ways; selling shareholders want cash. (Long-time readers of *Barron's* have been educated by Professor Briloff about dirty poolings.) Third, the detailed rules or prohibitions that we accountants and SEC staff use to try to make poolings look like true uniting of shareholder interests are arbitrary and don't have a business purpose and indeed interfere with and thwart legitimate business activity. Why, for example, should merged companies using pooling accounting be prohibited from buying back stock or selling significant assets for two years, which are two of those detailed prohibitions? (If any of these prohibited actions takes place, we accountants and SEC staff say that action contradicts the idea of uniting of shareholder interests and the pooling accounting gets undone, retrospectively, and purchase accounting is substituted, retrospectively, all with great *Sturm und Drang* because previously issued financial statements, on which investors relied in making investment decisions, have to be recalled and restated.) Fourth, the newly constituted International Accounting Standards Board in London, the FASB, the SEC, and SEC counterparts in various countries are trying to harmonize accounting around the world, and no one outside the USA has any fondness for poolings. So poolings have to go.

What to do? Well, the FASB and American business need to suck up their gut, charge goodwill to expense at the date of acquisition, and get on with tending to business and earning some CASH.

24 Accounting for financial instruments with characteristics of liabilities, equity, or both

Director of Research and Technical Activities
File reference No. 213-B
File reference No. 213-C
Financial Accounting Standards Board
401 Merritt 7; P.O. Box 5116
Norwalk, CT 06856-5116
1 May 2001

Dear sir,
This letter concerns the board's exposure draft of a proposed standard dated 27 October 2000 entitled *Accounting for Financial Instruments with Characteristics of Liabilities, Equity, or Both* (No. 213-B) and the board's exposure draft of a proposal to revise the definition of liabilities dated 27 October 2000 entitled "An amendment of FASB Concepts Statement No. 6" (No. 213-C).

File reference No. 213-C

I disagree with the board's proposal to expand the definition of liabilities to include "obligations" that require or permit the issuance of the enterprise's own equity shares in certain situations that do not establish an ownership relationship, as for example in the case where shares must be issued to satisfy an "obligation" stated at a fixed monetary amount. If, for example, a contract requires that the enterprise issue shares having a market value of $100,000 at the date the shares are issued, the amount of $100,000 would be reported as a liability.

It should go without saying that a corporation's own shares cannot be an asset of the corporation. Otherwise, a corporation's assets would be limitless and infinite. By saying that certain "obligations" that may or must be settled in shares are liabilities, the board implies that a corporation's shares, which will be used to settle the "obligation," are assets of the corporation. That is an incorrect implication that should be avoided.

If a corporation's owners, either by corporate charter or through other explicit or implicit approval, allow managers of the corporation to use the corporation's shares as currency, that act does not give rise to an expense. The issuance of shares dilutes the ownership of current owners of the corporation but does not give rise to an expense. Decreases in assets, or expenses, arise through the using up of assets or a decline in the market prices of assets, not through the issuance of shares. It seems that this proposed expansion of the definition of liabilities is an attempt by the board to force the recognition of expenses in cases where shares are issued. Just as the board tried to force the recognition of compensation cost and expense in the 1993 exposure draft related to employee stock options, the board here again is trying to force expense recognition just because a corporation issues shares.

The board has a misguided, incorrect view of what assets are and therefore what expenses are. In its Statement 123, *Accounting for Stock-based Compensation*, paragraphs 8 and 10, the board seems to say that assets arise because shares are issued. In its exposure draft dated 14 February 2001 entitled *Business Combinations and Intangible Assets – Accounting for Goodwill*, the board says in paragraph 46 that an asset called "goodwill" arises because it was "paid for." Not so. Assets – real assets, not FASB-created assets such as goodwill, direct-response advertising costs, and deferred taxes – exist separate and apart from whether anyone "paid for" them either by disbursement of cash, assumption of a liability, or issuance of stock or an option. Real assets – things like cash, securities, land, buildings, oil and gas reserves, patents, copyrights, equipment – exist in the real world. Real assets have a market price. The using up of real assets or a decline in their market prices causes expenses. The issuance of stock (or an option) does not create real assets; nor does the issuance of stock (or an option) cause an expense.

File reference No. 213-B

I also disagree with the board's proposal to require that proceeds received on the issuance of a compound instrument be allocated to the various parts. For example, on the issuance of a convertible bond, the board would require that the proceeds be allocated to the debt feature and the option feature. That's "as-if" accounting – as if a corporation had issued two instruments, a debt instrument and an option to buy shares of the corporation, when in fact only one instrument was issued. Financial statements should report what happened and what is, not what might have happened and what might be.

Take the following hypothetical case. Corporation DEF issues convertible debt; proceeds are 100. DEF allocates 90 to debt and 10 to equity. What is going to happen when the board requires that liabilities be reported at fair value? Assume that DEF's convertible debt trades in the marketplace at 100. Won't DEF's liability be reported at 100? What will happen to the 10? I assume that the 10 will disappear, as it should. Just as in accounting for hypothetical, as-if "deferred income taxes," the board is engaging in another time-consuming, money-consuming, hypothetical, as-if allocation that has no real-world meaning.

Yours truly,
Walter P. Schuetze

25 Accounting for stock options issued to employees

Senator Charles E. Schumer
United States Senate
Washington, DC 20510
25 March 2002

Dear Senator Schumer,

<u>Accounting for stock options issued to employees</u>

At the hearing of the Senate Committee on Banking, Housing, and Urban Affairs on Tuesday, 26 February 2002, in response to your question, I said that, for technical accounting reasons, I would not charge expense for stock options issued to employees. I said that I would explain why.

First, I will define a term. The word "expense" means (1) a decline in the value of an owned asset, as for example when an account receivable, which was thought to be collectible, goes bad; or (2) the using up of an owned asset, as for example, using cash to pay for advertising. (Technically, an expense arises when an obligation to transfer assets (to use up assets) arises, for example on the receipt of goods or services where payment of cash in satisfaction of the obligation is delayed in accordance with normal business terms.)

The Financial Accounting Standards Board, in one of its Concepts Statements, defines assets as "probable future economic benefits obtained or controlled by a particular entity as a result of past transactions or events." (That definition is followed by six paragraphs of more than 600 words explaining the definition.) The International Accounting Standards Board's definition of assets is similar to the FASB's in that it is based on "economic benefits." Under that definition of assets, the receipt of services from employees is an economic benefit, and the using up of that economic benefit is an expense. (For FASB mavens, see paragraphs 25–31 of Statement of Financial Accounting Concepts No. 6, *Elements of Financial Statements*, especially paragraph 31, and paragraph 88 of Statement of Financial Accounting Standards No. 123, *Accounting for Stock-based Compensation*.) The value of that economic benefit is hard if not impossible to measure directly, so it is measured indirectly by reference to the cash paid to the employee by the employer, state and federal taxes paid by the employer on account of the employee–employer relationship, and the cost of medical insurance, maternity leave, child care, vacation, sick leave, and other benefits furnished to the employee by the employer.

Defining assets as probable future economic benefits, as the FASB does, results in an expense on the receipt and use of services from employees in exchange for stock or stock options. The value of the economic benefit received is measured indirectly by reference to the fair value of the stock or stock options issued to the employees. If, as is generally the case, the stock is restricted stock or if restricted options are issued, the measurement of the fair value of the stock or the options is generally done by formula, because reference cannot be made to a market price of the stock or option.

So if you like the FASB's definition of assets, that is, economic benefits, you get an expense when stock or stock options are issued to employees as the FASB recommended in its Statement 123 issued in 1995, unless you think that it results in "double counting," which I will explain later on.

I do not like the FASB's and the IASB's definition of assets; "economic benefits" is too ambiguous, amorphous, and indeterminate. It is not workable. Only FASB and IASB accountants know what the term "economic benefits" means, but they cannot explain the term in words that ordinary folk and investors and creditors understand. When I was on staff at the Securities and Exchange Commission as chief accountant and as chief accountant of the commission's Division of Enforcement, I found "economic benefits" to be so pliable that almost any expenditure, cost, or debit can be said to qualify as an asset, or at least so it is asserted by registrants and their auditors, lawyers, and expert witnesses when challenged by the commission's staff or the commission itself, either informally or in court. (For proof, I can show you the court filings by respondents and their very distinguished expert witnesses.) Moreover, using that definition of assets allows junk, rusty junk, to get onto corporate balance sheets – junk that cannot be sold to anyone and therefore has no market value whatsoever – for example, goodwill, deferred income taxes, income tax benefits of operating loss carry forwards, development costs, direct-response advertising costs, debt issue costs, and capitalized interest cost said to relate to the acquisition of fixed assets. The FASB and the IASB say that that junk has probable future economic benefits. I say nonsense. That junk does not and cannot earn a penny. When it comes time to pay bills or make contributions to employees' pension plans, that junk is worthless. Showing that junk as assets on corporate balance sheets misleads investors. Showing that junk as assets allows stock prices to soar when the corporate balance sheet is bloated with hot air.

In my accounting model, which I have recommended to the FASB and the IASB, I define assets as follows: CASH, claims to CASH (for example, accounts and notes receivable), and things that can be sold for CASH (for example, securities, inventory, trucks, buildings, oil and gas reserves, and patents). Ordinary folk and investors and creditors understand my definition of assets. Nothing ambiguous about it. There are no rusty junk assets on balance sheets prepared using my definition of assets. And when assets, as I define assets (and liabilities, as I define liabilities), are shown on corporate balance sheets at their market prices as I have recommended to the FASB and the IASB, the balance sheet presents the corporation's true economic financial condition, not a financial position that is determined by reference to the FASB's mountain of rules and formulas for computing or determining asset and liability amounts, the result of which is not understandable by investors, creditors, and other users of financial statements.

In my accounting, I do not get an expense for the issuance of stock options (or stock for that matter) to employees in return for their services. No asset, as I define assets, is used up and no asset, as I define assets, declines in value as the result of the issuance of a stock option – thus no expense. I will use a simplified example to explain why no corporate expense arises on the issuance of a stock option to employees or on the vesting or exercise of the option. For simplicity, I use stock instead of stock options, but the result is exactly the same as if I had used options.

Year 1. Assume that on day 1 of year 1, all 100 US senators form the Senate Investment Club (hereinafter "SIC"), and each senator contributes $100 cash, making a total of $10,000, in exchange for 100 shares of SIC, making a total of 10,000 shares. During the 250 business days of year 1, each senator takes her/his turn at the wheel managing SIC for 2.5 days, making investment decisions, collecting cash dividends and interest, and reinvesting the cash. At the end of year 1, the combination of cash dividends and interest and increases in the market value of SIC's stocks and bonds brings total assets to $10,900.

Assume that a professional investment manager would charge 1 percent of average assets to manage a mutual fund such as SIC. Question: should SIC have a charge to expense of $105 (10,000 + 10,900 = 20,900 × 0.5 = 10,450 × 0.01 = 105), representing the value of the services contributed by the 100 senators during the year managing SIC as measured by what an investment manager would have charged, along with a corresponding contribution to capital of $105? The answer is "No." There was no asset, as I define assets, having a value of $105 that SIC owned during year 1 that was used up. There was no asset, as I define assets, that SIC owned during year 1 that declined in value by $105. Thus no expense.

Year 2. Assume that on day 1 of year 2, the 100 senators decide to hire Warren Buffett to manage SIC for year 2 and to pay him, at the end of year 2, cash equal to 1 percent of average assets during year 2. Assume that at the end of Year 2, SIC's assets have increased in value from $10,900 to $11,700, before a reduction for the 1 percent of average assets (or $113) paid to Mr Buffett.

Question: is the $113 paid to Mr Buffett an expense in year 2? Answer: Yes. An asset – namely cash of $113 – was used up. The using up of an asset is an expense.

Year 3. Assume that on day 1 of year 3, Mr Buffett and the senators agree that at the end of year 3, in return for Mr Buffett's managing SIC for year 3, each of the senators will convey to Mr Buffett one share of the stock of SIC instead of paying him cash equal to 1 percent of the average assets of SIC during year 3. (Or, as an alternative, SIC will issue 100 shares of SIC stock to

Mr Buffett.) Come the end of year 3, SIC's assets stand at $15,000, and each senator conveys to Mr Buffett one share of stock of SIC. Thus Mr Buffett receives SIC stock worth $150 from all of the senators at the end of year 3. Had Mr Buffett and SIC continued with the 1 percent of average assets arrangement as in year 2, SIC would have paid Mr Buffett cash of $133 (11,700 − 113 = 11,587 + 15,000 = 26,587 × 0.5 = 13,294 × 0.01 = 133).

Question: In Year 3, should SIC have an expense of $150, $133, or zero? If there is an expense of either $150 or $133, there is a contribution to capital of like amount. The answer is zero. No asset, as I define assets, of SIC having a value of either $150 or $133 was used up during Year 3. No asset, as I define assets, that SIC owned during Year 3 declined in value by either $150 or $133. Thus no expense.

Showing an expense, as would be done using the FASB's and the IASB's definition of assets, in either year 1 or year 3 is, in my opinion, as-if or pro-forma accounting. As if something was done that was not done. As if cash had been paid out. I think that accounting should be based on the facts of what was and what is, not what might have been if something that was not done had been done.

What happened in year 3 was that 100 senators had their ownership in SIC reduced by 1 percent by each conveying one share of stock of SIC to Mr Buffett. (If SIC had issued 100 shares of SIC stock to Mr Buffett, exactly the same result would have obtained.) After year 3, there are 101 owners of SIC. Each of the senators – in her/his personal income statement for year 3 – has an expense of 1 percent of $150, or $1.50, but SIC has no expense. The expense of the owners of SIC is not imputed to SIC. SIC accounts for its assets and expenses, not its owners' assets and expenses. Some say that the corporation has a cost when stock or options are issued to employees in return for services and that cost must be accounted for. What cost? There is no cost to the corporation. The cost is that of the owners of the corporation, as shown in the reduction of their percentage ownership of the corporation.

Remember the definition of an expense: the using up of an asset or the decline in value of an asset. Imputing reductions in 100 owners' (the senators) interests in SIC to SIC as an expense in year 3 implies that SIC's stock is an asset of SIC. That is fundamentally wrong. The stock of an entity is never an asset of that entity. Were the stock of an entity an asset of the entity, the entity's assets would be infinite and unlimited. The stock of an entity is an asset of the owners of the entity. How owners of an entity use their ownership interests, or what happens to the value of their ownership interests, does not affect the corporation's assets or the value of those assets. The corporation does not account for its owners' assets or changes in its owners' assets.

The rearrangement of the ownership interests in SIC in year 3 is exactly what happens when a corporation issues options to employees and the employees exercise the options – there is a rearrangement of the ownership interest of the corporation. But, importantly, no asset of the corporation is used up and no asset of the corporation declines in value when an option is issued or when an option vests or is exercised. Indeed, when an option is exercised, cash equal to the exercise price comes into the corporation.

Importantly, the issuance of a stock option to an employee does not change the market capitalization of the corporation as measured by the market value of the outstanding shares and the value of the outstanding option; any decline in the market value of outstanding shares shifts to the option. Thus no expense. If there had been a true expense – the using up of an owned asset or the decline in the value of an owned asset – then the market value of the outstanding shares and option should have declined. For example, if the market value of the stocks and bonds owned by SIC declined by 1 percent, that decline would be an expense of SIC. And that decline would be reflected – dollar for dollar – in the value of the SIC shares held by the senators. But, if the 100 senators convey 1 percent of their shares to Mr Buffet, or if SIC issues 100 shares to Mr Buffett, there is no decline in the value of SIC's assets – thus no expense. And, finally, on the exercise of an option by an employee, the market value of the corporation's outstanding shares should increase by at least the amount of cash that is received by the corporation on the exercise of the option – again, no expense.

Now take a look at the issue of double counting. Although net income in my accounting model is not reduced for an expense equal to the value of stock or stock options issued to employees, the number of shares in the earnings per share computation is the same in my model as in the FASB's model. Thus the dilutive effect of the issuance of options or shares is reflected in the earnings per share. Reducing net income by way of an expense charge for the value of stock or stock options issued to employees – as per FASB methodology – inappropriately counts the effect twice; that is, the corporation's shareholders see net income (the numerator in the earnings per share computation) reduced and the number of shares (the denominator in the earnings per share computation) increased – thus double counting. I will illustrate using year 3 above.

	Expense	No Expense
Net income (15,000 –11,587)	3413	3413
Deduct value of shares issued to Mr Buffett	(150)**	0
	3263	3413
Number of shares	10,150	10,150
Earnings per share	.3215**	.3363

** The effect of the expense deduction will be more pronounced in situations where the number of stock options (and therefore the value of the stock options) exceeds 1 percent of outstanding shares as in the SIC example.

Then, if there were a requirement to impute the value of stock options granted to employees to the corporation as an expense, as in year 3 of SIC above, a further question would arise: what should be done in those cases, as in year 1 of SIC above, where employee/owners of corporations are paid no cash compensation, or nominal cash compensation, and there is no expense, or nominal expense, in today's income statements for their services? For example, Mr Buffett of Berkshire Hathaway and Mr Gates of Microsoft are paid nominal cash salaries by those corporations. Should there be a pro-forma charge to expense in the income statements of those corporations for the true value of Mr Buffett's and Mr Gates' services, that is, the "economic benefit," along with a contribution to capital of like amount? My answer is that no amount beyond the cash salaries paid should be charged to expense. If an amount in addition to the cash paid should be charged to expense, that amount would have to be measured directly by reference to the value of the services of Mr Buffett and Mr Gates. What would that amount be – $25 million? $50 million? $100 million? A yet greater amount? Who would make that measurement? I assume, but do not know, that the FASB and the IASB would require an expense. I do not know how the FASB or the IASB would measure the value of those services and thus the expense.

If it would be appropriate to require a charge to expense in the case of an owner/employee being paid little or no cash salary, as in the case of Mr Buffett and Mr Gates, what would be done in the obverse case – where owner/employees are being paid more in cash salaries, bonuses, and the like than they are worth? To be consistent, would there be a requirement to measure directly the true value of their services, that is, the "economic benefit," and charge any excess to capital as a preferential dividend, thereby reducing the expense charge that is measured by cash salary, bonus, and the like? Not the way I would do the accounting, but perhaps yes in the FASB's and the IASB's accounting.

My example above – an investment club – is simplified for the purpose of illustration. But exactly the same concepts would apply to a manufacturing company, a service/entertainment company, a high-tech company, or any other company.

I hope this letter is helpful. I will be pleased to elaborate or explain further.

Yours truly,
Walter P. Schuetze

cc: other members of the Committee on Banking, Housing, and Urban Affairs

26 Proposed interpretation: guarantor's accounting and disclosure requirements for guarantees, including indirect guarantees of indebtedness of others

TO: Director of Major Projects and Technical Activities
File Reference No. 1124-001
Financial Accounting Standards Board

FROM: Walter P. Schuetze
8940 Fair Oaks Parkway
Boerne, TX 78015

SUBJECT: Proposed interpretation: guarantor's accounting and disclosure requirements for guarantees, including indirect guarantees of indebtedness of others

DATE: 14 July 2002

The board proposes, in paragraph 8 of the proposed interpretation, that guarantors *initially* measure and report guarantee liabilities at fair value. But then the board declines, in paragraph A17, without explanation and without giving its rationale, to give guidance on how the guarantee liability should be measured and reported *subsequently*. Guarantee liabilities should always be measured and reported at fair value, and the board should say so. If the board leaves the matter open, as in the proposed interpretation, practice will likely be mixed, which obviously is not in the best interest of financial reporting. That's no way to run a railroad.

The proposed interpretation is brimming with exclusions, with the result that many guarantees will not be covered by the final interpretation. A guarantee is a guarantee, and the board should include all guarantees within the final interpretation. Otherwise, financial reporting will be further diversified, needlessly. The board itself should not be a contributor to diversity in financial reporting. Again, no way to run a railroad.

27 Your proposed interpretation

Consolidation of certain special-purpose entities

TO: Director of Major Projects and Technical Activities
Financial Accounting Standards Board
File Reference No. 1082-200

FROM: Walter P. Schuetze
8940 Fair Oaks Parkway
Boerne, TX 78015
Tel: 210-698-0968
Email: schuetzewalterp@aol.com

SUBJECT: Your proposed interpretation: consolidation of certain special-purpose entities
DATE: 6 September 2002

This proposed interpretation by the board is incredibly complex and arcane. I have great difficulty figuring out to which entities the interpretation is supposed to apply, and then how to apply the interpretation. I don't know whether the word "entities" is even the right word. Half a dozen examples, written in plain English, sure would help.

But, assuming that I have correctly figured out what the board is saying, then I can't believe what the board is proposing. In its determination and rush to get off-balance-sheet liabilities of SPEs onto someone's balance sheet after Enron's implosion last year and the subsequent publicity about Enron's off-balance-sheet activities and the publicity about the board's inaction for a decade or more about accounting for SPEs, the board now proposes to contaminate the liability side of corporate balance sheets by putting onto corporations' balance sheets "debt" that the reporting corporations do not owe. In the process, the board now also proposes to contaminate the asset side of corporate balance sheets by putting onto corporations' balance sheets "assets" that the reporting corporations do not own, cannot sell, cannot pledge as collateral, cannot give to charity, and cannot distribute to shareholders – assets that belong to SPEs. Not only will that accounting not improve financial reporting, it will also confuse and potentially mislead investors.

The board says, in paragraph 14, that the assets (of the SPE) initially shall be reported (measured) by the "primary beneficiary" at fair value. The term "fair value" means the amount of cash that an asset would produce in a sales transaction. "Fair value" has no meaning with respect to an asset that the reporting enterprise does not own and therefore cannot sell; it is a *non sequitur*. Investors who read corporate balance sheets are entitled to assume that when an asset is reported at fair value (or at cost for that matter) that the reporting enterprise owns the asset and can sell it for cash. No amount of disclosure to the effect that the reporting enterprise really does not own the asset and therefore cannot sell it will cure the misleading impression given by reporting the asset in the balance sheet.

The board says in the summary of the proposed interpretation that "The relationship between an SPE and its primary beneficiary results in control by the primary beneficiary of the future benefits from the assets of the SPE even though the primary beneficiary may not have the direct ability to make decisions about the uses of the assets." What a strange meaning and use of the word "control" that statement by the board is. How can one control something and yet "not have the direct ability to make decisions about the uses of" that something? That does not make sense.

The board says, in paragraph 184 of its own Concepts Statement 6, that "an asset of an entity is the future economic benefits that the entity can control and thus can, within limits set by the nature of the benefit or the entity's right to it, <u>use as it pleases</u>. The entity having an asset is the one that can <u>exchange</u> it, <u>use</u> it to <u>produce</u> goods or services, <u>exact</u> a price for others' <u>use</u> of it, <u>use</u> it to <u>settle</u> liabilities, <u>hold</u> it, or perhaps <u>distribute</u> it to owners" (underlining added by me). Reporting enterprises can do none of those things with assets of SPEs. So how can the board square the words in its own Concepts Statement 6 with the proposed interpretation? I can't. Under the board's proposed interpretation, reporting enterprises that are "primary beneficiaries" will report phantom assets and liabilities, phantom revenues and expenses, and phantom cash flows. The board is going to make a yet further hash of already horribly complex financial reports that are produced by application of the encyclopedia of Byzantine FASB rules already in place – financial reports that are not understandable by or comprehensible to investors. That is not just my opinion; read speeches by the chairman of the Securities and Exchange Commission wherein he makes the same point. See, for example, Chairman Pitt's speeches of 22 October, 8 November, and 29 November 2001 on the SEC's website.

What is it that is the problem with accounting for SPEs? The problem is that guarantors are not reporting on their balance sheets as liabilities the fair value of guarantees (or undertakings) that they have issued. When an SPE is created, the creator thereof often guarantees the value of the assets, or a portion of the assets, held by the SPE. Or guarantees that the assets in the SPE will produce a certain level or amount of cash flow. Or undertakes to perform services related to the SPE at less than a fair rate for those services. Or the creator of the SPE guarantees the payment of the interest and principal, or some of the interest and principal, of the debt of the SPE. The solution to the problem is for the board to require that the guarantor, on its balance sheet, report as a liability the fair value of its guarantee at the date of the issuance of that guarantee, with a corresponding charge to earnings. Then, at each balance sheet date thereafter, the fair value of that guarantee would be redetermined, with the change, plus or minus, entered into earnings. Along with disclosure of the pertinent facts about the guarantee or undertaking, this is a simple, straightforward solution to the problem – a solution that will be understandable by and comprehensible to investors. And this solution to the problem will not have corporations reporting phantom assets and liabilities, phantom revenues and expenses, and phantom cash flows.

As to leases, lessees often guarantee the residual value of the leased asset, which guarantee becomes operative at the end of the lease. But most leases that I have seen also impose on the lessee a termination penalty, which penalty generally becomes operative immediately upon signing the lease. Payment of periodic amounts under the lease by the lessee (so-called lease payments) generally is optional in that the lessee need not make the periodic payment but may terminate the lease and pay the termination penalty. Thus the termination penalty is the amount that the lessee unconditionally must pay, and that is the amount (undiscounted) that the lessee should report as its liability under the lease, with a corresponding charge to earnings, not the amount of the guaranteed residual value or the present value thereof.

If, as to lessees, the board requires that some measure of the lessee's commitment to disburse cash, say the termination penalty amount, be reported as an asset, then the board will be repeating the mistake that it made in FASB Statement 142, where it said that the cost of goodwill is an asset. Unless the amount recognized as an asset for a lease can be realized in cash through a sublease, that amount is just like goodwill in that it represents hoped-for future profits. Leased assets differ from owned assets in that owned assets can be converted into cash through a sale. If the lessee may not sub-let the leased asset, the only way that any amount represented as an asset for a lease can be realized in cash is through future use of the leased asset. Thus the realization of that amount depends on customers buying the lessee's services or product at a price that yields a profit. Lessees obviously do not control their customers' actions; thus to a lessee the asset is a contingent asset – just like goodwill. Contingent assets are not recognized until realized in cash.

The board should not require, or even permit, primary beneficiaries of SPEs or lessees to report as assets on their balance sheets things that they do not own, cannot sell, cannot pledge as collateral, cannot give to charity, and cannot distribute to shareholders. Investors will be confused and potentially misled by that reporting.

Part II

The implications of accounting practices for auditing

28 Schuetze on the implications of accounting practices for auditing

Peter W. Wolnizer

This section comprises four articles and two speeches. They cover a variety of matters, including the role and legal liability of auditors, audit committees, peer reviews, and internal control.

However, Walter Schuetze makes the following vital, but seldom made, observation – accounting rules and practices have profound implications for the function and reliability of auditing and, indeed, for the independence of auditors. Accounting rules determine whether financial statements are of a kind that can be audited or verified by recourse to evidence that is external to the reporting enterprise and hence beyond the control of the managers who prepare financial statements. Schuetze demonstrates how conventional accounting rules give managers significant discretion in how they account for assets, liabilities, and income. He shows how conventional cost-based accounting yields many elements in financial statements that cannot be verified by auditors by recourse to evidence outside the reporting enterprise: to commercial evidence in the marketplace. He also shows how mark-to-market accounting would be good for auditors, because it would require the reporting enterprise to substantiate elements of financial statements by independent evidence. Schuetze advocates that the names of the persons or entities that provide the market price information should be disclosed in the financial reports.

These are important ideas, ones that are largely ignored in the auditing literature. Mark-to-market accounting, auditing by reference to corroborable evidence drawn from the marketplace, and disclosure of the persons or entities that provide the evidence would strengthen the independence of auditors in far more significant ways than the myriad of *déjà vu* proposals that are currently being advanced. Without detracting in any way from the proposals that are designed to strengthen auditor independence, Schuetze argues that until the control of the information reported in financial statements is taken out of the hands of the management of reporting enterprises, by an accounting that requires assets to be marked to market and liabilities valued at settlement prices, audit judgment will never be independent of management. It is for this reason that he argues that a fundamental problem underlying contemporary auditing is a technical accounting problem.

By explaining the connection between the rules that govern financial accounting and reporting and the reliability (and independence) of audit evidence and hence of the auditing function itself, Walter Schuetze has elevated auditing to the rigorous safeguard over the quality of financial information that it was intended to be.

The articles

The first article, "Disclosure and the impairment question," published in the *Journal of Accountancy* (1987), deals with the impairment of asset values, how such impairment should be disclosed and the problems associated with surprise large-scale write-downs of asset values. "Many believe that either the management or the independent auditors, or both, should have warned users of financial statements about the possibility of these write-downs or foreseen the necessity for write-downs and reported them earlier. Such beliefs erode confidence in financial reporting."

Lacking definitive guidance in the literature or in the accounting standards, accounting practices are inconsistent: "There is no uniform practice in selecting the circumstances that justify or require a write-down, and there is no uniform practice in measuring the amount of such write-downs." Reflecting on his experience of implementing the "probability approach" recommended in FASB Statement 5, which, as a member of the AICPA's Accounting Standards Executive Committee, he endorsed in 1980, Schuetze concludes: "Unless the [FASB] simply requires that assets be written down to fair value whenever fair value is less than cost, the task of developing definitive, operational criteria for recognition and measurement of write-downs will be extremely difficult to complete."

As an interim solution, while the FASB works on the "recognition and measurement problems," Schuetze proposes that "The FASB should require disclosure of the fair value [estimated price in an immediate, but not forced, sale for cash] of a non-monetary asset, or reasonable groupings of such assets, whenever the fair value of the asset at the date of the most recent balance sheet is less than its cost."

It is here that Schuetze makes the vital association between the quality of accounting numbers and their auditability or verifiability: "The rule would be unambiguous. Whether fair value of an asset is less than its cost is – at least in theory – a question of fact, not a judgment. ... From the independent auditor's perspective, this would be a tremendous improvement over the current state of affairs. As it is today, we do not search for facts. Rather, we rely on management's assertions about its judgment about recoverability of cost, and then we apply our judgment to that judgment." Schuetze goes on to make the second vital connection – he links auditability with evidence: valuing assets at their fair value "would mean that the preparer of the financial statements would have to produce evidential matter about the fair value of assets to satisfy the auditor."

Because the idea of getting fair value for all non-monetary assets may be costly, Schuetze, in this paper, suggests an alternative accounting treatment: "a standardized measure of cash flow to be disclosed in all cases when it is negative, along with the cost of the asset. The standardized measure of cash flow would be the net amount of annual operating revenue of the asset, minus the annual related cash operating costs, both based on the most recent year's results, minus one year's hypothetical interest to carry the cost of the asset with that interest to be measured using the 30-year US Treasury bond rate at the balance sheet date. This disclosure would allow users to make their own subjective determinations about the fair value of the asset and whether a write-down is necessary." He recommends that this disclosure requirement be "tested in the field" and argues that it "would alleviate considerably the surprise that frequently accompanies business failures."

It is apparent from his later papers, notably "What is an asset?" (1993) and "True north" (2001), that Schuetze subsequently takes a more rigorous approach to the determination of fair value – what an asset or collection of assets would fetch if sold on the balance sheet date – and the extent of asset impairment would be determined by the difference between fair value at two dates. Only the initial write-down would be determined relative to cost, since assets would thereafter be valued at fair value. Asset impairment in mark-to-market accounting is synonymous with depreciation – a diminution in the market selling price of the asset (or collection of assets).

This is the first paper in which Schuetze makes the vital, but commonly and widely overlooked, association between accounting rules, independent evidence, and the function of auditing as independent verification. That is, auditors cannot authenticate financial statements independently of those who prepare them unless the accounting numbers are supported by evidence external to the reporting enterprise: by evidence from the marketplace. In the case of fair value, that means by recourse to independent evidence of current selling prices for assets and current settlement prices for liabilities.

That association is the subject of the second article in this section: "The liability crisis in the USA and its impact on accounting." First delivered as a speech at a conference on the "liability crisis" held at Northwestern University on 7 April 1992 soon after he was appointed chief accountant to the SEC, the paper was published in *Accounting Horizons* in June 1993. It was written against the backdrop of the savings and loan (S&L) crisis. It is one of relatively few pieces of literature that addresses the liability of auditors and audit risk in terms of accounting rules: "For ten to fifteen years, I have contended that until generally accepted accounting principles are unambiguously defined, auditors of financial statements cannot see clearly the target they intend to strike. So long as asset and liability recognition and measurement standards are fuzzy, auditors of financial statements do not always hit the ball and indeed sometimes strike out when at bat."

Referring to the S&L catastrophe, Schuetze argues that "the cost of the savings and loan bailout and the related litigation are in significant part due to ambiguity in accounting standards regarding revenue recognition on loans and loss recognition on loans … and ambiguity, or outright contradiction, in loan loss recognition rules postponed too long the recognition of losses on those ADC loans." He concludes: "To my mind, the ADC loan case is the perfect case for saying that ambiguous accounting principles, not auditing failure, are to blame for the litigation and resultant auditor liability arising out of the S&L catastrophe."

In the context of ADC loans, he provides numerous examples where current accounting standards are so ambiguous as to allow management significant discretion and judgment in determining the accounting for loans. He examines the substance over form argument and concludes that "If we follow a substance over form rule, we will have anarchy in financial accounting. Substance over form itself is so ambiguous that if people are instructed to use that general rule instead of specific rules or standards, then financial statements will become highly individualized."

Next, he examines the argument that those who prepare financial statements should be allowed to exercise their judgment within broad, general financial accounting and reporting standards. He concludes: "That approach will not work either. A lot of people applied their judgment to accounting for ADC loans. That process produced a judgmental mess that is costing untold, uncounted billions."

Addressing the judgment applied to the identification of impaired loans (the "probable" criterion in FASB Statement 5), he argues: "We can see in current practice that the probable criterion has not worked. Identification of impaired loans under that criterion is all over the map, which produces wide non-comparability in financial statements." That same ambiguity extends to the identification and measurement of the impairment of the cost of marketable securities (when a decline in value is "other than temporary" where "other than temporary" is undefined in the accounting standards) and to the cost of long-lived assets. And many other examples are given.

In confronting the conventional wisdom that ambiguous accounting standards have little or nothing to do with auditor liability, Schuetze concludes: "I disagree. I think plaintiffs and their lawyers clearly see that any time an issuer or an issuer's auditor is in the dock, that person is vulnerable. That person is vulnerable because he or she relies on fuzzy notions such as 'probable' and 'cost' is recoverable through the ordinary operation of a going concern, 'realization' of tax benefits is 'more likely than not,' and market value declines are 'temporary.' Those terms, and others of similar ambiguity, are red meat for the plaintiff's bar." Returning to a recurrent theme, he argues that "if financial statement amounts were required in the case of assets to be not in excess of market values, or fair values, and not less than settlement amounts in the case of liabilities, these amounts would be relevant to investors. Investors would more readily understand the financial statements. … Likewise, it seems to me that, from the standpoint of auditors protecting themselves from the risks of litigation, they too should welcome simple and unambiguous accounting standards that produce financial statements that can be easily understood by reasonable investors and by the courts."

The third article, "Reporting by independent auditors on internal controls" (*The CPA Journal*, October 1993), was adapted from a speech given by Schuetze, as chief accountant to the SEC, at a symposium in 1993 sponsored by *The CPA Journal* on the topic "In the Public Interest." The article is a response to a proposal by the AICPA and the AICPA's Public Oversight Board (POB) that the SEC should require public companies to report publicly on the effectiveness of their internal controls over financial reporting, and that auditors should be required to express an opinion on those representations by management. The AICPA and POB argued that such a requirement would militate against fraudulent financial reporting.

Again, Schuetze questions the conventional wisdom:

> I question whether public reporting on internal controls over financial reporting by registrants and their independent auditors would reduce so-called fraudulent financial reporting and litigation against external auditors. ... No amount of reporting on internal controls will ferret out any more fraud or provide any better techniques to find it than the audit of the financial statements should have done in the first instance. ... I question ... how reporting on internal controls by independent auditors is going to deter fraudulent financial reporting resulting from "cooked books" when management was not deterred by the requirement for an annual audit and was able in the first instance to conceal the fraud from the auditors during the audit.

He then homes in on the critical issue:

> Another, and more prevalent, cause of improper financial reporting is the use of ambiguous accounting principles to overstate assets, equity and income. ... Auditors suggest that they cannot stop this kind of misconduct because, under existing accounting principles, assets may be recognized even though there is no way to audit or verify, with reasonable assurance, that any future benefit exists or that the asset amounts will be recovered or realized. This kind of improper reporting occurs, therefore, not because of a failure of auditors to discover crooked schemes, but because of a failure in the way accounting principles are written. No amount of internal controls reporting can cure this problem.

He provides several examples from current accounting standards to illustrate the point, but the critical observation in the paper is that internal control systems, being designed and implemented by management, will not militate against fraudulent or misleading financial statements if there is managerial collusion to perpetrate a fraud or where management has wide discretion in determining the reported financial values of assets, liabilities, equities, and income.

The fourth article in this section, "A mountain or a molehill?" (*Accounting Horizons*, March 1994), was also first delivered as a speech – on this occasion, to the AICPA's 21st Annual National Conference on Current SEC Developments,

11 January 1994. It was a powerful and influential speech, for it prompted the AICPA's Public Oversight Board to appoint an Advisory Panel on Auditor Independence, chaired by Donald Kirk, former chairman of the FASB, to examine Schuetze's charges. The article concerns auditor independence.

Schuetze acknowledges the importance and propriety of auditors being, and being seen to be, independent of their clients: "In the last analysis, therefore, it is his independence which is the certified public accountant's economic excuse for existence." However, he quickly turns "to an issue that has vexed and bewildered me since I came to the commission two years ago. I refer to situations in which auditors are not standing up to their clients on financial accounting and reporting issues when their clients take a position that is, at best, not supported in the accounting literature or, at worst, is directly contrary to existing accounting pronouncements. To me, auditors giving way to their clients, subordinating their view to their clients', raises a nasty issue about independence in appearance and in fact. In my opinion, an auditor's independence … is jeopardized as much by his or her subordinating judgment about a financial accounting and reporting issue as it is by investing in securities issued by a client, lending money to a client, or borrowing money from a client – perhaps even more so. At least insofar as money matters are concerned, if there were disclosure to the investor about that fact, then the investor would be on notice and could be guided by the facts, although I would not – definitely not – advocate such an approach. Not so with subordinated judgment, which is insidious. There is no way to communicate impaired or colored judgment."

Referring back to a speech he gave to the 1992 annual meeting of the American Accounting Association, where he raised, among other things, the issue of auditor independence (see the section "Accounting for assets and liabilities"), Schuetze acknowledges that some senior members of the profession "suggested privately that I was making a mountain out of a molehill." Not so, says Schuetze. Rather, he provides several telling examples of "incredible accounting proposals" that have been put forward, even since 1992, by registrants and their auditors. Those examples make for fascinating, indeed incredulous, reading. In respect of accounting for stock options, Schuetze argued that "It also appears to me, and other outside observers, that CPAs may have become cheerleaders for their clients." A bold statement, perhaps, but one for which there was, and remains, compelling evidence.

Having sustained the argument, Schuetze then poses the question: "Could continuation of such a trend be anything other than an invitation to Congress, the SEC, and other regulators to regulate more heavily, and directly, the auditing profession in particular and financial reporting in general? Could continuation of such a trend lead investors, particularly institutional investors, to find alternative ways to corroborate issuers' representations in their financial statements?" These are thought-provoking questions. In the wake of the most significant unheralded corporate collapses and retrospective financial restatements in corporate history, following the demise of Enron, Schuetze's first question was prophetic, for that is precisely what has happened in the Sarbanes–Oxley Act of 2002. Will his second question, likewise, be prophetic?

The strength of the arguments put in this article is enhanced by Schuetze's closing statement:

> As many of you know, these comments do not come from an ivory tower. I have lived and worked in the accounting profession for more than 30 years. I know the realities of saying "no" to a client. I know the disappointment some clients express when the auditor makes a decision to support an accounting proposal that may reduce those clients' reported earnings. I know the long and often heated telephone calls and client visits, the emotional strain, and the financial cost that follow such decisions. But I also know the rewards – a clean conscience, not having to worry about losing lawsuits based on the merits, and pride in the profession and the credibility of financial accounting and reporting.

As a consequence of this speech and article – and the consequent establishment of the Kirk Panel – that panel recommended, on page 2 of its report of 13 September 1994, as follows:

> [The panel] urges the accounting profession to look to the board of directors – the shareholders' representative – as the audit client, not corporate management. It calls for direct interface between the entire board and the auditor at least annually, and an expanded interface with the audit committee.
>
> To increase the value of the audit, the [panel] calls for a new level of candor from the auditor. Auditors would not only apprise the board of what is acceptable accounting, they would be expected to express their views, as accounting experts, on the appropriateness of the accounting principles used or proposed by the company.

That expansion of the auditor's responsibilities is a far-reaching, perhaps revolutionary, proposal, one that is responsive to complaints about "lowest common denominator" accounting principles often applied with "rose-colored glasses."

Subsequently, in 2000, the AICPA's Auditing Standards Board issued Statement on Auditing Standards No. 90, *Audit Committee Communications*, which requires the auditor to "discuss with the audit committee the auditor's judgment about the quality, not just the acceptability, of the entity's accounting principles as applied in its financial reporting ... The discussion should be open and frank." That requirement is consistent with the recommendation of the Kirk Panel in 1994.

In "True north" (2001) and the R.J. Chambers Memorial Research Lecture (2001), Schuetze develops the notion of independence much further, linking it strongly with the "competence" of the evidence to which auditors have recourse in forming their opinions. That is, he articulates a complete notion of independence in auditing: the evidentiary underpinning for the establishment of an independent auditor opinion as well as the ethical dimensions of the auditor–client relationship.

The speeches and addresses

There are two unpublished speeches in this section. The first, "Comments on certain aspects of the special report of the AICPA's Public Oversight Board of 5 March 1993," was delivered on 27 May 1993 at the University of Southern California's SEC and Financial Reporting Institute. The speech focuses on those three of the twenty-five recommendations contained in that report that were addressed to the SEC. The POB believes that the recommendations, if implemented, would improve the quality and reliability of financial statements and increase the likelihood of auditors detecting fraud and other illegal acts.

The first of these recommendations – that the SEC should require SEC registrants to disclose whether their auditors have had a peer review, the date of the most recent peer review, and its results – is similar to a proposal by the SEC as part of a comprehensive review of the proxy rules in 1985. Twenty of the thirty-eight commentators on that proposal, including the American Bar Association, were opposed to it. Schuetze questions the "benefit investors and potential investors would get from such a disclosure standing alone."

The second recommendation concerns audit committees: "The SEC should require registrants to include in a document containing the annual financial statements a statement by the audit committee (or by the board if there is no audit committee) that describes its responsibilities and tells how they were discharged." The POB cites the 1987 *Report of the National Commission on Fraudulent Financial Reporting* (the Treadway Commission) as support for this recommendation. Schuetze also questions this recommendation: "The information already required to be disclosed about audit committees, the commission's decision not to implement the Treadway recommendation in 1988, and the anticipated states' rights issues involved, will have to be reviewed carefully before the commission makes any determination on whether to proceed with this recommendation."

The third recommendation deals with registrants' disclosure about the effectiveness of internal control systems related to financial reporting. Schuetze admits to being "in two minds" about an independent auditor's reporting on management's assessment of its internal controls: "I recognize the argument that the more managements, audit committees, internal auditors, and external auditors think about, talk about, and focus on internal controls, the better the internal controls will be and will become." On the other hand, "I know … that there are in this world a certain number of people with dishonest bones in their bodies. All the reporting on internal controls in the world is not going to stop those people from defrauding the public and, in the process, the external auditor as well. … In addition, I am told that there will be a cost, perhaps a significant cost, to registrants, especially the smaller ones, to get their external auditors to report publicly on their internal controls. … So I do not know which way to lean."

The second speech, with the tantalizing title "Enforcement issues: good news, bad news, Brillo pads, Miracle-Gro, and Roundup," was delivered to the Twenty-sixth Annual AICPA National Conference on SEC Developments in Washington on 8 December 1998. Speaking as the chief accountant of the

Enforcement Division of the SEC, Schuetze tackles questions pertaining to auditor independence head on. Referring to his observations "that some issuer registrants are turning not to their regular auditors but to 'forensic' auditors from other firms when questions are raised about the issuer's financial statements," he observes: "The forensic auditors then take their Brillo pads and scrub the issuer's balance sheet until it looks like a newly minted copper penny, and the restatements to assets, liabilities, equity, and income are the size of an elephant." He then asks the critical question: "Which firm did the real audit? Which firm's partners and staff did not have their objectivity clouded or enveloped by relationships developed at picnics or golf outings or at sports events with their clients? Which firm's partners and staff did not have their skepticism dulled by the fact that a former partner of the audit engagement partner is now the client's CFO? That the audit partner and the CFO are also doubles partners at the tennis club on Saturday mornings?" Compelling and timely questions, indeed. He then raises an interesting query: "Should auditors have to follow the same rules with respect to their public company audit clients that I as an employee of the US federal government have to follow with respect to regulated entities or persons? Would there be fewer restatements if there were not such fraternizations?"

Turning to the accounting issues with which the Enforcement Division of the SEC deals, he states: "The Enforcement Division was formed in the 1970s. ... I have heard every one of the division's chief accountants give speeches wherein they described their cases. Well, nothing has changed. Registrants are still doing the same things." What things? Cooking the books – by "premature revenue recognition"; "deferral in the balance sheet of costs that should have been reported in income as operating expenses"; "assigning inflated, often outrageously inflated, dollar values to exchanges of non-monetary assets, particularly with related parties"; "not disclosing the existence of related parties and transactions with related parties"; "recognizing officers' salaries as receivables"; "recognizing cash taken from the corporation by officers as cash in the bank or as a direct reduction of stockholders' equity instead of a charge to expense"; "including brass bars that look like gold bars in an inventory of gold"; "bleeding into income, without disclosure, 'reserves' established in business combinations or in so-called restructurings." In several recent cases, he observed, "the bleeding [of reserves into income] turned into a hemorrhage from a severed carotid artery!"

Examining the use and abuse of reserves, Schuetze states:

> I thought that the "reserves" issue had been resolved in 1975, when the FASB issued its Statement 5 on *Accounting for Contingencies*, but nowadays general reserves are like crab grass. They are everywhere. Tax liability cushions. Deferred tax asset cushions. Inventory reserves. Bad debt reserves. Merger reserves. Restructuring reserves. They are like dirt. Some companies keep a 55-gallon drum of Miracle-Gro in the garage, and they irrigate their crab grass general reserve accounts with a garden hose hooked up to the

> drum. Then along comes the Division of Corporation Finance, in its review of filings by issuers, and squirts Roundup from a spritzer bottle on issuers' balance sheets, but the crab grass general reserves keep re-emerging. And the reserves are being used to manipulate earnings.

Whither auditing amid this shoddy and defective accounting?

> I have now seen several non-audits … Auditors accepting, with little or no evidential support, values ascribed to both monetary and non-monetary assets. … Auditors not doing substantive audit work but relying on so-called analytical procedures where the evidence, or lack thereof, cries out for substantive audit work. … Auditors not doing cut-off work for sales and purchases, with the result that sales of the next period are booked in this period with a corresponding increase in receivables from customers, and accounts payable for purchases of inventory in this period not booked until next period with the inventory recognized in the balance sheet resulting in understated costs of sales and overstated margins.

Here again, Schuetze makes the vital connection: poor accounting spawns poor auditing. Poor accounting produces financial statements for which there is a lack of commercial – independently corroborable – evidence. Poor accounting gives great discretion to the preparers of financial statements in the determination of the classification and quantification of assets, liabilities, equities, and income. Poor accounting renders auditors dependent upon the management of the reporting enterprise for all of those matters. In the end, there is the risk that investors will lose confidence in the integrity and reliability of auditing as the rigorous process of quality assurance that is intended by law.

And it is on that sobering note that Schuetze concludes his speech:

> Will investors stop drinking from the well called audits by "independent certified public accountants" and sample the water in other wells? You may say there are no other comparable wells. Not so. When investors begin to believe that their interests are not being protected by external auditors, those investors will find an alternative to protect their interests, in ways other than an audit by independent certified public accountants.

29 Disclosure and the impairment question

Journal of Accountancy, December 1987

In the short run, here's the way to go: disclosure of the fair value of long-lived, non-monetary assets.

Walter Schuetze

Accounting for impaired long-lived, non-monetary assets is an old problem, one of the acknowledged imperfections of financial accounting and reporting. The problem is when to recognize "impairment" – the inability to recover the carrying amount – by a write-down and how to measure it. Practice is inconsistent, and rules that would establish consistency thus far have eluded standard setters. In view of the confusion, this article proposes an interim solution: required disclosure of the fair value of non-monetary assets when fair value is less than cost.

Impairment and the winds of change

The first feature of the problem is its urgency. Economic change is now so rapid that various assets all too frequently lose some or all of their capacity to recover cost. This is obvious in the case, say, of a dramatic drop in the price of oil, which impairs the cost, or value, of oil and gas drilling rigs. The conditions that lead to such events can be treated as unique, but ongoing conditions also lead to asset impairment. Technological advances that create obsolescent plant, equipment, patents, and licenses are common events today, and rapid technological progress is a condition that will continue to be with us. Similarly, intense competition and rapid changes in market demand are standing rather than temporary conditions, and both can impair asset values. Still other conditions that can impair asset values, most notably volatile interest and foreign exchange rates, have been around long enough to make their disappearance hard to anticipate.

All these factors suggest that users of financial statements would benefit from information on impaired long-lived assets.

The urgency of the problem is also illustrated by the sense of surprise that is sometimes expressed when huge write-downs are reported. Many believe that either the management or the independent auditors, or both, should have warned users of financial statements about the possibility of these write-downs or foreseen the necessity for write-downs and reported them earlier. Such beliefs erode confidence in financial reporting.

Little clarity in the literature

The second feature of the problem is that the authoritative literature contains no clear, operational guidance on accounting for impaired long-lived assets.

In fact, the absence of a rule on when to write down impaired long-lived assets was explicitly acknowledged by the Financial Accounting Standards Board in 1977 in Statement No. 19, *Financial Accounting and Reporting by Oil and Gas Producing Companies*: "The question of whether to write down the carrying amount of productive assets to an amount expected to be recoverable for future use of those assets is unsettled under present generally accepted accounting principles. This is a pervasive issue that the Board has not addressed."

Despite the support that one can find in various places in the literature for the concept of mandatory write-downs of impaired long-lived assets, serious practical problems have made it difficult to establish a rule for consistent practice:

- How does one know when the cost of an asset is sufficiently impaired to necessitate a write-down?
- Should the write-down be mandatory if there is a chance that the asset will regain its stature or only when impairment is permanent?
- How does one distinguish with confidence between temporary and permanent impairments?
- How does one disaggregate impaired individual assets from other elements in an operating unit?
- Should write-ups be permissible for assets that have become unimpaired?
- Under what circumstances, if any, would a shortened amortization period or an accelerated depreciation method coupled with a reduction in residual value be more appropriate than a write-down (for example, a change from units-of-production depreciation to an accelerated depreciation method for facilities operating significantly below normal levels)?
- How should write-downs to recognize impairments be measured?

The measurement alternatives include fair value, replacement cost, undiscounted future cash flows, and discounted future cash flows using a choice of several possible interest rates. The measurement base can assume break-even, a normal profit margin, or less than a normal profit margin. The discount rate can be the enterprise's incremental borrowing rate, its cost of capital, a risk-free rate, or some other rate.

Inconsistencies in practice

Current practice is marked by two types of inconsistency. There is no uniform practice in selecting the circumstances that justify or require a write-down, and there is no uniform practice in measuring the amount of such write-downs. As of this writing, the FASB's Emerging Issues Task Force has discussed the issue three times but has reached a consensus on only one point: that the dominant practice is to recognize permanent rather than temporary impairment.

There are some hard data on inconsistencies in practice. The Financial Executives Institute (FEI) surveyed a number of companies reporting unusual charges in 1985. Of twenty-four companies reporting write-downs of fixed assets retained by the business (either idle or still in use), 60 percent of the decisions to write down the asset were based on a probability test similar to that in FASB Statement No. 5, *Accounting for Contingencies*, and 36 percent of the decisions were based on the permanent decline test. Thirteen of the write-downs (46 percent) were measured by net realizable value, five (18 percent) by undiscounted expected future cash flows, four (14 percent) by the net present value of future cash flows, and three (11 percent) by some combination of these methods. The remaining three write-downs were based on current replacement cost, percentage of historical cost based on expected long-term capacity, and historical cost reduced by the cost of holding a building that could not be sold.

These and other data in the FEI survey show inconsistencies in practice, but a plurality of the participating companies (48 percent) responded in the negative to a question asking whether additional guidance from the FASB on accounting and reporting on the impairment of fixed assets was desirable; 38 percent responded that additional guidance would be useful. What the survey does not point out explicitly is that, in the absence of a decision to abandon or dispose of assets at a loss, the timing and amount of any write-down are largely discretionary.

Proposals and projects

In 1980, the AICPA's Accounting Standards Executive Committee (ASEC) recommended that the probability approach in FASB Statement No. 5 be used to determine whether to report the inability to recover fully the carrying amounts of long-lived assets. Under this approach, declines would be recorded in the accounts if the inability to recover cost is probable and the amount can be reasonably estimated. This proposal was an explicit rejection of the concept that declines should be recognized only if the assets are permanently impaired. The ASEC concluded that the concept of permanent decline in value was too subjective and restrictive. However, the ASEC also recommended that no one method of measurement be prescribed for determining the amount of the write-down.

Looking back on the ASEC's conclusions in 1980 – which I endorsed at the time – one can understand the rejection of subjective determinations of permanent impairment. But it is harder, now that our experience with Statement No. 5 has more than doubled, to agree that its probability test could serve as a replacement because it is sufficiently less subjective than the permanent impairment test. In both cases, the preparer of the financial statements and the independent auditor must foretell the future.

The FASB's staff is now considering whether to recommend that the board add to its agenda a project on accounting for the inability to recover fully the carrying amounts of long-lived assets. One immediate issue for the FASB's staff is to define the project's objective. The objective could be to develop guidance on recognition and measurement of impairment of long-lived assets, or it could be to develop disclosure requirements that minimize the likelihood that users are taken by surprise when long-lived assets are written down. Unless the board simply requires that assets be written down to fair value whenever fair value is less than cost, the task of developing definitive, operational criteria for recognition and measurement of write-downs will be extremely difficult to complete. The board will have to answer many difficult questions, some of which are offered in the following.

Roadblocks to recognition and measurement criteria

In order to develop operational criteria as to *when* to recognize and *how* to measure impairments of long-lived assets, the Financial Accounting Standards Board will have to answer the following questions, among many others:

1 For an investment type of asset, for example a common stock, how long should the quoted market price stay below cost before a write-down is required? Six months? One year? Three years? May a write-down be reversed if the quoted price later bounces back?

2 For operating-type assets, such as plant, equipment, and patents,

- Should the presence of an operating loss (assuming "operations" is clearly defined) for some period of time require a write-down? How long? Six months? One year? Two years? When does an asset become *operational?*
- Should the management of an enterprise be entitled to assume improved future cash flows from the asset or from reasonable grouping of assets?
- Should the future cash flows be discounted? At what rate?
- Once write-downs have been made, may those write-downs be reversed if cash flows improve?
- Should the question of a write-down be considered in tandem with the amortization/depreciation policy related to the assets? Estimated useful lives? Residual values?

3 How does one deal with the intangible asset that arises from the application of FASB Statement No. 87, *Employers' Accounting for Pensions*, in relation to pensions?

4 For how long should losses or "subnormal" earnings be allowed to run before goodwill should be written down?

5 May assets be grouped? (This question is larger than it may seem, involving more than just write-downs.) What is the unit of accounting – individual assets or groups of assets?

An interim solution

I suggest an interim solution while the FASB works on the recognition and measurement problems or before it adds the item to its formal agenda. The FASB should require disclosure of the fair value (estimated price in an immediate, but not forced, sale for cash) of a non-monetary asset, or reasonable groupings of such assets, whenever the fair value of the asset at the date of the most recent balance sheet is less than its cost.

This proposal has several things going for it:

1 The rule would be unambiguous. Whether fair value of an asset is less than cost is, at least in theory, a question of fact, not a judgment. I do not deny that the facts may be hard to come by (and perhaps in some instances costly), but at least we know how and where to look for facts. And in some instances the facts are easy to come by, for example price quotations in newspapers for marketable equity securities. From the independent auditor's perspective, this would be a tremendous improvement over the current state of affairs. As it is today, we do not search for facts. Rather, we rely on management's assertions about its judgment about recoverability of cost, and then we apply our judgment to that judgment.

I also acknowledge that fair value of an asset is often not a clear-cut, indisputable fact, but at least we would be making judgments about facts, not speculating about future events and their outcomes, as we do today in trying to decide when and by how much to write down assets.

2 The disclosure would not be discretionary.
3 If there were no disclosure about cost being in excess of fair value, the user of the financial statement would be entitled to assure that fair value of the asset was at least equal to or in excess of cost at the date of the balance sheet. (One day later, however, fair value might be less than cost.)
4 If there were no disclosures and if the auditor's report was unqualified, the user of the financial statement would be entitled to assume that the independent auditor was satisfied that fair value of the asset was at least equal to or in excess of cost. This would mean that the preparer of the financial statement would have to produce evidential matter about the fair value of assets to satisfy the auditor.
5 Preparers and their independent auditors would not have to speculate, as they do today in assessing the need for write-downs, about future events and their outcomes, such as:

- Will the fair value – for example, the quoted market price of a common stock listed on the New York Stock Exchange – bounce back above cost? How likely is it to bounce back? How long will it take?
- Will cash flows from operations, but before interest charges, improve for an asset such as plant? Even if such cash flows do improve, will interest rates hold steady, decline, or rise?
- How will cash flows from operations be affected by local, regional, national, and international competition?
- How will cash flows from operations for operating assets be affected by foreign exchange rate changes?

This proposal probably cannot be applied to goodwill, or most goodwill. Unless goodwill attaches to specific assets or groupings of assets (for example, to separate divisions), it cannot be sold and has no separate value. I would exclude goodwill from the disclosure requirement.

How much would it cost to implement this proposal? I don't know. Business people generally know, sometimes only intuitively, the fair value of their assets; they know what the marketplace would pay for the assets. However, I doubt that independent auditors will accept intuition and unsupported assertions by management. The degree of auditor association with the disclosure will have to be worked out. However, if auditor association appears to be a significant hurdle, it should be sacrificed, at least at the outset. The disclosures could be labeled "unaudited" or could be placed outside the basic financial statements and notes.

A practical alternative

Because obtaining objectively determined fair values of non-monetary assets is often difficult and costly, I suggest an alternative required disclosure that would be more practical for some assets. The alternative would be a standardized measure of cash flow to be disclosed in all cases when it is negative, along with the cost of the asset. The standardized measure of cash flow would be the net amount of annual operating revenue of the asset, minus the annual related cash operating costs, both based on the most recent year's results, minus one year's hypothetical interest to carry the cost of the asset, with that interest to be measured by using the 30-year US Treasury bond rate at the balance sheet date.

This disclosure would allow users to make their own subjective determinations about fair value of the asset and whether a write-down is necessary.

A field test for disclosure

Given the support for mandatory write-downs of impaired long-lived, non-monetary assets, the serious practical problems already cited must be considered the major obstacle to achieving a definitive, operational standard that would result in consistent practice and comparability for recognizing and measuring write-downs. The FASB may solve these problems, but we cannot assume that the answers will come quickly. Until the answers are in hand, users of financial statements would benefit from disclosures. However, the disclosures will not be comparable or consistent if they entail the same practical problems that have beset recognition and measurement in the accounts. In other words, the disclosures cannot be based on predicting future events and their outcomes. For this reason, I suggest consideration of required disclosures of fair value when it is below cost.

The relationship of costs to benefits for this disclosure may or may not be favorable, but we need to find out. One way to do this would be to subject the proposal to a test in the field.

I believe that such disclosure would also alleviate considerably the surprise that frequently accompanies business failures. A business failure is almost always preceded by a decline in the fair value of the assets of the enterprise. Disclosure of those declines should help to serve as a harbinger of failure and thus reduce surprise and shock, unless the declines are sudden, as in the case of the price of oil in 1986. Such disclosure should all but eliminate surprise related to write-downs, sometimes involving huge amounts, in the absence of a business failure.

30 The liability crisis in the USA and its impact on accounting

These remarks were presented at a conference on the liability crisis held at Northwestern University, 7 April 1991, and subsequently published in *Accounting Horizons*, Vol. 7, No. 2, June 1993, pp. 88–91

For ten to fifteen years, I have contended that until generally accepted accounting principles are unambiguously defined, auditors of financial statements cannot see clearly the target they intend to strike. So long as asset and liability recognition and measurement standards are fuzzy, auditors of financial statements do not always hit the ball and indeed sometimes strike out when at bat. We need to have clearly articulated standards that result in financial statement descriptions of assets and liabilities and amounts for those assets and liabilities that are clearly understood and, in addition, are relevant.

I think that the cost of the savings and loan bailout and the related litigation are in significant part due to ambiguity in accounting standards regarding revenue recognition on loans and loss recognition on loans. Better accounting could not have prevented the S&L catastrophe; the seeds for that catastrophe were sown when thrifts were permitted to leave the staid business of long-term residential loans so they could compete with businesses offering uninsured investments with wider returns. One significant way thrifts found they could compete was by using insured funds to lend builders and developers 100 percent of the acquisition price of risky assets by way of what have come to be known as "acquisition development and construction," or "ADC," loans. But ambiguous revenue recognition accounting rules allowed revenue recognition on those loans to extend too far and too long. And ambiguity, or outright contradiction, in loan loss recognition rules postponed too long the recognition of losses on those ADC loans.

ADC loans became prevalent in the thrift industry in the early 1980s. At that time, the only pertinent words on or about revenue recognition in the literature, which did not constitute an accounting rule or even guidance, were contained in old Accounting Principles Board Statement 4, paragraphs 150 and 151, which said in part:

> Revenue is generally recognized when the earnings process is complete or virtually complete ... Revenue from permitting others to use enterprise

> resources, such as interest ... is recognized as time passes ... at the amount expected to be received.

The guidance in the then existing AICPA *Savings and Loan Audit and Accounting Guide* (page 33) regarding recognition of income on loans was consistent with the words in APB Statement 4. In fact, the words in the 1979 guide almost assume that interest income is recognized on loans as per the loan contract and do not suggest much caution regarding revenue recognition.

Even though the drafters of APB Statement 4 and the 1979 guide had never heard of or seen an ADC loan when those documents were written, the revenue recognition words in those documents were applied to ADC loans, and interest income was recognized on those loans based on the contractual terms; so was fee income. Fee income and interest income were recognized by the thrift holders of ADC loans, and the loan balances and accrued interest on those balances kept growing and growing even though in most cases no cash was ever received by the thrifts.

During that time, there was the general provision in the literature that loan losses should be recognized when it was probable that such losses had occurred and could be estimated, which is from FASB Statement 5. This statement, issued in 1975, addresses when losses should be recognized, not how those losses are to be measured, a point to which I will return. Statement 5 was followed closely by Statement 15, which was issued in 1977. It addresses troubled debt restructurings.

In paragraph 1 of Statement 15, the FASB said that Statement 15 does not address allowances for estimated uncollectible amounts and does not prescribe or proscribe particular methods for estimating amounts of uncollectible receivables. Statement 5 is in place, and presumably Statement 5 governs when there is a loss, but Statement 5 does not define how to measure any loss. But, after appearing to defer to Statement 5, Statement 15 then goes on to say that if the holder of a troubled receivable expects to collect the entire carrying amount of the receivable, whether through the medium of interest or principal collection, no loss is to be recognized, no matter how long the collection might take. This means that economic losses may be retained in balance sheets and called assets so long as there is some expectation that some day the amount of the loan will be collected. As a result, we have Statement 5 saying to recognize a loss when it is "probable" that a loss has occurred, we have Statement 15 saying not to recognize a loss if the carrying amount of the loan may ultimately be collected, and we have no guidance, in any event, on how to measure such a loss. Talk about confusion. Talk about contradictory guidance. Talk about ambiguity. An entire generation of accountants was plunged into darkness by Statement 15. Those who prepared financial statements did not know whether to go forward, backward, sideways. Whether to put their left foot first or their right foot first. Independent auditors were similarly confused.

The thrift industry was in stress, so it opted to recognize the fee income and interest income on ADC loans and not to recognize any losses on those loans until the project assets were foreclosed, even though the fair values of the ADC projects were known to be less, often far less, than the ADC loan carrying amount and accrued interest. Independent auditors more or less agreed that the authoritative literature either required, or at least permitted, that accounting. Regulators, who were trying to keep an entire industry afloat, turned a blind eye to the accounting. Ultimately, equity investors were done in, and the American taxpayer is footing the bill through the bail-out of the deposit insurance system, and accountants are paying millions to the government and others in legal judgments.

To my mind, the ADC loan case is the perfect case for saying that ambiguous accounting principles, not auditing failure, are to blame for the litigation and resultant auditor liability arising out of the S&L catastrophe.

Some may say that if issuers of financial statements and their independent auditors had put on their thinking caps and looked at the substance of the ADC rather than their form, then the ADC loan asset would have been accounted for as an investment in real estate rather than as a loan and all of the fee income and interest income would not have been recognized and the problem would not have gotten as serious as it finally did. Well, maybe so, but think about that for a minute.

If accounting for the substance of events, circumstances, arrangements, and transactions is indeed the overarching guiding rule, then there is no need for standards. Or a standard-setting body. Presumably, all of us can see, clearly see, the substance of things, and will account for the substance of them, and everything will be fine. Not so. If we follow a substance-over-form rule, we will have anarchy in financial accounting and reporting. Substance over form itself is so ambiguous that if people are instructed to use that general rule instead of specific rules or standards, then financial statements will become highly individualized. I will prepare financial statements for my company the way I perceive the substance of things. You will prepare yours your way. And soon the financial statements that are presented to investors will have little comparability or consistency or understandability or meaning.

By like token, some people say that preparation of financial statements ought to be left, in large part, to the judgment of those who prepare and audit financial statements. That we should have broad, general financial accounting and reporting standards emanating from the FASB, with their implementation being left to the issuer of the financial statement and its auditor. That approach will not work either. A lot of people applied their judgment to accounting for ADC loans. That process produced a judgmental mess that is costing untold, uncounted billions. Before Accounting Research Bulletin 51 and FASB Statement 94 on consolidation were issued, issuers of financial statements consolidated the financial statements of whichever subsidiaries they wanted to. Before FASB Statements 8 and 52 on foreign currency translation were issued, issuers of financial statements did their foreign currency translation in a multitude of ways. Before FASB Statement 2 was issued, some issuers of financial statements capitalized R&D costs, some capitalized selected R&D costs, and others capitalized none. Before FASB Statement 5 was issued, some issuers of financial statements charged to expense additions to catastrophe reserves and so-called self-insurance reserves, and others did not. These examples prove that broad general rules left to the judgment of issuers and their auditors have not worked and will not work.

Currently, judgment is applied to the identification of impaired loans (the "probable" criterion in FASB Statement 5) and to the measurement of losses on impaired loans under Statement 5. We can see in current practice that the probable criterion has not worked. Identification of impaired loans under that criterion is all over the map, which produces wide non-comparability in financial statements. The General Accounting Office has found that the criterion does not work. Likewise, because Statement 5 does not address measurement of loan impairment, there is wide non-comparability on that score in financial statements as well. At least the FASB is working on the measurement aspects of loan impairment, but despite the warnings of the GAO and others, the FASB is retaining the "probable" criterion.

In the area of impairment of cost of marketable debt and equity securities, FASB Statements 12 and 60 require that the cost of marketable securities be written down when a decline in value of the security is "other than temporary." That literature does not define "other than temporary," so it is left up to the judgment of the issuer of the financial statement.

Judgment is also applied to the identification and measurement of impairment of the cost of long-lived assets, such as land, plant and equipment, and patents. The questions the accountant asks are "will the carrying amount of the asset be recovered through operations, and if not, what is the shortfall?" The Financial Executives Institute and the Institute of Management Accountants have performed or sponsored research work that has found wide variability in both the identification and the measurement of impairment of the cost, or recoverability of the cost, of long-lived assets, resulting in wide non-comparability in financial accounting and reporting.

We can see, for example, that full-cost oil and gas companies must write down the cost of their oil and gas assets whenever the so-called ceiling limitation is exceeded by cost. Successful oil and gas companies do not have such a constraint, and their capitalized costs sometimes exceed what would be allowed for a full-cost company. We also see that some companies, but not full-cost oil and gas companies, in identifying the impairment of the cost of assets and then measuring that impairment, assume that the state of the world that surrounds the assets will improve. That idle drilling rigs, for example, will go back to work drilling oil wells. However, this assumption is not based on an assumption of a continuation of the current price of oil of, say, $19 a barrel but an assumed increase to $25 or $30 a barrel. That a plant producing at 45 percent of capacity will increase its production runs to 85 percent of capacity or the assumption that consumers will buy more of the product in the future despite prior reluctance. That buildings currently having only 30 percent occupancy in two to three years will be 80 percent occupied, even though there is seven to ten years of vacant space to be absorbed. That's what we get when we allow judgment to enter the accounting process in a major way; management puts on its rose-colored glasses and the auditor is unable to prove that his or her client is wrong.

Accountants and investors are currently seeing judgments being applied in another area, namely the recognition of deferred tax assets. Under FASB Statement 109, the tax benefits of future tax-deductible amounts such as bad debts, warranties, post-retirement benefits other than pensions, and operating loss carryforwards and tax credit carryforwards are recognized as assets. If it is "more likely than not" that a tax benefit, in whole or in part, will not be realized, a valuation allowance is recognized that reduces the amount of the related tax asset. I recently saw the 1992 balance sheet of a registrant where the deferred tax assets are more than 400 percent of shareholders' equity. The deferred tax asset related just to healthcare benefits of retirees from that corporation is more than 200 percent of shareholders' equity. We all know that those benefits will be paid many years in the future and will not represent a tax deduction until paid. In a sense, this company's balance sheet and fortunes are based on anticipated future taxable income, and the company has concluded that it is "more likely than not" that future taxable income is sufficient to absorb tax deductions that arise in the future and those on hand today. The auditor is hard put to second-guess that judgment.

Well, so what, you may say. Ambiguous accounting standards have little or nothing to do with auditor liability. I disagree. I think plaintiffs and their lawyers clearly see that anytime an issuer or an issuer's auditor is in the dock, that person is vulnerable. That person is vulnerable because he or she relies on such fuzzy notions as "probable" and "cost is recoverable through the ordinary operation of a going concern," realization of tax benefits is "more likely than not," and market value declines are "temporary." Those terms, and others of similar ambiguity, are red meat for the plaintiff's bar. After an issuer has failed and it is found that the historical cost of its fixed assets or patents cannot be recovered through a sale of those assets, the issuer's assertion that it thought it could recover its cost of those assets on a going-concern basis is indeed weak. When an issuer's receivables turn out to be no good, but the receivables were thought not to be sour under a notion of "probability," the assertion that there was compliance with the literature is indeed weak. When income tax benefits are ultimately not realized, using the literature as a crutch will be of little help.

I think that it is in the best interests of investors to have financial statement descriptions and amounts of assets that are relevant and that flow from simple and unambiguous accounting standards. For example, if financial statement amounts were required, in the case of assets, to be not in excess of market values, or fair values, and not less than settlement amounts in the case of liabilities, these amounts would be relevant to investors. Investors would more readily understand the financial statement. Investors would be able to evaluate and compare the financial position and results of operations of companies A, B, and C with greater ease and with more certainty than is possible today. Likewise, it seems to me that, from the standpoint of auditors protecting themselves from the risks of litigation, they too should welcome simple and unambiguous accounting standards that produce financial statements that can be easily understood by reasonable investors and by the courts. Simple and straightforward standards may be the only way to end costly legal debates over the reasonableness of judgment calls made, oftentimes, many years in the past in a world of conflicting pressures and rapidly changing circumstances.

31 Reporting by independent auditors on internal controls

Adapted from a speech given by Walter Schuetze in 1993 at a symposium sponsored by *The CPA Journal* on "In the Public Interest"

Both the Public Oversight Board and the AICPA have endorsed a number of proposals to strengthen the profession. Among them is a recommendation that the SEC require management and auditors of public companies to report on the company system of internal control relating to financial reporting. The chief accountant of the SEC responds.

According to the SEC's Office of Public Affairs, more than 13,400 public companies and 4,000 investment companies file various reports with the SEC. The SEC requires that most of these reports include audited financial statements and that those financial statements be made available to investors. The audit reports attached to these entities' financial statements enhance the public's confidence in the reliability of these statements, lessen the public's fear that the financial statements are incomplete or biased, and encourage the public to invest in securities issued by public companies and investment funds. This concept of an independent audit of the financial statements of enterprises that seek to raise money from the public is one of the cornerstones of the Securities Act of 1933. Significantly, under the Securities Act, an enterprise wishing to offer its securities to the public need not engage counsel or have an underwriter, but it must have an independent auditor. That independent auditor must audit and report on the registrant's financial statements and consent to the inclusion of his or her report in the offering document.

The commission requires audited financial statements for other purposes as well. For example, 8,200 broker/dealers file reports with the commission. More than half of these reports include audited financial statements, which are required to be mailed to the broker/dealers' customers. Audited financial statements in this situation increase customers' confidence in the creditworthiness and solvency of the entity that holds their funds and securities and transacts their business.

The auditing function is thus of great importance to investors, the commission, and the general process by which corporations raise capital and conduct their business affairs.

Our capital market is the best in the world. I never cease to marvel at the capital-raising and capital-allocation capability of our debt and equity markets.

And audited financial statements and related disclosures are the lubricant that allows the capital market engine of this country to turn at very high RPMs. So, when the Public Oversight Board says that the auditing profession is threatened by a lack of public confidence litigation, or other risks, I am concerned, and when the profession makes recommendations for improvements in financial reporting, I consider those recommendations seriously.

However, I am not a lawyer, so I cannot speak to the legal issues raised by the profession, the Public Oversight Board, and others, such as joint and several liability versus proportional liability, how contribution works or ought to work, or when or how Rules 9 and 11 of the Federal Rules of Civil Procedure work or ought to work.

I am an accountant/auditor, so I want to address one aspect of the proposals made by the Public Oversight Board and the AICPA's board of directors that concerns auditing and accounting, namely auditor reporting on registrants' internal controls related to financial reporting to the public. I am particularly interested in statements that these bodies have made about how such auditor reports relate to what is commonly referred to as "fraudulent financial reporting." In addition, as I will discuss later, I am concerned that investors and others may rely on such reports.

Who wants it?

The AICPA and the POB would have the SEC put in place a mandatory reporting system so that the 13,400 public companies would have to state publicly whether their internal controls over financial reporting are effective and their independent auditors would have to opine, publicly, on that assertion by management. I think most public company registrants would be opposed to such a requirement. When the commission exposed that idea for comment in 1979 and again in 1988, it received substantial adverse comment. More recently, public company registrants formally or informally (mostly informally), have said they oppose the idea of public reporting on internal controls by their independent auditors. The registrants are saying that the additional costs involved would outweigh the benefits. Indeed, I have heard some of those registrants say, informally, that there would be no benefit whatsoever to the registrants or to investors. As well, I have not heard any private user group arguing for public reporting on internal controls or indicating concern over the magnitude or level of fraudulent financial reporting. For example, in its July 1992 position paper entitled *Financial Reporting in the 1990s and Beyond*, the Association for Investment Management and Research does not mention public reporting on internal controls or the issue of fraudulent financial reporting.

Is there a cost benefit?

On the cost side, I have heard, again informally, that public reporting by independent auditors on the effectiveness of registrants' internal control systems over financial reporting will involve additional costs to registrants. For smaller companies, I have heard that the cost might be substantial, relatively speaking. So, if one is favorably disposed toward such reporting, the age-old cost–benefit trade-off would have to be considered.

One could argue that management and auditor reports on the quality of a registrant's internal control systems are desirable for two reasons: one, to prevent fraudulent financial reporting; and, two, to improve financial reporting in general. I have not heard much argument in favor of the second reason, namely to improve financial reporting in general. The POB asserts, on page 53 of its Special Report, that requiring auditors to assess management reports will lead to improvements in systems, and I suppose that could improve financial reporting generally. Auditors are now required to gain an understanding of the registrant's internal controls, so what the POB literally suggests is not new in that sense. Public reporting on those controls would be new, however. The more registrants and their external auditors think about, talk about, and work on improving internal control systems the better those systems will probably become.

Aside from the POB's statement and the position of the General Accounting Office that led to the requirements for management and auditor reports on internal control as part of the Federal Deposit Insurance Corporation Improvement Act of 1991, I have not heard any recent argument that public reporting by public companies and their independent auditors will improve financial reporting in general. I question whether the financial reporting by honest managements, who run the vast majority of public company registrants, is going to be improved significantly by public reporting on internal controls. However, I will reserve judgment on that reason for public reporting on controls until I see or hear more evidence or argument.

Will it prevent fraud?

The other reason for public reporting on internal controls is to prevent or deter dishonest management from "cooking the books." The AICPA has stated quite plainly and directly that it is the independent auditor's responsibility to detect such fraud. The AICPA says, on page 2 of the White Paper:

> Fraudulent financial schemes are the stuff of headlines and spicy news reports. Fraud justifiably engenders public outrage. While few business failures involve fraud, their corrosive effect on public confidence is widespread. The public looks to the independent auditor to detect fraud, and it is the auditor's responsibility to do so.

The only argument by the board of directors of the AICPA for reporting on internal controls over financial reporting is that it would reduce fraudulent financial reporting. On page 4 of the June 1993 White Paper, the AICPA says "The internal control system is the main line of defense against fraudulent financial reporting," and "The investing public deserves an independent assessment of that line of defense." The POB agrees. It says, on page 53 of its Special Report, that "improved systems will make management fraud and manipulation of financial reporting more difficult."

After considerable informal discussions with practitioners, preparers of financial statements, and other regulators, and a year and a half of reviewing accounting and auditing enforcement cases as they wind their way to the commission, I question whether public reporting on internal controls over financial reporting by registrants and their independent auditors would reduce so-called fraudulent financial reporting and litigation against external auditors.

The Treadway Commission found, in 1987, that fraudulent financial reporting arises primarily because management is "cooking the books." The POB, on page 49 of its Special Report, made a similar finding, to wit, "every fraudulent financial statement for which an [independent] auditor has been held responsible was prepared by executives who were intentionally committing a fraud, not only upon their shareholders, investors and the markets, but also on the auditor."

I agree that fraudulent financial reports arise principally when management of an enterprise has deliberately falsified the facts by mis-stating assets, liabilities, equity, or income. For example, management may report bogus receivables or non-existent inventory as assets, or it may overprice existing inventory, or omit liabilities from the balance sheet. These kinds of irregularity – namely lying and cheating by "cooking the books" – may be difficult to identify if there is widespread collusion, but a well-designed and well-executed audit provides the best means of detecting these frauds. Indeed, the White Paper, as noted above, says that auditors have the responsibility to find such fraud. No amount of reporting on internal controls will ferret out any more fraud or provide any better techniques to find it than the audit of the financial statements should have done in the first instance. Some argue that, although reporting on internal controls may not uncover fraud, it will deter fraud by having management and auditors focus on the internal control system and the checks and balances placed on each management employee by such a system of controls. However, I question how reporting on internal controls by independent auditors is going to deter fraudulent financial reporting resulting from "cooked books" when management was not deterred by the requirement for an annual audit and was able in the first instance to conceal the fraud from the auditors during the audit.

The problem of ambiguous accounting principles

Another, and more prevalent, cause of improper financial reporting is the use of ambiguous accounting principles to overstate assets, equity, and income. Some registrants use the lack of specific guidance in some accounting standards, or the absence of a standard that directly addresses the registrant's situation, to argue for the presentation of uncertain facts in their most ambitious and favorable light instead of presenting the facts in the financial statements in a neutral and objective way. Auditors suggest that they cannot stop this kind of misconduct because, under existing accounting principles, assets may be recognized even though there is no way to audit or verify, with reasonable assurance, that any future benefit exists or that the asset amounts will be recovered or realized. This kind of improper reporting occurs, therefore, not because of a failure of auditors to discover crooked schemes but because of a failure in the way accounting principles are written. No amount of internal controls reporting can cure this problem.

The S&L crisis provides a prime example. The savings and loan crisis and certain bank and insurance company failures went undetected, or at least unreported, by the auditing profession because of such a failure of accounting principles. S&Ls recognized interest income and fee income and related assets on acquisition, development, or construction loans because revenue-recognition standards were so general, so vague, and so judgmental that they amounted to no standards at all; and this problem continues today. Even with SFAS No. 91, adopted in 1986, there is no truly objective standard in place for recognition of fee income, or interest income for that matter. In Statement 91, the FASB stated: "Deferred net fees or costs shall not be amortized during periods in which interest income on a loan is not being recognized because of concerns about the realization of loan principal or interest." The phrase "concerns about realization" is not a standard that can be applied objectively. How can anyone audit the results of its application?

If it is believed that the practice regarding the recognition of fee and interest income that went on in S&Ls is no longer going on, that belief is wrong. Insurance companies that hold payment-in-kind (PIK) bonds or PIK preferred stocks, today, with the blessing of their auditors, are recognizing interest or dividend income on those assets even though no cash is being received and even though the market value or fair value of the PIK bond or PIK preferred stock may be less than the cost plus the amount of the so-called accrued interest or accrued dividend.

Observers of this scene also should not be lulled into believing the newly issued SFAS No. 114, which deals with loan impairment, will necessarily improve the matter. Unfortunately, the new standard suffers in some respects from the same lack of bright lines as the previous practice. For example, in SFAS No. 114, the FASB states that loan impairment should be recognized when it is probable that contractual principal and interest will not be collected as stipulated in the loan contract. While Statement 114 is, in certain other respects, a significant improvement over the prior literature, the *probable* standard in Statement 114 for the identification of impaired loans is the same standard as was in effect when the S&L problems arose. The probable standard is too judgmental and leads to wide non-comparability among issuers' financial statements.

By like token, under new SFAS No. 115, companies that invest in marketable debt and equity securities are not required to write down the cost of their impaired investment through income until any decline in value below cost is "other than temporary." Unfortunately, the standard does not define "other than temporary," so it is left to the judgment of the issuer of the financial statement. Auditors are not able to enforce that standard, or at least have not enforced it, until the investee company is draped in black crepe.

There is no written accounting standard at all for identifying and then measuring impairment of cost of fixed assets and intangible assets. In practice, companies may look at the undiscounted cash flows of assets to identify and measure impairment. That seldom leads to write-downs of fixed assets or intangible assets short of a decision to sell or abandon the asset. The cost of plant and equipment can sit in the balance sheet for years even if fair value is below cost, even far below cost, because management of the enterprise can assert, and generally does, that the state of the world surrounding the assets is only temporarily depressed, that markets for the company's products will improve, or that the company will be able to reduce its costs over time and that margins will improve. Thus cash flows will improve, and no write-down is necessary.

I have suggested that the auditing profession go to the Financial Accounting Standards Board and encourage it to write standards that provide numbers that can be tested, verified, and reported on with a true sense of objectivity and reliability.

Reports by auditors regarding registrants' internal controls, therefore, would not address what I believe to be the basic cause of fraudulent financial reporting – dishonest managements, or the application of subjective accounting principles.

The potential for over-reliance

In addition, there is a more fundamental concern I have with auditor reporting on internal controls, which is the potential for over-reliance on the reports by investors and the public generally. I have heard investors, and even members of Congress, say that if a bank or savings and loan had better internal controls, they would not have made loans that went bad. I have also heard some say that effective internal controls result in more effective decision making by management, and others have gone so far as to state that effective internal controls may prevent bad business decisions.

Unfortunately, the truth is that even companies with good internal controls make mistakes. Internal controls related to financial reporting typically relate to the recording of transactions, the authorization of transactions, and the safeguarding of assets. No amount of internal controls will keep banks from making loans that later go bad, prevent managements from entering into contracts that become loss contracts, or make each decision to fund research and development pay off. Investors will be disappointed. And, in their disappointment, investors and others may point to the "clean" audit report on the effectiveness of the issuer's internal controls and ask "How could this happen?" Proponents of auditor reporting on internal controls should make sure that there is an obvious and readily understandable answer to this question before asking the commission staff to consider the imposition of more costly reporting requirements on public companies.

Not a solution

I believe that auditor reporting on internal controls will not stop the crooks of the world, who are going to make the financial statements say what they want them to say regardless of the facts, and that auditor reporting on internal controls will not solve the more pervasive and more important problem of managements pushing pliable accounting standards. Further, while I believe that the proposition has yet to be proved that auditor reporting on internal controls would result in a significant improvement in financial reporting in general, I am certainly willing to have further discussions on the issue.

Reproduced with the permission of the copyright owner; further reproduction prohibited without permission.

32 A mountain or a molehill?

American Accounting Association,
Accounting Horizons, Vol. 8, No. 1,
March 1994, pp. 69–75

The commission has stated repeatedly that the independence of auditors, both in appearance and in fact, is crucial to the credibility of financial reporting and, in turn, the capital formation process.

However, I want to emphasize that these remarks represent my views and not necessarily those of the commission or other members of the staff. This routine disclaimer is perhaps more appropriate today because, in a moment, I am going to discuss an independence issue that, as the commission's chief accountant, I have found personally very troubling when dealing with registrants' accounting issues.

John L. Carey was, for many years, the senior staff officer of the American Institute of Certified Public Accountants. In his 1946 book, *Professional Ethics of Public Accountants*, Mr Carey wrote as follows about independence:

> Only a moment's reflection is necessary to perceive why independence is the keystone in the structure of the accounting profession ... The prime purpose of ... [the audit] opinion is to add to the credibility of the statements in the eyes of outsiders who for one reason or another are interested in the financial position and operating results of the business – for example, credit grantors, stockholders, government regulatory agencies, potential investors and financial analysts. Clearly they would set no great store by the certified public accountant's opinion or certificate if they were not confident of his independence of judgment, as well as his technical competence. Technically competent accountants may be employed by corporations as part of their own staffs to keep accounts and make up their statements. The basic differentiation between privately employed accountants and professional practitioners is in their responsibilities, moral or legal, to the corporation or the public, and in the extent to which their relationship may tend to influence their judgment. In the last analysis, therefore, it is his independence which is the certified public accountant's economic excuse for existence.

Independence is an abstract concept, and it is difficult to define either generally or in its peculiar application to the certified public accountant. Essentially it is a state of mind. It is partly synonymous with honesty, integrity, courage, and character. It means, in simplest terms, that the certified public accountant will tell the truth as he sees it and will permit no influence, financial or sentimental, to turn him from that course. Everyone will applaud this ideal, but a cynical world requires more than a mere declaration of intent if it is to stake its money on the accountant's word. Therefore the profession has publicly laid its heaviest penalties on those who breach the unwritten contract of independence and, in addition, it has proscribed specific acts and models of behavior that might raise a question as to the independence of its members. In other words, the rules not only provide for punishment of members who are not independent but also prohibit conduct that might arouse suspicion of lack of independence. Objective standards of independence have thus been introduced into the code. It is not enough for the member to do what he thinks is right. He must also avoid behavior that could lead to an inference that he might be subject to improper influences. The accounting profession must be like Caesar's wife. To be suspected is almost as bad as to be convicted.

Not long after I arrived at the commission in January 1992, the chairman of a special committee of the AICPA asked for an appointment with my staff and me to discuss auditor independence and, more specifically, to discuss a draft of a new approach to determining auditor independence. The proposed approach would have replaced the reasonable outside investor's approach to independence with the approach that a well-informed auditor would take to the question of independence. The draft would have done away with the concept of auditors maintaining the appearance of independence from their clients and would have focused solely on independence in fact. That focus would have been achieved by eliminating much of the specific guidance contained in current AICPA independence requirements.

My office reacted negatively to that draft. While I personally do not like the present situation, where there is a large volume of detailed rules relating to independence issues, principally issues arising out of family relationships between auditors, auditing firms, and their audit clients, I do not see a practical way out of this situation.

Moreover, I think that eliminating the concept of appearance of independence is not viable. I personally would not favor its elimination. Prior commissions have looked at the need for auditors to avoid being "suspected of improper influences," to use John Carey's words, and concluded that requiring auditors not only to be independent in fact but also to be independent in appearance was appropriate and necessary if investors are to maintain confidence in the reliability of the financial statements that daily provide the basis for investment and lending decisions. Moreover, the Supreme Court emphasized appearance in the Arthur Young case in 1984 as follows:

> The SEC requires the filing of audited financial statements in order to obviate the fear of loss from reliance on inaccurate information, thereby encouraging public investment in the nation's industries. It is therefore not

> enough that financial statements be accurate; the public must also *perceive* them as being accurate. Public faith in the reliability of a corporation's financial statements depends upon the public perception of the outside auditor as an independent professional.

The concept of auditor independence under federal securities laws was therefore designed not only as a means to have better financial information reported to the public but also to enhance investors' perceptions regarding the reliability and accuracy of that information. Starting from this vantage point, it is easily understood why the staff resisted the approach taken by the AICPA committee that independence issues should be viewed from the standpoint of a "reasonable auditor." To the staff, the key question is whether a reasonable investor, knowing all the facts and circumstances, would consider the independent accountant to have impartial and objective judgment on the questions confronting him or her during the audit.

I want to turn now to an issue that has vexed and bewildered me since I came to the commission two years ago. I refer to situations in which auditors are not standing up to their clients on financial accounting and reporting issues when their clients take a position that is, at best, not supported in the accounting literature or, at worst, directly contrary to existing accounting pronouncements. To me, auditors giving way to their clients, subordinating their views to those of their clients, raises a nasty issue about independence both in appearance and in fact. In my opinion, an auditor's independence, whether called appearance or fact, is jeopardized as much by his or her subordinating judgment about a financial accounting and reporting issue as it is by investing in securities issued by a client, lending money to a client, or borrowing money from a client – perhaps even more so. At least insofar as money matters are concerned, if there was disclosure to the investor about that fact, then the investor would be on notice and could be guided by the facts, although I would not – definitely not – advocate such an approach. Not so with the subordinated judgment, which is insidious. There is no way to communicate impaired or colored judgment. No disclosure about it could ever be complete, or be trusted. Nor is there any way for an investor to make judgments about the effect of impaired or colored judgment on the part of the auditor.

In a speech in August 1992 to the annual meeting of the American Accounting Association, I raised the issue of auditor independence in connection with what I called "incredible" accounting proposals. By incredible accounting proposals, I meant unsupportable conclusions regarding accounting issues that were being proposed by registrants with the support of their auditors. These accounting proposals, in my opinion, were wrong – not just debatable or arguable, but wrong. Sometimes that support was in the form of a signed and unqualified opinion, and sometimes that support was in written or oral presentations to the SEC's staff before the registrant's financial statements were issued and the independent auditor reported on those financial statements.

Some senior people in the profession privately suggested that I was making a mountain out of a molehill in that 1992 speech. Some, including the AICPA's Public Oversight Board in its March 1993 special report entitled *In the Public Interest*, suggested that a few engagement partners, on their own and without consultation within their firms, might have inappropriately supported some liberal accounting proposals. Others privately suggested that the few incredible accounting proposals that were put forward to SEC staff had to be taken in the context of the thousands of audits of public companies' financial statements that take place every year, where those companies' financial statements are based on good and thorough applications of generally accepted accounting principles.

It is true, as some have suggested, including the Public Oversight Board, that many new and complex issues reach my desk because there is an honest difference of opinion based on well-reasoned positions on all sides. In these cases, the staff works with the registrants and their auditors to resolve those issues through discussion, analysis of analogous literature, and compromise in many cases. Addressing those kinds of issue is a challenging and interesting part of my job, and I encourage registrants and their auditors to continue to bring these issues to the staff. I am also aware, because I practiced in public accountancy for many years, of the thousands of decisions that are made by auditors in their work where they insist on adjustments to financial statements that reduce net assets and income or otherwise insist on financial statement reporting and disclosures that managements of their clients would rather not make – none of which is ever publicized.

However, there have been too many times where accounting arguments made by registrants lack any reasonable foundation and, without being able to cite any authoritative support for the registrant's position, the auditor has acquiesced.

I was hopeful, after the August 1992 speech, that the profession would have gotten the message and would have stopped the practice of supporting their clients' incredible accounting proposals. My hopes have not been fulfilled, however. Since then, we have had the following proposals, among others, by registrants and their auditors. These have been supported not just by an engagement partner in a firm without consultation within the firm but also by partners from the national offices of the firms.

1 An airline company spends money to overhaul aircraft engines and airframes. Some airline companies defer those overhaul costs and amortize the costs over the estimated future benefit period. One such airline, with the support of its auditor (actually two auditors, because one auditor was being succeeded by another), proposed to classify as a current asset at the most recent balance sheet date the portion of the deferred costs that was to be amortized to expense in the following year. I cannot fathom how an equipment expenditure made in a prior period can credibly be said to be a current asset at any subsequent balance sheet date.

2 A registrant was committed to making cash payments under a non-cancellable lease for the use of a building. For accounting purposes, the lease was classified as an operating lease. The lease payments were based on a rental rate of, say, $25 a square foot, which was the fair market rental when the lease was entered into some years ago. Because of an oversupply of commercial real estate, the market rental rate for comparable space over the remaining lease term is not $25 but, say, $15 a square foot. The registrant was going to sub-let the building to another company and receive from the sub-lessee so-called barter credits that could be exchanged for, among other things, advertising by the company and discounts from certain vendors. The company asserted that the value of the barter credits for the advertising and the discounts was equal to the value of the lease payments based on a rental rate of $25 a square foot. The registrant, with the support of its auditor, therefore proposed not to recognize the loss of $10 a square foot. The problem is the company's assigning a value to the barter credits based on the subjective nature of the value of the right to advertising and trade discounts, rather than basing the value of the barter credits on the more objective, and independently verifiable, current rental value for comparable property – $15 per square foot. How could anyone credibly support the argument that a sub-lessee would pay something of value worth $25 a square foot when a fair value of the rent was $15 a square foot?

3 Registrant A acquired Company X. When A delved into Company X's records, it found that Company X's liabilities for certain payroll taxes were understated. A and X, with the auditor's support, proposed that adjustment to X's payroll tax liability not be reported in X's income statement in periods prior to the business combination but be included in the adjustments arising in purchase accounting. How could anyone credibly support a proposal that X's payroll costs did not need to include the necessary payroll taxes in X's income statements for periods prior to the business combination?

4 Company H acquired majority, but not total, ownership of Company Z. Company Z had outstanding stock options held by employees, which if exercised would have had adverse tax consequences for Company H. The options were deep in the money and were vested and exercisable. Company H wanted to enter into new contracts with Z's employees, which would have postponed exercise of the options and protected the amount by which the options were in the money if the value of the underlying stock declined. Companies H and Z argued, with the support of their auditor, that the terms of the outstanding options had not been changed, no new measurement date had occurred under Accounting Principles Board Opinion 25, and therefore no amount of compensation cost need be recognized. How can anyone credibly argue that a new agreement that protects an employee holding a stock option deep in the money from any decline in the price of the stock is not a new stock option agreement that triggers a new measurement date and consequent compensation cost?

Those are a few specific registrant examples, of which there are more. If these were the only examples, they perhaps could be excused as anomalies. But there are other cases that are more broadly applicable, and they involve many companies. And, in these cases, it is again clear that the auditors' actions are not individual engagement partners acting on their own but that the actions are undertaken with the knowledge of the national offices of the firms. For instance, last year the FASB's staff and the SEC's staff had to force prompt consideration of the issue of "funded catastrophe covers" by the Emerging Issues Task Force, which is reported in EITF Issue 93-6. This issue involves companies in the property casualty industry paying reinsurers premiums for catastrophes such as Hurricane Andrew and Typhoon Iniki in years before, during, and after the year of the catastrophic event. The reinsurance contract was such that, if no catastrophe happened, a portion of the amount of the premium, say, 85 percent, went from the reinsurer back to the insurer in the form of cash. If a catastrophe happened, the reinsurer paid the loss but then the insurer had to repay the amount of the loss to the reinsurer plus interest. The insurers were recognizing expenses for the catastrophe losses in years before the catastrophic event, the year of the event, and years after, as premiums were paid to the reinsurers, instead of in the year or quarter in which the catastrophe happened, all with the concurrence of their auditors. FASB Statement 5, *Accounting for Contingencies*, issued in 1975, specifically deals with the accounting for such events and says that a loss should be recognized in expense in the year in which the event happens – not sooner or later. A number of registrants have changed their accounting as a result of the FASB staff's and SEC staff's intervention. This episode led to an article in *The New York Times* on 5 September 1993 entitled "Cooking books: how hurricane losses vanished." The article said, in part:

> How, you might wonder, could any companies have gotten away with this obvious phoney accounting, given that all the Big 6 Accounting firms agree it is wrong. In fact, auditors from each of those firms accepted the accounting, although some tried to resist and allowed slightly less liberal accounting.
>
> "When there is somebody down the street who will say yes," commented one accountant who studied the issue, "other firms find themselves under enormous pressure to also say yes."

I do not see how registrants and their auditors credibly could argue that they did not have to pay attention to the official accounting literature.

Another issue arose last year that affected many companies. Our staff began to question the rates that registrants were using to discount their estimated future cash payments for pensions and healthcare benefits for retirees. The official literature explicitly requires that the discount rate be based on the current level of interest rates, and the literature refers to the yield on high-quality corporate bonds. Many registrants were instead using old, outdated interest rates that were much higher than current rates on high-quality corporate bonds. Consequently, their pension and healthcare benefit obligations were significantly understated. As our staff got into the issue, it became clear that many registrants, without objection from their auditors, were not following the authoritative literature in selecting their discount rates. It took a letter from the chief accountant to the FASB's Emerging Issues Task Force dated 20 September 1993 to challenge both registrants and their auditors to pay attention to the literature. In many cases, the effect of not following the literature was, without any doubt, material. The press has covered this issue extensively in recent months. *USA Today*, on 18 November 1993, wrote as follows, in part, about corporations using a too high rate to measure pension liabilities:

> It's an open secret in the pension field that companies have been using out-of-date assumptions about interest rates, says Gordon Webb, a pension consultant at Foster Higgins in San Francisco. "Employers are playing it fast and loose, and the auditors are letting them get away with it," he says.

There are now a substantial number of companies that will be changing their discount rates as a result of the SEC staff's intervention. This non-compliance with the literature comes on the heels of what we observed in 1992, when many banks, thrifts, and insurance companies, with the concurrence of their auditors, were not following the literature in classifying their debt securities holdings as between "held for investment" and "held for sale," which was corrected only through SEC staff intervention. How can registrants and their auditors ignore the literature and then expect investors, regulators, Congress, and the public generally to put credence on what they say?

It also appears to me, and other outside observers, that CPAs may have become cheerleaders for their clients on the issue of accounting for stock options issued to employees. (I should make it clear here that the commission has not considered the issue of the accounting for stock options issued to employees.) In 1978, in response to a proposed interpretation by the FASB of the existing accounting rules for stock options granted to employees, six of the Big Eight accounting firms wrote to the FASB suggesting that the board reconsider the accounting rules for stock options granted to employees. In the early and mid-1980s, the AICPA, through its Accounting Standards Executive Committee, twice asked the FASB to re-examine the accounting for stock options issued to employees. In 1982, the AICPA said "the principles [of Accounting Principles Board Opinion 25] should be changed so that compensation expense is recognized for most plans." In 1984, the AICPA said "AcSEC is pleased that the FASB has undertaken a project on a broad reconsideration of the principles that underlie APB Opinion 25 ... AcSEC believes a major change in accounting for compensation plans is necessary." The AICPA, in the 1984 letter, went on to say that compensation cost should be based on the fair value of the option at the grant date and recommended that the so-called minimum-value method be used to measure the value of the option.

In 1984 and 1985, in response to the invitation to comment that began the FASB's reconsideration of the existing accounting rules for stock options granted to employees, all except one of the then Big Eight accounting firms wrote to the FASB supporting (1) reconsideration of the accounting rules and (2) a charge to compensation cost/expense for all options granted to employees.

But, in February 1993, even before the FASB issued its exposure draft on the subject on 30 June 1993, all of the Big Six accounting firms joined forces with certain members of industry and a group of users to recommend to the FASB that there be no formal recognition for the cost of stock options. (I understand that the AICPA's Accounting Standards Executive Committee recently changed its mind and now will recommend to the FASB that there be no recognition for the cost of fixed stock options.) The Big Six accounting firms did not, in February 1993, offer an explanation for their change of mind. I would be the first to say that anyone could change his or her mind. I have changed my mind on several accounting issues over the years. But I think that the public deserves an acknowledgment of that change of mind by the firms and the reason why. Such a change in position, without a corresponding change in the underlying concepts and issues that led the firms and the AICPA initially to support the FASB's project, has left some members of the public with the impression that the switch was in response to the fear of losing clients or other forms of retaliation. I do not know if this is true. However, if public companies are pressuring their outside auditors, and the Accounting Standards Executive Committee of the AICPA, to take particular positions on financial accounting and reporting issues, and outside auditors are subordinating their views to their clients' views, can the outside auditor community continue to claim to be independent? Could continuation of such a trend be anything other than an invitation to Congress, the SEC, and other regulators to regulate more heavily, and directly, the auditing profession in particular and financial accounting and reporting in general? Could continuation of such a trend lead investors, particularly institutional investors, to find alternative ways to corroborate issuers' representations in their financial statements?

The independence rules promulgated by the AICPA and the SEC principally address the appearance of independence because it is impossible to regulate an individual's state of mind. However, the independent mindset is the most basic independence requirement. The advocacy of weak and unsupported client accounting positions speaks loudly about independence in fact. The preceding examples have been gleaned from the numerous issues that have been considered by the Office of the Chief Accountant since August 1992. In that context, the specific and general examples cited represent a small – some might even argue, insignificant – number of exceptions to the generally outstanding manner in which the accounting profession carries out its duties as "public watchdog." However, individual practitioners and firms need to be mindful that the number of such instances that may poison the well with regulators, legislators, investors, and the general public is small indeed.

I make these comments with a heavy heart. As many of you know, these comments do not come from an ivory tower. I have lived and worked in the accounting profession for more than 30 years. I know the realities of saying "no" to a client. I know the disappointment some clients express when the auditor makes a decision to support an accounting proposal that may reduce those clients' reported earnings. I know the long and often heated telephone calls and client visits, the emotional strain, and the financial cost that follow such decisions. But I also know the rewards – a clear conscience, not having to worry about losing lawsuits based on the merits, and pride in the profession and the credibility of financial accounting and reporting. I hope that the profession and registrants will, through self-restraint, take a fresh look at these independence issues and, as John Carey suggested, let nothing stand in the auditor's way of telling the truth as he or she sees it.

Reproduced with permission of the copyright owner; further reproduction prohibited without permission.

33 Comments on certain aspects of the special report by the AICPA's Public Oversight Board of 5 March 1993

Address to University of Southern California, SEC and Financial Reporting Institute, 27 May 1993

The major firms in the public accounting profession say that they are in a crisis, a liability crisis. They say that when there is a business failure, they are being asked by the government and by the courts to pay huge amounts of money to the government or to investors. Moreover, they say, they are being asked to pay, and forced to pay, amounts of money that are not in proportion to any fault that they may have had in reporting on the correct or incorrect financial statements of the business that failed.

Representatives of a number of accounting firms asked the Public Oversight Board of the American Institute of Certified Public Accountants[1] to consider whether that board could support the profession's efforts to obtain relief from what the profession believes to be an excessive burden of litigation. In studying this issue, the POB became concerned that attacks on the accounting profession from a variety of sources suggested a significant public concern with the profession's performance. The POB has therefore issued a report addressing more than the isolated issue of litigation reform. The report includes twenty-five recommendations that the POB believes, if implemented, would improve the usefulness and reliability of financial statements and enhance the auditor's ability to detect fraud and other illegal acts.[2]

It is time to begin the discussion and debate about the recommendations in the POB's special report, and I will address here today the three recommendations that are addressed to the Securities and Exchange Commission. I wish to make it clear that I have not discussed my analysis with any of the commissioners and that the commissioners have reached no conclusions, tentative or otherwise, about the POB's recommendations. What follows is my analysis and very, very tentative conclusions, and mine alone. I would not be surprised if I were to change my mind about these matters as this discussion and debate goes forward in the coming months. As is often the case, as I learn more about something and as I think more about it, I change my mind.

Recommendation II-1: the SEC should amend its rules to require SEC registrants to disclose whether their auditors have had a peer review, the date of the most recent peer review, and its results.

In 1985, the commission proposed such disclosure as part of a comprehensive review of the proxy rules: Securities Act Release No. 6592, Exchange Act Release No. 22195 (1 July 1985). Specifically, the proposal would have required each registrant's proxy statement to include:

> (i) a statement of whether or not the principal accountant ... is a member in a professional organization which has both a peer review program and independent oversight function, both of which are subject to review by the Commission and (ii) if such a member, a statement whether or not the principal accountant has had such a peer review, and if so the date of the most recent peer review report.

While the proposed disclosure did not address the results of the peer review, the text of the proposing release stated:

> (ii) if the results of the peer review were other than unqualified, however, registrants would need to consider whether they should disclose the nature of any qualifications and the status of the principal accountant's efforts to correct deficiencies which were the basis for such qualifications. Such disclosure might be material to an informed voting decision, where, for example, the deficiencies uncovered were of a significant or pervasive nature and have not yet been corrected.

A footnote at the end of this paragraph stated:

> See Rule 14a-9(a), which prohibits, inter alia, the use of proxy material that "omits to state any material fact necessary in order to make the statements therein not false or misleading."

Thirty-eight commentators addressed the proposal. Five supported the proposal, thirteen suggested modifications, and twenty opposed it. Those suggesting modifications, and those opposing the proposal, stated that they were concerned with putting such information about the accountant in the registrant's "liability document." They stated that the proposal opened questions regarding a registrant's duty to inquire, verify, and evaluate any information provided by the accountant regarding its participation in the peer review program, its categorization of the peer review report, and the status of the accountant's efforts to correct deficiencies. Commentators emphasized that registrants were not experts in performing peer review evaluations. They said that the proposal would place a "compliance burden" on registrants without providing an equivalent benefit to security holders. The American Bar Association, in its opposition to the proposal, said that requiring registrants to make judgments on disclosure of deficiencies noted in peer review reports, and to ascertain the status of corrective efforts by their accountants, "imposes burdens on registrants that border on the unseemly."

Other positions advanced by several commentators to show that the proposal would be an inappropriate burden on registrants were that (1) the proposal was superfluous (as most SEC registrants already had auditors who were members of the SECPS) and that (2) others were in a better position than registrants to review the peer review process. In addition, other commentators said that the disclosure was an inappropriate method of coercing membership in the SECPS, especially because, in their opinion, SECPS members were no better qualified to perform audits than non-members. Others said that the disclosure might give shareholders an unwarranted sense of confidence. Still other commentators said that the costs of membership in the SECPS were material to small and medium-sized firms and that the proposal therefore tipped the "competitive balance" in favor of large firms.

I question what benefit investors and potential investors would get from such a disclosure standing alone. Should the disclosure be accompanied by any "comments" that the reviewer had on quality controls of the firm being reviewed? Suppose the peer review report was not unqualified and that fact was disclosed – what would investors do then? Should the disclosure be accompanied by additional disclosure about litigation against the firm generally or about SEC Rule 2(e) proceedings against the firm or certain of its partners?

Recommendation V-10: the SEC should require registrants to include in a document containing the annual financial statements a statement by the audit committee (or by the board if there is no audit committee) that describes its responsibilities and tells how they were discharged. This disclosure should state whether the audit committee members (or, in the absence of an audit committee, the members of the board): (1) have reviewed the annual financial statements; (2) have conferred with management and the independent auditor about them; (3) have received from the independent auditor all information that the auditor is required to communicate under auditing standards; (4) believe that the financial statements are complete and consistent with information known to them; and (5) believe that the financial statements reflect appropriate accounting principles.

The POB report cites the 1987 report of the National Commission on Fraudulent Financial Reporting (the Treadway Commission) as support for this recommendation. In line with the Treadway Commission's "tone at the top" approach, the POB report states, "The responsibility of corporate boards and their audit committees for the integrity of management and financial reports should be pinpointed and reinforced and the appropriate authorities should adopt measures to assure that it is."[3] The POB states, "in too many instances the audit committees do not perform their duties adequately and in many cases do not understand their responsibilities."[4] The proposed disclosure is intended to encourage audit committees (or boards) to fulfill the listed responsibilities. The POB cites the recent compensation committee reports as a precedent for this kind of reporting.

As noted by the POB, the Treadway Commission similarly recommended that all public companies should be required by SEC rule to include in their annual reports to stockholders a letter signed by the chairman of the audit committee describing the committee's responsibilities and activities during the year.

When then Chairman Ruder testified before Congress on the Treadway recommendations in 1988, he noted that companies that have securities registered under section 12 of the Exchange Act are subject to the commission's proxy rules, and that these rules require disclosure concerning the existence of and the functions performed by audit committees. Specifically, pursuant to item 7(e) of Schedule 14A, a company making a proxy solicitation must state whether it has an audit committee, and if so, must "identify each committee member, state the number of committee meetings held ... during the last fiscal year and describe briefly the functions performed" by the audit committee. Chairman Ruder's testimony noted that the Treadway Commission report acknowledged that certain of the information in the proposed audit committee letter would duplicate existing proxy statement disclosures. The testimony then states, "The Commission believes that the proposed audit committee letter would not provide investors with significant additional information and is thus unnecessary." The disclosure described by Chairman Ruder continues to be required today.

Other information about audit committees, not mentioned in Chairman Ruder's testimony, that must be disclosed in commission filings includes whether a registrant's audit committee recommended or approved a change in accountants, and whether it consulted with the former accountant concerning disagreements with management and certain other matters.[5]

The POB's analogy to the compensation committee report may not be on all fours. The compensation committee report disclosure item does not require any particular actions or procedures. It is designed to require a description of the rationale of the compensation committee for the reported compensation and its relationship to company performance. Even so, it attracted negative comment.[6]

The audit committee disclosure proposed by the POB, essentially requiring the performance of designated procedures, surely would be more controversial than the compensation committee disclosure.

The POB admits that the proposed disclosure is designed primarily for its behavioral impact and not for the relevance of the information being disclosed.[7] I understand that courts have generally opposed the commission's imposing such corporate governance standards and suggested that how audit committees operate should remain a matter of state law. The information already required to be disclosed about audit committees, the commission's decision not to implement the Treadway recommendation in 1988, and the anticipated states' rights issues involved, will have to be reviewed carefully before the commission makes any determination on whether to proceed with this recommendation.

Recommendation V-12: the SEC should require registrants to include in a document containing the annual financial statements: (1) a report by management on the effectiveness of the entity's internal control system relating to financial reporting; and (2) a report by the registrant's independent accountant on the entity's internal control systems relating to financial reporting.

On 19 July 1988, the commission published for comment proposed rules that would have required a report from management on its responsibilities for the registrant's financial statements and internal controls to be included in annual reports to shareholders, in forms 10-K, and in investment companies' semiannual reports.[8] The commission received approximately 190 comment letters in response to this release. A review of these letters indicated that a majority of the commentators supported a management report on its responsibilities for the preparation of the registrant's financial statements and for establishing and maintaining a system of internal controls for financial reporting.

However, reservations were expressed about other aspects of the commission's proposed management report. Commentators noted concerns regarding proposals for a management assessment of the effectiveness of the registrant's internal controls, disclosure of how management has responded to significant recommendations concerning the registrant's internal controls made by its internal auditors and independent accountants, and a requirement that the report be signed by the registrant's principal executive, financial, and accounting officers. Some commentators questioned whether a report noting deficiencies in a registrant's internal controls would constitute an admission of a violation of the Foreign Corrupt Practices Act (FCPA). Commentators also expressed concerns about the potential for over-reliance by investors on the proposed report. On 16 April 1992, the commission withdrew this proposed rule from its Regulatory Flexibility Act agenda.[9]

Although this was not included in the proposed rule, the commission requested specific comments on whether independent accountants should be required to report directly on either the registrant's internal controls or the proposed management report. Almost all of the commentators addressing this issue opposed such direct auditor reporting.[10]

Under the commission's 1988 proposal, the management report would have been included in an annual report of the registrant containing audited financial statements. Thus the registrant's independent accountant would have been required, under current auditing standards, to read the management report and to inform the registrant of anything in that report that the accountant concluded constituted a material inconsistency with the financial statements or a material mis-statement of fact or material omission. In the event that an issuer failed to correct such mis-statements or inconsistencies, Statement on Auditing Standards No. 8 would have required the auditor to take appropriate steps to ensure disclosure of its concerns or, failing that, to consider other actions including withdrawal from the audit engagement. If the audit engagement ended (through the auditor's resignation or discharge), the accountant's concerns would have been reported publicly pursuant to the disclosure requirements regarding changes in accountants included in form 8-K and item 304 of Regulation S-K.[11]

Legislative proposals have been made in this area. On 5 October 1990, the US House of Representatives passed an amendment to the then proposed Comprehensive Crime Control Act of 1990 that, among other things, would have required virtually every issuer subject to the reporting requirements of the Securities Exchange Act of 1934 to set forth, in its form 10-K and annual report to shareholders, (1) a description of management's responsibilities for maintaining an adequate internal control structure and (2) an assessment of whether that structure reasonably assures the preparation of annual and quarterly reports in conformity with generally accepted accounting principles. Management would also have been required to disclose the existence of any material weakness in the control structure that had not been substantially corrected as of the date of filing the annual report. Under this proposed amendment, the issuer's independent public accountant would have examined and reported on management's assessment of its internal control structure, and the independent accountant's opinion would have been included in the issuer's annual reports. However, this amendment was not made part of the enacted Crime Bill.

In 1991, a bill was introduced in the US House of Representatives that, if enacted, would have mandated an SEC study on the extent to which companies are complying with the accounting and internal control provisions of the FCPA. The required study would also have examined the extent to which registrants' compliance with the FCPA, and the reliability of registrants' financial statements, would be improved by a requirement for annual public reports by managements and registrants' independent accountants on the adequacy of registrants' internal control structures. However, this bill was also not enacted.

Finally, the Committee of Sponsoring Organizations of the Treadway Commission has completed a study that is intended to provide guidance in conducting assessments of public companies' internal control structures, entitled *Internal Control – Integrated Framework*.

I am of two minds about an independent auditor's reporting on management's assessment of its internal controls. I recognize the argument that the more managements, audit committees, internal auditors, and external auditors think about, talk about, and focus on internal controls, the better the internal controls are likely to be and will become. That argument says that management should report publicly about the effectiveness of the registrant's internal controls and that the external auditor should report publicly about management's representations about the effectiveness of the registrant's internal controls.

The commission's experience in requiring auditor reports on the internal controls of certain broker/dealers,[12] transfer agents,[13] and investment companies[14] would support the argument for mandatory internal control reports for public companies as well. However, the reports that are currently required have been motivated primarily by the fact that these entities are custodians of their customers' funds and securities, and by the need to ensure that these funds and securities are safeguarded. In a sense, all public companies are custodians of their investors' funds, and it could be argued that the same type of report should be required of all registrants.

However, I know that there are in this world a certain number of people with dishonest bones in their bodies. All the reporting on internal controls in the world is not going to stop those people from defrauding the public and, in the process, the external auditor as well. Invariably, there are going to continue to be cases where, despite reports on internal controls by external auditors, inventories are missing, receivables are bogus or not good, and not all the accounts payable or other liabilities are recorded in the books and recognized on the face of the balance sheet. When those cases happen, and they will, the public's expectations will be dashed.

In addition, I am told that there will be a cost, perhaps a significant cost, to registrants, especially smaller ones, to get their external auditors to report publicly on their internal controls. So I do not know which way to lean.

The POB should be commended for the hard work and insight that is reflected in the special report. The issues covered in the report, although not necessarily new, are important not only to the accounting profession but also to preparers and users of financial statements and to the legislators, courts, and regulators that administer and enforce the financial reporting system in this country. Without any prediction on what actions, if any, the commission may take, I hope that the report will continue to fuel the public debate on these issues. I look forward to hearing your thoughts throughout this and other conferences, in articles in the press, and in other forums. Thank you.

Notes

1 The AICPA determined in 1977 that public confidence in the profession's, then newly established, peer review program would be increased if an independent oversight board composed of prominent individuals oversaw and reported on that program. The Public Oversight Board (POB) was created to serve this purpose. The POB also reports on other matters bearing on the integrity of the audit process. The POB maintains its independence from the AICPA by selecting its members and staff, setting their compensation, and choosing its own chairman. Current members of the POB are Chairman A.A. Sommer, former SEC commissioner; Robert Mautz, professor emeritus of the University of Illinois and the University of Michigan; Robert Froehlke, former Secretary of the Army; Melvin Laird, former Secretary of Defense; and Paul McCracken, former chairman of the President's Council of Economic Advisers.

2 Public Oversight Board, *In the Public Interest: A Special Report by the Public Oversight Board of the SEC Practice Section*, AICPA (5 March 1993), at 1.

3 POB report, at 49–50.

4 POB report, at 50.

5 Item 304 of Regulation S-K, 17 CFR 229.304.

6 See Securities Act Release No. 6962 (16 October 1992).

7 See generally, POB report, at 49–51, which states, among other things, "In the Board's opinion, audit committees should assume defined responsibilities, as outlined in the recommendation set forth below."

8 Securities Act Release No. 6789 (19 July 1988) [53 FR 28009].

9 See Securities Act Release No. 6935 (24 April 1992) [57 FR 18424].

10 Congressional testimony by the commission in February 1993 notes that mandatory auditing of internal controls could result in "enormous costs with relatively few real benefits." Statement of Chairman Richard C. Breeden before the Subcommittee on Telecommunications and Finance of the House Committee on Energy and Commerce, Concerning H.R. 574, The Financial Fraud Detection and Disclosure Act, at 35 (18 February 1993).

11 17 CFR §229.304. See Financial Reporting Release No. 31 (12 April 1988) [53 FR 12924].

12 17 CFR §240.17a-5(j).

13 17 CFR §240.17Ad-13.

14 Form N-SAR, sub-item 77B.

34 Enforcement issues

Good news, bad news, Brillo pads, Miracle-Gro, and Roundup

Address to Twenty-sixth Annual AICPA National Conference on SEC Developments, Grand Hyatt Hotel, Washington, 8 December 1998

There is nothing new under the sun on the accounting side at the Division of Enforcement. Over the years, I have heard every chief accountant of the division speak at forums like this one, and they all said the same things. I have been the chief accountant of the Enforcement Division since November 1997, and I have seen nothing new. There are only so many ways to cook the books. I, too, am going to sound like a broken record.

I bring both good news and bad news. I will start with what should be good news. From my perspective as chief accountant of the Enforcement Division, looking only at our statistics, financial accounting and reporting would appear to be in good shape. I say this based on the number of financial accounting and reporting cases that the commission completes every year. These are the cases involving accounting issues, financial statement disclosure issues, MD&A disclosure issues, auditing issues, and auditor independence issues. These cases do not involve insider trading, stock price manipulations, yield burning, or supervision of registered representatives.

Our statistics show that the commission completes about 100 accounting cases a year. If I divide 100 cases by 16,000 commercial and industrial public companies who file documents with the commission, the result is about 0.6 percent. A very small percentage. To be sure, the percentage is not Six Sigma, but nonetheless it is very small. What that statistic taken in isolation says to me is that, by and large, the issuer/participants in our vast public marketplace are conforming to the rules.

The value of 0.6 percent would be cut about in half were I to include broker/dealers and investment companies in the statistics. In addition to the 16,000 public company issuer/registrants that file financial statements and audit reports with the SEC, there are about 7,000 broker/dealers and about 7,000 investment companies that also file financial statements and audit reports with the SEC. So if I add 7,000 broker/dealers and 7,000 investment companies to the 16,000 issuer/registrants, the total is about 30,000. Then, 100 cases divided by 30,000 opportunities equals 0.3 percent. Over the years, we have had only a limited number of accounting cases involving broker/dealers and mutual funds. I think that it is instructive to observe why that is. I think that there are not many cases involving broker/dealers and investment companies because those companies mark their assets to market. Many of our accounting cases not related to broker/dealers and investment companies involve accounting for various kinds of deferred costs. One cannot mark to market a cost. One can mark to market only something that has value in the marketplace.

While the above should be good news and welcome news, I have bad news. Bad news that makes me suspect that the inferences I draw from the numbers above are incorrect. In the 13 July 1998 issue of *Business Week*, there is a special advertising section reporting on the magazine's Seventh Annual Forum of Chief Financial Officers. The 160 delegates at the forum were polled electronically and anonymously on twenty-seven questions. Question 10 reads as follows:

> As CFO, I have had to fight off other executives' requests that I misrepresent results:
>
> 1 Yes, it has happened, but I said "no" and fought them off.
>
> 2 I yielded to the requests.
>
> 3 No such pleas ever received by me.

Sixty-five of the 160 CFOs responded to that question. Listen now to the responses. Only twenty-one CFOs, or one-third of the sixty-five respondents, said they had not been asked to misrepresent results. But forty-four of the sixty-five said they had been asked to misrepresent results. Thirty-six of those forty-four fought off the requests, but eight of the respondents said that they had yielded to the requests to misrepresent results. I repeat: 67 percent of the CFOs had been asked to misrepresent results, and 18 percent of those who were asked did so. Those statistics are staggering. Given that we have about 16,000 commercial and industrial companies as issuer/registrants, and assuming that the answers given of the sixty-five respondents are representative of the entire population, this means that in almost 11,000 cases CFOs were asked to misrepresent results, and in almost 2,000 cases the CFOs yielded to the request to misrepresent results. Those statistics boggle my mind.

Let me raise with you another troublesome development regarding financial accounting and reporting. While I have not counted the cases, I see, just by reading the newspapers, that some issuer/registrants are turning not to their regular auditors but to "forensic" auditors from other firms when questions are raised about the issuer's financial statements. The scenario is as follows: The issuer says in a press release that it has uncovered facts that indicate previously issued financial statements may be wrong. The issuer's audit committee then retains counsel to investigate. Counsel retains "forensic" auditors to help in the investigation. The forensic auditors are a different firm from the issuer's regular auditors. The forensic auditors then take their Brillo pads and scrub the issuer's balance sheet until it looks like a newly minted copper penny, and the restatements to assets, liabilities, equity, and income are the size of an elephant. The question is: which firm did the real audit? Which firm's partners and staff did not have their objectivity clouded or enveloped by relationships developed at picnics or golf outings or at sports events with their clients? Which firm's partners and staff did not have their skepticism dulled by the fact that a former partner of the audit engagement partner is now the client's CFO? That the audit partner and the CFO are also doubles partners at the tennis club on Saturday mornings?

Which brings me to the issue of fraternization between auditors and their clients. It appears to me that some auditors and their families, through social contacts, are getting so close to and so involved with their clients and their clients' families that a disinterested observer would question whether the auditor's objectivity had not been clouded or perhaps even enveloped. Let me give you two examples. In *Business Week* (23 February 1998), there is an article that talks about auditors and their families having social contacts with their clients and their clients' families through such joint activities as picnics and baseball games.

The Enforcement Division recently came across an audit planning memorandum of a Big Five firm wherein social events between the auditor and client are explicitly set forth. I quote from that memorandum (I have not used the names of sports teams actually used in the memorandum but have substituted other names).

Summer and Other Social Events

- Golf
- The University of Texas football games (Oklahoma, Texas A&M, and Arkansas)
- NCAA Basketball final four tickets
- San Antonio Spurs tickets
- Houston Astros tickets
- Shopping

I wonder what "shopping" means. Alpaca sweaters? Golf clubs? Bally leather jackets?

I wonder how investors or potential investors would react if they were aware of these facts. Would investors believe that the auditor's objectivity is not affected when the auditor and his or her family are engaged in periodic baseball games and picnics with the client and the client's families? Would investors believe that the auditor's objectivity is not affected if the auditor and client personnel regularly attend sporting events together? Go shopping together? Whether paid for by the auditor or paid for by the client? Would investors perceive that gift giving, whether from auditor to client or client to auditor, can go on for very long without compromising the auditor's objectivity? How would an underwriter who is about to underwrite an offering of $500 million of stock of that company react to these facts? A mutual fund investment manager who is about to invest

$100 million in the stock of that company? Query: should auditors have to follow the same rules with respect to their public company audit clients that I as an employee of the US federal government have to follow with respect to regulated entities or persons? Would there be fewer restatements if there was not such fraternization?

Let me now turn to the kind of problem that we accountants in the Enforcement Division actually work on. In the year that I have had to look at the problems, I see that we do not deal much with esoteric accounting problems such as foreign currency translation or the ins and outs of pension accounting or post-retirement benefits other than pensions. We deal with more pedestrian issues. For example, on the auditor independence issue, we have one case where the outside auditors of a company wanting to raise money went around to their other clients and promoted the stock of the issuer, passed out the subscriptions for the issuer's stock, and then took the checks that their clients wrote for the shares of the issuer's stock and delivered the checks to the issuer. The SEC has a rule that says that the external auditor may not be a broker for his or her client and remain independent. So does the AICPA.

Another independence case that we have is the one involving KPMG Peat Marwick, which the commission filed in December 1997 and which has been well publicized. This case has several moving parts, which I will not recite here. KPMG has responded by denying the commission's assertions about its lack of independence. The matter was heard recently by an administrative law judge. The judge's opinion will follow in due course.

We also have other independence cases in the works involving ownership by audit and tax partners and staff of securities issued by audit clients and ownership of securities issued by the audit client and held indirectly by a trust where a partner in the CPA audit firm is also a co-trustee of the trust. These cases are not yet resolved.

Let me move on to some of the accounting issues with which we are dealing. The Enforcement Division was formed in the 1970s. As I said earlier, over the years, I have heard every one of the division's chief accountants give speeches wherein they described their cases. Well, nothing has changed. Registrants are still doing the same things.

Premature revenue recognition appears to be the recipe of choice for cooking the books. Recognizing revenue when an undisclosed right of return exists. Recognizing consigned inventory as sold inventory. Shipping products to company warehouses or employees' homes and recognizing sales revenue. Recognizing revenue in advance of the customer's acceptance of the product. Keeping the sales journal open after the end of the quarter or year but back-dating sales invoices. The following is quoted from the commission's AAER 1020, dated 25 March 1998, *In re Sensormatic Electronics Corporation*:

> The Commission Order finds, among other things, that from at least the start of its 1994 fiscal year through July 10 1995, Sensormatic manipulated its quarterly revenue and earnings in order to reach its budgeted earnings

> goals and thereby meet analysts' quarterly earnings projections. During the relevant period, Sensormatic consistently met, within one cent, the analysts' forecasts of quarterly earnings per share, even for the third quarters which were Sensormatic's seasonally weaker quarter.
>
> Sensormatic carried out this fraudulent scheme by improperly recognizing revenue through several different practices. The conduct, which occurred over a number of years and involved employees throughout the organization, primarily involved recognizing and recording revenue in one quarter from product shipped in the next quarter. At the end of each quarter Sensormatic turned back its computer clock that recorded and dated shipments so that out-of-period shipments, and consequently revenue, would be recorded in the prior quarter. According to the Order, revenue also was recognized through the following improper practices: recognizing revenue in one quarter, when products were shipped to warehouses leased by Sensormatic, instead of in the next quarter, when the products were shipped to the customers; slow shipments, whereby revenue was recognized on shipments which were made during the last days of a quarter but which were not scheduled to arrive at the customers' location until well into the next quarter; and recognizing revenue on goods at the time that they were shipped to customers even though the customers' contracts with Sensormatic contained an FOB destination provision. The amount of out-of-period revenue that Sensormatic recognized in quarters ranged from $4.6 million to $30.2 million.

Sensormatic's income statement should have been headed up as follows: "Year ended June 35, 1994."

Deferral in the balance sheet of costs that should have been reported in income as operating expenses. Assigning inflated, often outrageously inflated, dollar values to exchanges of non-monetary assets, particularly with related parties. Assigning inflated, often outrageously inflated, dollar values to non-monetary assets contributed to the corporation in exchange for debt or stock of the corporation. Not disclosing the existence of related parties and transactions with related parties. Recognizing officers' salaries as receivables. Recognizing cash taken from the corporation by officers as cash in the bank or as a direct reduction of stockholders' equity instead of as a charge to expense. Including brass bars that look like gold bars in an inventory of gold.

Bleeding into income, without disclosure, "reserves" established in business combinations or in so-called restructurings. In several recent cases, the bleeding turned into a hemorrhage from a severed carotid artery. How I dislike that word "reserve." It is terribly misleading. Most non-accountants, including lawyers, judges, and journalists, think that "reserves" have green money in them. For example, the *New York Times* of November 16, in an article by Melody Petersen, says that federal banking regulators often worry that banks have not set aside enough MONEY to cover expected loan losses. The *Wall Street Journal* of November 17, in an article by Elizabeth MacDonald, also equates "reserves" with MONEY. Even the *New York Times* and the *Wall Street Journal* think that reserves are vessels containing money.

I thought that the "reserves" issue had been resolved in 1975, when the FASB issued its Statement 5 on *Accounting for Contingencies*, but nowadays general reserves are like crab grass. They are everywhere. Tax liability cushions. Deferred tax asset cushions. Inventory reserves. Bad debt reserves. Merger reserves. Restructuring reserves. They are like dirt. Some companies keep a 55-gallon drum of Miracle-Gro in the garage, and they irrigate their crab grass general reserve accounts with a garden hose hooked up to the drum. Then along comes the Division of Corporation Finance, in its reviews of filings by issuers, and squirts Roundup from a spritzer bottle on issuers' balance sheets, but the crab grass general reserves keep re-emerging. And the reserves are being used to manipulate earnings. Need a penny a share to meet Wall Street's expectations? Need two pennies? A nickel? A dime? Two bits? Dip into the chocolate chip cookie jar reserve. The mere existence of reserves is a chocolate chip cookie jar that management finds hard to resist when the earnings need a sugar high.

Let me read to you from the transcript of a September telephone call between an issuer/registrant and Wall Street analysts:

Analyst: A couple of questions for you Jack. [Jack is the issuer's CEO.] One on the conservative accounting. Actually it surprises me that people have any doubts about the accounting. All the work we've done shows it's really conservative. Let me ask you about a couple of aspects of the conservatism. One, it looks like you're probably over-reserving for indirect sales and that's one aspect of the conservatism. If you want to give any clarity on that, that's terrific. And two, it looks like your deferred revenues shot up a lot in the last quarter so it looks like you were holding back revenue recognition, so if you want to offer anything on that.

Jack: Well you're absolutely right on both counts. We've been extremely conservative and that's how you build little honeypots that you can go to, because when you make these acquisitions in our business planning, we always project a sequential decline in the revenue of the acquired company, and we have to go back to our core businesses to get faster growth to cover up the potential 10–15 percent decline in revenue. And that's where you see the releasing of backlog, and that kind of thing, you can only do that if you've created those acorns out there.

Honeypots! Acorns! We need another pass at "reserves." We need a Year 2000 version of FASB Statement 5.

How about treasury stock carried as an asset in the balance sheet at market, with gains on sale of treasury stock credited to income. (I'm not making this up.) Counting on-hand but consigned inventory as owned inventory. How about increasing fixed assets and crediting cost of sales. Not booking all of the accounts payable; just put the invoices from suppliers into a desk drawer. Not writing down or writing off uncollectible receivables. Booking barter trade credits as if they represented *bona fide* US dollars. Such is the grist of our accounting mill. Not very esoteric stuff. If I draw an analogy with police work, what we see is stolen automobiles with fingerprints on the door handles, not murders where there are no clues except for dogs that did not bark.

On the audit side, I have seen several non-audits since I came on board last year. Auditors accepting, with little or no evidential support, values ascribed to both monetary and non-monetary assets. Artwork by unknown artists booked as assets at huge amounts but without any support for the assigned value and no inquiry by the auditor about independent valuation of the artwork. (One registrant did get an opinion about the value of artwork it had acquired from an artist through the issuance of stock. The registrant asked the artist the value of the artwork and the artist, without modesty, gave his opinion.) Receivables acquired from collection agencies for pennies but booked at dollars without any documentation and no auditor inquiry as to the basis for the value. Auditors not doing substantive audit work but relying on so-called analytical procedures where the evidence, or lack thereof, cries out for substantive audit work. In one case, the physical inventory test counts showed a large shortfall from the inventory amount in the general ledger. Rather than requiring a complete physical count of the inventory or qualifying the audit opinion, the auditor relied on so-called "analytical procedures," which led to acceptance of an erroneous book amount for the inventory. Auditors not doing cut-off work for sales and purchases, with the result that sales of the next period are booked in this period with a corresponding increase in receivables from customers, and accounts payable for purchases of inventory of this period not booked until next period with the inventory recognized in the balance sheet, resulting in understated costs of sales and overstated margins. And we see cases where the auditors were lied to or were not given all of the documentation that they should have been given. But sometimes I wonder whether the auditors asked the right questions.

I realize that what I have talked about today is the dark side of financial accounting and reporting, the side that is not nice to look at. And that the dark side is very small in relation to the universe. But when we see a steady stream of restatements by all manner and kind of registrants, not just microcaps, and when we see a steady stream of articles in business journals entitled "hocus-pocus earnings," "abracadabra accounting," "pick a number, any number," we regulators take notice. Investors also take notice. While the numerical count of enforcement cases is small, a hundred or so a year, one has to ask how much cyanide will poison a well. Will it take long before investors bid down the prices of securities in our markets to factor in the uncertainty arising from possible bad numbers and inadequate disclosures? Perhaps the bidding-down process is already silently taking place. Will investors stop drinking from the well called audits by "independent certified public accountants" and sample the water in other wells. You may say that there are no other comparable wells. Not so. When investors begin to believe that their interests are not being protected by external auditors, those investors will find an alternative to protect their interests, in ways other than an audit by independent certified public accountants.

Postscript

As material for this book was being assembled in April 2003, I reread this speech, which I gave in 1998, for the *n*th time. I wish that I had not implied in this speech, in the third paragraph, that a failure rate of 0.6 percent was acceptable. (Failure rate determined as a result of retrospective restatements of financial statements because of errors and irregularities.) Those who prepare and issue financial statements, and those who audit those financial statements, should strive for a failure rate of zero. Investors expect a failure rate of zero. If numbers in financial statements were to be based on market prices as I have advocated, and were those numbers to come from sources outside the reporting enterprise as I have also advocated, the failure rate would be zero. There would be no retrospective restatements of financial statements.

Part III

Accounting standard setting and regulation

35 Schuetze on accounting standard setting and regulation

Peter W. Wolnizer

This section comprises eleven speeches and addresses and a letter to Sir Bryan Carsberg, then Secretary-General of the International Accounting Standards Committee. The speeches include Walter Schuetze's distinguished lecture at the University of Texas (Austin), the R.J. Chambers Memorial Research Lecture at the University of Sydney, and his testimony before the US Senate Committee on Banking, Housing, and Urban Affairs hearing on "Accounting and Investor Protection Issues Raised by Enron and Other Public Companies: Oversight of the Accounting Profession, Audit Quality and Independence, and Formulation of Accounting Principles."

While comprehensive in their scope and extensively illustrated with examples from regulation and practice, four major themes emerge in these speeches. To set these themes in the overall context of Schuetze's work, however, it needs to be appreciated that the majority were delivered in his capacity as the chief accountant to the Securities and Exchange Commission (SEC) or as chief accountant of the Enforcement Division of the SEC. Consequently, those speeches addressed specific topics of contemporary interest to the particular audiences to whom they were presented.

1 The harmonization or internationalization of accounting standards is ideal when companies seek to list their securities in foreign countries, provided those standards yield financial statements that are as relevant, reliable, and transparent as those produced under US generally accepted accounting principles. However, the recent implosion of Enron, WorldCom, and other corporations in the USA may have caused many outside the USA to question seriously whether financial statements prepared pursuant to US generally accepted accounting practices are indeed the best.
2 The function of accounting is to inform financial decision making by investors and creditors. Consequently, accounting standard setters and corporate regulators should adopt a "capital markets perspective" in determining the kind of financial information that should be provided to investors.
3 While applauding the achievements and work of the FASB, investors would be better served if there was a more simple, relevant, and transparent

accounting whereby assets and liabilities are marked to market; and a more reliable style of auditing, which required auditors to authenticate financial statements by recourse to evidence outside the reporting enterprise – to commercial evidence from the marketplace.

4 In the particular context of a potential intervention by the US Congress on the matter of accounting for stock options awarded to executives, Schuetze argued that the setting of accounting standards should remain the distinct responsibility of the private sector – of the FASB overseen by the SEC – and that the US Congress should not override or interfere with the accounting standard-setting process. However, in his testimony before the US Senate Committee on Banking, Housing, and Urban Affairs in February 2002, he argued that accounting needs "deep and fundamental reform" and that Congress should require mark-to-market accounting, the implementation of which should be the responsibility of the SEC.

The reformist views of Walter Schuetze are brought together comprehensively in "A memo to national and international accounting and auditing standard setters and securities regulators," the title of his address delivered as the R.J. Chambers Memorial Research Lecture on 27 November 2001. They are in crisp focus in his testimony before the US Senate Committee on Banking, Housing, and Urban Affairs hearing on "Accounting and Investor Protection Issues Raised by Enron and Other Public Companies: Oversight of the Accounting Profession, Audit Quality and Independence, and Formulation of Accounting Principles" on 26 February 2002. Particular reference to that lecture and testimony is made in the introductory chapter.

The speeches and addresses

The speeches and addresses in this section were delivered over a decade, from October 1992 to March 2003. With the exception of the R.J. Chambers Memorial Research Lecture (2001), his testimony before the US Senate (2002) and his address to the Southwest Regional Meeting of the American Accounting Association (2003), these addresses were given when Schuetze was chief accountant to the SEC or chief accountant of the Enforcement Division of the SEC.

The first speech, titled "The setting of international accounting standards," was delivered to the members and observers of the IASC in Chicago on 7 October 1992. Here he responds to several inquiries made of him as to whether he supports the efforts of the IASC to harmonize or internationalize financial accounting and reporting standards for application by issuers of financial statements around the world. He responded in the affirmative, believing that investors will benefit. But his positive answer is conditional: international accounting standards have to be comparable with US generally accepted accounting practices; otherwise, he predicts, overseas companies will not be successful in raising capital and trading in US capital markets.

He explores and analyses the pros and cons of each of three ways in which regulators such as the SEC can deal with financial reports of foreign companies when considering their listings of securities. One approach is to require that "the foreign issuers report financial position, results of operations or income, and cash flows and related disclosures … as the host country would require of host country issuers." An alternative is to "allow net income and shareholders equity to be reconciled from that which is produced using home-country accounting standards to that which would have resulted using host-country accounting standards if the issuer does not prepare its basic financial statements using host-country accounting standards." That is the current situation in the USA. A second approach is the multi-jurisdictional disclosure system whereby "the SEC accepts, for investment-grade debt offerings and related periodic filings, financial statements of Canadian issuers based on Canadian accounting standards, and the Canadian Securities Commissions accept financial statements of US issuers prepared using US accounting standards." The third approach, which is followed in many European and Far Eastern countries, "is to allow foreign issuers to issue and list securities, both debt and equity, based on financial statements using home-country accounting standards."

After examining the advantages and disadvantages of each of these, he explores a fourth possibility, namely "International financial accounting Esperanto promulgated by the IASC or something like the IASC." For such an accounting Esperanto to succeed and become acceptable to investors and regulators around the world, "it must result in financial statements that have relevance and reliability, and obviously transparency, as their foundation. The Esperanto must be supportable in concept and should be simple and practical to implement. It should be fairly prescriptive and not allow for too much judgment on the part of issuers so as to maintain a high degree of reliability."

With his distinctive insight and incisiveness, he compares two recent IASC proposals with "the beacons of relevance and reliability" – the exposure draft on research and development and the exposure draft on financial instrument assets – and finds that they fail those tests based on the IASC's definition of an asset as a "resource controlled by the enterprise." In the case of research and development, he notes the IASC's view that a cost *per se* is an asset and demonstrates that costs fail the test of control. In the case of financial instrument assets, he notes that the IASC proposes that financial instrument assets be recognized based on who has the risks or rewards inherent in the financial asset rather than on who controls it.

He concludes by saying that the IASC has "a tough and delicate job." Standard setters, he says, "must have patience and resolve. Most of all they must have extraordinarily keen hearing. Standard setters must be able to discern the voice of the investor – sometimes the small, faint voice of the investor – in the din of voices of all of the supplicants making entreaties to the standard setter."

In the second speech, "What is the future of mutual recognition of financial statements and is comparability really necessary? (Information is king)," delivered to the Third Congrès Fédération des Experts Comptables in Copenhagen on 10 September 1993, he analyzes the mutual-recognition approach whereby regulators and investors in the host country adopt as adequate whatever financial statements and related disclosures are acceptable in the issuer's home country. The issue, he believes, turns on the question: "What is the objective of the financial statements and reports being issued by those companies wishing to offer their securities to investors?" Recognizing the disparities of financial reporting objectives around the world, Schuetze comes down firmly on the side of a capital-markets approach, one that is directed towards informing investment and credit decisions. This has been the approach in the USA since the establishment of the SEC in 1934: "Our public companies lay out the facts and let marketplace participants decide on how the facts should affect securities prices and how capital should be allocated." He observes that the IASC "has adopted much the same approach" and suggests that "the capital markets approach is the wave of the future for those companies in Europe and elsewhere that wish to offer their debt or equity securities in worldwide markets." Information is "king and queen," says Schuetze. "Keeping information private has a cost. That cost is reflected in reduced securities prices."

Under the mutual-recognition approach, the regulator in the host country accepts as adequate the financial disclosures that the issuer makes in its home country. Schuetze argues that while this approach may be less costly and may, on the surface, appeal to issuers, it places a great burden on investors:

> Under that approach, investors have to learn and become familiar with the accounting requirements of the country of the issuer. … The aim of regulation should be to help investors, not burden them. Moreover, the mutual-recognition approach has another drawback, which I call the lowest common denominator syndrome. By that I mean that managers of some corporations may not necessarily act in the best interests of investors by factually and openly reporting financial information.

He concludes:

> I think that issuers of financial statements will resolve the conflict between the desire to keep information private along with the desire to publish only home-country information and the need to get a full price for their securities in the way that they see is in their best self-interest. If the issuers want to maintain closeness about their business affairs, they will opt for less than transparent disclosures. If, on the other hand, their current owners demand that the best price possible be obtained for new issues of securities so that current owners' values are not diluted, and if current and prospective owners want full pricing of securities in their portfolios, they will choose transparency, which is the approach to regulation of securities offering we take in the USA.

In the third speech, "A note about private-sector standard setting," delivered to the Fourth Annual Conference on Financial Reporting at the University of

California at Berkeley on 29 October 1993, Schuetze tackles the important question of public versus private accounting standard-setting arrangements. He is particularly concerned about private-sector accounting standard setting, and specifically with the relationship between the SEC and the FASB and the FASB's standard-setting process. At the time of this address, the FASB had outstanding a proposal that would have required that the value of stock options issued to employees be reported as a cost/expense in the financial statements of companies issuing such options. Several members of Congress had proposed legislation that, in various ways, would have set aside any final decision by the FASB to require that accounting. (Subsequently, in 1994, the FASB dropped its proposal to require companies to recognize as an expense the value of stock options issued to employees.)

The purpose of the speech was not to take sides on the substantive issue of whether the value of stock options issued to employees should or should not be recognized as a compensation expense and, if so, at what value. Rather, Schuetze was concerned with the standard-setting process. In particular, he argued that the accounting standard-setting process. which is in the hands of the FASB and overseen by the SEC, should not be politicized. Referring to the financial disclosure objectives of the federal securities laws of the 1930s, and the fact that the SEC, without abrogating its responsibilities in the area of financial accounting and reporting, "has looked to the accounting profession for leadership in establishing and improving accounting standards." As a result, the USA has "what are widely recognized as the most comprehensive accounting standards in the world." Schuetze goes on to explain, in detail, how the FASB goes about setting accounting standards.

While critical of the fundamental foundations of modern accounting – the historical-cost doctrine – Schuetze is highly supportive of the work and achievements of the SEC and FASB working collaboratively. And it is against the background of that achievement of private-sector accounting standard setting and commercial auditing that Schuetze argues strongly against the intervention of Congress in setting accounting standards. "If the effort to legislate in this area [accounting for employee stock options] is successful, and Congress indeed sets aside an eventual FASB decision, where does it stop?" He illustrates his argument by reference to several examples of accounting in which those with strong vested interests could, potentially, lobby Congress to the detriment of investors, and concludes: "I don't know how long this piece of yarn is, once Congress starts pulling on it."

Most persuasively, he sets forth his argument by analogy. "I think that it is quite appropriate for Congress to decide, after consultation with the medical profession, that the health of US citizens would be improved if there was less emission of pollutants from automobiles and to pass a law saying that emissions should be reduced. But I think that Congress should leave the design of fuel injection systems, catalytic converters, and exhaust systems to automotive engineers." Acknowledging that the "standard-setting process in the United States, although the best in the world, is not perfect," and that there is "room for constructive advice from Congress, the business community, investor groups, and others on how the process may be improved and strengthened," Schuetze concludes that "it is best to use the technical expertise available in the process that currently is in place and has worked for decades, rather than pre-empting that process through congressional action."

In "Take me out to the ball game," a speech delivered to the Eighteenth Annual AICPA National Conference on Banking on 5 November 1993, Schuetze adopts baseball jargon to compliment the FASB on some of its recent pronouncements and willingness to re-examine some prior standards. In so doing, he reinforces his views about the wisdom of having an independent standard-setting apparatus like the FASB.

Reflecting on his experience of accounting and auditing standard setting over thirty years – with the AICPA's Committee on Accounting Procedures, the Accounting Principles Board, the Accounting Standards Executive Committee of the AICPA, and the FASB – Schuetze states: "In this world of standard setting, things take time, sometimes lots of time, and change tends to come in small chunks. In terms of singles instead of home runs … I think that FASB Statements 114 [on loan impairment] and 115 [on debt and equity securities] were line-drive singles, not bouncers through the infield." While retaining the fuzzy notion of "probable" for identifying impairment, Statement 114 recognized the importance of the time value of money. While still based on management intent, Statement 115 requires marketable securities to be recognized at market value instead of cost:

> The standard on pension funds (Statement 87), aside from its complicated deferrals, which level the hills and valleys of changes in asset and liability valuations, is a double … The standard on post-retirement healthcare benefits (Statement 106), aside from its complicated deferrals and its permissible drawn-out transition provision, is a bases-clearing double. … Had the standard on cash flow information (Statement 95) required direct reporting of operating cash flows, it would have been a home run; as it is, it is a stand-up triple.

Those successes, "along with others such as FASB Statement 14 on segment and geographical reporting, Statement 52 on foreign currency translation, and Statement 94 on consolidation, demonstrate the wisdom of having an independent, full-time, well-funded Financial Accounting Standards Board." A further strength of the FASB system, he notes, is shown by its willingness to re-examine prior standards, "as was done with foreign currency translation where Statement 52 replaced Statement 8, as was done with income taxes where Statement 109 replaced Statement 96, and as the board is now doing with its re-examination of reporting disaggregated information, which in effect is another look at segment reporting."

In the second half of his speech, Schuetze looks at one of the FASB's unfinished projects – the financial instruments project – which has been on the board's agenda since 1986. Recognizing the enormous size and importance of the project, Schuetze compliments the board on breaking it down into "manageable bites": for example, Statement 105 on disclosure about financial instruments with off-balance-sheet risk and concentrations of credit risk; Statement 107 on disclosure about fair value of financial instruments; Statement 114 on the recognition and measurement of loan impairment; and Statement 115 on accounting for and disclosure of investments in debt and equity securities. And he acknowledges the work that the FASB is doing on derivative contracts. He concludes: "Given the disclosures with respect to on-balance-sheet financial instrument items, investors have the necessary ingredients to make judgments about a bank's future earnings and cash flows." However, he argues that the information provided to investors about derivatives that are used to manage a bank's off-balance-sheet assets and liabilities as an end user "is not nearly so robust." Schuetze recommends that banks "should consider giving investors as much information about the off-balance-sheet items used by banks as end users to manage on balance-sheet assets and liabilities as banks give for the on-balance-sheet items." He elaborates in some detail what information he would like to see disclosed to investors.

The fifth speech, "Financial accounting and reporting in our worldwide economy" was delivered in the Distinguished Lecture Series at the University of Texas at Austin on 12 November 1993. There are two parts to the speech. In the first part, he describes in some detail the function, workings, and structure of the SEC – the laws it administers, the composition of the commission, and the work undertaken by its various divisions (Enforcement, Corporation Finance, Market Regulation, and Investment Management) and offices (of the General Counsel, Chief Accountant, International Affairs, Economic Analysis, Administrative Law Judges, Secretary, and Inspector General).

In the second part of the speech, he discusses the function of accounting standard setting in the context of the role of financial accounting and reporting in US capital markets. He goes on to trace the history and development of accounting standards from 1938, when the SEC stated that financial statements that were not prepared in accordance with principles having "substantial authoritative support" would be presumed to be misleading. The accounting profession quickly moved to establish principles that had such authoritative support: the fifty-one Accounting Research Bulletins issued by the AICPA Committee on Accounting Procedures (1939–59), "some of which, in one form or another, are still applicable today"; the thirty-one opinions issued by the APB (1959–73), "many of which survive today in one form or another"; and the 117 Statements on Financial Accounting Standards and sixty interpretations and technical bulletins issued by the FASB since its inception in 1973 to the date of his speech.

In his strong advocacy of the capital-markets approach to accounting standard setting, he argues that "One of the reasons for this country's deep and highly liquid financial markets is relevant, reliable, transparent, and credible financial statements. We have over fifty million individual investors in this country and many thousands of institutional investors, ranging from the likes of the trust department of the local bank to the huge pension funds," all of whom "use financial statements issued by public companies to make investment decisions, and those investors are able to rely on those financial statements." He also argues that financial statements issued by public companies in Canada, Great Britain, Australia and New Zealand, while "fairly transparent," "are not comparable with those issued by companies in the USA."

In "An SEC accounting update," delivered to the AICPA's Nineteenth Annual Conference on Banking in Washington on 4 November 1994, Schuetze addresses three topical subjects: disclosures about derivatives; accounting for derivatives; and internal audit outsourcing by banks. He compliments the FASB on Statement 119 for requiring disclosures about the nature, terms, and financial-statement effects of derivatives. However, he suggests "that disclosures about derivatives and cash positions be supplemented with information that brings the entire risk management function together so that investors can understand better how the company manages its overall financial risks." In particular, he "would like to encourage registrants to concentrate on quantitative disclosures about market risks inherent in on- and off-balance-sheet financial instruments and to discuss how these risks are managed."

One of the quantitative measures used by companies in their internal risk management systems is "value at risk" – a measure recommended by the Group of 10 and the Group of 30 and endorsed by the Financial Executives Institute. "Value at risk is a measure of the potential loss resulting from hypothetical changes in market factors, such as interest rates and foreign currency exchange rates, for a given time period. It is used to measure the potential changes in the fair values of financial instruments arising from changes in market prices or yields." Schuetze provides an example of what a "value at risk" disclosure might look like.

He indicated that the SEC's Division of Corporation Finance had formed a task force that was then reviewing derivative disclosures by approximately 100 banking registrants and 400 non-banking registrants. The particular interests of the task force were to "(1) learn why and how companies are using derivatives, (2) understand better the current types of disclosures about derivatives, (3) improve disclosures about derivatives, and (4) form a basis from which the commission could develop guidance regarding disclosures about derivatives."

He concludes the speech by addressing the increasing trend by banks and other financial institutions to outsource their internal audit work, in addition to other functions such as legal work, data processing, mutual fund back-office work, and property management. In particular, he cautioned banks not to outsource their internal audit work to the external auditor as that may compromise that auditor's professional independence.

The seventh speech in this section, "A review of the FASB's accomplishments since its inception in 1973," was delivered at the AICPA's Twenty-second National Conference on Current SEC Developments in Washington on 10 January 1995. The timing of this speech is important: Schuetze had announced his retirement as chief accountant of the SEC, his final day being 31 March

1995. (He returned to the SEC in November 1997 as chief accountant to the Enforcement Division.) This is important for at that time, Walter Schuetze – being the forthright advocate for accounting reform that he is – had no institutional or professional reason to praise the work of the FASB. Yet he did. That is the measure of the integrity and professionalism of the man. His opening remarks on that occasion were: "I have on occasion been critical about certain financial accounting and reporting issues. Today, I want to mention some of the positive things in financial accounting and reporting."

In this speech, he quotes Sir David Tweedie, his former partner at KPMG and standard setter: "There's only three things wrong with accounting – the balance sheet, the income statement, and the cash flow statement." Says Schuetze: "That was about five years ago, and I am pleased to report that Sir David's Accounting Standards Board is making good headway in improving accounting in the UK. I am pleased to say that the FASB is also making good headway in improving accounting here in the United States." In his speech, he goes on to say that, in his opinion, the FASB has been "very good for investors."

The eighth speech, addressing current developments at the SEC, was delivered at the Seventeenth Annual SEC and Financial Reporting Institute Conference at the Leventhal School of Accounting in the University of South California on 14 May 1998. He brought the audience the "good news" that, having regard to the number of registrants, relatively few open cases were being investigated by the division: "Although the issues that we deal with in the Enforcement Division are messy and quite distasteful, they are a very small fraction of the universe." He made the same observation in "Good news, bad news, Brillo pads, Miracle-Gro, and Roundup," reproduced in the previous section. He arrived at the same conclusion in that speech, on the following basis: "Our statistics show that the commission completed about 100 accounting cases a year. If I divide 100 cases by 16,000 commercial and industrial public companies who file documents with the commission, the result is about 0.6 percent." This he attributes to the effectiveness of the Enforcement Division in overseeing and monitoring the financial reporting practices of registrants and the severity of penalties that may be imposed for infractions.

Matters that come before the division are seldom "esoteric accounting problems such as foreign currency translation or the ins and outs of pension accounting or post-retirement benefits other than pensions." The most recurrent problems are "pedestrian" matters such as those described in the section on the "Implications of accounting practices for auditing."

On the auditing side, he notes that the Enforcement Division often investigates matters pertaining to auditor independence. Indeed, he states, "I have now seen several non-audits." Under that caption, he includes many of the scenarios described in the section on the "Implications of accounting practices for auditing." Referring to some cases where "the auditors were lied to or were not given all of the documentation that they should have been given," he observes that "sometimes I wonder whether the auditors asked the right questions."

The speech concludes with an observation about the "fraternization between auditors and their clients" and an exhortation to auditors to be diligent and prudent in relation to their professional independence.

In a postscript added to "Good news, bad news, Brillo pads, Miracle-Gro, and Roundup" for this volume, written after he delivered the following address to the Southwest Regional Meeting of the American Accounting Association on 7 March 2003, he said "I wish that I had not implied in this speech that a failure rate of 0.6 percent was acceptable. Investors expect a failure rate of zero." He relates failure rate "to the result of retrospective restatements of financial statements because of errors and irregularities." He suggests that under mark-to-market accounting the failure rate would be zero.

In his address titled "Watching a game of three-card monte on Times Square" to the Southwest Regional Meeting of the American Accounting Association on 7 March 2003, Schuetze examines the notion of serviceability – "fitness for intended use" – of financial statements. He does so by using commonly understood analogies:

> Consumers here in the USA, and around the world as well, are used to the "serviceability" of the things that they buy and use every day. For example, we buy Hershey's candies and Kellogg's corn flakes and know they are fit to eat. We fly around the world in Boeing and Airbus airplanes and know that the planes are safe. We buy IBM and Dell desktop and laptop computers that run on Microsoft software and are delighted with their performance. Caterpillar tractors that we take to construction job sites, John Deere combines that we take into the wheat fields, and Honda automobiles that we drive home from the showroom perform flawlessly. We buy a GE toaster at the department store, knowing that the toaster will not give us a shock when we plug it into the electricity socket at home. We know these products are "fit for their intended use." Not so for financial reports.

Referring to the Huron Consulting Group Report, dated January 2003, which found 330 retrospective restatements of financial statements in 2002, Schuetze observes that "Assuming 15,000 public company registrants, that is a failure rate of about 2 percent." Against the view that such a failure rate might be considered acceptable, he asks the following question: "Suppose Airbus and Boeing had a failure rate of 2 percent, or 1 percent, or 0.5 percent, or even 0.1 percent. Would any of us fly in their airplanes? No! Suppose Hershey or Kellogg had that kind of failure rate. Would any of us eat the candy or the cereal? No!"

He then considers whether the Sarbanes–Oxley Act of 2002, which he calls "the mother of all securities laws," is likely to reduce the failure rates in corporate financial reporting. After examining the three requirements of Section 302(a) pertaining to the SEC-required certifications of the quality of financial statements by CEOs and CFOs, Schuetze concludes that the Sarbanes–Oxley Act "is of no help," because it "does not touch the real issues, which are accounting issues." For this reason, it will not stop earnings management and its by-products: unheralded corporate failure and the retrospective restatements of financial statements. It is an incomplete solution to the problem of Enronitis. A complete solution to the corporate governance dilemmas illustrated by the Enrons and WorldComs mandates fundamental accounting and auditing reform. Schuetze goes on to examine the accounting profession's agenda of "principles-based standards and standards that refer to the substance of transactions." He demonstrates how that approach also will not work and concludes that the vital solution lies in the formulation of mark-to-market accounting, which he has described as "true north." While he does not claim that true north would solve all of the problems in financial reporting, he argues that "at least we would be working toward getting relevant numbers. Numbers that are real and have their foundation in the marketplace."

The address concludes with the identification of the following six benefits associated with the implementation of mark-to-market accounting:

1 Financial reports would be understandable to retail and institutional investors, Congress, and the public at large.

2 Financial reports would have increased usefulness in making investment, lending, corporate governance, and public policy decisions.

3 We would do away with today's mountain of accounting rules that nobody understands.

4 We could do away with the FASB and the IASB.

5 We could do away with the 150-hour education requirement for CPAs – no mountain of rules to memorize.

6 And, finally, continuing professional education requirements for CPAs could be scrapped.

The implementation of mark-to-market accounting would also solve the independence problem in auditing and transform auditing into the rigorous safeguard of the quality of financial statement information that the corporations and securities laws intended it to be.

The letter

The letter of 12 August 1997 to Sir Bryan Carsberg, then Secretary-General to the IASC, addressed matters of due process in the deliberations and reporting of the IASC. In particular, Schuetze urged the IASC to enhance the transparency of its operations and reporting. He recommended that "future exposure drafts of standards and final standards include (1) the reason for issuing the standard, (2) a basis for conclusions setting forth why the proposed standard or final standard requires what it does and why any dissenters' reasons are insufficient or incorrect, (3) identification of the dissenters and the reasons for their dissent, (4) a brief explanation of other plausible approaches that could have been taken in the proposed standard or final standard even if none of those approaches is supported by a dissenter and why the IASC board believes such approaches would be insufficient or incorrect, and (5) the reasons for changes in the final standard from the exposure draft."

After acknowledging the importance of the IASC as a successful standard-setting body, Schuetze concludes that "The IASC needs to help to guarantee its own success by issuing standards that, first, produce relevant and reliable information for use by investors and, second, stand on their own feet by reason of persuasion by the IASC board in the published basis for conclusions."

Sir Bryan Carsberg responded indicating general agreement with the recommendations. They are recommendations that might, with good effect, be adopted by Sir David Tweedie and his colleagues on the recently established successor to the IASC, the International Accounting Standards Board.

36 The setting of international accounting standards

Remarks to the International Accounting Standards Committee, Chicago, 7 October 1992

Your chairman, Arthur Wyatt, graciously asked me to come here today to discuss with you the setting of international accounting standards from the perspective of the new chief accountant of the USA's Securities and Exchange Commission. I thank him and you for this opportunity and this platform.

Since I took up my new post in January of this year, I have been asked several times whether I support efforts by your committee, the International Accounting Standards Committee, to "harmonize" or "internationalize" financial accounting and reporting standards for application by issuers of financial statements around the world. The short answer to that question is "yes." I say yes because I think that investors around the world will benefit therefrom.

Let me explore with you, conceptually and philosophically, the choices that regulators around the world have as they address the question of differing or different accounting standards in different countries. One approach as to what regulators could do is what we in the USA have done. That is, the regulator of the host country, faced with filings by foreign issuers, could require the foreign issuers to report financial position, results of operations or income, and cash flows and related disclosures such as related party transactions, loss contingencies, segments, asset pledges, and the like, as the host country would require of host-country issuers. Alternatively, the regulator could, as we also do in the USA, allow net income and shareholders' equity to be reconciled from that which is produced using home-country accounting standards to that which would have resulted using host-country accounting standards if the issuer does not prepare its basic financial statements using host-country accounting standards. In the USA, we have 481 SEC registrants who either follow US generally accepted accounting practices in preparing their basic financial statements or reconcile.

The host-country presentation and reconciliation approach has the advantage of presenting information in a way that is familiar to investors in the host country. Those investors are used to seeing things dealt with in a particular way in the financial statements, and they are comforted by this approach. Those investors can compare a foreign issuer's financial statements with those of issuers in the host country. It has the drawback of requiring the issuer to incur the cost, at a minimum, of developing information necessary to provide disclosures that are incremental to those required in the home country and, at the extreme, to keep two sets of records. It also requires the issuer's auditors and other financial advisers to become knowledgeable in the accounting standards and disclosure requirements of the host country. Another drawback is that the issuer must follow standards in which it had no say and to which it may object as a matter of principle or on other grounds, such as the cost of gathering information.

A second approach would be along the lines that the USA's Securities and Exchange Commission and Canada's Securities Commissions agreed to several years ago, the so-called multi-jurisdictional disclosure system. Under this system, the SEC accepts, for investment-grade debt offerings and related periodic filings, financial statements of Canadian issuers based on Canadian accounting standards, and Canadian Securities Commissions accept financial statements of US issuers prepared using US accounting standards. That approach has the benefit of not requiring issuers to spend the money to keep two sets of records and employ accounting and auditing experts who are knowledgeable in both countries' financial accounting and reporting standards. That approach has the drawback that it requires investors in both countries to learn the accounting standards in both countries and keep up to date with changes in those standards. Of course, in the case of Canada and the USA, the accounting standards and disclosure requirements are fairly close together, and the SEC found, after lengthy study, that the Canadian requirements satisfied the requirements of our securities laws.

Another approach is that which I understand is followed in many European countries, and in many Far Eastern countries, which is to allow foreign issuers to issue and list securities, both debt and equity, based on financial statements using home-country accounting standards. This approach allows for the greatest possible flexibility on the part of an issuer and correspondingly imposes the greatest burden on investors and creditors, for they have to learn and keep current with changing accounting standards around the world. This latter approach seems to me to be the least efficient way possible. It just does not seem possible, even given the communications technology currently available, for investors in all the countries to be able to understand all the ins and outs and nuances of the accounting standards and the way or multiple ways in which those standards are applied in practice in the various countries. A US investor, for example, is unlikely to understand fully how and why companies in other countries, even those geographically close by, apply accounting standards the way they do. The accounting standards and disclosure practices of a country derive from commercial business practices in that country, the civil law in that country, contract law in that country, tax law in that country, and custom in that country. It seems to me that it is asking a lot of investors in a country to know and understand what underlies other countries' accounting standards and disclosure practices or requirements. Although many assert that the price of an issuer's securities is set by investors in the issuer's home country, it seems to me, intuitively, that an issuer's securities will not be priced efficiently around the world if investors around the world do not fully understand the issuer's financial statements.

That then leads to the fourth possibility, namely international financial accounting Esperanto promulgated by the IASC or something like the IASC. I think that, in the long run, agreement on such an accounting Esperanto holds out the most promise for international investors and creditors and perhaps for international issuers as well.

In order for such an accounting Esperanto to succeed and become acceptable to regulators around the world, and indeed to investors and creditors around the world, it seems to me that it must result in financial statements that have relevance and reliability, and obviously transparency, as their foundation. The Esperanto must be supportable in concept, and it should be simple and practical to implement. It should be fairly prescriptive and not allow for too much judgment on the part of issuers so as to maintain a high degree of reliability. If those qualitative characteristics of the information produced by the accounting Esperanto are present, then it seems to me that regulators such as the USA's Securities and Exchange Commission will be favorably disposed to its acceptance. That will be because investors and creditors will be both protected by and benefit from financial accounting information having such qualities. We have fifty-one million individual investors in the USA. Our commission will have to be satisfied that those investors are protected and will benefit before it will be inclined to allow international accounting Esperanto to replace US generally accepted accounting principles in the preparation of financial statements disseminated to our public.

Let me take two of your recent proposals and compare them with the beacons of relevance and reliability.

In your conceptual framework, you define an asset as a "resource controlled by the enterprise." Yet, in your proposal on research and development, you have tentatively concluded that a cost *per se* is a resource, in that development cost may qualify for recognition as an asset if certain conditions are met. To me, a resource, or an asset, in order to be controlled, is something that can be identified and sold, or pledged to a bank as collateral for a loan. A cost as such cannot be sold, or pledged to secure a loan. A cost cannot be controlled. Furthermore, the conditions for cost capitalization are quite judgmental and will be very difficult to verify. Indeed, it appears that the conditions are so judgmental that capitalization may be optional. So it seems to me that that proposal does not measure up on the counts of relevance or reliability. However, I might note that what you are proposing for development cost is not unlike what the Financial Accounting Standards Board did with respect to software costs in FASB Statement 86.

In your financial instruments exposure draft, you would have financial instrument assets initially recognized and subsequently de-recognized based not on who controls the financial instrument but on who has the risks or rewards inherent in the financial instrument. Using risks or rewards as the criterion for recognition and de-recognition instead of control will result in the reporting of phantom assets, phantom liabilities, phantom revenue, and phantom expense. That criterion will also result in written credit puts not being recognized as liabilities at fair value by transferors and not reducing shareholders' equity by the amount of that fair value. Commercial banks and thrift banks in the USA have sold upward of $1.5 trillion of receivables with recourse. Under the criterion of risk, those banks would have to reinstate the unpaid/uncollected portion of those receivables, along with an equal liability, to their balance sheets, whereas, under the notion of control, those receivables are not on the face of the balance sheets. I do not think it is relevant to balloon banks' balance sheets with receivables that they do not own and do not control.

Moreover, under the exposure draft on financial instruments, management intent plays an important role in the accounting. We have seen in the USA that relying on management intent with regard to marketable securities does not produce reliable financial statements; management intent cannot be verified.

Finally, that exposure draft would continue to favor historical cost for long-term investments in marketable securities as opposed to market value.

My assessment is that the exposure draft would not meet the twin tests of relevance and reliability. But I would have approximately the same comment about the FASB's recent exposure draft on debt and equity securities, which relies on management intent and, to some extent, on historical cost for marketable securities.

That said, however, I am hopeful that the IASC can, in the future, promulgate standards that meet the twin tests of relevance and reliability along with the companion tests of simplicity and practicality. If that happens, it may force national standards to converge along the lines of international standards. And that convergence would be good. I can even see the day where we at the commission would conclude that a foreign issuer would not necessarily have to follow every jot and tittle of one of our very complex US accounting standards if compliance with international accounting Esperanto produced financial statements that both protected and benefited fifty-one million US investors.

Let me close by saying that you have a tough and delicate job. Standard setters must have patience and resolve. Most of all they must have extraordinarily keen hearing. Standard setters must be able to discern the voice of the investor – sometimes the small, faint voice of the investor – in the din of voices of all of the supplicants making entreaties to the standard setter.

37 What is the future of mutual recognition of financial statements, and is comparability really necessary?

Information is king

Remarks to Third Congrès Fédération des Experts Comptables, Copenhagen, 10 September 1993

The main heading for today's panel discussion is "What is the future of mutual recognition of financial statements, and is comparability [of financial information] really necessary?"

The detailed subheading for the discussion is: "Can changes be expected to the accounting, presentation, and disclosure requirements imposed by capital market regulators in foreign companies wishing to raise finance in their jurisdictions? Should comparability be a necessary precondition for the mutual recognition of financial statements? How can the role of the IASC enhance and influence these issues? Should not current practices in Europe be accepted by regulators elsewhere?"

In accordance with the commission's policy, I must tell you that my answers to these questions and my other remarks today will be my views, and will not necessarily reflect the views of the commission or my colleagues on the commission's staff.

The answers to those questions, to me, depend on how one answers an unasked question, namely, what is the objective of the financial statements and reports being issued by those companies wishing to offer their securities to investors? Is the objective to make decisions about income to be reported to taxing authorities? Is the objective for state planners outside the enterprise to make decisions about tax policy, labor policy, or other state matters? Is the objective to determine the amount of cash that may safely be distributed to owners of the business while maintaining sufficient resources within the enterprise to provide jobs for the present workforce and possibly additional workers? Is the objective to state net assets and income with a downward bias so as to minimize demands by owners for dividends? Or is the objective one that is oriented primarily toward the capital markets, that is, toward investors and creditors and making investment and credit decisions?

In the United States of America, starting in the 1930s after the Great Depression and then after World War II, we embarked on a course of preparing financial statements for use by those who make investment decisions. The American Institute of Certified Public Accountants' Committee on Accounting

Procedures, in the introduction to Accounting Research Bulletin No. 43, *Restatement and Revision of Accounting Research Bulletins*, wrote as follows in the early 1950s:

> In the past fifty years there has been an increasing use of the corporate system for the purpose of converting into readily transferable form the ownership of large, complex, and more or less permanent business enterprises. … As a result of this development, the problems in the field of accounting have increasingly come to be considered from the standpoint of the buyer or seller of an interest in an enterprise, with consequent increased recognition of the significance of the income statement. … The fairest possible presentation of periodic net income, with neither material overstatement nor understatement, is important, since the results of operations are significant not only to prospective buyers of an interest in the enterprise but also to prospective sellers.

Writing in 1978, the Financial Accounting Standards Board, in its Concepts Statement 1, said:

> the objectives in this Statement are focused on information for investment and credit decisions [for those] who generally lack the authority to prescribe the information they want … [paragraph 30].
>
> The objectives are those of financial reporting rather than goals for investors, creditors, or others who use the information or goals for the economy or society as a whole. The role of financial reporting in the economy is to provide information that is useful in making business and economic decisions, not to determine what those decisions should be. For example, saving and investing in productive resources (capital formation) are generally considered to be prerequisite to increasing the standard of living in an economy. To the extent that financial reporting provides information that helps identify relatively efficient and inefficient users of resources, aids in assessing relative returns and risks of investment opportunities, or otherwise assists in promoting efficient functioning of capital and other markets, it helps to create a favorable environment for capital formation decisions. However, investors, creditors, and others make those decisions, and it is not a function of financial reporting to try to determine or influence the outcomes of those decisions. The role of financial reporting requires it to provide evenhanded, neutral, unbiased information. Thus, for example, information that indicates that a relatively inefficient user of resources is efficient or investing in a particular enterprise involves less risk than it does and information that is directed toward a particular goal, such as encouraging the reallocation of resources in favor of a particular segment of the economy, are likely to fail to serve the broader objectives that financial reporting is intended to serve [paragraph 33].
>
> Financial reporting should provide information that is useful to present and potential investors and creditors and other users in making rational investment, credit, and similar decisions [paragraph 34].

> Financial reporting should provide information to help present and potential investors and creditors and other users in assessing the amounts, timing, and uncertainty of prospective cash receipts from dividends or interest and the proceeds from the sale, redemption, or maturity of securities or loans [paragraph 37].

In fulfilling that capital-markets objective, financial accounting and reporting in the United States of America has developed into a system where public companies present the facts surrounding their businesses and operations with great transparency. The degree of the transparency is bounded or constrained only by the necessity to summarize information so as to get the information into a report of manageable size that may be sent to owners and creditors and may be understood and digested and used by them. In this system, information is king, and also queen. Our public companies lay out the facts and let marketplace participants decide on how the facts should affect securities prices and how capital should be allocated.

The International Accounting Standards Committee, in its *Framework for the Preparation and Presentation of Financial Statements*, has adopted much the same approach to deciding what should go into financial statements, that is, an investor-oriented, capital-markets approach. In paragraph 10 of its framework, the IASC said, "as investors are providers of risk capital to the enterprise, the provision of financial statements that meet their needs will also meet most of the needs of other users (such as, employees, lenders, trade creditors, customers, governments, and the public) that financial statements can satisfy." The IASC, in its framework, also lists most of the same qualitative characteristics of financial information as does the FASB: for example, relevance, reliability, neutrality, and comparability.

I think that the capital-markets approach is the wave of the future for those companies in Europe and elsewhere that wish to offer their debt or equity securities in worldwide markets. If those companies are unwilling to provide to the investing public the same information that they provide privately to their major debt and equity holders, then those companies cannot, it seems to me, expect worldwide investors to bid the full price for their securities. Keeping information private has a cost. That cost is reflected in reduced securities prices. I have heard and understand the argument that the price of an issuer's securities is set in the home-country market and is accepted by participants in other markets and therefore there is no need to make any more disclosures than are considered necessary by the home-country regulator. But that argument ignores the fact that an issuer's securities may not be fully priced by participants in the home-country marketplace if disclosures in that marketplace are opaque. It also seems to me, intuitively, that if worldwide investors have a choice as to whether to buy the securities of two issuers – one whose disclosures are great and transparent and one whose disclosures are minimal and opaque – the investor will select the securities of the issuer whose disclosures are great and transparent, all other things being equal.

Under the mutual-recognition approach to regulation of securities offerings, the regulator in the country where the securities are sought to be offered and listed would accept as adequate whatever disclosures the issuer makes in its home country. While this approach may, on the surface, appeal to issuers, it places a great burden on investors. Under that approach, investors have to learn and become familiar with the accounting requirements of the country of the issuer. That approach burdens rather than helps investors. I do not see as practical the proposal that investors in another country know enough about the disclosure requirements and accounting rules or practices in the issuer's country so as to make informed decisions about prices of the issuer's securities. The aim of regulation should be to help investors, not burden them.

Moreover, the mutual-recognition approach has another drawback, which I call the lowest common denominator syndrome. By that I mean that managers of some corporations may not necessarily act in the best interests of investors by factually and openly reporting financial information. If some companies in worldwide markets smooth their earnings, or indeed determine the amounts of their earnings, on an undisclosed and discretionary basis through the use of hidden accounting reserves, other companies may be motivated to report in a similar way so as to preserve perceived competitive advantage. If some companies, selectively and without disclosure of relevant details, omit cash, working capital, plant, and debt from their financial statements by not consolidating the financial statements of subsidiaries, or some subsidiaries, other companies may be motivated to report in a similar way. If some companies, on the acquisition of other companies, recognize liabilities or asset-valuation allowances that have no basis in fact, so as to allow the release of those amounts into earnings in periods after the acquisition, other companies may want to do likewise. If this syndrome became widespread, financial accounting and reporting could sink to a very low level. Although this condition probably would not persist over the long term, I think that any movement of this sort would harm investors.

There is a large body of academic research and literature that says that the accounting numbers that are disclosed by reporting companies can affect stock prices. That accounting numbers make a difference. That accounting numbers are important. I think that issuers of financial statements will resolve the conflict between the desire to keep information private along with the desire to publish only home-country information and the need to get a full price for their securities in the way that they see is in their best self-interest. If the issuers want to maintain closeness about their business affairs, they will opt for less than transparent disclosures. If, on the other hand, their current owners demand that the best price possible be obtained for new issues of securities so that current owners' values are not diluted, and if current and prospective owners want full pricing of securities in their portfolios, they will choose transparency, which is the approach to regulation of securities offerings we take in the USA.

In closing, I would like to share with you some statistics that I believe demonstrate the success of complete and transparent financial reporting systems, such as the system used in the United States. Last year alone, equity trading volume in the USA grew by 18 percent to nearly (US)$3 trillion. The growth of securities registered for public offering in the USA was also exceptional, increasing more than 37 percent in 1992 to $610.5 billion. Registered initial public offerings for debt and equity rose by nearly 43 percent to about $52 billion. More significant to this audience, securities registered for public offering in the United States by foreign issuers grew 32 percent from $25 billion to $33 billion between 1991 and 1992. In the first seven months of 1993, foreign company registrations reached $26.5 billion. Since 1 January 1990, 228 companies from thirty-one countries have entered the US public securities markets for the first time. Over that period, foreign issuers registered approximately $94 billion of securities for issuance to the public. Today, a total of thirty-nine countries, including all major markets except Germany, are represented among the 557 foreign issuers having securities registered with the commission. And earlier this year, Daimler Benz announced that it will be the first German company to list its shares on the New York Stock Exchange.

I believe that it is, in large part, the SEC's commitment to a financial reporting system with the objective of providing full disclosure to investors that has made the US securities markets attractive for global as well as domestic capital formation. Such transparency must, in my personal view, be a primary ingredient in any standards that are to receive worldwide recognition.

I would like to thank the federation for inviting me to participate in today's panel discussion, and I look forward to hearing the other participants' views.

38 A note about private-sector standard setting

Remarks to Fourth Annual Conference on Financial Reporting, Haas School of Business, University of California at Berkeley, San Francisco, 29 October 1993

Thank you very much for inviting me to be the luncheon speaker at this fourth annual conference on financial reporting. Let me say at the outset that my remarks represent my views and mine alone and that I do not speak for the commission or other members of the staff.

I want to speak today about private-sector standard setting and specifically the relationship of the commission to the Financial Accounting Standards Board and the FASB's standard-setting process. The occasion for these remarks is that Congress is considering whether it should intervene in the standard-setting process because the FASB's tentative conclusions, if ultimately adopted, would result in the value of stock options issued to employees being reported as a compensation cost/expense in companies' financial statements.

On the one hand, Senator Levin and Representative Bryant have been concerned that the use of stock options to compensate high-level management employees has resulted in hundred million dollar pay days for certain CEOs, which are never reflected in their companies' financial statements. On the other hand, Representative Eshoo and Senator Bradley have introduced "sense of the House" and "sense of the Senate" resolutions objecting to the FASB's tentative conclusion, and Senator Lieberman *et al.* have introduced a bill that would set aside any decision that the FASB may reach. Senator Lieberman's bill would preclude the recognition of the value of employee stock options as an expense, as a matter of law. Those who have supported Senator Lieberman's bill say that a requirement to recognize a cost/expense for stock options issued to employees would be harmful to business and would put US businesses at a competitive disadvantage with foreign companies.

However, my purpose today is not to take a side in the substantive debate on whether the value of stock options issued to employees should or should not be recognized as a compensation cost/expense and, if so, how that value should be measured. What I want to do today is talk about the standard-setting process.

As you know, the federal securities laws, enacted in the 1930s, are intended to protect investors through the disclosure of reliable, material information. Financial statements, prepared by managements and audited by outside independent accountants, are a central feature of this disclosure system. Indeed, I think that financial information – financial information having a high degree of relevance, reliability, and, most of all, transparency – is the lubricant that allows the engine of our system here in the United States to run at a very high rate of RPMs. To be sure, products have to be manufactured, services have to be available, and products and services have to be packaged, distributed, and sold for businesses to be successful, and no amount of financial maneuvring or engineering will be able to turn poor or substandard products or services into successes. Similarly, no amount of financial reporting should turn a good product or quality services into business failures. However, the way we recognize, measure, and report these business activities to investors and potential investors is crucial to the turning of the wheels of commerce and business.

Since 1938, the commission, without abdicating its responsibilities in this area, has looked to the accounting profession for leadership in establishing and improving accounting standards. Working in partnership, the SEC and the accounting profession have established what are widely recognized as the most comprehensive accounting standards in the world. These standards provide for transparency of the economic conditions, events, and transactions affecting public entities and allow investors to decide how the underlying facts should affect securities prices and the allocation of capital. I believe that it is, in large part, the commitment in this country to an accounting system that has the objective of providing complete and unbiased financial information to investors that has made the US securities market attractive to both domestic and global capital formation.

The Financial Accounting Standards Board has been the private-sector body designated by the accounting profession to set accounting standards since 1973. The FASB's concepts statements, which set forth the fundamental precepts that the FASB uses in setting standards, stress that financial reporting should not be viewed as an end in itself but as a means to provide information that is useful in making economic and business decisions. In order to achieve this objective, the FASB listens to the concerns of all of its constituents and then writes and issues, without bias or favoritism, standards that are designed to reflect economic conditions, events, and transactions as objectively as possible. The FASB's mission statement accents this approach by stating that the FASB must, among other things: (1) be objective in its decision making; (2) weigh carefully the views of its constituents; (3) promulgate standards only when the expected benefits exceed the perceived costs; and (4) bring about needed changes in ways that minimize disruption to the continuity of reporting practice.

To implement the concepts statements and mission statement, the meetings of the FASB concerning proposed standards are open to the public, and prior to acting on any significant proposed standard, a discussion memorandum or similar initial document exploring all the issues is published for public comment, public hearings are held, drafts of the proposal are published for public comment, and the proposal may be field tested. After studying information from all of these sources, the FASB then re-deliberates the proposal. The commission staff, through the Office of the Chief Accountant, reviews each standard-setting proceeding carefully by reading comment letters, observing FASB meetings and public hearings, and expressing its concerns and interests to the FASB and its staff. Once a standard is adopted, the SEC staff continues to consult with the FASB staff on implementation issues and whether interpretations or changes in the standard may be necessary to achieve the objective of the standard. I strongly endorse this process for setting accounting standards and believe that it should continue, unabated, in the future.

The success of this process is of vital concern not only to the commission, investors, and the accounting profession but also to Congress. In my view, it is certainly appropriate for Congress to question whether this standard-setting process fulfills the goals of the federal securities laws and to oversee the efforts of public and private standard-setting bodies in implementing those laws. It is also appropriate for Congress to be concerned with whether the accounting profession is acting in the best interests of investors.

However, setting accounting standards is a complex task. Very often, in seeking to address one question, the FASB and the SEC must be careful that they are not creating new, tougher questions. And should the neutrality of the process even temporarily be overshadowed by the interests of one industry or group, or one set of interests over another, accounting standards may result that make it difficult not only for investors but also for public policy officials to make informed decisions based on the facts. Examples may be found on both sides – where actual economic conditions were shielded from the public's view and appropriate decision making was delayed (such as through the use of regulatory accounting principles and the construct of "net worth certificates" for certain thrifts), and where economic conditions were portrayed more accurately and fueled what many consider appropriate and timely public policy debates (such as the recognition and quantification of post-retirement healthcare costs).

If the effort to legislate in this area is successful, and Congress indeed sets aside an eventual FASB decision, where does it stop? For example, would those who opposed timely recognition of costs and liabilities for employee pension benefits and post-retirement healthcare benefits now want to go to Congress and ask it to overturn FASB Statements 87 and 106 on pensions and post-retirement benefits? US manufacturers can say that having to recognize those costs and liabilities on a timely, accrual basis instead of on the cash basis is incorrect because it decreases income and equity before cash flows out. That it puts them at a disadvantage with foreign competitors who are not directly burdened with those costs and liabilities but pay for such benefits indirectly through income tax regimes on a cash basis.

Would those who have to mark to market certain of their marketable securities now wish to go to Congress and ask for relief from the requirements of FASB Statement 115? US commercial banks and insurance companies can say that their shareholders' equities are too volatile because of that requirement. That foreign banks and insurance companies do not have to mark to market their holdings of certain marketable securities and therefore are at a competitive advantage.

Would those who have to recognize foreign currency transaction gains and losses currently in income now wish to go to Congress and ask for relief from the requirements of FASB Statement 52? US companies can say that their incomes and stockholders' equities are either under- or overstated because of that requirement. That foreign companies are allowed to defer such gains and losses and thus have an advantage over US companies.

Would those who have to charge research and development costs to expense when incurred now wish to go to Congress and ask for relief from FASB Statement 2? US companies can say that companies should be able to defer such costs if, in their judgment, the amounts will be recovered in the future through royalties or sales of products. That foreign companies may defer such costs and therefore enjoy an advantage over US companies.

I do not know how long this piece of yarn is, once Congress starts pulling on it.

I do not mean to be disrespectful to those who have asked Congress to step into this debate on the accounting for stock options issued to employees. Nor do I mean any disrespect to any members of Congress for entering this debate. I just believe that Congress is not the forum to determine the specific accounting standards that are necessary for the protection of investors and that provide for the smooth and efficient functioning of our capital markets. Let me use an analogy. I think that it is quite appropriate for Congress to decide, after consultation with the medical profession, that the health of US citizens would be improved if there were less emission of pollutants from automobiles and to pass a law saying that emissions should be reduced. But I think that Congress should leave the design of fuel injection systems, catalytic converters, and exhaust systems to automotive engineers.

The FASB, with its technical expertise, and the SEC and its staff, are uniquely positioned to perform the task of setting accounting standards. Based on my experiences as the chief adviser to the commission on accounting and auditing issues, as one of the original FASB members, and as a practicing accountant for over thirty years, this process achieves its best results when the establishment of specific accounting standards is left to those bodies having technical expertise.

The standard-setting process in the United States, although the best in the world, is not perfect. There is room for constructive advice from Congress, the business community, investor groups, and others on how the process may be improved and strengthened. In designing specific standards, however, in my opinion, it is best to use the technical expertise available in the process that is currently in place and has worked for decades rather than pre-empting that process through congressional action.

39 Take me out to the ball game

Remarks to the Eighteenth Annual AICPA National Conference on Banking, Washington, 5 November 1993

I am pleased to share this session with my former partner, John Shanahan, and with Denny Beresford, chairman of the FASB. My remarks represent my views and mine alone, and I do not speak for the commission or other members of the staff.

At the outset, let me commend the FASB for working long, hard hours to issue Statement 114 on loan impairment and Statement 115 on debt and equity securities earlier this year. I think that investors are and will be the beneficiaries of that work, and I applaud the FASB.

I have been working in the auditing and accounting standard-setting business for a long time. In 1963, when I was at Peat Marwick, I started working with that firm's representatives on the AICPA's Committee on Auditing Procedures and the Accounting Principles Board. Starting in 1966 through 1970, I was one of the technical advisers to a member of the Accounting Principles Board. From 1973 to mid-1976, I was one of the original members of the FASB. And, off and on from 1979 through 1991, I was a member of then chairman of the Accounting Standards Executive Committee of the AICPA. So I think that I know something about this business.

In the accounting standard-setting business, one has to deal with things emotional and things psychological as much as with things technical. Standard setting in accounting is as much about managing change as it is about understanding technical financial accounting and reporting. Accounting standard setting is the process of making changes to recognize shifts in business practice and economic situations and sometimes to reflect changes in accounting thought. Some people, especially preparers of financial statements, might welcome less change. I have heard a few of them say that the FASB should take a long holiday. But that is not the way the world is.

In this world of standard setting, things take time, sometimes lots of time, and change tends to come in small chunks, in singles instead of home runs. Sometimes in bunt singles. Sticking with the baseball vernacular, I think that FASB Statements 114 and 115 were line-drive singles, not bouncers through the infield. In Statement 114, while retaining the indefinite standard of "probable" for identifying impairment in Statement 5, the board recognized the importance of the time value of money. That required the elimination of part of old Statement 15, which had allowed, indeed required, that the time value of money be ignored in accounting for troubled debt restructurings. FASB Statement 115, although still based on management intent as to debt securities, requires marketable securities to be recognized at market instead of cost, making the financial statements more relevant. Based on Statements 114 and 115 and other recent board actions, I think that the FASB has been doing quite well. The standard on pension benefits (Statement 87), aside from its complicated deferrals, which level the hills and valleys of changes in asset and liability valuations, is a double; research studies have shown that investors are demonstrably taking the pension disclosures and impounding them into stock prices. The standard on post-retirement healthcare benefits (Statement 106), aside from its complicated deferrals and its permissible drawn-out transition provision, is a bases-clearing double. Research also shows that investors are using information produced by that standard. Indeed, not since line-of-business/segment reporting was introduced in the 1970s has an accounting standard so dramatically and forcefully communicated so much information to so many people as has Statement 106 on post-retirement benefits. Had the standard on cash flow information (Statement 95) required direct reporting of operating cash flows, it would have been a home run; as it is, it is a stand-up triple. Investors are more than cheering spectators when the FASB scores; investors are the very real winners in a very real game affecting their fortunes.

Those successes by the FASB, along with others such as FASB Statement 14 on segment and geographical reporting, Statement 52 on foreign currency translation, and Statement 94 on consolidation, demonstrate the wisdom of having an independent, full-time, well-funded Financial Accounting Standards Board. They demonstrate the wisdom of the board's having a mission statement and concepts statements that drive toward financial information that is relevant, reliable, complete, neutral, free from bias, and even-handed – that will produce financial information that is useful for making economic and business decisions. That will produce financial information that is transparent and credible.

A further strength of the FASB system is shown by the fact that the FASB is willing to, and does, re-examine prior standards, as was done with foreign currency translation, where Statement 52 replaced Statement 8; as was done with income taxes, where Statement 109 replaced Statement 96; and as the board is now doing with its re-examination of reporting disaggregated information, which in effect is another look at segment reporting. This demonstrates the wisdom of having a standard-setting apparatus that is the finest of its kind – one that works.

That said, let me now turn to one of the FASB's unfinished projects, namely the financial instruments project, which is of much interest to this audience. That project has been on the board's agenda a long time, since 1986. In fact, the longer the board works on that project, the more we learn how significant it is and how large it is. To give you some idea of how large I think it is, I think it is larger than a bread box and larger than my Buick. It's about as large as the *Queen Mary*. The board has broken the project down into manageable bites; we have a standard on disclosure about financial instruments with off-balance-sheet risk and concentrations of credit risk (Statement 105), a standard on disclosure about fair value of financial instruments (Statement 107), a standard for recognition and measurement of loan impairment (Statement 114), and a standard on accounting for and disclosure about investments in debt and equity securities (Statement 115). And now the board is working on what to do about forwards, exchange-traded futures, options, and swaps, or generally speaking, the so-called derivative contracts, of which there are now hundreds.

As things stand now, investors know a lot about what appears on a bank's balance sheet and what went on during the year about cash financial instruments that are recognized on a bank's balance sheet. Taking a bond, for example, the investor can see the bond's cost, its maturity date and amount, and its market value. The coupon interest rate may not be disclosed explicitly but may be inferred. The investor sees the interest income recognized on the bond in the income statement. And if there were sales and purchases of bonds, the investor sees cash receipts coming in and cash payments going out in the cash flow statement. With respect to liabilities like deposits and debentures, investors can see the maturity amount, the fair value, and maturity dates. Coupon rates, if not explicitly disclosed, may be inferred. The income statement shows an amount representing interest expense, and the cash flow statement shows activity in issuances and extinguishments of debentures payable.

Given the disclosures with respect to on-balance-sheet financial instrument items, investors have the necessary ingredients to make judgments about a bank's future earnings and cash flows. The investor can make his or her own judgment about the course of interest rates in the future, how quickly the bank can react to changes in interest rates, the prospects of bad debts in the bank's customer base, the bank's cost structure, competition, regulatory changes, and the like, and come up with some fairly good ideas about a bank's future income and cash flow streams.

The information given to investors about derivatives that are used to manage a bank's on-balance-sheet assets and liabilities as an end user is not nearly so robust, however. Even as to futures contracts, where there is daily mark to market for changes in value, there is not always disclosure about those on-balance-sheet cash items related to "hedging" of assets or liabilities. Disclosure about the realized and unrealized gains and losses on non-exchange-traded forwards and options and swaps is also often not robust. The explanation of why the contracts are entered is often slight. Disclosure about open contracts and contracts settled or offset with other contracts is also often less than robust. In short, the disclosures need to be improved so that investors may make better and more well-informed decisions.

I recently attended a meeting at the FASB where the participants were discussing accounting for hedging instruments and off-balance-sheet derivatives that are used by banks as end users. One banker said that the off-balance-sheet instruments are like on-balance-sheet instruments but involve no initial cash outflow, or cost, or no initial cash inflow, or proceeds. That description is, I think, apt. What it suggests to me is that banks should consider giving investors as much information about the off-balance-sheet items used by banks as end users to manage on-balance-sheet assets and liabilities as they give for on-balance-sheet items. Notional amounts. Strike prices. Interest rates. Due dates. The amounts of cash that will flow in and out depending on where interest rates go. When cash receipts will come in. When cash payments will go out. Activity in contracts. Unrealized gains and losses or replacement value of contracts. Deferred gains and losses. When, period by period, deferred gains and losses will be recognized in income, and the amounts thereof. The effect of those instruments on net interest income or margin. Why the bank is entering into such contracts. Whether it will enter into such contracts in the future. What the bank is doing to prevent counterparty credit loss. The effects of netting agreements including disclosure about legal enforceability. With that information, investors can make judgments about future income and future net cash flow both for what is on the balance sheet and what is not on the balance sheet. Until the FASB decides what the accounting and related disclosures should be for the derivatives used by banks as end users, I think voluntary disclosure of these kind of item will be most helpful to investors.

At the 23 September 1993 meeting of the Emerging Issues Task Force, I made an announcement of SEC staff positions on (1) the discount rate used to measure the amount of defined pensions benefits under FASB Statement 87, *Employers Accounting for Pensions*, and post-retirement benefits other than pensions under FASB Statement 106, *Employers' Accounting for Post-retirement Benefits other than Pensions*; (2) the classification of in-substance foreclosed assets; and (3) the reclassification of securities in anticipation of the adoption of FASB Statement 115.

The SEC staff expects registrants to use discount rates to measure obligations for pension benefits and post-retirement benefits other than pensions that reflect the current level of interest rates at each measurement date. Interest rates have declined substantially and are at levels not seen in twenty years. In reviewing various filings, we have found that registrants are not updating the discount rate assumption, and we have required that it be done. We will be looking at future filings to make sure that registrants are updating their assumption about discount rates. In that announcement, we also said that we would expect the rate to be the rate of high-quality bonds, which are the equivalent of AA-rated bonds.

Financial Reporting Release 28, *Accounting for Loan Losses by Registrants Engaged in Lending Activities*, requires that in-substance foreclosed assets be classified and accounted for as "other real estate owned." On 10 June 1993, the banking regulators jointly issued a regulatory credit initiative that is not consistent with the guidance provided in FRR 28 because the regulatory initiative permits the classification of ISF assets as loans rather than as real estate owned. Registrants have asked whether SEC staff would object to the classification of ISF assets as loans in financial statements and other financial information filed with the commission.

Even though the classification of ISF assets as loans is not consistent with the guidance contained in FRR 28, it is the position of SEC staff that the main objective of FRR 28 is to require a systematic methodology to be applied to the recognition and measurement of ISF assets, and that this objective should be met even if the classification pursuant to the regulatory credit initiative is adopted by registrants. Therefore, the SEC staff would not object to the reclassification of ISF assets as loans, provided that:

1 Registrants do not change their recognition and measurement accounting policies for ISF assets.
2 Registrants file with the commission, in a current report, financial statements and other financial information, including Guide 3 disclosures and management's discussion and analysis, that reflect the effects of the new classification policy for ISF assets for each period for which such statements and other financial information were provided in the most recent 10-K and subsequent interim reports. This means that the staff would like registrants to present the impact of the new reclassification policy on (a) the financial statements for each of the latest three years, (b) each quarterly period since the last form 10-K as well as comparable quarters for the preceding fiscal year, and (c) all other financial information, including Guide 3 disclosures and management's discussion and analysis, for each period for which such statements and other financial information were provided.
3 There is disclosure of the reclassification and its effects.

The SEC staff will object if, because of the adoption of this new regulatory initiative, ISF assets are not classified consistently. Therefore, registrants should not adopt this initiative on a prospective basis, because the financial statements and other financial information would not be presented in a consistent manner.

FASB Statement 114 is silent on the issue of classification. Paragraph 26 of FASB Statement 114 states that annual financial statements shall not be restated, but it does not state whether annual financial statements should be retrospectively reclassified to present ISF assets consistently. I think that investors would be better informed if the financial statements for all periods had the amounts for ISF assets classified and displayed consistently, rather than having a disjointed presentation that may confuse investors.

Statement of Financial Accounting Standards No. 115, *Accounting for Certain Investments in Debt and Equity Securities*, requires an investment in a security to be classified as held to maturity, available for sale, or trading, based on an enterprise's intent with respect to holding the security. The staff understands that the anticipated adoption of Statement 115 and possible changes in regulatory capital requirements may have caused registrants to change their intent with respect to holding certain securities. As a result, for financial reporting purposes, these registrants may need to change their classification of certain securities to reflect that revised intent.

The SEC staff has been asked whether such a change in classification would call into question the prior accounting for securities. The staff will not challenge a registrant's prior accounting for securities as a result of a one-time change in the classification of securities on, or prior to, the date of adopting Statement 115 if that change is caused by a change in intent because of the anticipated adoption of Statement 115 and possible changes in the regulatory capital requirements. However, registrants should not change the measurement principles for securities prior to the adoption of Statement 115.

40 Financial accounting and reporting in our worldwide economy

Remarks in the Distinguished Lecture Series at the University of Texas at Austin, 12 November 1993

Thank you very much for inviting me to speak in this Distinguished Lecture Series. My remarks represent my views and mine alone, and I do not speak for the commission or other members of the staff.

I want to talk today about financial accounting and reporting in the United States and in our worldwide economy and how important that reporting is. Before I launch into that topic in general, it may be helpful if I set the stage by a brief description of what the Securities and Exchange Commission is and does.

The US Securities and Exchange Commission's mission is to administer federal securities laws that seek to provide protection for investors. The purpose of these laws is to ensure that the securities markets are fair and honest and to provide the means to enforce the securities laws through sanctions where necessary. Laws administered by the Commission are the Securities Act of 1933, Securities Exchange Act of 1934, Public Utility Holding Company Act of 1935, Trust Indenture Act of 1939, Investment Company Act of 1940, and Investment Advisers Act of 1940.

Congress created the Securities and Exchange Commission in 1934 in the Securities Exchange Act. The SEC is an independent, non-partisan regulatory agency.

The commission is composed of five members, a chairman and four commissioners. Commission members are appointed by the President, with the advice and consent of the Senate, for five-year terms. The chairman is designated by the President. Terms are staggered; one expires on June 5th of every year. Not more than three members may be of the same political party.

Under the direction of the chairman and commissioners, the staff ensures that publicly held entities, broker/dealers in securities, investment companies and advisers, and other participants in the securities markets comply with federal securities laws. These laws were designed to facilitate informed investment analysis and decisions by the investing public, primarily by ensuring adequate disclosure of material information. However, conformance with federal securities laws and regulations does not imply merit. The commission does not pass on the merits of a particular security. If information essential to an informed investment analysis is properly disclosed, the commission cannot bar the sale of securities that analysis may show to be of questionable value. It is the investor, not the commission, who must make the judgment of the worth of securities offered for sale.

The commission's staff is composed of lawyers, accountants, financial analysts and examiners, engineers, investigators, economists, and other professionals. The staff is divided into divisions and offices (including twelve regional and district offices), each directed by officials appointed by the chairman. At this time, the staff numbers about 2,700. The commission's annual budget is about $260 million, which works out to about $96,000 per person.

The commission staff is organized into divisions and offices with specific areas of responsibility for various segments of the federal securities laws.

The divisions are Enforcement, Corporation Finance, Market Regulation, and Investment Management. The Office of General Counsel serves as the chief legal officer for the commission. As such, it is responsible for appellate litigation and conducting disciplinary proceedings against professionals, as well as certain other legal matters.

Other offices are those of the Chief Accountant, International Affairs, Legislative Affairs, Economic Analysis, Administrative Law Judges, Secretary, and Inspector General.

The Corporation Finance Division has overall responsibility for reviewing disclosure documents filed by publicly held companies registered with the commission. This division has about 325 lawyers, accountants, analysts, and administrative staff. Its work includes reviewing registration statements for new security issuances, secondary offerings of securities, proxy material, and annual reports that the commission requires from publicly held companies, documents concerning tender offers, and mergers and acquisitions in general. About 13,400 public companies file registration statements, annual reports, and proxy statements with this division.

The Market Regulation Division is responsible for oversight of activity in the secondary markets – registration and regulation of broker/dealers, oversight of the self-regulatory organizations (such as the nation's stock exchanges), and oversight of other participants in the secondary markets (such as transfer agents and clearing organizations). This division employs about 175 people.

The financial responsibility of broker/dealers, trading and sales practices, policies affecting operation of the securities markets, and surveillance fall under the purview of this division. In addition, it carries out activities aimed at achieving the goal of a national market system set forth in the Securities Act Amendments of 1975. The division also oversees the Securities Investor Protection Corporation and the Municipal Securities Rulemaking Board.

The Investment Management Division, with about 165 people, has basic responsibility for the Investment Company Act of 1940 and the Investment Advisers Act of 1940. In 1985, it assumed responsibility for administering the Public Utility Holding Company Act of 1935.

The division staff ensures compliance with regulations regarding the registration, financial responsibility, sales practices, and advertising of mutual funds and investment advisers. New products offered by these entities are also reviewed by the staff in this division. This division also processes investment company registration statements, proxy statements, and periodic reports under the Securities Act. If you look in your daily newspaper, *USA Today*, you will see listed about 4,000 mutual funds, all of which are overseen by the Investment Management Division.

The Enforcement Division, employing about 315 lawyers and accountants, but mostly lawyers, is charged with enforcing federal securities laws. Enforcement responsibilities include investigating possible violations of federal securities laws and recommending appropriate remedies for consideration by the commission. Possible violations may come to light through the Enforcement Division's own inquiries, through referrals from other divisions of the commission, from outside sources such as the self-regulatory organizations, or by other means.

When possible violations of federal securities laws warrant further investigation by its staff, the commission is consulted before proceeding. The commission's decisions may result in issuing subpoenas, formal orders of investigation, or other means of proceeding with actions. At the conclusion of investigations, the commission may authorize the staff to proceed with injunctions preventing further violative conduct, with administrative proceedings in the case of entities directly regulated by the commission, or with other remedies as appropriate.

In recent years, the Enforcement Division has been involved with such matters as the Drexel Burnham Lambert affair, which resulted in disgorgements and fines of more than $600 million; Salomon Bros and the US Treasury bond market affair, which resulted in fines and other payments totalling $290 million; and, just two weeks or so ago, the Prudential Securities matter, involving limited partnerships where Prudential will create a fund of more than $330 million for settlement with investors.

The Office of the Chief Accountant comprises the chief accountant, the deputy chief accountant, four associate chiefs, five assistant chiefs, five professional accounting fellows, one academic fellow, the chief accountant's counsel, one individual who is our liaison with state boards of accountancy and other bodies, and four secretarial/administrative staff. We spend about 30 percent of our time on registrant issues concerning accounting, 10 percent in rule making, 15 percent in enforcement, 30 percent in oversight of private-sector standard-setting bodies, the Financial Accounting Standards Board, and the American Institute of Certified Public Accountants' Accounting Standards Executive Committee and the Auditing Standards Board, and the remainder on congressional and administrative matters.

The chief accountant consults with representatives of the accounting profession and the standard-setting bodies designated by the profession regarding the promulgation by those bodies of new or revised accounting and auditing standards. This implements a major SEC objective to improve accounting and auditing standards and to maintain high standards of professional conduct by independent accountants.

This office also drafts rules and regulations prescribing requirements for financial statements. Many of the accounting rules are embodied in Regulation S-X, adopted by the commission. Regulation S-X, together with the generally accepted accounting principles promulgated by the profession's standard-setting bodies and a number of opinions issued by the commission as "Accounting Series Releases" or "Financial Reporting Releases," govern the form and content of most of the financial statements filed with the SEC by public companies, broker/dealers, and mutual funds.

This office administers the commission's statutes and rules requiring that accountants auditing financial statements filed with the SEC be independent of their clients. This office also initiates proceedings under Rule 2(e) of the commission's rules of practice, which specifies reasons why an accountant may be denied the privilege of practicing before the commission. These reasons include lack of character or integrity, lack of qualifications to represent others, unethical or unprofessional conduct, or the willful violation of (or the willful aiding and abetting of a violation of) any of the federal securities laws, rules, or regulations. The chief accountant also reviews the procedures followed in other accounting investigations conducted by commission staff.

Let me now turn to the function of accounting standard setting and the place it occupies in our financial markets. Financial statements and related disclosures, as we know them here in the United States, are the lubricant that allows our capital markets engine to turn at very high RPMs without overheating. There are about 13,400 public companies here in the USA, running from giants like General Motors, General Electric, General Mills, General Dynamics, and General Reinsurance with billions in assets and revenues and millions of shareholders down to the small limited partnership that has perhaps only 500 owners and a million or two in assets and revenue. There are about 4,000 mutual funds like Fidelity's Magellan and Vanguard's Windsor, which are giants managing many billions in assets. And about 8,000 broker/dealers like Merrill Lynch and Charles Schwab. They are all required to prepare financial statements in conformity with generally accepted accounting principles, file those financial statements with the SEC, and send them to shareholders or customers.

After the market crash in 1929 and the subsequent depression – the Great Depression – when the Dow Jones average lost 89 percent of its value, Congress, in setting up the SEC, looked at the question of whether financial statements of public companies should be audited by government auditors. The public accounting profession persuaded Congress that audits should be left in the private sector. However, Congress specifically empowered the SEC to prescribe accounting standards for the preparation of financial statements. In 1938, the commission stated that financial statements that were not prepared in accordance with principles having "substantial authoritative support" would be presumed to be misleading. The American Institute of Certified Public Accountants promptly created the Committee on Accounting Procedure to set standards that would provide the "substantial authoritative support" sought by the commission. That committee, during its lifetime from 1939 through 1959, issued fifty-one Accounting Research Bulletins, some of which, in one form or another, are still applicable today. For example, the bulletins on inventory costing and consolidation continue in force. The essence of the bulletins on deferred income tax accounting, although amended many times, survive today, that is, there should be accounting recognition of differences between taxable income and financial statement income reported to shareholders.

The Committee on Accounting Procedure was succeeded in 1959 by the Accounting Principles Board. The APB was also an arm of the AICPA and in fact turned out APB opinions much the same way the Committee on Accounting Procedure turned out bulletins. The APB, which lasted from 1959 through 1973, turned out thirty-one opinions, many of which survive today in one form or another. For example, APB Opinion 15 on earnings per share and APB Opinion 16 on business combinations continue to be used today, every day.

The independence of the APB began to be questioned in the late 1960s and early 1970s, and it gave way to the Financial Accounting Standards Board in 1973. The FASB is not an arm of the AICPA or any other organization. It is independent. It is funded by contributions from AICPA members, corporations, and, to a very small extent, individuals, and the sale of its publications and research documents.

Since 1973, the FASB has issued 117 statements on financial accounting standards and about sixty interpretations and technical bulletins. I signed the first twelve statements and nine interpretations.

Pursuant to an ethics rule, members of the AICPA must, in reporting on the financial statements of their clients, determine that those clients observed those various bulletins, opinions, and statements in the preparation of their financial statements in order for those financial statements to be in conformity with generally accepted accounting principles. The SEC's rules require that public company registrants, mutual funds, and broker/dealers prepare their financial statements in conformity with those same generally accepted accounting principles, which include those bulletins, opinions, and statements.

These standard-setting bodies have, in the preparation and issuance of standards, expressly said that financial statements should be prepared for use by investors in, and prospective investors in, the securities issued by the enterprise preparing and issuing the financial statement. This perspective is called the capital-markets perspective. The FASB has said that financial statements, in order to be useful for decision making by users of financial statements, should be relevant, reliable, neutral, comparable, free of bias, even-handed, and representationally faithful. The FASB, when it explicitly set out these qualitative characteristics, added powerfully to the capital-markets perspective. Today, financial statements prepared by companies following US generally accepted accounting principles are highly transparent and credible. These financial statements are relied on by investors.

One of the reasons for this country's deep and highly liquid financial markets is relevant, reliable, transparent, and credible financial statements. We have over fifty million individual investors in this country and many thousands of institutional investors, ranging from the likes of the trust department of the local bank to the huge pension funds. For example, here in Texas there is the Texas State Teachers Retirement System, which manages upwards of $31 billion of assets.

The California Public Employees Retirement System manages $69 billion of assets. TIAA/CREF, the college school system retirement vehicle, has assets of about $110 billion; it is the largest in the world. The various pension and retirement plans of General Motors manage assets of more than $40 billion; General Electric's various pension plans' assets exceed $36 billion. The open-ended mutual fund industry manages $1.9 trillion in assets. All of these fifty million individuals, and all of these mutual funds and institutions, use financial statements issued by public companies to make investment decisions, and those investors are able to rely an those financial statements.

In most other English-speaking countries, for example Canada, Great Britain, Australia, and New Zealand, accounting systems and the resulting financial statements are also fairly transparent. However, the financial statements issued by companies in those countries are not comparable with those issued by companies here in the USA. For example, companies in Great Britain often write up their fixed assets from historical cost to theoretical replacement value, and companies in Canada defer transaction gains and losses on their debts denominated in foreign currency, whereas US companies do not.

There are other major differences between what US companies do and what companies in those countries do. However, financial statements issued by companies in those countries are somewhat transparent, and the investor can see what the accounting is and make whatever adjustments considered necessary or desirable so as to make informed investment decisions. These countries have also adopted a capital-markets perspective, although they may not yet have advanced the capital-markets ideas as far as we have here in the United States. There are, in fact, many substantial differences between US accounting standards and the standards followed in other English-speaking countries.

However, many other countries have not yet adopted the capital-markets perspective in the preparation of financial statements. They have other objectives in mind. For example, in Japan, determining taxable income may take precedence over determining income from the perspective of investors. I recently saw an article in the business press to the effect that a major Japanese bank was going to recognize in income its losses from bad loans over five years. It is widely reported that many Japanese financial institutions have yet to recognize the decline in the value of their investments in stocks and real estate, some of which have declined in value by 50 percent or more in the past three years. Japanese companies, as I understand it, do not consolidate some or all subsidiaries' financial statements and account for the investments in stocks of subsidiaries at cost without elimination of inter-company profits on asset transfers such as inventory.

In Europe, particularly in Germany, the use of so-called hidden reserves and other practices such as not consolidating the financial statements of subsidiaries mask the true financial position and income of German companies. We recently saw a dramatic example of that. Earlier this year, Daimler Benz, the auto manufacturer, became the first and so far only German company to have its shares listed on the New York Stock Exchange. The SEC's rules require that, when foreign companies come to our shores to list their securities, they must prepare their financial statements in conformity with US accounting standards or reconcile their home-country financial statements to what the results would be using US accounting standards. Daimler Benz reconciled its financial statements. Here are the results. Under German accounting, Daimler Benz's shareholders' equity at 31 December 1992 was 11.5 billion Deutschmarks; under US accounting, equity was DM16 billion, an increase of about 40 percent. For the six months ended 30 June 1993, net income under German accounting was DM168 million; under US standards, Daimler Benz reported a net loss of DM949 million – a swing of more than DM1 billion, or $600 million.

While we have over fifty million individuals here in the USA who are investors in their own right, and many more indirect investors through retirement plans, individuals in Japan, Germany, and other European companies do not invest very much of their assets in securities issued by public companies in those markets. There is now quite a drive going on for companies in those countries to adopt accounting policies that will result in more relevant, reliable, and transparent financial statements. More than 550 foreign companies, including as Daimler Benz, Royal Dutch Shell, Smithkline Beecham, Telefonos de Mexico, Glaxo, Akzo, Sony, Toyota, and Honda, now have securities listed and traded in this country. I think that number will increase.

In the USA, we have one of the largest pools of capital available in the world. I believe that as companies in Europe need money for expansion, as European countries privatize some of their state-owned companies, as countries in the old Soviet bloc privatize their industries, as companies in less developed countries reach for capital to build things like roads, bridges, and telephone systems, not to mention factories that will produce consumer goods, they will increasingly come to US capital markets and prepare their financial statements under, or reconcile those statements to, US generally accepted accounting standards, which produce relevant, reliable, and credible information. Working with those companies is a high priority at the commission. The staff would like to bring as many of these investment opportunities to the USA as possible while maintaining the high-quality disclosures and accounting practices that investors in US capital markets have every right to expect.

In summary, the current accounting and disclosure operations of the SEC are premised on the need to provide clear, comparable, and understandable information to capital markets. Since the 1930s, the commission has worked with registrants and the accounting profession in this country to achieve that objective, and in more recent years we have begun to work with companies and standard setters around the world. And I am convinced that the capital-markets perspective will be adopted, not because the US Securities and Exchange Commission wants it, but because investors around the globe need it to make informed investment decisions.

Thank you. I will be happy to answer any questions.

41 SEC accounting update

Remarks to the Nineteenth Annual AICPA National Conference on Banking, Grand Hyatt Hotel, Washington, 4 November 1994

Introduction

I am pleased to speak at this conference again and to share this session with my former partner, John Shanahan, and the chairman of the FASB, Denny Beresford.

These remarks represent my views and mine alone. I do not speak for the Commission or other members of the staff. I will be making remarks regarding disclosures about derivatives, accounting for derivatives, and internal audit outsourcing

Disclosures about derivatives

Dealing first with disclosures about derivatives, I want to compliment the FASB for its speed in addressing additional disclosure issues in FASB Statement 119. From start to finish, that document took the FASB less than a year to complete. While I have not gone back and looked at prior FASB statements, I doubt that many have been started and finished in less than a year. In addition to the speed of issuing Statement 119, I think that 119 is a significant step in improving disclosures about derivative financial instruments.

In Statement 119, the FASB prescribed disclosures about the nature, terms, and financial statement effects of derivatives. Statement 119 encourages, but does not require, disclosure of quantitative information about market risks inherent in derivative financial instruments. In May 1994, the SEC's chairman, Arthur Levitt, testified before the US House of Representatives Subcommittee on Telecommunications and Finance on issues relating to financial derivatives. In that testimony, Chairman Levitt stated that, for companies that file with the commission, it is essential to disclose quantitative information about derivatives. He also stated that the commission would be publishing guidance on disclosures about derivatives and risk-management activities. The SEC's staff is working on that disclosure requirement. At this time, I do not know when it will be issued or what form it will take.

At this conference last year, I commented that companies that use derivatives for purposes other than trading should provide disclosures about these instruments that are similar to the disclosures required for on-balance-sheet financial instruments, such as debt securities held as assets. I mentioned that the purpose of these disclosures is to provide investors with an appropriate amount of information about derivatives so they can make judgments about future income and future net cash flows from both derivatives and on-balance-sheet financial instruments. Based on the filings that I have looked at, it appears that many banks have improved, or at least are well on their way to improving, their disclosures about derivatives. Investors will thus be able to make more informed judgments about the banks' cash and derivatives positions and future earnings and future cash flows.

This year, I would like to focus on improving the way that registrants describe their overall risk-management activities, not just their derivatives activities. In other words, I would like to suggest that the disclosures about derivatives and cash positions be supplemented with information that brings the entire risk-management function together so that investors can understand better how the company manages its overall financial risks. Specifically, I would like to encourage registrants to concentrate on quantitative disclosures about market risks inherent in on- and off-balance-sheet financial instruments and to discuss how these risks are managed.

Quantitative measures of market risk are used frequently by many banking and non-banking registrants for internal risk-management purposes; however, disclosures about these market risk-management techniques are generally not contained in filings with the commission. Therefore, a gap often exists between the way a company measures and assesses its market risks and the way investors think a company may measure and assess its market risks. I suggest that this gap be closed. The Group of 10 encourages this disclosure and suggests that this information gap can cause a misallocation of capital among companies and can also amplify market disturbances. That conclusion by the Group of 10 seems intuitively to be correct.

While several quantitative measures are used by companies in their internal risk-management systems, the Group of 10 and the Group of 30 recommend "value at risk" as a measure of market risk. The Financial Executives Institute also recently endorsed disclosures about value at risk. Value at risk is a measure of the potential loss resulting from hypothetical changes in market factors, such as interest rates and foreign currency exchange rates, for a given time period. It is used to measure the potential changes in the fair values of financial instruments arising from changes in market prices or yields. For example, value at risk would be an estimate of loss for a statistically calculated hypothetical change in interest rates of, say, 100 basis points.

Although this measure may initially sound complex and potentially costly to calculate, at least one large bank is making much of the data needed for this computation available at little or no cost. I'm sure that we will hear more about the potential costs and benefits of making these computations and of disclosing them.

An abbreviated sample of a value-at-risk disclosure might be something like the following:

As of 31 December 1994, the value at risk for all financial instruments, including derivatives, amounted to $*x* million for interest rate movements and $*y* million for foreign exchange movements. Value at risk is defined by the company as the potential loss from adverse market movements that would cover 99 percent of possible adverse movements during a one-day period.

From that disclosure, investors would have an indication that for ninety-nine days out of a hundred the value of the portfolio would be expected to lose no more than $*x* million because of adverse interest rate changes and no more than $*y* million because of adverse changes in foreign currency exchange rates.

This information, supplemented with a qualitative discussion about how a company manages risk and how much risk the company is willing to tolerate, would allow investors to understand better the market risks of a company's portfolio. Also, investors would be better able to compare, quantitatively, the market risks of one company with the market risks of another. This type of information should improve an investor's understanding of the potential risks and returns of two or more potential investments.

Accounting for derivatives

Next, let's discuss accounting for derivatives. At or about the time of Chairman Levitt's testimony to Congress in May 1994, the Division of Corporation Finance formed a task force to review derivative disclosures for approximately 100 banking registrants and 400 non-banking registrants. The primary objectives of this task force are to (1) learn why and how companies are using derivatives, (2) understand better the current types of disclosure about derivatives, (3) improve disclosures about derivatives, and (4) form a basis from which the commission could develop guidance regarding disclosures about derivatives.

One of the outcomes of the Corporation Finance Division's project on derivatives is that the SEC staff has learned more about how registrants account for derivatives. We have learned that companies that are parties to highly leveraged interest rate swaps are marking those swaps to fair value and including the mark in income. Companies that are parties to interest rate swaps with some form of mild embedded written option are accounting for those swaps more or less on the cash basis in that the swap is not being marked to fair value, even though, if the written option portion of the swap were a free-standing instrument, it would be marked to fair value as are other written options. The SEC staff is following closely developments by the FASB in its project on hedge accounting. Until these issues are resolved, registrants are encouraged to disclose descriptive numerical information about swaps and other instruments that have embedded written options so that investors can come to grips with what the entity is doing.

There was some publicity, about a month or two ago, that the commission or its staff was about to issue some guidance or rules on the accounting for certain kinds of swap. That position was somehow inferred from some informal discussions with our staff. Although we are considering additional quantitative disclosures at this time, the staff does not plan to issue guidance or recommend specific accounting rules in this area. That is not to say that we will not find that a registrant, in its specific circumstances, has not accounted for certain swaps correctly, which accounting may require revision. But that determination will have to be made on a case-by-case basis.

Internal audit outsourcing

The last issue I will discuss is internal audit outsourcing. With increasing worldwide competition from financial intermediaries, banks and other financial institutions are forced to work smarter and become more cost-efficient. To do this, several have begun to contract out, or "outsource," various functions. For example, I recently read an article that indicated that several banks were outsourcing their legal work, data-processing functions, mutual fund back-office work, and property management. Moreover, some banks are beginning to outsource their internal audit function.

I understand that many different alternatives are available to a company that wishes to outsource its internal audit function. One alternative being considered by some is for a company to replace completely its internal audit function with an "expanded" external audit function. As a result, the external auditor would perform both the external audit functions and the functions previously performed by the internal audit department. That is, the external auditor would be responsible for (1) performing audit procedures and issuing an opinion on whether the financial statements were prepared in conformity with generally accepted accounting practices, (2) issuing another opinion on management as assertions regarding the effectiveness of the company's internal controls, and (3) designing and executing audit procedures that traditionally were performed by the internal auditors. Because external auditors must be independent, in fact and in appearance, of the company being audited, external auditors attempting to attend to both the responsibilities of the external auditor and the responsibilities traditionally performed by the internal audit function must exercise great care.

In 1993, the AICPA issued Ethics Ruling 97, *Performance of Certain Extended Audit Services*, which addresses independence issues relating to internal audit outsourcing. That ruling highlights that external auditors (1) cannot perform management functions or make management decisions, (2) cannot be part of the client's approval process, or (3) cannot be part of the internal control system, without impairing their independence.

The guidance in Ruling 97, read carefully, is very restrictive. The auditor cannot perform management functions or make management decisions. This means, for example, that the auditor cannot determine the projects to be performed under the scope of the "internal audit" work. Also, the auditor cannot become part of the approval process for specific transactions, such as the loan-approval process, because that is a management function. In addition, to the extent that federal or state banking regulations require an internal auditor to be under the control of management, the agreement by an outsourcer to function in that employee role is fundamentally inconsistent with the notion that for external audit purposes this same auditor would be considered independent from that management.

The SEC staff has informally advised external auditors that it would question independence, consistent with Ruling 97, when external auditors perform procedures that are management functions or internal control functions. Practitioners are advised to give careful consideration to the implications that attend such outsourcing arrangements and the resulting effect on the accountant's independence.

That concludes my prepared remarks. I would be happy to respond to questions.

42 A review of the FASB's accomplishments since its inception in 1973

Remarks to the Twenty-second Annual AICPA National Conference, Washington, 10 January 1995

Good morning. I am pleased to be invited to speak at this national conference on SEC developments. I need to give the standard disclaimer. I am speaking for myself and not for the commission or any of the other staff.

I have on occasion been critical about certain financial accounting and reporting issues. Today, I want to mention some of the positive things in financial accounting and reporting.

When David Tweedie, now Sir David, commenced his chairmanship of the UK's equivalent of our Financial Accounting Standards Board, he quipped: "There are only three things wrong with accounting – the balance sheet, the income statement, and the cash flow statement." That was about five years ago, and I am pleased to report that Sir David's Accounting Standards Board is making good headway in improving accounting in the UK. I am pleased to say that the FASB is also making good headway in improving accounting here in the United States.

The FASB's mission statement says that its mission is to "improve standards of financial accounting and reporting for the guidance and education of the public, including issuers, auditors, and users of financial information." I think that the FASB is doing just that.

Last month, the FASB hit a pothole in its road to improving the accounting here in the USA. As most of you know by now, and no doubt will hear more about today and tomorrow, the FASB decided to back away from its proposal to require that the value of fixed stock options issued to employees be charged to expense. Instead, the board decided to require disclosure of that value if a company chooses not to formally recognize that value as an expense in its income statement. Many who had opposed expensing favored explicit disclosure of the value of stock options granted to employees. Given the great degree of opposition to its proposal and the clear danger that Congress would get involved with legislation, I believe that the FASB acted wisely to end the controversy by requiring disclosure instead of formal recognition in expense of the value of stock options. The FASB has, in my opinion, been good for investors. Very good for investors. I want the FASB to continue to do good work for investors. I do not want the FASB legislated out of existence. Were that to happen, I think that investors would get the short end of that stick.

Let me briefly review some of the FASB's major outputs since its inception in 1973. Time does not permit a review of all of them. When the FASB got started in 1973, a lot of the tires on the accounting vehicle were flat or very low on air. A few had ruptured, blown out so to speak.

Some companies were capitalizing research and development costs, and some were charging the costs to expense when incurred. Disclosures were non-existent or not very clear. FASB Statement 2 was quickly issued in 1974, and since then all R&D costs have been charged to expense when incurred, except for those costs incurred on R&D contracts for third parties. And there is disclosure by companies in their annual reports of the amount of R&D costs for the year.

Some insurance companies were recognizing, in advance of the event and maybe even in advance of writing a policy and collecting a premium, losses from future catastrophes such as hurricanes and ice storms. Some commercial and industrial companies were also recognizing other types of loss in advance of the event. FASB Statement 5, issued in 1975, precluded the recognition of those kinds of loss in advance of the event triggering the loss. I will note, in passing, that there has been some backsliding on this score recently in so-called "restructuring charges," where losses are being recognized in advance of the event, but I will not get into that matter here today.

How to account for operations in foreign countries and how to translate foreign currency monetary items and what to do with foreign currency transaction gains and losses was quite muddled when the FASB started business in 1973. Statement 8 quickly resolved that very complex area in 1975. However, Statement 8 produced results that were thought to be extreme, so it was changed by Statement 52 in 1981, and the world seems to be fairly well satisfied with how Statement 52 works and the results it produces. Statement 52's "hedging" provisions will be changed based on the direction the FASB is going on its hedging project, and we will hear about that this afternoon from Jim Leisenring.

Segment disclosures were covered by the board in Statement 14, issued in 1976. This is probably the one FASB standard that has not measured up to what financial statement analysts believe ought to be reported by issuers. The FASB and the Canadian Institute of Chartered Accountants, working together, are considering again what companies should report by way of segment data. At the same time, the International Accounting Standards Committee is also working on an international standard on segment reporting.

When one looks at income statements of corporate America, one sees that employee-related costs comprise more than 50 percent of total costs. In Statements 87 and 106, the FASB has improved tremendously the recognition, measurement, and disclosure rules for pension and post-retirement healthcare costs. There is now, happily, great transparency in corporate America's financial statements regarding pension and post-retirement healthcare costs.

In Statement 57, the board required the disclosure of the existence of related party relationships and related party transactions. That required disclosure had previously been contained only in the AICPA's auditing literature. Many issuers of financial statements were reluctant to provide related party disclosures prior to the issuance of Statement 57. Now that the requirement is part of the formal body of generally accepted accounting principles, it is easier to persuade issuers of the necessity of the disclosures. Users of financial statements have been the beneficiaries of the related party disclosures.

In Statement 91, on loan fees, the FASB rejected a most objectionable practice, that is, crediting to income a fee received at the time a loan is originated. Prior to that time, savings and loan associations and some banks and insurance companies were recognizing income on the acquisition of an asset instead of when the asset itself produced the income.

In Statement 95 on cash flow statements, the FASB hit a bases-clearing triple. The old funds statement required by APB Opinion 15 simply was not very good, although in its time it was a move forward in financial reporting. Had the board required the direct method of reporting operating cash flows in Statement 95 as investors and creditors wanted, as opposed to allowing the indirect method as requested by issuers, the hit would have been a grand slam home run. But, in issuing Statement 95, the board accepted the proposition that the costs of gathering the data for presenting operating cash flows on the direct basis exceeded the benefits.

I must say that I have never understood the argument by issuers of financial statements that excessive implementation costs are involved in gathering operating cash flow information by type or source. All that is required is that cash payments be coded as to type and then sorted. For example, cash payments to vendors for raw materials. Cash payments to employees. Cash payments to advertisers. That seems simple enough to me, especially in this day of computers. Likewise, cash receipts can't be hard to sort by type.

Inasmuch as investors and creditors believe that the information revealed by the direct method of presenting operating cash flows is extremely relevant and inasmuch as the costs of gathering the information cannot possibly be large, it seems to me that a good case can be made for revising Statement 95 to require the direct method of presenting operating cash flows. Moreover, I do not understand why issuers of financial statements do not, of their own volition, provide operating cash flows using the direct method. If the suppliers of capital want something, then the users of capital, it seems to me, would, in their own best interests, give that something to the suppliers of capital. In the end, those who furnish desired information to suppliers of capital will see their cost of capital reduced by supplying that information.

In Statements 105, 107, and now 119, the board made good progress on disclosures about financial instruments. Although I wish the board had required more specific, numerical-type disclosure by end users of their derivatives positions, which the SEC will now have to require, the disclosure package is obviously becoming more robust. The 1994 reporting season is now upon us, and I look forward to seeing some rich disclosures about both cash and derivatives positions.

The critical thing now is to nail down the accounting for derivatives. As we all know, the accounting literature that exists is inconsistent, and the existing literature does not deal with many of the accounting issues that issuers and their auditors encounter. We will hear from Jim Leisenring this afternoon where the board stands in the accounting for derivatives. Let me simply say at this point that I think it is critical that the board move forward on the accounting issues as speedily as possible.

All of that said, the analysts – those who use financial reports – seem pretty content with the current state of affairs, with a few exceptions. In 1993, the Association for Investment Management and Research published a report entitled *Financial Reporting in the 1990s and Beyond*. As I read that report in constant flow from cover to cover, I have the impression that the AIMR folks are fairly well pleased with the current state of affairs. They don't want to move to more market value accounting, although they favor disclosures about market values. They would like more disaggregated information and would like it more often, say quarterly. They would like more information about derivatives. They would recognize liabilities for all executory contracts, and they would deduct goodwill from shareholders' equity. Now that really is not a very long wish list.

We will hear tomorrow from Ed Jenkins, who chaired the AICPA's Special Committee on Improving Business Reporting. Jenkins talked with a large number of analysts and other users of financial reports. My impression is that he also found that users of financial reports are pretty well pleased with the current state of financial reporting, but his conclusions differ somewhat from the inferences that I draw from the AIMR report.

Let me deal with one final issue in my remarks here this morning. At this conference last year, I spoke critically about public accountants' independence from their clients and the objectivity of public accountants. The Public Oversight Board, much to its credit, promptly appointed a distinguished panel to look into my criticisms and make recommendations. The panelists were George Anderson, formerly chairman of the AICPA, Don Kirk, formerly chairman of the FASB, and Ralph Saul, formerly chairman of the American Stock Exchange. Don Kirk chaired the panel, which reported its findings and recommendations in September.

The centerpiece of the Kirk Panel report is what is described as a three-part package. I quote from page 23 of the report:

> In summary, the Panel's suggestions for strengthening the relationship between the board of directors and the auditor are a three-part package. All three steps are needed to ensure that the company's financial reports meet the shareholders' need for relevant and reliable information. (1) The board must recognize the primacy of its accountability to shareholders. (2) The auditor must look to the board of directors as the client. (3) The board must expect and the auditor must deliver candid communication about the appropriateness, not just acceptability, of accounting principles and estimates and the clarity of the related disclosures of financial information that the company reports publicly.

I was pleased to hear, when the POB met with the commission about a month ago, that the SEC Practice Section of the AICPA has appointed a task force to consider the Kirk Panel's report and make recommendations. I understand that this task force has met several times and is considering what to do. I am pleased about the promptness of the response to the criticisms that I raised at this conference last year.

That concludes my remarks.

43 Current developments at the SEC

Remarks to the Seventeenth Annual SEC and Financial Reporting Institute Conference, Leventhal School of Accounting, University of Southern California, Los Angeles, 14 May 1998

There is nothing new under the sun on the accounting side at the Division of Enforcement. Over the years, I have heard every chief accountant of the division speak at forums like this one, and I have heard nothing new. There are only so many ways to cook the books. I too am going to sound like a broken record.

Actually, I bring good news. Despite what we occasionally read in the press about accounting lapses, from my perspective as chief accountant of the Enforcement Division, financial accounting and reporting is in good shape. I say this based on the number of open cases that the accounting staff is working on. These are the cases involving accounting issues, financial statement disclosure issues, MD&A disclosure issues, auditing issues, and auditor independence issues. And there are one or two cases that potentially involve bribes paid by public companies to government officials. We have between 200 and 250 open cases involving accounting staff of the home office in Washington and the regional offices. Of the 200–250 cases, 120 are in the home office. Those 120 cases came onto our work program as follows: 1991 – two cases, one of which is on hold because there is an ongoing criminal investigation and one of which is on appeal; 1992 – one case, which is in settlement negotiations; six cases were opened in 1993; twelve cases originated in 1994; twenty-one started in 1995; twenty-four in 1996; forty-one began in 1997; and to date in 1998, thirteen cases have been opened. These years are calendar years, not commission years, which run from October through September. In the home office, we have twenty accountants, so the workload is about six cases per accountant.

When I look at the statistics of about 250 open accounting cases across the entire commission, that compares very favorably with the total number of possible cases. Those 250 cases arose over about a five-year period. Assuming that as many cases were closed as were opened during that period (and I do know the actual number), the 250 becomes 500. During that five-year period, approximately 15,000 registrants filed financial statements with the commission. Thus, over the five years, there were 75,000 opportunities to get the accounting, auditing, and independence right. Then, when I divide 500 cases by 75,000 opportunities, the result is about 0.7 percent. One of the old hands in the Enforcement Division tells me that it seems to him that we bring about 100 accounting cases each year. If I divide 100 cases by 15,000 opportunities, the result is about 0.7 percent. These percentages are very small. To be sure, the percentages, whatever they are, are not Six Sigma, but nonetheless they are very small. What that says to me is that, by and large, the participants in our vast public marketplace are conforming to the rules.

The percentages would be cut about in half were I to include broker/dealers and investment companies in the statistics. In addition to the 15,000–16,000 public company registrants that file financial statements and audit reports with the SEC, there are about 7,000 broker/dealers and about 7,000 investment companies that also file financial statements and audit reports with the SEC. So if I add 7,000 broker/dealers and 7,000 investment companies to the 15,000–16,000 issuer/registrants, the total is about 30,000. Then 100 cases divided by 30,000 opportunities equals 0.3 percent. Over the years, we have had only a limited number of accounting cases involving broker/dealers and mutual funds. I think that it is instructive to observe why that is. I think that there are not many cases involving broker/dealers and investment companies because those companies mark their assets to market.

Let me now turn to the kind of problem that we accountants in the Enforcement Division actually work on. In the six months that I have had to look at the problems, I see that we do not deal much with esoteric accounting problems such as foreign currency translation or the in and outs of pension accounting or post-retirement benefits other than pensions. We deal with more pedestrian issues. For example, on the auditor independence issue, we have one case where the outside auditors of a company wanting to raise money went around to their other clients and promoted the stock of the issuer, passed out the subscriptions for the issuer's stock, and then took the checks that their clients wrote for the shares of the issuer's stock and delivered the checks to the issuer. The SEC has a very clear rule that says that the external auditor may not be a broker for his or her client. So does the AICPA.

Another independence case that we have is the one involving KPMG Peat Marwick, which the commission filed in December 1997. The assertions by the commission are as follows (I am quoting from the Commission's order):

8 As described in detail below, in approximately January 1995, KPMG Peat Marwick organized and capitalized KPMG BayMark, a purportedly independent firm owned by Edward R. Olson and three others. KPMG Peat Marwick planned to use KPMG BayMark as a vehicle to engage in new lines of business, including the "corporate turnaround" business. Later in 1995, as part of a turnaround engagement, KPMG BayMark installed its principal Olson as the President/COO of Porta, a financially troubled audit client of KPMG Peat Marwick's Long Island office.

9 When KPMG Peat Marwick audited Porta's 1995 year-end financial statements and prepared its audit report, KPMG Peat Marwick's financial and business relationship with its audit client Porta and with KPMG BayMark impaired KPMG Peat Marwick's independence from its audit client, in both fact and appearance. In particular, KPMG Peat Marwick lacked independence because: (1) KPMG Peat Marwick loaned $100,000 to the President/

COO of its audit client Porta; (2) KPMG Peat Marwick capitalized the separate business owned by the President/COO of its audit client Porta; (3) KPMG Peat Marwick capitalized the "affiliate" of its audit client Porta; (4) KPMG Peat Marwick was entitled to a percentage of the earnings, disposed inventory and restructured debt of its audit client Porta; and (5) by reason of their contractual ties and interdependence, KPMG Peat Marwick and KPMG BayMark should be considered a single entity for independence purposes.

10 Despite warnings from the Commission's OCA staff concerning independence issues arising from its relationship with KPMG BayMark, KPMG Peat Marwick completed its audit of Port's 1995 year-end financial statements and issued its "Independent Auditors' Report," dated March 22 1996, which represented that it had conducted our audits in accordance with generally accepted auditing standards' ("GAAS"). Porta incorporated KPMG Peat Marwick's report as part of its 1995 annual report on Form 10-K, filed with the Commission on April 2 1996.

KPMG has responded by denying the commission's assertions about its lack of independence. The matter will soon be heard by an administrative law judge.

Let me move on to some of the accounting issues with which we are dealing. The Enforcement Division was formed in the 1970s. As I said earlier, over the years, I have heard every one of the division's chief accountants give speeches wherein they described their cases. Well, nothing has changed. Registrants are still doing the same things.

Premature revenue recognition. Deferral in the balance sheet of costs that should have been reported in income as operating expenses. Assigning inflated, often outrageously inflated, dollar values to exchanges of non-monetary assets, particularly with related parties. Assigning inflated, often outrageously inflated, dollar values to non-monetary assets contributed to the corporation in exchange for stock of the corporation. Not disclosing the existence of related parties and/or transactions with related parties. Recognizing officers' salaries as receivables. Recognizing cash taken from the corporation by officers as cash in the bank or as a direct reduction of stockholders' equity instead of as a charge to expense. Bleeding into income, without disclosure, "reserves" established in business combinations or in so-called restructurings. Treasury stock carried as an asset in the balance sheet at market, with gains on sale of treasury stock credited to income. (I'm not making this up.) Increasing fixed assets and crediting cost of sales. Recognizing sales revenue when right of return exists. Shipping products to company warehouses or employees' homes and recognizing sales revenue. Recognizing revenue in advance of the customer's acceptance of the product. Keeping the sales journal open after the end of the quarter or year but backdating sales invoices. Not booking all of the accounts payable; just put the invoices from suppliers into a desk drawer. Not writing down or writing off uncollectible receivables. Booking barter trade credits as if they represented *bona fide* US dollars. Such is the grist of our accounting mill. Not very esoteric stuff. If I draw an analogy with police work, what we see is stolen automobiles with fingerprints on the door handles, not murders where there are no clues except for dogs that did not bark.

On the audit side, I have now seen several non-audits. Auditors accepting, with little or no evidential support, values ascribed to both monetary and non-monetary assets. Artwork by unknown artists booked as assets at huge amounts in non-monetary exchanges but without any support for the assigned value and no inquiry by the auditor about independent valuation of the artwork. Receivables acquired from collection agencies for pennies but booked at dollars without any documentation and no auditor inquiry as to the basis for the value. Auditors not doing substantive audit work but relying on so-called analytical procedures where the evidence, or lack thereof, cries out for substantive audit work. Auditors not doing cut-off work for sales and purchases, with the result that sales of the next period are booked in this period with a corresponding increase in receivables from customers, and accounts payable for purchases of inventory of this period not booked until next period with the inventory recognized in the balance sheet, resulting in understated costs of sales and overstated margins. And we see cases where the auditors were lied to or were not given all of the documentation that they should have been given. But sometimes I wonder whether the auditors asked the right questions.

Let me return to my major theme. Although the issues that we deal with in the Enforcement Division are messy and quite distasteful, they are a very small fraction of the universe. Maybe that is because marketplace participants know that the Enforcement Division is paying attention to what goes on and that the penalty for infractions is or can be quite severe. I am fairly well satisfied that the number of transgressions that we see is quite small given the size of the population from which they arise. The state of financial accounting and reporting is good, and we need to keep it that way through constant vigilance.

The SEC's enforcement program regarding practicing accountants is accomplished primarily but not completely by bringing cases against accountants under rule 102(e) of the SEC's Rules of Practice. Rule 102(e) reads as follows:

> The Commission may censure a person or deny, temporarily or permanently, the privilege of appearing or practicing before it in any way to any person who is found by the Commission after notice and opportunity for hearing in the matter:
>
> (i) Not to possess the requisite qualifications to represent others; or
>
> (ii) To be lacking in character or integrity or to have engaged in unethical or improper professional conduct; or
>
> (iii) To have wilfully violated, or wilfully aided and abetted the violation of any provision of the federal securities laws or the rules and regulations thereunder.

The Washington Court of Appeals, on 27 March 1998, remanded a case, the Checkosky and Aldrich case, to the commission and instructed the commission to dismiss the case. Briefly, the facts in the Checkosky case are as follows. Savin Corporation, a Coopers and Lybrand client, in its 1981, 1982, 1983, and 1984 financial statements, deferred in its balance sheet "start-up" costs related to Savin's effort to develop and bring to market a copying machine. In 1985, pursuant to an SEC enforcement action, Savin restated its 1983 and 1984 financial statements, writing off the deferred start-up costs as R&D costs. The commission then brought an administrative action against the Coopers' audit partner and manager, asserting that they had engaged in unprofessional conduct by allowing Savin to capitalize start-up costs that should have been charged to expense as R&D costs.

In 1989, after a lengthy hearing, an administrative law judge found that Checkosky and Aldrich had engaged in improper professional conduct by violating generally accepted accounting practices and standards in five audits over four years (1981–4) by allowing Savin to improperly defer $37 million of research and development costs as start-up costs, and by failing to adequately audit the deferred costs. The judge suspended the two auditors from practice before the commission for five years. Checkosky and Aldrich appealed against the judge's decision to the commission. In 1992, the commission upheld the judge's findings, determined that Checkosky and Aldrich had acted recklessly, and stated that "a mental awareness greater than negligence is not required for improper professional conduct" but reduced the sanction to a two-year suspension. Two years later, in 1994, the DC Circuit Court of Appeals remanded the Checkosky and Aldrich case back to the commission with instructions to address its interpretation and application of rule 2(e)(1)(ii). Over two years later, in January 1997, the commission issued an opinion and order that affirmed its first opinion and order, based on Checkosky's and Aldrich's reckless conduct, but added some language to which Commissioner Johnson in January 1997 and the Court of Appeals on 27 March 1998, took exception. The commission's majority opinion stated: "We believe that Rule 2(e)(1)(ii) does not mandate a particular mental state and that negligent action by a professional may under certain circumstances constitute improper professional conduct." The Court of Appeals, in its decision pursuant to the second appeal, said that "elementary administrative law norms of fair notice and reasoned decision making demand that the Commission define those circumstances with some degree of specificity. It has not done so." The court went on to state "there are strong signs that the Commission is unlikely to settle on a uniform theory as to the necessary mental state for a violation of Rule 2(e)(1)(ii) anytime soon," pointing to Commissioner Johnson's dissent in Checkosky, his separate concurrence in Potts, and to Commissioner Wallman's dissent in Potts. (Potts is another 2(e) case that is on appeal.) The court concluded: "it would be futile to allow the SEC a third shot at the target." The case was remanded with instructions to dismiss the charges against Checkosky and Aldrich.

Since Checkosky was handed down on March 27, the staff has been considering a number of recommendations to the commission on how to respond to Checkosky. One way, but it is only one way, would be for the commission to issue for review and comment by the public a revised rule 102(e) wherein the commission would set forth the standard that it will use in applying rule 102(e) against professionals. Just last week, the American Institute of Certified Public Accountants petitioned the commission to issue such a rule for review and comment. The AICPA's petition was accompanied by its proposed rule, which reads as follows:

> "Improper professional conduct" as used herein shall mean conduct showing that the professional is

1 substantially unfit to practice before the Commission by reason of:

   a the commission of a knowing violation of applicable professional standards, or

   b conduct showing a conscious and deliberate disregard of applicable professional standards, or

   c a course or pattern of conduct showing repeated failure to conform to applicable professional standards; and

2 constitutes a current threat to the integrity of the Commission's processes or to the financial reporting system; in each case found after due notice of the conduct charged and a fair hearing thereon.

These criteria suggested by the AICPA would be very high hurdles indeed.

I obviously do not know how the commission is going to come down on this matter or the form that a commission decision will take. All I can suggest is that you stay tuned to this frequency.

The final matter that I want to raise today relates to fraternization between auditors and their clients. It appears to me that some auditors and their families through social contacts are getting so close to and so involved with their clients and their clients' families that a disinterested observer would question whether the auditor's objectivity had not been clouded or perhaps even enveloped. Let me give you two examples. In *Business Week* (23 February 1998), there is an article that talks about auditors and their families having social contacts with their clients and their clients' families through such joint activities as picnics and baseball games. The Enforcement Division recently came across an audit planning memorandum of a Big Six firm wherein social events between the auditor and client are explicitly set forth. I quote from that memorandum (I have not used the names of sports teams actually used in the memorandum. I have substituted other names.)

- Summer and Other Social Events
- The University of Texas football games (Oklahoma, Texas A&M, and Arkansas)
- NCAA Basketball final four tickets
- San Antonio Spurs tickets
- Houston Astros tickets
- Shopping

I wonder what "shopping" means. Alpaca sweaters? Golf clubs? Bally leather jackets?

I wonder how investors or potential investors would react if they were aware of these facts. Would investors believe that the auditor's objectivity is not affected when the auditor and his or her family are engaged in periodic baseball games and picnics with the client and the client's family? Would investors believe that the auditor's objectivity is not affected if the auditor and client personnel regularly attend sporting events together? Whether paid for by the auditor or paid for by the client? Would investors perceive that gift giving, whether from auditor to client or client to auditor, can go on for very long without compromising the auditor's objectivity? How would an underwriter who is about to take $100 million of stock of that company react to these facts? A mutual investment manager who is about to invest $100 million in the stock of that company? Should auditors have to follow the same rules with respect to their public company audit clients that I as an employee of the US federal government have to follow with respect to regulated entities or persons? I leave you to ponder those questions.

Postscript

Readers should refer to the postscript on page 230.

44 A memo to national and international accounting and auditing standard setters and securities regulators (a Christmas pony)

The 2001 R.J. Chambers Memorial Research Lecture, delivered in the Great Hall, University of Sydney, Australia, 27 November 2001

Chancellor, Vice-Chancellor, distinguished guests. Thank you, Chancellor, for those kind introductory words, and thank you Dean Wolnizer for the invitation to present the R.J. Chambers Research Lecture. It is indeed a pleasure for me to be here in Sydney delivering this lecture. I have long admired Professor Chambers' work. I wish I had met him.

I graduated from the University of Texas in Austin in the summer of 1957. I went to work on 1 August 1957 for an accounting firm in San Antonio, Texas, by the name of Eaton & Huddle. Tom Holton, one of the partners of Eaton & Huddle, hired me. After Eaton & Huddle merged with Peat, Marwick, Mitchell & Co., now KPMG, Tom Holton eventually became chairman of KPMG. Holton will attest that I have been talking about, making speeches about, and generally advocating and promoting market-value accounting since the late 1950s. By "market-value accounting," I mean estimated selling price for assets and estimated settlement price for liabilities. Without knowing it, I was sounding like Chambers in the 1950s, although not so eloquent.

I had not read Chambers until I joined the Financial Accounting Standards Board. I was at the FASB from March 1973 through June 1976. While I was there, I read Chambers' book *Accounting, Evaluation and Economic Behavior* and discovered that he and I shared the same view about accounting for assets. Unfortunately, there was no way to get market-value accounting adopted by the FASB in its early days. The climate was just not right. In fact, in 1975, when the FASB issued Statement 12 on *Accounting for Certain Marketable Securities*, the FASB could muster only three out of seven votes for mark-to-market accounting of marketable equity securities.[1] Similarly, in 1985, in FASB Statement 87 on *Employers' Accounting for Pensions*, the mark-to-market accounting for off-balance-sheet pension plan assets, mostly stocks and bonds, is smoothed out so as not to affect employers' pension plan expense too much in any particular year.

The climate for introducing market-value accounting into financial statements did not change until 1990, in the aftermath of the savings and loan crisis and the consequent US government bail-out of insolvent savings and loan associations. On 10 September 1990, the US Securities and Exchange Commission, in testimony by its chairman before the US Senate's Committee on Banking, Housing, and Urban Affairs, described how faulty accounting and the consequent improper measurement of regulatory capital contributed to lax regulatory oversight of the S&Ls, which ultimately led to the bail-out. The commission in that testimony took the position that banks and thrifts should mark to market their bond portfolios. At that time, Richard Breeden was chairman of the SEC. Chairman Breeden is a lawyer, not an accountant. But he strongly believed that thrifts and banks were presenting false pictures of their financial positions and results of operations, and importantly the amounts of their regulatory capital, through the use of historical cost accounting for their bond portfolios and through selective timing of sales of bonds so as to trigger gains but not losses, a practice called "gains trading."

When I was interviewed by Chairman Breeden for the position of chief accountant in December 1991, it turned out that his and my thoughts on market-value accounting were in sync, At least as far as bond portfolios were concerned. Chairman Breeden did not want to go further than the bond portfolio. I wanted to mark all assets to market, but in the early 1990s, I was glad to start with the bond portfolios of thrifts and banks. So, in January 1992, I started as chief accountant to the SEC. As it turns out, I was the commission's foot soldier getting thrifts and banks to mark to market their bond portfolios. Of course, there was no stopping with depository institutions. Insurance companies and other "float" companies also had bond portfolios, and they also had to mark to market their bonds. I was chief accountant from January 1992 to April 1995. I spent a considerable portion of 1992 and 1993 promoting the commission's view that banks, thrifts, and insurance companies should mark to market their bond portfolios.

In May 1993, the FASB, in Statement 115, required that all marketable equity securities be marked to market. Statement 115 went part of the way on bonds, requiring that trading and held-for-sale bond portfolios be marked to market, but it allows a held-to-maturity bond portfolio to be reported at cost. (Determining which bond is in which portfolio is a metaphysical, serendipitous determination that has always eluded my understanding.) Since 1993, the accounting for bonds, mortgages, mortgage-backed securities, derivative instruments, and hedging has become more incredibly complex than I can or want to describe, but gains trading out of the held-to-maturity portfolio is still possible. However, the FASB is moving forward to require mark-to-market accounting of all financial assets and liabilities.

Few people know that to the extent that we have mark-to-market accounting today, the credit for that belongs to the Securities and Exchange Commission, and primarily to Chairman Breeden. Incidentally, none of those commissioners in 1990 was an accountant. (To my knowledge, only one accountant, James Needham, has served as a commissioner since the commission was established in 1934. Most, but not all, of the commissioners have been lawyers. An exception is Arthur Levitt, the immediate past chairman, who is not an attorney. Chairman Levitt, prior to his appointment to the SEC, was head of the American Stock Exchange.)

When the SEC endorsed marking to market of bonds in 1990, the banking, thrift, and insurance companies community had to be dragged, kicking and screaming, into the world of relevant, mark-to-market accounting. In a sense, the FASB was also dragged along by the SEC, because none of the FASB's constituencies was in favor of mark-to-market accounting, and the FASB itself was not out in front leading the charge for mark-to-market accounting. But come around it did, and now the FASB is moving forward on mark-to-market accounting for all financial assets and liabilities.

I think that it is now time for the SEC, the FASB, and the reconstituted International Accounting Standards Board to extend mark-to-market accounting to the rest of the balance sheet – to all assets and liabilities. Why do I say that? Well, to begin with, there is no question that mark-to-market accounting produces relevant information that investors and creditors can use to make investment decisions. Not only is the information relevant, its quality is undisputed. The two ideas – relevance of information and quality – go hand in glove. There is no relevance to a datum called cost or cost minus amortization – it is just a number, a number having no information content. The "quality" of the datum called cost or cost minus amortization for assets such as inventory, factories, mines, oil and gas reserves, salmon farms, machinery and equipment, copyrights, and patents is indisputably awful; worse, it can be and often is misleading. We have seen many situations in the USA, and I'm sure you have seen them in Australia as well, where corporations have been reporting earnings and an excess of assets over liabilities using our current generally accepted accounting principles just before going bust. We now have the case where after the tragic events of September 11th some US airlines are teetering on the brink of bankruptcy and the market prices of their aircraft have fallen into the cellar. Yet the historical cost of those aircraft continues on the airlines' balance sheets because, under the FASB's rule in Statement 121 and now Statement 144 of looking to the undiscounted future cash flows from the aircraft, the carrying amount of the aircraft is not impaired. What an awful rule. Historical cost of assets and representations as assets of FASB-approved junk such as goodwill, deferred income taxes and tax benefits of operating loss carryforwards, and capitalized direct-response advertising costs have misled investors for years. I will have more on quality later.

The second reason to adopt mark-to-market accounting for all assets and liabilities is to go back to basics – to go back to first principles – and to simplify the accounting. First, we need a definition of assets that we can all understand. The FASB's definition of assets in paragraph 25 of its Concepts Statement 6 is as follows: "Assets are probable future economic benefits obtained or controlled by a particular entity as a result of past transactions or events." That is followed by six paragraphs of about 600 words explaining the definition. There are 330,000 members of the American Institute of Certified Public Accountants. It is my experience that a very large majority of those CPAs do not understand the FASB's definition of an asset. I have seen litigation involving alleged fraudulent financial statements because of improper asset and income recognition where both parties to the litigation and both of their expert witnesses, in their briefs and at trial, quoted the very same words from the FASB's Concepts Statements saying that a debit balance on the balance sheet was, or was not, a fit and proper asset under the FASB's definition. The judge has not yet decided the case, even though three years have gone by.

Not only do most practicing accountants not understand the FASB's language about assets; ordinary folk are also mystified by that babble. The financial statements that are produced as a result of all of the FASB's rules, which is now a veritable mountain of rules, are impenetrable. Go to the Internet and look at the financial statements and related notes to the financial statements of US companies in their annual reports. There are pages and pages of jargon, understandable to a few highly indoctrinated accountants but not to most investors and other ordinary folk. This is not just my opinion. The new chairman of the SEC, Mr Harvey Pitt, is quoted on page 92 in the 5 November 2001 issue of *Business Week* as saying that quarterly and annual reports are "not always capable of being deciphered by sophisticated experts, much less ordinary investors."

Using the FASB's definition of an asset, a thing that most of us call a truck is not that which is the asset. The asset is the economic benefit, whatever that is, that will arise from using the truck to haul lumber or coal or bread. Using the FASB's definition, the truck is an abstraction. I think that we should define assets by reference to real things, not abstractions. I think that we should define assets as follows: cash; claims to cash, for example accounts and notes receivable; and things that can be sold for cash, for example a truck. I'll bet that this audience understands my definition of an asset.

The FASB's definition of a liability in paragraph 35 of Concepts Statement 6 is as murky as its definition of an asset, to wit: "Liabilities are probable future sacrifices of economic benefits arising from present obligations of a particular entity to transfer assets or provide services to other entities in the future as a result of past transactions or events." That paragraph is followed by five paragraphs of more than 700 words that explain the definition. Included in those five paragraphs is a sentence that says liabilities include, in addition to legal obligations, "equitable or constructive obligations," but it does not define what those are. Most accountants do not understand, at the margin, what the FASB's definition of a liability means, leading to great diversity in practice. In practice, if the management of a corporation says that it has a liability under a so-called restructuring plan, a liability may be, but need not be, booked. In practice, year-end bonuses to employees are sometimes, but not always, booked as liabilities as the year progresses, even though there is no contractual obligation to pay the bonuses. We are seeing in 2001 that many US corporations are not going to pay bonuses or are going to pay reduced amounts of bonuses. (See the *Wall Street Journal*, 2 October 2001, p. B1; I doubt that there is much disclosure in financial statements about those liability reversals.) In corporate acquisitions, liabilities are booked if the acquiring corporation declares that it will pay out cash for this or that even though there is no contractual requirement to pay cash; no liability is booked if the corporation makes no declaration. Consequently, liability recognition, and the amount thereof, is subject to great management discretion and abuse.

I think that liabilities should be defined as follows: cash outflows required by negotiable instruments, by contracts, by law or regulation, and by court-entered judgments and agreements with claimants. I'll bet that this audience understands my definition of liabilities. Nothing murky about it.

The third reason to adopt mark-to-market accounting for all balance sheet items is to stop – to stop dead in its tracks – earnings management. Earnings management is a scourge in the USA. The disease called earnings management is endemic. I am not being shrill or alarmist when I say that I think that it threatens the very soul of financial reporting. What we get under our present reporting system is earnings as determined by management, not as determined by transactions and economic events and conditions that actually happened and exist. Many people, indeed many accountants, are fond of saying that financial statements should portray economic reality. But, in fact, except for the financial statements of investment companies (mutual funds) and broker/dealers, where all assets are marked to market every evening at the close of business, today's financial statements come nowhere close to achieving that goal because, except for stocks, and bonds in some cases, non-cash assets are not marked to market.

In the spring of 1998, a national business magazine in the USA – *Forbes* – had the following banner on its cover: "Pick a Number, Any Number." That was followed by articles in the national press, such as *USA Today*, about "Abracadabra accounting," "Hocus-pocus accounting," and the like. The gist of these articles was that the accounting numbers were being managed or manipulated by corporations and certified as being OK by their external auditors. This national outrage moved Chairman Levitt of the SEC into action. On 28 September 1998, Chairman Levitt gave a speech entitled "The numbers game" (this speech is available at www.sec.gov). In that speech, he gave examples of ways in which corporations are managing their earnings – big bath restructuring charges, creative acquisition accounting, cookie jar reserves, improper revenue recognition, and abuse of materiality. (I would point out that under our current accounting rules there are dozens of ways to manage earnings. Chairman Levitt gave only a few examples.) Chairman Levitt made numerous suggestions for improvement. The upshot of that speech was (1) the SEC's staff produced staff accounting bulletins on restructuring charges, revenue recognition, materiality, and banks' loan loss allowances; (2) the New York Stock Exchange and the NASDAQ charged a blue-ribbon panel chaired by two prominent business leaders, Ira Millstein and John Whitehead, with making recommendations about corporate audit committees; and (3) the Public Oversight Board of the American Institute of Certified Public Accountants charged the Panel on Audit Effectiveness chaired by Shaun O'Malley, formerly CEO of PricewaterhouseCoopers, with making recommendations about improving the effectiveness of external audits.

The Millstein–Whitehead Blue Ribbon Committee issued its report on 8 February 1999 (the report is available at www.nyse.com). Among the committee's recommendations are that (1) there be a discussion between the audit committee and the external auditor about the quality of the company's accounting and (2) that the audit committee represent in the company's annual report that, based on discussion with management and the external auditor, the company's financial statements are fairly presented in conformity with generally accepted accounting principles. The second recommendation attracted massive negative comment from the corporate and legal communities. Commentators stated that audit committee members are not accountants and do not have the expertise to determine whether the company's financial statements conform to generally accepted accounting principles. When the SEC adopted its revised rules on audit committees on 22 December 1999 (see SEC Release No. 34.42266 at www.sec.gov), the commission did not adopt that recommendation. Instead, the SEC merely required that the audit committee state, in the annual report, that, after discussion with the external auditor, the audit committee "recommended to the Board of Directors that the audited financial statements be included in the Annual Report," thereby implicitly acknowledging that members of audit committees don't know whether the financial statements comply with generally accepted accounting principles.

The recommendation that the audit committee discuss with the external auditor the quality of the company's accounting has been acted on by the auditing profession in the USA. In December 1999, the AICPA's Auditing Standards Board issued Statement on Auditing Standards No. 90, *Audit Committee Communications*, which requires, as to public companies, that the auditor "discuss with the audit committee the auditor's judgments about the quality, not just the acceptability, of the company's accounting principles as applied in its financial reporting." I would like to be a fly on the wall when such discussions take place in the corporate boardroom. I can just imagine the auditor saying to his/her client, "My firm has audited your financial statements. My firm is prepared to report without qualification that your financial statements have been prepared in conformity with generally accepted accounting principles, but my grade on the quality of your financial statements is C−." In my opinion, this requirement by the Auditing Standards Board is worse than a joke. It is farcical. The large auditing firms have hundreds, some thousands, of partners in the USA and still more worldwide. There are no objective standards by which the individual partner in San Francisco, Sydney, Seoul, Singapore, or Southampton can make a judgment about the quality of a client's accounting. Following the Auditing Standards Board's rule, opinions about the quality of clients' accounting would be based on the idiosyncratic judgments of hundreds or thousands of individual partners. The practical upshot will be that every client's grade on quality will be an A. There are two reasons for that. First, given the highly competitive nature of the public accounting business, few if any audit partners are going to jeopardize a client relationship by telling the client that its accounting is not of high quality. The second reason is that the accounting rules under which financial statements are prepared allow the management to use its judgment in preparing those financial statements, and the auditor has no basis on which to make a different judgment except personal preference.[2]

The O'Malley Panel issued its 255-page report on 31 August 2000 (that report may be viewed at www.pobauditpanel.org). The panel's major recommendations are as follows:

- Auditors should perform some "forensic-type" procedures on every audit to enhance the prospects of detecting material financial statement fraud.
- The Auditing Standards Board should make auditing and quality control standards more specific and definitive.
- Audit firms should put more emphasis on the performance of high-quality audits in communications from top management, performance evaluations, training, and compensation and promotion decisions.
- The Public Oversight Board (POB) of the AICPA, the AICPA, the SEC Practice Section (SECPS) of the AICPA, and the SEC should agree on a unified system of governance for the auditing profession under a strengthened Public Oversight Board that would oversee standard setting (for auditing, independence, and quality control), monitoring, discipline, and special reviews.
- The SECPS should strengthen the peer review process, including requiring annual reviews for the largest firms, and the POB should increase its oversight of those reviews.
- The SECPS should strengthen its disciplinary process.
- Audit committees should pre-approve non-audit services that exceed a threshold amount.
- The International Federation of Accountants should establish an international self-regulatory system for the international auditing profession.

As I understand it, the Auditing Standards Board and other AICPA entities are working on the panel's recommendations. And I have no doubt that the SEC's staff is watching over their shoulders to make sure that all of the details are implemented to the SEC staff's satisfaction. Maybe the number of financial statement frauds that the SEC periodically has to investigate and address through enforcement actions will be reduced if more "forensic-type" audit work is done by external auditors as recommended by the panel. But the earnings management game won't stop even if every one of the panel's recommendations is implemented immediately. And the dismaying, surprise corporate collapses – such as HIH Insurance here in Australia – that happen about once a month won't stop even if every one of the panel's recommendations is implemented immediately.

There have been similar panels, committees, and even Royal Commissions in the past, all with more or less similar recommendations. We now have O'Malley. We had the Kirk Panel in the 1990s. We had Treadway about fifteen years ago. We had the Cohen Commission in the late 1970s. We had Metcalf.

Canada had MacDonald. Great Britain had Cadbury. Australia has had similar committees, I'm sure. In the 1970s, we in the USA introduced peer reviews of audit firms. Concurring audit partner reviews are also now a requirement in the USA. We have the AICPA's Quality Control Inquiry Committee looking into external auditor performance when financial statements are restated. We have the AICPA's Public Oversight Board breathing hard, looking over everyone's shoulder. All for nought. What we have is layers on top of layers on top of layers of regulation. After O'Malley, we no doubt will have another layer of regulation.

We had the AICPA's Committee on Accounting Procedure writing the accounting rules from 1939 to 1959. That didn't work, and that committee was replaced by the AICPA's Accounting Principles Board, which wrote the accounting rules until 1973. In 1973, the Accounting Principles Board was replaced, with great hope and fanfare, by the Financial Accounting Standards Board.[3] Things were supposed to get better. But nothing has changed. Earnings management continues to flower.

Corporations today continue to manipulate their earnings without objection from their external auditors. SEC Commissioner Hunt, in a speech on 26 October 2001, discussed earnings management (see www.sec.gov). *Business Week*, on page 71 of its 23 July 2001 issue, reported that "In today's financial climate, auditors' reports have about as much credibility as buy recommendations from Wall Street analysts." The June 2001 issue of the *Harvard Business Review* has a twelve-page article entitled "The Earnings Game: Everyone Plays, Nobody Wins." On 19 October 2001, on a Friday night TV program called *Wall Street Week*, I heard and saw a prominent Wall Street investment manager say something along the following lines: "Corporations are writing off assets right and left in the quarter ended September 30 2001. Comparative earnings statements in 2002 will be wonderful." His implication was that the write-downs are arbitrary. The Levy Institute Forecasting Center, in a special research report dated September 2001, describes in twenty-three pages of detail "two decades of overstated corporate earnings," which its chairman, David Levy, previewed on TV on CNBC on 24 October 2001. *Business Week*, on pages 46 and 47 of its 15 October 2001 issue, reported:

> Brace yourself for what may be the ugliest quarter ever for corporate earnings. For years, companies used every trick in the book to make their results look better than they really were. Now, many will be taking the opposite tack: loading costs and charges onto their income statements in an all-out effort to make an already horrid year look even worse. To make next year's results look stronger companies may load losses into 2001 by slashing values of physical assets, which will cut depreciation charges in the future; overestimating likely bad debts, thus boosting future profits when customers pay up; and charging impending restructuring costs immediately, so as to benefit if they're less than expected.

It's not just in *Business Week* and the *Harvard Business Review.* I see it in *Forbes.* I see it in *Barron's.* I read the earnings reports of corporations on their websites and in the *Wall Street Journal*, and I see the earnings management. It is going on in bright daylight and not behind closed doors. Everyone on Wall Street knows it is going on. The stock exchanges know it is going on. The SEC knows it is going on. Every sell-side security analyst knows it is going on. Every institutional investor knows it is going on. But the individual investor who is not part of the Wall Street in-the-know crowd doesn't know it is going on. John and Jane Q. Public don't know it is going on. Maybe members of Congress don't know it is going on. The external auditors can't stop it. Even if the external auditors were US federal government auditors, whose independence would be unquestionably pure, they could not stop it, because the accounting rules allow for earnings management. External auditors have no ground on which to stand to stop it because of the way the accounting rules are constructed. The stock exchanges can't stop it. Because the accounting rules allow for earnings management, the SEC can't stop it through its Division of Corporation Finance, which reviews and clears registration statements and other filings by issuers of securities. The SEC's Office of the Chief Accountant and Division of Enforcement can't stop it, because the accounting rules allow it. I could not stop it when I was chief accountant at the SEC.

I have been in this business since 1 August 1957. I think that I have seen every side and dimension of this problem. In my opinion, the only way that earnings management will be stopped is as follows: the SEC, or the SEC and the FASB, or the SEC and the FASB and the IASB, must change the accounting rules. The SEC must make deep and fundamental changes to the system. Unless and until the SEC requires that assets be reported at estimated selling prices, which of course means that only things that have a market price could be represented as assets, nothing will change. Unless and until the SEC requires that liabilities be reported at estimated settlement prices, nothing will change. Unless and until the SEC requires that reported asset and liability amounts be based on estimated selling and settlement prices and that external auditors get evidence about those selling and settlement prices from persons or entities outside the reporting enterprise, nothing will change.

So long as management controls the numbers, nothing will change. For example, so long as management decides on the amount of inventory obsolescence, the amount of bad debts, or the amount of the warranty liability, nothing will change. So long as management decides on the assumed rate of return on pension plan assets, nothing will change. So long as management decides on the estimated useful lives and salvage values of capital assets without regard to the selling prices of those assets as determined by the marketplace, nothing will change. So long as management decides on what will be future undiscounted cash flows from capital assets, and can change those numbers at will in determining whether the carrying amounts of capital assets are impaired, nothing will change. So long as management is allowed to recognize liabilities for restructuring the business whenever it wants to, and in an amount determined solely by management, nothing will change.

The reported numbers for assets and liabilities must be such that they can be verified by external auditors (and by regulators and courts) by reference to sources outside the enterprise. By reference to competent evidence.[4] The SEC must make deep and fundamental change to the system. Only by requiring that assets and liabilities have a reference point in the marketplace and that the amounts representing those assets and liabilities be verifiable by reference to sources, competent sources,[5] outside the enterprise will we be able to produce financial statements that include reliable numbers. As a practical matter, neither the FASB nor the IASB can accomplish such deep and fundamental change on its own. Or even together. Only the SEC can accomplish such change. And only if such change is made will the financial statements be of high quality.

This idea that financial statements be of high quality, or that accounting standards be of high quality, has attracted a lot of attention recently. The term "high quality" is on everyone's lips. It is high-sounding. The IASB's website says that the IASB "is committed to developing, in the public interest, a single set of high-quality, understandable, and enforceable accounting standards that require transparent and comparable information in general purpose financial statements." The US House of Representatives' Subcommittee on Capital Markets, Insurance, and Government Sponsored Enterprises, on 7 June 2001, held a hearing on "Promotion of International Capital Flows through Accounting Standards." Representatives Baker, Oxley, LaFalce, Kanjorski, and Mascara made "opening statements." Paul Volcker, chairman of the trustees of the IASB, Philip Ameen, VP and comptroller of General Electric, representing Financial Executives International, and Robert Elliott, a KPMG partner representing the AICPA, testified before the subcommittee about international accounting standards. By my count, the US representatives, Mr Volcker, Mr Ameen, and Mr Elliott, in their prepared remarks, used the term "high quality" no fewer than twenty-three times. Sometimes high-quality standards, sometimes high-quality financial statements, and sometimes high-quality information. Mr Lynn Turner, the SEC's chief accountant from mid-1988 to mid-2001, used the term frequently in his speeches when describing financial statements prepared under FASB standards and when he described what he hopes will result under IASB standards. But I can't tell what it is that these people are describing. These people are obviously not describing what Chairman Levitt described in his September 1998 speech, what Commissioner Hunt described in his speech on 26 October 2001, and what Chairman Pitt meant when he said that quarterly and annual reports are indecipherable by ordinary investors. These people are obviously not describing what I see in the *Harvard Business Review*, *Business Week*, *Forbes*, and *Barron's* about earnings management. To me, these people sound like my seven-year-old granddaughter, who is wishing that Santa Claus will bring her a pony on Christmas morning.

What is it that we want for investors when we say "high-quality financial statements" or "high-quality information?" I'll tell you what I want. I want financial statement amounts (numbers) that are relevant and reliable. Historical costs of assets and historical proceeds of liabilities are not relevant to an investor for the purpose of making an investment decision – or to any business person wanting to make a decision about an asset or a liability. Only current selling prices for assets and current settlement prices for liabilities are relevant. The only reliable measures of these prices are those that come from the marketplace, from persons or entities unrelated to the reporting enterprise. Selling prices of assets and settlement prices of liabilities can be verified by external auditors by reference to marketplace sources. If the SEC requires that assets and liabilities be measured, and be verified by external auditors, by reference to selling and settlement prices that exist in the marketplace, and requires disclosure of the names of persons or entities that furnished those prices, the resulting financial statements will be of high quality. And that standard, unlike what we have today, will be enforceable by external auditors, regulators, and ultimately the courts.

There is a new chairman, Harvey Pitt, and a new chief accountant, Robert Herdman, at the SEC. Mr Pitt made a speech on 22 October 2001 (see www.sec.gov) before the governing council of the AICPA in which he spoke of "simplifying financial disclosures to make accounting statements useful to, and utilizable by, ordinary investors" and that "we [the SEC] may need to reconsider whether our accounting principles provide a realistic picture of corporate performance." The SEC's press release on 19 September 2001 (see www.sec.gov) announcing Mr Herdman's appointment as chief accountant says, "Mr. Herdman will lead us [the SEC] in revising and modernizing our accounting and financial disclosure system." Those words are promising. Maybe Mr Pitt and Mr Herdman will surprise investors with the equivalent of a pony on Christmas morning – that is, high-quality financial statements.

Postscript: 9 December 2001

After I presented this lecture, I received in the mail a brochure advertising a two-day course entitled "How to Manage Earnings in Conformance with GAAP." "This Intensive Two-day, Skill-based Workshop Features over 50 Illustrations, Applications and Case Studies to Make GAAP Work for Your Company or Client." "Earn 16 Hours of A&A CPE Credit and CLE Credit." This course is sponsored by the National Center for Continuing Education, 967 Briarcliff Drive, Tallahassee, FL 32308, and it costs $995. I rest my case about earnings management being a disease.

Notes

1 FASB Statement 12, issued in 1975 and now superseded by Statement 115, required lower of cost or market accounting for the portfolio of marketable equity securities held, which is awful accounting. In Statement 12, I wanted to require mark-to-market accounting for every security in the portfolio, as did two other board members, Messrs Litke and Sprouse, who dissented to the issuance of Statement 12. But because we needed five votes to issue a standard, and because our constituents were telling us that practice was so diverse that a standard, some standard, was necessary, I bit my tongue and signed the document without dissenting.

2 For an excellent discussion and analysis of why the presence of audit committees cannot and will not improve the quality and reliability of today's financial statements, see "Are audit committees red herrings?" by P.W. Wolnizer, *Abacus*, Vol. 31, No. 1, March 1995, pp. 45–66.

3 I know. I was a charter member of the FASB. My wife and I were present at the FASB's inauguration dinner in the spring of 1973. Reginald Jones, chairman of General Electric, delivered the inaugural address. He held out great hope for the FASB.

4 This style of auditing – obtaining competent evidence – is exactly what P.W. Wolnizer describes and recommends in his book *Auditing as Independent Authentication*, Sydney University Press, 1987.

5 The SEC should require (1) disclosure, either by the reporting enterprise or the external auditor, of the names of the persons or entities that furnished the selling and settlement prices and (2) the consent of those persons or entities to the use and disclosure of their names.

45 Hearing

"Accounting and Investor Protection Issues Raised by Enron and Other Public Companies: Oversight of the Accounting Profession, Audit Quality and Independence, and Formulation of Accounting Principles"

Prepared statement by Mr Walter P. Schuetze, chief accountant, Securities and Exchange Commission 1992–5, before the US Senate Committee on Banking, Housing, and Urban Affairs, 26 February 2002

Thank you, Mr Chairman. Senator Gramm. Members of the Committee. My name is Walter P. Schuetze. My brief resumé is attached hereto.

Just a few comments about my experience and background. I was on the staff and a partner with the public accounting firm KPMG and its predecessor firms for more than thirty years. I was one of the charter members of the Financial Accounting Standards Board from April 1973 through June 1976. I was a member and chair of the Accounting Standards Executive Committee of the American Institute of Certified Public Accountants in the 1980s. I was chief accountant to the Securities and Exchange Commission from January 1992 through March 1995 and chief accountant of the SEC's Division of Enforcement from November 1997 through mid-February 2000.

I need to mention that although I am retired, I am a consultant to the Securities and Exchange Commission and several other entities under consulting contracts. In addition, I have one remaining tie with my former firm KPMG in that I am insured under a group life insurance contract obtained and administered by that firm; I pay the premium attributable to me. The views I express here today are my personal views.

I appreciate very much the opportunity to testify here today. Your letter of 16 January 2002 inviting me to testify at this hearing says:

> A number of high-profile business failures in recent years, including, most recently, the collapse of Enron Corp., have involved significant accounting irregularities, and the February 26 hearing will examine the issues raised by those failures for financial reporting by public companies, accounting stan-

> dards, and oversight of the accounting profession. You should feel free to address those issues as you see fit. The committee would also appreciate any recommendations you may have about ways to deal with the issues you discuss.

I indeed have a major recommendation, which I will get to at the conclusion of my remarks.

The public's confidence in financial reports of and by corporate America, and in the audits of those financial reports by the public accounting profession, has been shaken badly by the recent surprise collapse of Enron, by recent restatements of financial statements by the likes of Enron, Waste Management, Sunbeam, Cendant, Livent, and MicroStrategy, and by the SEC's assertion of fraud by Arthur Andersen in connection with its audits of Waste Management's financial statements in the 1990s, which Andersen did not admit or deny in a settled SEC action last summer. The public's confidence needs to be regained and restored. If that confidence is not regained and restored, the result will be that investors will bid down the price of stocks and bonds issued by both US and foreign corporations; we have seen evidence of that phenomenon in recent weeks. That is an investor's natural response to increased risk or the perception of increased risk. This will reduce the market capitalization of corporations, which in turn will negatively affect capital formation, job creation and job maintenance, and ultimately our standard of living. So, we are concerned today with a very important matter.

You will hear or have heard many suggestions for improvement to our system of financial reporting and audits of those financial reports. Some will say that auditor independence rules need to be strengthened. That external auditors should not be allowed to do consulting work and other non-audit work for their audit clients. That external audit firms should be rotated every five years or so. That external auditors should be prohibited from taking executive positions with their corporate clients for a number of years after they have been associated with the audit firm doing the audit unless the firm resigns as auditor. That peer reviews of auditors' work need to be improved and done more frequently if not continuously. That auditors should be engaged by the stock exchanges and paid from fees paid to the exchanges by listed companies. That the oversight of auditors needs to be strengthened. That punishment of wayward auditors needs to be more certain and swift. In that regard, Chairman Pitt of the SEC has proposed that there be a new Public Accountability Board overseeing the external audit function; this board would, as I understand it, have investigative and disciplinary powers. And so on and on. In my opinion, those suggestions, even if legislated by Congress and signed by the President, will not fix the underlying problem.

The underlying problem is a technical accounting problem. The problem is rooted in our rules for financial reporting. Those financial reporting rules need deep and fundamental reform. Unless we change those rules, nothing will change. The problems will persist. Today's crisis as portrayed by the surprise collapse of Enron is the same kind of crisis that arose in the 1970s when Penn Central surprisingly collapsed and in the 1980s when hundreds of savings and loan associations collapsed, which precipitated the S&L bail-out by the federal government. Similar crises have arisen in Australia, Canada, Great Britain, and South Africa. There will be more of these crises unless the underlying rules are changed.

Under our current financial reporting rules promulgated by the Financial Accounting Standards Board, management of the reporting corporation controls and determines the amounts reported in the financial statements for most assets. For example, if management concludes, based on its own subjective estimates, that the cost of an asset – say equipment – will be recovered from future cash flows from operations without regard to the time value of money or risk, no write-down is required even when it is known that the current market price of the asset is less than the cost of the asset. The external auditor cannot require that the reported amount of an asset be written down to its estimated selling price; the external auditor cannot even require the corporation to determine the estimated selling price of the asset and disclose that price in its financial statements. So when it comes time to sell assets to pay debts, there are often surprise losses that investors then see for the first time. Management also makes similar assessments in determining the amount of inventory obsolescence, the allowance for bad debts, and whether declines in the values of investments below cost are "other than temporary."

Under our current accounting rules, corporate management often records sales and trade receivables at 100 cents on the dollar even though a bank or a factor would pay only pennies on the dollar for those trade receivables. We have seen that phenomenon in the past few years in the telecom rage, where sales and receivables were recorded, followed several months later by write-offs of the receivables. On another front, we are currently seeing swaps of assets and the recognition of gains in what is effectively a barter transaction, even though the fair value of what was exchanged is apparently negligible.

Except for inventories and marketable securities, none of these asset amounts in the financial statements – trade receivables, commercial and consumer loans receivable, real estate loans, oil and gas reserves, mineral deposits, pipelines, plant, equipment, investments – is subjected to the test of what the cash market price of the asset is. Yet we know that most individual investors and, in my experience, even many sophisticated institutional investors believe that the reported amounts of assets in corporate balance sheets represent the current market prices of those assets; nothing could be further from the truth.

And under the FASB's definition of an asset, corporations report as assets things that have no market price whatsoever; examples are goodwill, direct-response advertising costs, deferred income taxes, future tax benefits of operating loss carryforwards, costs of raising debt capital, and interest costs for debt said to relate to acquisition of fixed assets. I call these non-real assets. Today's corporate balance sheets are laden with these non-real assets; this is the kind of stuff that allows stock prices to soar when in fact the corporate balance sheet is bloated with hot air. Of course, when it comes time to pay bills or make contributions to employees' pension plans, this stuff is worthless.

The same goes for liabilities. Corporate management determines the reported amount of liabilities for such things as warranties, guarantees, commitments, environmental remediation, and restructurings. Again, this is as per the FASB's accounting rules.

The upshot is that earnings management abounds. Earnings management is like dirt; it is everywhere. SEC commissioners have made speeches decrying earnings management. *Business Week*, *Forbes*, *Barron's*, the *New York Times*, the *Wall Street Journal*, and the *Harvard Business Review* carry hand-wringing articles about earnings management. Earnings management is talked about matter-of-factly on *Wall Street Week* and Bloomberg TV, on CNBC, CNNfn, and MSNBC. Earnings management is a scourge in this country. Earnings management is common in other countries as well because their accounting rules, and the accounting rules promulgated by the International Accounting Standards Board, are much the same as ours.

We need to put a stop to earnings management. But until we take control of the reported numbers out of the hands of corporate management, we will not stop earnings management and there will be more Enrons, Waste Managements, Livents, Cendants, MicroStrategies, and Sunbeams. How do we take control of the reported numbers out of the hands of corporate management? We do it by requiring that the reported numbers for assets and liabilities, including guarantees and commitments, be based on estimated current market prices – current cash selling prices for assets and current cash settlement prices for liabilities. And by requiring that those prices come from, or be corroborated by, competent, qualified, expert persons or entities that are not affiliated with, and do not have economic ties to, the reporting corporate entity. And by requiring that the names of the persons or entities furnishing those prices, and the consents to use their names, be included in the annual reports and quarterly reports of the reporting corporate entity so that investors can see who furnished the prices.

Let me give you an example of what I am talking about. Pre-September 11, 2001, the major airlines, to the extent that they own aircraft instead of leasing them, had on their balance sheets aircraft at the cost of acquiring those aircraft from Airbus and Boeing. Let's say that cost was $100 million per aircraft. The market prices of those aircraft fell into the basement post-September 11 to about $50 million per aircraft and remain there today, although prices have recovered somewhat. Yet, under the FASB's rules, those airlines continue to report those aircraft on their balance sheets at $100 million and are not even required to disclose that the aircraft are worth only $50 million. Under mark-to-market accounting, the aircraft would be reported at $50 million on the airlines' balance sheets, not $100 million.

I could give you many more examples, but I will add just one more. In the late 1970s, this country was experiencing great inflation. The Federal Reserve Board raised short-term interest rates dramatically. Long-term rates shot up. As a consequence, the market value of previously acquired residential mortgage loans and government bonds held by savings and loan associations declined drastically. But the regulations of the Federal Home Loan Bank Board and the FASB's accounting rules said that it was OK for the mortgage loans and bonds to be reported at their historical cost. Consequently, the S&Ls appeared solvent but really were not. This mirage allowed the S&Ls to keep their doors open and in so doing they incurred huge operating losses because their cost of funds far exceeded their interest income on loans and bonds in their portfolios. Some of the S&Ls decided to double down by investing in risky real estate projects, also accounted for at historical cost, and proceeded to lose still greater amounts, which losses were also hidden on the balance sheet under the historical cost label. The Federal Home Loan Bank Board even went so far as to allow S&Ls to capitalize and report as assets losses on sales of assets, but the FASB said no to that procedure. Of course, when the federal government had to bail out the insolvent S&Ls in the 1980s, the federal government paid for the losses that were hidden in the balance sheet under the historical cost label and the operating losses that had been incurred while the S&Ls kept their doors open because of faulty accounting. Had mark-to-market accounting been in place and had the Federal Home Loan Bank Board computed regulatory capital based on the market value of the S&Ls' mortgage loans, government bonds, and real estate projects, the S&L hole would not have gotten nearly as deep as it ultimately did.

Various members of Congress have said in recent hearings about Enron that a corporation's balance sheet must present the corporation's true economic financial condition. A corporation's true economic financial condition cannot be seen when assets are reported at their historical cost amounts. The only objective way that the true economic financial condition of a corporation can be portrayed is to mark to market all of the corporation's assets and liabilities. Recall my earlier example about the cost of aircraft being $100 million and the current market value being $50 million. Mr Chairman and members of the committee: is there any question that the $50 million presents the true economic financial condition and the $100 million does not? Moreover, following today's FASB's accounting rules produces financial statements that are understandable only to the very few accountants who have memorized the FASB's mountain of rules. "Indecipherable" is the word Chairman Pitt has used in recent speeches. On the other hand, marking to market will produce financial statements that investors, members of Congress, and my sister, who also happens to be an investor, can understand.

The various proposals that have been made to cure Enronitis will not cure the problem. I liken our current accounting system to bridges built from timber, which bridges keep collapsing under the weight of eighteen-wheelers. The public demands that expert consulting engineers be called in to oversee the building of replacement bridges. But the replacement timber bridges keep collapsing under the weight of eighteen-wheelers. More expert consulting engineers will not make the timber bridges any stronger. What needs to be done to fix the problem is build bridges with concrete and steel. The same goes with accounting. In the 1970s, after the surprise collapse of Penn Central, the auditing profession instituted peer reviews, where one auditing firm reviews the work and quality controls of another auditing firm. In the 1970s, auditing firms also instituted concurring partner reviews, where a second audit partner within the public accounting firm looks over the shoulder of the engagement audit partner responsible for the audit. These procedures have been ineffectual, as shown by the dozens of Enrons, Waste Managements, Sunbeams, MicroStrategies, Cendants, and Livents that have occurred since then. Coincidentally, the Financial Accounting Standards Board also came on the scene in the 1970s; it was going to write accounting standards that would bring forth financial statements based on concepts. What happened was that the FASB wrote a mountain of rules that produce financial statements that nobody understands and that can be and are gamed by corporate management. What all of that amounted to was continuing to build timber bridges that keep collapsing under the weight of eighteen-wheelers. We need to stop building timber bridges. We need to build concrete and steel bridges. We need to mark to market all assets and liabilities.

Now, you may ask, how much will concrete and steel bridges cost? Can we afford to build concrete and steel bridges? My response is that we cannot afford not to build concrete and steel bridges. How much of the cost of the S&L bailout was attributable to faulty accounting; the amount is unknowable but no doubt was huge. How much does an Enron or Cendant or Waste Management or MicroStrategy or Sunbeam cost? The answer for investors is billions, and that does not count the human anguish when working employees lose their jobs, their 401-k assets, and their medical insurance, and retired employees lose their cash retirement benefits and medical insurance. By some estimates, Enron alone cost $60–70 billion in terms of market capitalization that disappeared in just a few months. Waste Management, Sunbeam, Cendant, Livent, MicroStrategy, and the others also cost billions in terms of market capitalization that disappeared when their earnings management games were exposed. And these costs do not include the immeasurable cost of lost confidence by investors in financial reports and the consequent negative effect on the cost of capital and market efficiency.

By my estimate, annual external audit fees in the United States for our 16,000 public companies, 7,000 mutual funds, and 7,000 broker/dealers total about $12 billion. Let's say that $4 billion is attributable to mutual funds and broker/dealers. (Incidentally, mutual funds and broker/dealers already mark to market their assets every day at the close of business, and we have very few problems with fraudulent financial statements being issued by those entities. Mark-to-market accounting works and is effective.) That leaves $8 billion attributable to the 16,000 public companies. Assume that the $8 billion would be doubled or even tripled if the 16,000 public companies had to get competent, outside valuation experts (and not the public accountants, because they are not competent valuation experts) to determine the estimated cash market prices of their assets and liabilities. We are then looking at an additional annual cost of $16–24 billion. If we prevented just one Enron per year by requiring mark-to-market accounting, we would easily pay for that additional cost. And, when considered in relation to the total market capitalization of the US corporate stock and bond markets of more than $20 trillion, $16–24 billion is indeed a small price to pay.

The question arises: who should mandate mark-to-market accounting? I recommend that there be a sense of the Congress resolution that corporate balance sheets must present the reporting corporation's true economic financial condition through mark-to-market accounting for the corporation's assets and liabilities. I recommend that Congress leave implementation to the SEC, much the way it is done today by the SEC for broker/dealers and mutual funds. There will be many implementation issues, so the SEC will need more staff and money.

My testimony today is a summary of a lengthy article that I wrote about the definitions of assets and liabilities, earnings management, and mark-to-market accounting that was published last year in *Abacus*, a University of Sydney publication, and that was the basis for the R.J. Chambers Research Lecture that I presented last year at the University of Sydney. That article and lecture are attached hereto.

I will be pleased to answer the committee's questions.

46 Watching a game of three-card monte on Times Square

Remarks to the Southwest Regional Meeting of the American Accounting Association, Houston, Texas, 7 March 2003

When Sandy Welch asked me in July of last year to speak here today, the Sarbanes–Oxley Act was being debated and shaped by Congress. President Bush signed that bill on 30 July 2002. I thought then, and I continue to believe, that Sarbanes–Oxley would not touch the real problem underlying the malaise that I call "Enronitis." The problem is a technical accounting problem, which I will describe.

Let me set the stage for my belief. I think that financial reports about assets and liabilities, and changes in assets and liabilities, should be based on current market prices. That is, current, immediate, cash selling prices of assets and current, immediate, cash settlement prices of liabilities. I assert, and I think it is a truism, that historical costs of assets and historical proceeds of liabilities, which is what financial reports are largely based on today, are always irrelevant and often misleading. In contrast, current, immediate, cash selling prices of assets and current, immediate, cash settlement prices of liabilities are never misleading and always relevant.

Consumers here in the USA, and around the world as well, are used to the "serviceability" of the things that they buy and use every day. By "serviceability," I mean that something is "fit for its intended use."[1] For example, we buy Hershey's candies and Kellogg's corn flakes and know that they are fit to eat. We fly around the world in Boeing and Airbus airplanes and know that the planes are safe. We buy IBM and Dell desktop and laptop computers that run on Microsoft software and are delighted with their performance. Caterpillar tractors that we take to construction job sites, John Deere combines that we take into the wheat fields, and Honda automobiles that we drive home from the showroom perform flawlessly. We buy a GE toaster at the department store, knowing that the toaster will not give us a shock when we plug it into the electricity socket at home. We know that these products are "fit for their intended use." Not so for financial reports.

Witness that most retail investors, through no fault of their own, do not understand the financial reports. Nor in my experience do many institutional investors. Nor do the men and women in Congress, which became obvious during the congressional hearings about Enron and WorldCom last year. The reports are incomprehensible. But, beyond lack of understandability, financial reports as we know them today affirmatively mislead investors, who are the consumers of those reports. Those reports are not "fit for their intended use."

Witness the surprise, elephant-size write-offs of accounts receivable, loans receivable, inventory, fixed assets, and goodwill, which are often followed by huge declines in the market prices of the securities of the reporting enterprises. Just last week, Royal Ahold, the Dutch grocer, disclosed accounting irregularities, and the stock lost almost 70 percent of its value in two days. Witness the surprise retrospective restatements of previously issued financial reports to correct errors and irregularities in those reports. Witness the recent surprise corporate collapses of Enron in 2001 and WorldCom in 2002 to mention only a few surprise collapses, where prior to the collapse the financial reports submitted to investors showed that those corporations' financial health appeared to be OK. All of this in the presence of unqualified certifications by outside auditors!

These recent surprises are just that – recent. But since I entered the practice of public accountancy in 1957, there have been hundreds, maybe thousands, of surprise corporate collapses and surprise retrospective restatements of financial statements, where prior to the collapse or the restatement the financial reports submitted to investors were just like those of Enron and WorldCom – they looked OK.[2] And investors relied on those reports. These financial reports looked OK, but only superficially so, because the numbers shown for assets were generally based on historical cost of assets and management's judgment as to whether those costs were recoverable through future operations, and the numbers shown for liabilities were generally the historical proceeds – all of which is as per the encyclopedia of Byzantine accounting rules issued by standard setters and regulators in various countries. That encyclopedia of Byzantine accounting rules did not forestall those collapses; nor did the unqualified audit reports.

Huron Consulting Group (see note 2) found 330 restatements in 2002. Assuming 15,000 public company registrants, that is a failure rate of about 2 percent. Some have defended the current state of affairs, saying that a failure rate of 2 percent is acceptable. Suppose Airbus and Boeing had a failure rate of 2 percent, or 1 percent, or 0.5 percent, or even 0.1 percent. Would any of us fly in their airplanes? No! Suppose Hershey or Kellogg had that kind of a failure rate? Would any of us eat the candy or the cereal? No! Enough said.

And now we have the mother of all securities laws, the Sarbanes–Oxley Act of 2002 and SEC-required certification by CEOs and CFOs that the financial statements of their corporate employer are OK. Or, more precisely, Section 302(a) of Sarbanes–Oxley requires that the SEC require by rule that the principal executive officer(s) and the principal financial officer(s) certify in each annual or quarterly report that:

1 the signing officer has reviewed the report;

2 based on the officer's knowledge, the report does not contain any untrue statement of a material fact or omit to state a material fact necessary in order to make the statements made, in light of the circumstances under which such statements were made, not misleading;

3 based on such officer's knowledge, the financial statements, and other financial information included in the report, present fairly the financial condition and results of operations of the issuer as of, and for, the periods presented in the report;

Let's look at three of those requirements. The first is that the report does not contain any untrue statement of a material fact. I think that requirement should cause lots of heartburn. For example, paragraph 13 of FASB Statement 107, *Disclosure about Fair Values of Financial Instruments*, requires disclosure of the fair value of trade receivables if the fair value does not approximate the carrying amount of the receivables. That requirement is often observed in the breach in today's financial reports, and I doubt that most CEOs and many CFOs know of that requirement. For example, Vice-President Dick Cheney, when he was the CEO of Halliburton, must not have known about it, because Halliburton booked receivables from clients for construction cost overruns but did not disclose that practice or that the receivables, some of which I understand to this day remain uncollected, did not have a fair value equal to carrying amount. And, as we saw from the disclosures last week about Royal Ahold's booking questionable receivables for promotional allowances, Royal Ahold's CEO must not have known about that requirement. Not only is that omitted disclosure a violation of generally accepted accounting principles, but now, in my opinion, it is also a violation of Sarbanes–Oxley. However, whether that will be seen as a violation of Sarbanes–Oxley will depend on interpretation by the courts, and that will take years to develop. So that piece of Sarbanes–Oxley will not be effective or will take years to be effective.

By way of further example, paragraph 7 of FASB Statement 142, *Accounting for the Impairment or Disposal of Long-Lived Assets*, requires that the carrying amount of long-lived assets (read, property, plant, and equipment) not exceed fair value of the asset if the carrying amount is not recoverable from future, undiscounted cash flows resulting from use and eventual disposal of the asset; any excess is recognized as an impairment loss. Well, guess what. The estimate of future cash flows from the asset is determined by the management of the enterprise, and FASB Statement 142 does not require that the estimate be grounded in economic reality or be based on estimates available in the marketplace. The best current example of impairment losses that are being carried in the balance sheet under the label of historical cost is commercial aircraft that are owned by US airlines. Lessors of commercial aircraft are also carrying losses in their balance sheets instead of reporting them as losses in income. Those losses were evident before September 11, 2001, because even before 9/11 airplanes were parked in the Arizona and California deserts, and airplane brokers and owners knew full well about the dismal market conditions for commercial aircraft. Post 9/11, the desert parking lots are overflowing, but still the losses have not been recognized by the owners of the airplanes, and the dismal market conditions for commercial aircraft have turned even worse. See, for example, page 79 of the 20 January

2003 edition of *Fortune*, which suggests that the losses for aircraft lessors are in the range of $20 billion. Another example is the current state of the telecoms. There is huge overcapacity in that industry, but I am aware of no impairment losses that have been recognized; it is as if no one wants to go near the issue. I doubt that courts are going to agree that non-recognition of those losses, or even the lack of disclosure about them, was not material just because of the way a nonsense accounting rule is written and interpreted by FASB accountants. But waiting for the courts to interpret those words in Sarbanes–Oxley will take years, so Sarbanes–Oxley will be years away in fixing this problem, if it ever does.

Now let's look at omissions to disclose material facts. There are many, many situations where the fair value of on- and off-book assets is materially different from book value. I think that whenever the known fair value of an asset is materially different from the reported carrying amount of that asset, and that would include unrecognized assets, that is a material fact that requires disclosure under Sarbanes–Oxley. For example, the value of unrecognized mineral deposits and patents is huge for some companies. But that this is a required disclosure is only my interpretation. I have talked with several lawyers and accountants about this provision of Sarbanes–Oxley, and they generally do not agree with me. It seems that lawyers and accountants are so set in their ways that they do not even want to think about and talk about meaningful disclosure that will help investors to understand the current state of affairs of reporting companies. So I don't see this Sarbanes–Oxley requirement bearing fruit.

The third requirement is that the financial statements, and other financial information included in the report, "present fairly" the financial condition and results of operations of the issuer. Those are high-sounding words. But nobody knows what they mean. The words are not qualified by reference to generally accepted accounting principles, deliberately so as I understand it from persons close to the drafting of the statute. Those words suggest that the term "present fairly" stands alone without regard to the technical accounting term "generally accepted accounting principles," which we find in every set of financial statements, generally in footnote 1, and in every audit report and in regulation S-X. Do those words, "presents fairly," mean something like "true and fair view," which are words used in Great Britain and Australia? Well, the people in Great Britain and Australia obviously don't know what those words mean, for they have had their Enrons and WorldComs, and the "true and fair view" was no help in those similar situations in those countries. Just look at HIH Insurance in Australia for a recent surprise corporate collapse accompanied by an unqualified audit report. Some have suggested that the words should be interpreted by reference to Judge Friendly's decision in Continental Vending in the 1960s, which said that auditors could not find a defense in reliance on generally accepted accounting principles. But that decision is more than thirty years old, and subsequent court cases and administrative decisions have not built on it and given it prominence. Suffice it to say, then, that there is no warp and woof to which we can refer for the meaning of "present fairly," and the legislative history of Sarbanes–Oxley offers no clues or help.

My bottom line about Sarbanes–Oxley is that it is of no help. Congress drilled a dry hole in Sarbanes–Oxley. In fact, I think the investing public was and is being misled about the efficacy of Sarbanes–Oxley. The mother of all securities legislation since the 1930s, and it does not touch the real issues, which are accounting issues. It will not stop future Enrons and WorldComs. Sure, maybe more miscreants in the future will go to jail because of Sarbanes–Oxley, but that will be after disclosure of irregularities, which will be of no help to investors who have lost money and to employees who have lost their jobs and related benefits as in Enron. Nor will Sarbanes–Oxley stop earnings management. Pre-Sarbanes–Oxley, earnings management was like dirt; it was everywhere. Earnings management will continue under Sarbanes–Oxley. Why is that? Well, it is because management of the reporting enterprise, under generally accepted accounting principles, which principles remain unchanged under Sarbanes–Oxley, has control of the accounting numbers. Management determines whether and when and in what amount receivables are booked, especially in service industries, and what the amount of allowance for uncollectible receivables is. Inventory amounts and obsolescence of inventory are determined by management. Cost of property, plant, and equipment is subject to considerable management discretion as well in that many items are not always capitalized, and the amount of construction interest capitalized is highly discretionary. As well, estimated useful lives, salvage values, and depreciation methods with respect to fixed assets are highly discretionary. As mentioned earlier, determining whether the carrying amount of fixed assets is recoverable is highly discretionary. Whether tax benefits from operating loss carryforwards will be realized is also up to management to decide, based on its gaze into the future. Take a look at the accounting for motion pictures if you would like to see management discretion in action. And if that is not enough for you, take a look at how banks determine their bad debt allowances and casualty insurance companies determine their claim liabilities, especially for their long-tailed lines – that is certainly management discretion in spades. Finally, take a look at how impairment of goodwill is determined; it is like watching a game of three-card monte on Times Square.

Determining liability amounts for other than accounts payable, salaries payable, and notes payable is also highly discretionary. Warranty allowances. Payables to vendors when volume allowances are in play. (And as we have seen just last week in the case of the Dutch grocer Royal Ahold, receivables from suppliers for volume purchases are also subject to great discretion.) Income taxes payable. All of these liability amounts are highly discretionary.

So, what to do? Well, the FASB, more or less at the insistence of the SEC and with prodding from Congress in Sarbanes–Oxley, is going to start writing principle-based standards. The thought is that the current set of FASB standards is too, too rule-driven, and that rules can be evaded by issuers of financial statements through financial engineering. That, for example, Enron would not have happened had the rule-driven model not been in play but instead a principle-based model had been in play.

Let's take a look at that proposal. I think that the current set of FASB standards is no good, and that is an understatement. I have so contended, in writing, for many years, but the FASB has not agreed with me. We have some 100+s FASB standards, plus forty-six interpretations of standards, plus FASB staff documents that expand on the FASB standards, plus I don't know how many Emerging Issues Task Force consensuses, plus a couple of dozen AICPA audit and accounting guides and statements of position, plus a number of SEC staff accounting bulletins – all making up the body of generally accepted accounting principles. It is more than most accountants can comprehend. The FASB's comprehensive publication on accounting for financial instruments, for example, runs to more than 800 pages. Reading that document, and financial statements that are produced by applying that document, is like reading the Old Testament written in Aramaic – not comprehensible to other than a very few scholars. And they often disagree on the meaning of the words. For example, according to the *Wall Street Journal* of 28 January 2003, page A2, Freddie Mac, one of the largest users of derivative financial instruments in the USA, will have to restate its 2002, 2001, and possibly 2000 financial statements because its new auditor disagreed with how Freddie Mac accounted for some hedging transactions in prior years. So the high priests at PricewaterhouseCoopers, the new auditor, disagreed with the high priests at Arthur Andersen, Freddie Mac's prior auditor. The *Wall Street Journal* says that "Many investors have expressed concern that Freddie Mac's financial statements are too complex, in part because the accounting rules it must follow are so complicated." Indeed, rules written in Aramaic interpreted by accountants wearing skull caps. It is little wonder that today's financial reports are not understood.

So now we will get broad-based, principle-based standards. Let's look at a current broad-based, principle-based standard. Take a look at FASB Statement 5, *Accounting for Contingencies*, issued in 1975 when I was a member of the FASB. That standard started out to stop casualty insurance companies establishing so-called catastrophe reserves in advance of the happening of the catastrophe, but it morphed into the broadest, most all-encompassing standard ever issued by the FASB. Statement 5 says that "An estimated loss … shall be accrued by a charge to income if *both* the following conditions are met: (a) Information prior to the issuance of the financial statements indicates that it is probable that an asset has been impaired or a liability has been incurred at the date of the financial statements … and (b) The amount of the loss can be reasonably estimated." Those are high-sounding words. When I signed FASB Statement 5 in 1975, I thought that those words, which I just read, would work in the everyday world of accounting. Would work in determining when, for example, to recognize and measure bad debts. Would work, for example, in determining when to recognize and measure losses arising from injuries to employees and customers and the public at large. Would work, for example, in determining when to recognize and measure tax liabilities. Would work, for example, in determining when to recognize and measure volume discounts to customers. But I found that the twin standards of "probable" and "reasonably estimable" are so judgmental that they amount to no standard at all. Finance companies and banks determine the timing and amounts of their loan loss allowances under FASB Statement 5 with great variability. Insurance companies are all over the lot in determining claim liabilities, both in timing and amount. Liabilities for year-end bonuses and vacation pay vary from company to company. Income tax liabilities are "ouija board" determinations, as are tax benefits from operating loss carryforwards. FASB Statement 5 is a simple, broad-based, principle-based standard that does not work in practice. Widespread adoption of that approach will result in great variability in financial reports company by company. Investors will not benefit from that approach. That approach will, in my opinion, reduce security prices in general, without regard to company-specific risk, because investors will be forced to take account of the variability in financial reports through downward pricing of securities.

In addition, the FASB has been urged by many commentators to write standards that require preparers of financial statements to look to the substance instead of the form of transactions, and then account for the substance accordingly. The chairman of the International Accounting Standards Board, in a memorandum submitted to the British parliamentary Treasury Select Committee on 5 April 2002, when speaking about accounting for special-purpose entities, said, with obvious approval, that the IASB's Standing Interpretations Committee had identified four situations where, *in substance*, the situation indicated that the financial statements of the SPE should be consolidated. I think that the IASB will be disposed to similar utterances in the future. The AICPA's Quality Control Inquiry Committee, in an October 2002 memorandum entitled "Recommendations for the profession based on lessons learned from litigation," recommended to the FASB that in its revenue recognition project and special-purpose entities project, the FASB place an emphasis of the substance of transactions rather than their form. Various commentators on accounting by lessees for leases have said that the substance of lease agreements is that the lessee has a property right that should be recognized as an asset, with, of course, a corresponding liability. The cry to account for the substance of transactions can be heard in many districts.

The approach of principle-based standards and standards that refer to the substance of transactions absolutely will not work. If the substance of transactions, economic conditions, and economic events is so clear that the substance can be discerned by any reasonable person, then there is no need for a standard-setting body. Think about it. If one can see, see clearly, the substance of transactions, there is no need for an FASB or an IASB. Much the same problem is inherent in principle-based standards. We have 15,000–17,000 public companies here in the USA. The ten largest accounting firms serving those public companies have perhaps 4,000 to 6,000 partners serving as engagement partners for those companies. In Great Britain and continental Europe, there are about 5,000 public companies and probably 1,000 audit partners serving as engagement partners for those companies. I don't know how many public companies there are in Canada, Mexico, Brazil, Japan, India, Australia, New Zealand,

Indonesia, South Africa, Israel, China, Hong Kong, Russia, and the rest of the world where there are public companies. So, then, we have the case where there are, let's say, 25,000–30,000 individual CEOs and a like number of CFOs all preparing their individual financial statements using their individual, idiosyncratic judgments – all based on principles and substance without reference to any descriptive, prescriptive accounting standards. On top of that, we then have, let's say, 6,000 individual audit engagement partners applying their individual, idiosyncratic judgments to the financial statements that their 25,000–30,000 clients have laid before them. Even if we assume that every one of those 50,000–60,000 individuals is honest and well intentioned, we will have anarchy in financial reporting.

So, then, what to do? Well, as I said at the beginning, I know how to fix this problem.

First, we need simple, explicit, understandable definitions of assets and liabilities instead of the FASB's "probable future economic benefits" for assets and "probable future economic sacrifices" for liabilities, which lets anything and everything be an asset or a liability. Which definitions are understood only by FASB accountants, but not by most other accountants and certainly not by ordinary folk. We need a simple, descriptive, and prescriptive approach that will be understood by accountants, men and women in Congress, and lay people, and which can be implemented from Boston to Miami to Minneapolis to Los Angeles to Honolulu and indeed around the globe. I would define an asset as cash, claims to cash, and things that can be sold for cash. I would define a liability as cash outflows required by negotiable instruments, contracts, law or regulation, and court-ordered judgments or decrees, and agreements with claimants. Notice the orientation to cash. Cash is understood by everyone. My sister understands cash.

Then we need to take control of the numbers out of the hands of management of the reporting enterprise by requiring that the numbers for assets and liabilities come from the marketplace. For non-cash assets, the amount of cash that the assets would fetch in an immediate sale. For liabilities, the amount of cash that the obligee would accept in immediate liquidation of his/her/its claim. You may ask where these prices will come from. They will come from persons outside the reporting enterprise – competent valuation experts having no familial or economic ties to the reporting enterprise. And the names of those persons will go into forms 10-Q and 10-K so that investors will know where the prices came from.

Will that approach cost more money than we are spending today for financial reports. Most assuredly yes. But let's look at the issue. How much does an Enron or WorldCom cost? By some estimates, Enron alone cost $60–70 billion in lost market value for investors. And that does not count lost 401(k) assets of employees, lost benefits, and lost jobs. If we add up Enron, WorldCom, Waste Management, Sunbeam, Cendant, Livent, MicroStrategy, Adelphia, Royal Ahold, and all the rest of just the last five years, the amounts are huge. Maybe more than $100 billion. And that does not count the immeasurable cost of lost investor confidence and the consequent effect on security prices and the consequent effect on our economy here in the USA and economies around the world. If, by way of further example, we look at the cost of the federal government S&L bail-out in the late 1980s and early 1990s, which bail-out was due, in significant part, to bad accounting, the cost to the US taxpayer was several hundred billion dollars. Bad accounting can cost, and has cost, mega bucks.

By my estimation, annual external audit fees in the USA for our public companies are of the order of $8–10 billion. That amount does not include fees for the audits of 7,000 mutual funds and 7,000 broker/dealers, which already mark to market every day at the close of business. If we assume that the $10 billion were to be doubled or even tripled if issuers had to go to outside experts to determine the cash market prices of their assets and liabilities, we would be looking at fees of $20–30 billion. If we prevented just one Enron per year by requiring mark-to-market accounting, we would easily pay for that additional cost. And when considered in relation to the total market capitalization of just the US corporate stock and bond markets of $15 trillion or so, the additional cost of $10–20 billion would be small indeed.

Will my proposal solve all of the problems in financial reporting? No. But, at least we would be working toward getting relevant numbers. Numbers that are real and have their foundation in the marketplace.

Let me list just a few of the benefits:

1. Financial reports would be understandable to retail and institutional investors, Congress, and the public at large.
2. Financial reports would have increased usefulness in making investment, lending, corporate governance, and public policy decisions.
3. We would do away with today's mountain of accounting rules that nobody understands.
4. We could do away with the FASB and the IASB.
5. We could do away with the 150-hour education requirement for CPAs – no mountain of rules to memorize.
6. And, finally, continuing professional education requirements for CPAs could be scrapped.

Thanks for your attention.

Notes

1. I am indebted to Professor Peter W. Wolnizer, University of Sydney, for "serviceability" and "fit for intended use." See Wolnizer, *Auditing as Independent Authentication*, Sydney University Press, 1987.
2. The US General Accounting Office, in GAO-03-138 dated 4 October 2002, found 919 retrospective restatements of financial statements for irregularities by 845 public companies between January 1997 and June 2002. Similarly, in a report dated January 2003, Huron Consulting Group found 1,207 retrospective restatements in the five years ended 31 December 2002. See huronconsultinggroup.com.

47 IASC due process

Sir Bryan Carsberg
International Accounting Standards Committee
167 Fleet Street
London EC4A 2ES
England
12 August 1997

Dear Sir Bryan,

This letter concerns the IASC's due process.

Last week, I inquired of Ms Rivat of your staff as to why IASC standards do not include dissents of member delegations who disagree with the standard. Ms Rivat told me that the IASC's constitution prohibits publication of dissents in exposure drafts and final standards. It is unbecoming and inappropriate for a body such as the IASC to preclude publication of dissent. Transparency is the hallmark of good financial reporting. Transparency should be the first principle of the IASC's operations. I urge you to do what is necessary to remove that prohibition from the constitution.

The IASC's final standards are issued bare of explanation. Standards do not include the reasons for the need for the standard. Because of the constitutional prohibition, standards do not include identification of dissenting delegations along with the reasons for their dissent. Also not included in final standards is a "basis for conclusions" wherein the assenters to the standards set out the reasons for concluding the way they did and why the assenters believe that the reasons put forth by the dissenters are insufficient or incorrect. I recommend that future exposure drafts of standards and final standards include (1) the reason for issuing the standard, (2) a basis for conclusions setting forth why the proposed standard or final standard requires what it does and why any dissenters' reasons are insufficient or incorrect, (3) identification of the dissenters and the reasons for their dissent, (4) a brief explanation of other plausible approaches that could have been taken in the proposed standard or final standard even if none of those approaches is supported by a dissenter and why the IASC board believes such approaches would be insufficient or incorrect, and (5) the reasons for changes in the final standard from the exposure draft.

The importance of the IASC as a successful standard-setting body is acknowledged. The IASC needs to help to guarantee its own success by issuing standards that, first, produce relevant and reliable information for use by investors and, second, stand on their own feet by reason of persuasion by the IASC board in the published basis for conclusions. As you know, standard setting is not easy. What would be the correct or best accounting treatment for a particular issue is generally not obvious or intuitive. Even among investors and financial analysts what would be the correct or best accounting treatment in a particular circumstance is generally contentious. That contention is vastly increased when investors, financial analysts, preparers of financial statements, preparers' outside auditors, and regulators are all involved in the standard-setting process, either by participating directly at the standard-setting table or indirectly by making their own proposals for consideration by the IASC, by commenting on discussion documents or exposure drafts issued by the IASC, by participating in field tests or at conferences where accounting issues are discussed, or by accepting, for regulatory purposes, the results of preparers of financial statements applying the final standard in the preparation of their financial statements with opinions thereon by their outside auditors. That contention generally will not go away just because the IASC issues a standard, but acceptance of and compliance with the standard will be enhanced if the IASC carefully and persuasively explains, in both the exposure draft and final standard, why the standard is necessary and why the IASC concluded the way it did and why the IASC did not find other approaches or proposals persuasive or appropriate.

People within the IASC's inner circle – IASC board members, steering committee members, IASC staff, and official observers of IASC board meetings – know why a particular standard was necessary, why the IASC board reached the conclusion it did, why other approaches were rejected by the IASC board, and why changes were made between the exposure draft and final standard. However, that inner circle of people is a very small number when considered in relation to all the people who are affected by IASC standards. Many people outside the IASC's inner circle are or will be vitally interested in the IASC's standards. Stock exchanges, federal and state securities regulators, and federal and state accountancy boards that license accounting practitioners and mandate continuing accounting education by licensed accounting practitioners obviously have a great interest in what the IASC board does and how it reaches its decisions; those bodies, who mostly are outside the IASC's inner circle, may be hesitant to embrace IASC standards as being in the best interests of investors if those standards are not fully completed with careful and persuasive reasoning. Likewise, most preparers of financial statements and their outside auditors are outside the IASC's inner circle; those people need to be informed as to why the standard was necessary and the IASC board's reason for the approach taken. Most investors and financial analysts are also outside the IASC's inner circle and similarly need to be informed. Lastly, and perhaps most importantly, teachers of accounting and their students need to be informed by the IASC as to why a standard was issued and the reason for the conclusion reached and why other approaches were rejected; if they are not so informed, then all they can do is memorize the standard and apply it in a robot-like fashion. Understanding of IASC standards by students, who will be tomorrow's accountants, depends on students being fully informed by the IASC through careful and persuasive reasoning and not by issuing standards bare of explanation.

I wrote to you earlier this year (May 27) about the IASC's due process. You responded by saying that you were referring the matter to the Strategy Working Party. I hope you will refer this letter as well and make such changes as you can on your own in advance of recommendations by the Strategy Working Party.

Yours truly,
Walter P. Schuetze

cc: Mr Arthur Levitt and Mr Michael Sutton, SEC
Ms Jane Adams, AICPA
Mr Anthony Cope, FASB

International Accounting Standards Committee
167 Fleet Street
London EC4A 2ES
United Kingdom
Email: iase@iase.org.uk
20 August 1997

Mr Walter P. Schuetze
8940 Fair Oaks Parkway
Boeme
TX 78015, USA

Dear Walter,
Many thanks for your letter of 12 August about IASC's due process. I share your view that there is room for improvement in our due process and that improvement is particularly important in the context of IASC's current objectives. I want to bring about the situation where IASC's procedures are regarded as being as good as we can make them, within unavoidable resource constraints, for the purposes of establishing internationally harmonized standards.

You focus particularly on the desirability of having a basis for conclusions and explanations of alternative approaches with arguments for and against the different approaches. As I have said before, and as you acknowledged in your letter, I have always intended that our Strategy Working Party should undertake a thorough review of all due process issues. I believe it is almost certain that the working party will agree that a basis for conclusions is desirable. On the basis of early discussions in the working party, it also seems likely that the working party will recommend that board meetings should be open to the public for attendance in person or by telephone. If that is the case, identifying dissenters is a very small step. We might prefer to adopt a slightly different approach towards explaining dissents from that adopted at the FASB simply because of the force of numbers. (Although this will have to be worked out in the context of the details of any changes in structure that are proposed.) We might agree that the views of dissenters would be explained by the staff as part of the basis for conclusions or in a separate section of the standard in consultation with the people who are the dissenters. In any case, something along these lines seems to be needed.

I will make sure that these issues are considered by the Strategy Working Party. I suspect that our board may wish to await the recommendations of the working party before making any changes in existing procedures, although we shall be keeping in mind the possibility of making some recommendations early and implementing them right away. Whatever the outcome, I am most grateful to you for taking the trouble to write about these matters.

Sir Bryan Carsberg
Secretary-General

cc: Mr Arthur Levitt
Mr Michael Sutton, SEC
Ms Jane Adams, AICPA
Mr Anthony Cope, FASB
255

Index

eBooks – at www.eBookstore.tandf.co.uk

A library at your fingertips!

eBooks are electronic versions of printed books. You can store them on your PC/laptop or browse them online.

They have advantages for anyone needing rapid access to a wide variety of published, copyright information.

eBooks can help your research by enabling you to bookmark chapters, annotate text and use instant searches to find specific words or phrases. Several eBook files would fit on even a small laptop or PDA.

NEW: Save money by eSubscribing: cheap, online access to any eBook for as long as you need it.

Annual subscription packages

We now offer special low-cost bulk subscriptions to packages of eBooks in certain subject areas. These are available to libraries or to individuals.

For more information please contact webmaster.ebooks@tandf.co.uk

We're continually developing the eBook concept, so keep up to date by visiting the website.

www.eBookstore.tandf.co.uk